BIG DADDY FROM THE PEDERNALES

LYNDON BAINES JOHNSON

TWAYNE'S TWENTIETH-CENTURY AMERICAN BIOGRAPHY SERIES

John Milton Cooper, Jr., General Editor

BIG DADDY FROM THE PEDERNALES

LYNDON BAINES JOHNSON

PAUL K. CONKIN

TWAYNE PUBLISHERS · BOSTON
A Division of G. K. Hall & Co.

Copyright © 1986 by Paul K. Conkin
All Rights Reserved
Published by Twayne Publishers
A Division of G.K. Hall & Co.
70 Lincoln Street, Boston, Massachusetts 02111

Twayne's Twentieth-Century American
Biography Series No. 1

Photographs courtesy of the
Lyndon Baines Johnson Library

Designed and produced by Marne B. Sultz
Copyediting supervised by Lewis DeSimone
Typeset in 10/12 Aster by Compset, Inc.

Printed on permanent/durable acid-free paper
and bound in the United States of America

First Printing

Library of Congress Cataloging in Publication Data

Conkin, Paul Keith.
Big Daddy from the Pedernales.

(Twayne's twentieth-century American biography series)
Includes index.
1. Johnson, Lyndon B. (Lyndon Baines), 1908–   . 2. Presidents—United
States—Biography.   I. Title.   II. Series.
E847.C53   1986   973.923'092'4 [B]   86-12149
ISBN 0-8057-7762-8
ISBN 0-8057-7772-5 (pbk)

CONTENTS

FOREWORD

"Larger than life" was the phrase most often used to describe Lyndon Baines Johnson, whether in praise or in blame. During the two highly successful periods of his political career—his time as Senate majority leader in the mid-1950s and the first two years of his presidency in the mid-1960s—he seemed an irresistible force whom no opposition could withstand, as he bulldozed through great legislative programs. During the unsuccessful periods, especially his latter days as president during the Vietnam war, he appeared by turns a malign bully intent on crushing the weak and powerless or a helpless giant ensnared in traps of his own making. Both kinds of mythology mistook the man badly, as Paul Conkin demonstrates in this extraordinarily insightful biography. He depicts Lyndon Johnson as a mortal with a mixture of gifts and flaws, strengths and weaknesses, and attractive and repellent sides of his personality, but never a creature of either Olympian or demonic proportions. Conkin's is a portrait of Johnson as a believable human being. As such, it is a major contribution to interpretations of him and twentieth-century America.

Perhaps Lyndon Johnson's greatest asset and liability as a political leader derived from his not belonging to the twentieth century in style and spirit. As a Texan, he evoked images of the South and the West. He alternately cultivated and cursed those images, according to whether they helped or hurt him politically. But he could not escape them. His frequent private invocations of a heroic Texan heritage, particularly the Alamo legend, indicated how faithfully his outward appearance as a nonmetropolitan, nonsophisticated, nonfashionable figure reflected inner reality. Actually, as Paul Conkin points out, Johnson was not out of place but out of time. He appeared to be and, in certain senses, was a throwback to a much earlier epoch of American history. He evoked memories of the frontier—not six-shooter, cowboy days, as he tried to suggest with his Stetson hats and ranch, but the still earlier era of woods clearing, fantastic dreams, and tall tales, the time of mythological creatures like Paul Bunyan and self-created characters like Davy Crockett.

As Paul Conkin portrays him, Lyndon Johnson belonged to the nation's remote past in both his simplicity of character and his belief that he could do everything and satisfy everybody. Those traits of a bygone era were what made him, in Conkin's telling phrase, a "big daddy." The American statesmen whom he resembled most closely were not his youthful idol, Franklin D. Roosevelt, or the champion of racial justice whom he emulated, Abraham Lincoln. Rather, Johnson harked back to a combination of Andrew Jackson and Henry Clay. Like Jackson, he was an imperious, domineering father figure, who similarly carried airs of crudity and rusticity. Like Clay, he was a compromiser, who always sought to harmonize conficting interests and who profited and suffered by turns from his reputation as a wheeler-dealer politician. These resemblances, combined with Johnson's unusual energies and driving personality, helped account for both his successes and his failures. Paul Conkin views Lyndon Johnson with penetrating understanding, dispassionate criticism, and imaginative sympathy. Thereby, he captures the man behind the myths.

John Milton Cooper, Jr.

PREFACE

Explaining Lyndon Baines Johnson has become a growth industry. Perhaps the biographies multiply because no one has yet fully understood the man. No one ever will. Admittedly, such a pessimistic judgment reflects a truism—every personality is, to some extent, opaque. The deepest sources of action remain hidden, often even to the actor, always to outside observers. Johnson poses unusual difficulties, although not for a lack of historical artifacts. A biographer soon flounders in the sheer mass of family memories, public documents, and transcripts of hundreds of interviews. Mothers, brothers, uncles, cousins, neighbors, colleagues, teachers, enemies, employees—all have had their say. But every new perspective seems only to blur the portrait.

Johnson, almost perversely at times, contributed to the confusion. Not that he neglected explanation and justification. Just the opposite. No one ever attended more carefully to his own image, offered more clues to a puzzling identity. But these clues are at the heart of the problem, not a solution to it. His stories about his own past included some truth and a great deal of fantasy; in time, legendary embellishments became, for him, the truth, forever obscuring much that really happened. And from those memories and legends no coherent body of beliefs, no clear hierarchy of preferences seemed to emerge. All one glimpsed, with any confidence, were a few controlling sentiments.

Now I have had my go at it. What follows is my developing portrait of Johnson. Inevitably, the portrait is shaded by my unique perspective, by what I brought to the effort. By choice, I have avoided any psychological explanations. Any adult is a product of genetic dispositions, culturally or linguistically transmitted beliefs and preferences, and learned behavior. We know, or think we know, regularities in genetics and patterns in learning. But even here the genetic complexity of any person, the diversity of stimuli that shapes what one learns, precludes any causal explanation of how any human personality develops the way it does. We have, in my judgment, no verified theories at all that encompass linguistically encoded beliefs or preferences. We confront plenty of purported theories of this type, but none is sufficiently clear for unambiguous verification. I include here all the competing theories in depth psychology, including those with a Freudian pedigree. Anyone who craves the specious certainties of psychoanalytic history will have to look elsewhere.

Since I am skeptical of theories that purport to explain personality development, I have not in any rigorous sense tried to "explain" Johnson. That is, I have not cited sufficient conditions or controlling influences that made him the man he became. I doubt there were such fully controlling conditions. Thus, like most people who knew him well, I stand in amazement and wonder before the phenomenon that was Lyndon Johnson. The very strength of his ego, the overwhelming power of his personality, argues eloquently for the irreducible uniqueness of each person. Thus, instead of explanation I have sought a more modest understanding. I have looked for developed personality traits, for patterns in his behavior. And under the illusion that I have correctly identified some of these, I have looked for the formative influences that at least help account for them. I have sought, in parentage and place, in family and schooling, the necessary conditions, the circumstances, without which an infant named Lyndon would have matured into a different adult, although, given the obvious influence of genetic endowment, perhaps not a completely different adult.

I have tried to capture the heart themes of this biography in my title. It is intended as fully descriptive, not in any way pejorative. Johnson's love for his home country, for the land along the Pedernales, was notorious. But the hill country of Texas that gave him a sense of identity, that served as a refuge and at times as a source of strength, also nourished a sense of inferiority. It contributed to deep insecurities that plagued Johnson's career and that lay behind the most persistent pattern of that career—periods of intense involvement and engagement followed by intervals of disengagement, retreat, and depression.

Even more critical for Johnson was the emotional support and the intimacy of an extended family. He created new, ever larger families throughout his career and never functioned well or was happy outside them. Sentiments and loyalties, not rules and principles, guided his life. With people older than himself, or those in positions of authority, he always tried to become a dutiful son, close and intimate. When he gained a leadership role, which he always craved, he became the protective, often magnanimous, but demanding father. He tried to pull as many people as possible into his families and then serve them as responsibly as he could. He craved their appreciation and love. He first established this role with his younger siblings. Later, he never really wanted, or sought, employees or a normal staff. Instead, he adopted sons and daughters, with all the emotional intensity, all the depths of loyalty, and all the forgiveness that such a relationship suggests. Although a committed public servant, he was never a public person, with the formalities, the conventions, the manners that this identity entails. Even in the public arena he usually presumed upon people in a way most of us would never dare except in the privacy of home and family. He let it all hang out. Thus, not only in the sense of paternal concern and dutiful service, which characterizes many politicians, but in the way he related to staff and constituents, he was the big daddy of American politics.

As an intellectual, reconciled to solitude, addicted to clarity and consistency, and committed to what I hope are universalist principles, I found Johnson quite a challenge. In almost all ways he seemed my opposite. Maybe, for that reason, I could not fully understand him. The visceral, earthy, primitive, impulsive, indulgent aspects of his personality seemed alien to me. But the more I worked at this biography, the more I moved toward a rather detached, somewhat whimsical view of Johnson. It became impossible either to love or to hate him. Such categories no longer applied. At one time, during the Vietnam War, I had hated Johnson, or at least I thought I did. I did not understand him. I measured him by my standards. They did not fit. Had I even then come within the enveloping sway of his personality, I might have succumbed, been seduced. I hope I would have resisted. Like so many of his associates, I probably would have ended up ambivalent, attracted by his occasional warmth and generosity, repelled by his occasional crudeness or by his need to dominate others. Fortunately, I did not have to experience such options. Distance is one of the consolations of historical scholarship. Insulated by time and distance from his powerful ego, I could watch Johnson operate. And enjoy the spectacle.

Most of my work has been in intellectual history. The challenge of this book was to dispossess myself of my normal skills and habits. I am often given to philosophical complication, to rather tedious analytical games. None of these fits Johnson. It made no sense to contemplate an intellectual biography. Even to ask him to stand still for an ideological examination would have been as incongruous, and as useless, as making detailed X rays of a helium-filled balloon. Thus, I have tried, more so than in any earlier historical work, to be simple, to be content with straightforward description, to navigate in communities bound together by unchallenged conventions and pure sentiment. The clearest exception to this hard discipline is my chapter on the Great Society. Here, briefly, I intentionally shifted my focus from Johnson to what he wrought. I indulged some of the abstractions of policy analysis to understand better not him but his America.

Enough confession. Perhaps too much. I turn, briefly, to praise. I had very limited time to do the archival work at the Lyndon Baines Johnson Library. Thus, I always came to Austin in a hurry, impatient, tense, all normal for me. What a wonderful response from the library staff—a bit of amazement, but then only calm, generous help. The knowledge, the help, of several staff members enabled me to do more work than I had ever hoped. By the third trip, I almost relaxed. I enjoyed it. Thus, I will always have a warm feeling for that architecturally cold, monumental library.

I

PARENTAGE
AND
PLACE

The Johnson story has to begin with a family heritage tied to a beloved and familiar landscape. Aided by his mother's genealogical explorations, Johnson eventually learned the names of distant progenitors. But as he grew up, the family heritage that was alive to him stretched back only to his great-grandparents. He learned about these from the reminiscences of parents or other relatives, or from well-rehearsed family legends, most embellished with the passage of time. Lost to memory were the more distant relatives, largely those who had not shared in the treasured drama of Texas history. Thus, the live past for a youthful LBJ was entirely a Texas past and, more recently, a past limited to the hill country of Texas, an unclearly delimited region known only locally before Johnson's presidency.

On his paternal side, young Lyndon Johnson grew up as part of an extended clan. Until the age of five he lived next to and enjoyed the love and attention of his paternal grandparents, Samuel Ealy Johnson, Sr., and Eliza Bunton Johnson. Through his grandfather's memory, Lyndon's heritage stretched back an additional genera-

1

tion to Samuel's father, Jesse Johnson, the first Texan of the family. In 1846 he had moved to Lockhart, to a farming area just south of Austin and only a few miles from the fault line that demarcates the hill country from the coastal plain. He and his immediate fore-bears had lived in Georgia, but were of English ancestry. Jesse acquired a large farm or plantation, farmed by slaves, and like so many of his descendants also joined in commercial undertakings. He had ten children, but at his death in 1856 his debts almost equaled the size of his estate, establishing an early and characteristic Johnson heritage—large ambitions but frequent failures.

His sons had to strike out on their own. This placed them on an equal footing with a steady stream of impoverished, yeoman, non-slave-owning migrants into Texas, mostly from the southern states east of the Mississippi. They came seeking cheap land and a proprietary status. By the very odds of the game, they could not compete for developed land with a smaller flow of moneyed slave-owning migrants. Typically, they ended up on thin soil, or on land on the edge of settlement or still vulnerable to Indian attacks.

Grandmother Eliza Bunton Johnson also grew up in the Lockhart area, but in a more illustrious family. Her father, Robert Holmes Bunton, first migrated from Tennessee to Kentucky and then moved on to Texas in 1858, there joining other members of his family. He fought on the Confederate side in the Civil War and in its aftermath joined hundreds of other Texans in the great cattle drives to Abilene, Kansas. With the profits he expanded his land-holdings. His reputation was overshadowed by that of his brother, John Wheeler Bunton, a hero of the Texas Revolution. Lyndon Johnson gladly incorporated this great great-uncle into his own gallery of heroes, at times confusing his exploits with those of other members of his family. John Wheeler Bunton came to Mexican Texas in 1835 and quickly enlisted in the cause of Texas independence. He signed the Texas Declaration of Independence, helped draft the constitution of the new republic, and fought in the climactic battle of San Jacinto under Sam Houston. After returning to marry his fiancée, he went back to Texas to serve in its first Congress. After an early retirement from politics, he built up one of the largest pre–Civil War plantations in central Texas, near Bastrop.

In 1856 two of the three sons of Jesse Johnson, Thomas and Samuel Ealy (Lyndon's grandfather), moved into the sparsely settled hill country west of Austin. The brothers settled along the Pedernales River in what, in 1858, became Blanco County. They began raising cattle near present-day Johnson City (named not for the brothers but for a nephew who later staked out the village). Subsequently, the two brothers fought for the South in the Civil War. After the war, they became the largest cattle drivers in a six-county area and grew wealthy on profits realized in sales at Abilene. Samuel retained a ton of memories about the long drives, memories he later shared with his grandson, Lyndon. In 1867 Samuel returned to Lockhart to marry his love, Eliza Bunton, a remarkable young woman in both appearance—dark hair, piercing black eyes, white skin—and personality—strong willed, intellectual, daring. She rode with her husband in some of the cattle drives, allegedly hid with her baby in a root cellar in one of the last Comanche attacks (this became a treasured family legend), and took over much of the management of the Pedernales farm.

These prosperous beginnings soon turned to ashes. After successful cattle drives, and an expanding empire of landholdings, the two Johnson brothers lost almost all their wealth in a disasterous drive in 1871. Glutted supplies and falling prices at Abilene forced them to sell their herds at a severe loss. When they returned home they did not have enough money to pay off the former owners. They failed in an effort to recoup in 1872 and by 1873 had lost all their holdings in the hills. Sam and Eliza moved back to Lockhart and then to nearby Buda, at the edge of but not in the hills. The new farm was in Eliza's name; her father had come to the aid of the bankrupt couple. They remained in Buda until 1887. There were born their first three children, including Samuel, Jr. (Lyndon's father), in 1877. Only in 1887 did the growing family move back into the nearby and beloved hill country. Sam and Eliza sold their farm in Buda in order to make a down payment on a 433-acre almost level farm back on the Pedernales at the eastern edge of Gillespie County. This exceptionally well located farm or ranch remained in the family until both Samuel and Eliza died.

From age ten, Sam, Jr., lived at the Pedernales ranch. As a young man he learned to cut hair and by this skill earned extra money. He had a lively mind and broad interests, particularly in the area of public affairs. He yearned to teach and by intense self-study passed the exams required for certification for those, such as himself, who had not finished high school. He taught in country schools for three years before returning to the farm. In 1904, at age twenty-seven, he ran successfully for the Texas House of Representatives (by informal agreement, the right of candidacy rotated among the four counties of the district). The campaign, and his much-applauded performance, established Sam as a leading citizen of the hill country. Highly personable, articulate, irresistibly

3

persuasive, he challenged the rotational system in 1906 and won reelection. As a Democratic representative (a part-time job), he proved honest and did his best to back the interests of the small farmers in the hills. This meant an antimonopoly and antiprivilege stance and support for improved education, for internal improvements, and for stricter regulation and taxation of large businesses. As a basis of another treasured family legend, Sam also drafted and supported legislation that enabled the state of Texas to purchase and restore the crumbling Alamo in San Antonio.

In the midst of his second term, Sam met a young reporter for local newspapers, Rebekah Baines. She lived in the county seat of Fredericksburg and interviewed him for an Austin newspaper. After a whirlwind courtship they married in August 1907. Since his ill-remunerated legislative duties (two dollars a day) diverted him from needed farming tasks, the newly married Sam decided to retire from politics and make it as a full-time farmer, husband, and, in only a year, father. He always romanticized farm life, tried it at intervals, but never really liked it or had the requisite discipline or skills. He was a gambler, a promoter, a salesman—too grandiose in schemes, too expansive in his dreams, and too incurably people centered for sustained success in farming.

Rebekah Baines's ancestors shared only one commonality with the Johnson clan—an intense emotional tie to the state of Texas. Lyndon's maternal grandmother, Ruth Ament Huffman Baines, had abundant reason to be proud of her ancestors. Her Huffman lineage stretched back to frontier Kentucky. Her grandfather, John Smith Huffman, Sr., moved his distinguished family from Bourbon County, Kentucky, to Collin County, Texas, in 1851. He had married an Ament, a family that would long remain among the most distinguished in Kentucky. Ruth's father, John Smith Huffman, Jr., was born in Kentucky in 1824 and received his education as a physician at the University of Louisville Medical College. He came to Texas with his father, served as a physician in the Confederate Army, and died shortly after the war from broken health. Thus, Lyndon's grandmother Baines grew up in the home of her widowed mother, Mary Elizabeth Perrin Huffman, who died at the age of ninety in 1916, when her great-grandson, Lyndon Johnson, was eight years old. The Huffman family was only slightly less fertile than the Buntons and Johnsons. Even in Texas alone, the descendants of Lyndon's eight great-grandparents numbered in the hundreds. He had cousins almost too numerous to count, and, more than most people, he tried to keep some contact with all of them. After he became president, an unusual amount of staff time

4

had to be devoted to genealogical updates, as purportedly distant relatives wrote the White House or tried, often unsuccessfully, to establish kinship.

Rebekah Baines's paternal ancestors were cultured, prudent, dependable, ambitious, and pious, the very opposite of the impulsive, risk-taking, exuberant Johnsons. Rebekah's grandfather—George Webster Baines—gained recognition not as a soldier in the army of Sam Houston but rather as the Baptist preacher who later baptized him. A leader of Texas Baptists, he served briefly as president of Baylor University, then located at Independence, Texas. Her father—Joseph Wilson Baines—also became one of Texas's leading citizens. His daughter stood in awe of him and always revered him as a model of good character. He moved from college to school-teaching to study of the law. He founded a newspaper, served as secretary of state for Texas, ran for the U.S. House of Representatives, and then held the seat in the Texas House just before Sam Johnson. In 1886 he moved his family to the village of Blanco in the hill country, and there lived as the town's, perhaps even the county's, wealthiest and most respected citizen—a leading layman in the Baptist church, literate and refined in taste, and by all accounts a person of unimpeachable integrity, although surely not up to Rebekah's later saintly descriptions. The Baineses lived in the best house in town. But even such a man was not exempt from economic disaster. In 1904, after years of disasterous crops and because of a speculative venture, he came close to bankruptcy. He had to sell the Blanco house to pay debts, and, a broken man, he moved his family to a smaller house in the largely German town of Fredericksburg. Two years later he died; his widow moved to San Marcos, where she rented rooms to college students.

During the painful collapse of the Baines family, Rebekah completed her college work at Baylor Female College (now Mary Hardin Baylor) at Belton, Texas. She eventually had to work to pay her way—not, one suspects, without psychic costs. She always kept up a front, concealed her insecurities behind a pose of gentility, camouflaged painful aspects of her past in Victorian homilies. After graduation, Rebekah taught elocution in Fredericksburg and wrote articles for a local and then an Austin newspaper. The courtship of Sam Johnson proved irresistible to such an incurable romantic as Rebekah. The couple at least shared an interest in politics and in the outside world. But in many ways the resulting marriage proved unfortunate. Despite all her pretense, Rebekah suffered a loss of self-esteem. She had married beneath her self-perceived station in life, or at least beneath the image of gentility and piety she struggled to maintain even in the worst of times. Sam's exuberance, his bursts of temper, his love of a good time with the boys, his occasional excessive drinking, his jokes and folksy but often coarse humor, his financial recklessness, even his lax church attendance all symbolized a major cultural gap. On her part, Rebekah placed unwanted demands or fetters on Sam, never played well the role of a political wife, at times came close to retreating into her romantic fantasies, and put a damper on the playful, convivial impulses of her husband and his family.

Even the first years for Sam and Rebekah were far from idyllic. Sam took his bride of twenty-six back to the Pedernales farm, to the original family house, now next to that of his parents and in the midst of the extended Johnson clan. Rebekah was the alien and soon felt it. Sam was often her only companion, almost the only one in the valley to share any of her "higher" interest in books or in the larger world outside Texas. The couple moved into a nice commodious house, at least for a newly married couple and by hill country standards. It enjoyed a new coat of paint, and had four rooms and a lovely setting in the broad river valley. But the housework demanded new skills, ones hard to acquire for someone of Rebekah's temperament and past experience.

The house, the work, matched that of rural wives everywhere. Recent biographers, with no firsthand experience, have enormously exaggerated the drudgery of rural homemaking before the advent of electricity. A mere litany of tasks does seem intimidating—drawing or hand-pumping water from wells or cisterns, heating water in outside cast iron kettles, laundering with a scrub board, and cooking on wood-fired ranges. Add to this the stove-heated flatirons, the human-powered churns, the constant demands of chickens and cows, the rigors of an outdoor privy, the hand labor of vegetable gardening, and the long hours of canning and preserving foods for winter. Washtub baths and reading by kerosene lamps add a primitive, at times even a romantic aura to it all. But the resulting picture can be misleading. It joins all the distorted legends about the unrelenting toil required on premechanized farms. In fact, the average farmer at the turn of the century, those such as Sam Johnson, did less in a year than the average factory worker today. Farm chores were constant and unremitting, but the pace of work generally quite relaxed. The same was true for housekeepers. Indeed, later machines have dramatically reduced the required labor of household tasks. But the main effect of this has been the upgrading of living standards, not reduced hours of work. Farm families able to enjoy higher standards of living always did so by the use of hired labor. In 1907 the chores tied to a small house and one husband were easily manageable for anyone at all proficient in homemaking. But little in her past prepared a newly married Rebekah for the role of farm wife. Undoubtedly she had to suffer through a period of adjustment, not because of the primitive conditions or the isolation of rural life generally, but because of her inexperience.

Place rivals family in most people's sense of identity. In America, where one comes from competes for attention with what one does or the status of one's parents. The where involves much more than mere geography; it involves a regional culture, distinctive and familiar beliefs and values. For Lyndon Johnson, the old home place remained peculiarly vivid and compelling. Few presidents have been more conscious of where they came from or introduced more images of place in their speeches. In part, this reflected both pride and a certain defensiveness about where he grew up. In part, it recorded how vivid and sustaining and solacing were the memories of the often idealized world of his youth.

Of course, almost anyone grows up with overlapping allegiances. Broader bases of identity—being an American—may overwhelm local ones—being a Texan—and typically will do so for those who are very mobile in their youth. What was so clear in LBJ was the depth of local loyalties. These did not necessarily lessen his broader allegiances, perhaps even at times reinforced them, but still provided him a convenient point of reference. In only one area did he reveal some confusion about his provincial allegiances. Born at the unclear boundaries of South and West, he never fully identified with either and, as political need dictated, alternatively claimed one or the other. In many contexts he could not escape the label and often the burden of being "southern," and he often did the best possible job exploiting the occasional assets that went with that imposed identity. Despite his Confederate progenitors, one suspects that he simply did not feel very southern. He transferred his regional loyalties to his home state. To him, Texas was his section and region and, in many ways, even his nation. As much as any Texan he identified with the state's unique history—its period of nationhood and its uniquely voluntary allegiance to the Union.

Generalizations about Texas are as numerous as jokes and in most cases as unfair. Texans are as varied, or more varied, than the people of any other state. Here merge Anglo, black, and Hispanic cultures, all leavened by a scattering of German, Czech, and other central European traditions. Of course, not all Texans are proud of their state or its heritage. But Texans are at least, by necessity, very self-conscious about state identity. Outsiders force them to be. Their own pride, or the overt boasting of a few, has invited such state consciousness. Being a Texan is often not just an accident of birth but a cause. A form of Texas nationalism is particularly beguiling for those who grow up in the center of such a large state. It is their middle kingdom, the center of their world. The world, the only one that counts, is almost all in Texas. LBJ could not escape this identity. He did not try, although he often tried to change outsiders' images of Texas. In most respects he suffered from the image and from his central Texas accent. People viewed him as a Texan and filled in all the images that they associated with that identity. Long before Texas became chic, or so prosperous and populous as to invite more jealousy than derision, the images of the state held by outsiders were largely pejorative.

LBJ came from the heart of Texas. His roots lay within the dramatic but resource-poor hill country, a geographical region with little national recognition until Johnson gained the presidency. In fact, even Texans at the fringe of the state often had no clear images of the hills. Johnson gave visibility to the region, even as his reputation, in subtle ways, helped shrink the recognized extent of the hill country to the areas immediately around his ranch or around Johnson City. The label comes from a line of dramatic, heavily eroded hills that rise rather abruptly from the Texas coastal plain. A major fault line (the Balcones Escarpment) gives clear definition to the eastern boundaries of the hills. This fault line, in a concave curve, bisects Texas from the Rio Grande to the Red River. But by "hill country," local Texans usually refer only to the hills and ridges that lie south of the Colorado River. Most clearly, the label now applies only to the hills between the Colorado and, roughly, the Medina rivers, or the area to the west and northwest of a line stretching southwestward along the fault from just west of Austin to just west of San Antonio. The two principal rivers draining this delimited hill country are the Colorado at its northern edge and the Guadalupe, which bisects it. Two lesser tributary rivers rise in the hills—the Pedernales, which joins the Colorado near Austin, and the Blanco, which flows from the hills and the coastal plain to join the San Marcos and then the Guadalupe at Gonzales. This attenuated but widely recognized hill country includes an area of approximately twelve thousand square miles (only 5 percent of Texas but still larger than Rhode Island, Delaware, or Connecticut).

The Texas hill country has suggested widely varied images to outsiders. Booth Mooney, who wrote both a laudatory campaign biography of Johnson and then a more restrained retrospective chronicle, has best articulated one negative image. He talks of a "bleak, dusty region not friendly to living things. It is a land where all forms of life must, for survival, go armed against one another. Rattlesnakes slither over the usually parched earth, hard as biscuits baked over a cowboy's campfire." He goes on to talk of javelinas, horned toads, terrapins, and buzzards in a fathomless sky, of stunted cedar and live oak, of a scorching sun, and of bare animal carcasses, here where the thin soil fights a losing battle with sun and wind. One thinks of the biblical book of Ezekiel and the valley of dry bones.

In actuality, the hills are more hospitable to man than fully half the rest of Texas. Johnson's later and more exaggerated claims about the poverty of the hills also helped conceal an obvious fact to anyone who has visited his birthplace. Johnson grew up securely within the hill country, in the sense of a geographical region, but was not really of the hills. The valley of the Pedernales is broad, level or gently rolling, and exceptionally fertile by hill country standards. A wide swath of countryside, from Johnson City west through Stonewall to Fredericksburg has always made up a peculiarly favored subsection of the hills. This valley is scarcely comparable, except in aridity, to the eroded, sharp hills and ridges that make up the distinctive terrain of the hill country and that are visible only at a distance from LBJ's birthplace. Early in this century the valley of the Pedernales, with its peach orchards, its extensive crop farming, its clustered population, resembled the coastal plains of Texas much more than typical hill country ranches.

The diverse images of the hills reflect seasonal or even rainfall cycles. The hills offer dramatic vistas throughout the year and in the spring can be as lovely as any area on earth. Then the more conical or self-standing hills or the watershed ridges (such as the Devil's Backbone, which marks the divide between the Blanco and Guadalupe rivers) burst forth in lurid dress. Dozens of wildflowers compete with blooming cacti, with bluebonnets often dominant. The usual moisture of springtime also feeds a lush cover of grass, creating hills as verdant as those in England. In a typical summer, midday heat, low humidity, and extended periods of insignificant rainfall brown the grasses on the thin-soiled and rocky higher ground. But a special beauty remains. The sky is often deep and blue, festooned on a typical afternoon by billowing cumulus clouds. Most of the hills are also punctuated by the shimmering

9

green of live oaks. Spotted through the hills are dense thickets of juniper (cedar). The valleys have enough moisture for deciduous trees, such as cottonwood, pecan, and Spanish oak. In the river bottoms a few cypress trees have survived man's deprivations.

Of course, the hills, usually so dramatic and beautiful, have more somber moods. The winters are normally mild, as befits a subtropical climate. Grasses remain green. But periodic northers bring deep freezes, with temperatures in rare years as low as zero. Every two or three years significant and beautiful snowfalls push this far south. The winds can make such northers feel colder than the temperatures indicate. Cattle, angora goats, and particularly sheep, require protection in barns and sheds. Along with the glory of the springtime come frequent floods, fed by the erosive runoff from the steep hills, with the water often channeled into narrow creek bottoms. But worst of all is summer drought. In extended drought cycles, such as in the 1950s, even the larger creeks, which normally meander through most of the valleys, dry up. Limestone springs and shallow wells go dry for extended periods. Vegetation, even the deep-rooted live oaks, wilt. And the monotony, the expectant but frustrating wait for rain, wounds and embitters the human occupants. After three or four years of drought, a type of depression settles on the people of the hills, by then one of the gloomiest places on earth. But despite all the hazards, the hill country is better suited for ranching than the more arid plains farther west. The climate allows grazing for all but a few days each year. And the first settlers, thinly scattered over the hills, profited from the favorable man-land ratio, from the well-developed native grasses, and from open grazing privileges. LBJ's grandfather reaped these benefits.

The meager resources of the hill country made it an identifiable pocket not of dire poverty but of low incomes, a low tax base, limited public services, marginal schools, and few cultural activities. The exceptions, such as the valley of the Pedernales, only highlight the rule. Overall, the marginal soils attracted, or at least retained, marginal people—those with less capital, less education, fewer skills. No more remarkable cultural fault lines exist in America than these separating poor soils from rich ones, which often means flatlands from hills and mountains.

Who moved into the hill country? The first large-scale migration involved the Germans who settled in the area around Fredericksburg. And in this case, special circumstances led to an early, compact settlement of skilled people with exceptional cultural resources. To this day, Fredericksburg is the gem of the hill country, a lovely town that retains its German architecture and culture and is surrounded by orchards and well-tended farms. The Germans, by coming first (1846), chose the best site. As part of a mass migration, first to New Braunfels at the edge of the hills, and then into the hills, they bypassed the normal filtering and screening process of frontier settlement. People of varied skills came together and very quickly created a thriving community tied to artisanship and commerce as well as to agriculture. From Fredericksburg, German farmers spread throughout most of the hills, but those on more isolated or hilly homesteads eventually suffered from the same economic and cultural backwardness as their non-German neighbors.

The English-speaking settlers came into the hills not in organized groups but as single families seeking the best land their often meager resources would allow. The names of the early farmers suggest largely an English or Scottish ancestry and a more recent residence in the upland areas of the South. Many had already lived for a time in the eastern parts of Texas. This is the exact pattern of the Johnson family. The early, pre–Civil War settlers faced pioneer hardships, even a few belated Indian raids, but enjoyed a plentitude of land and excellent grazing. First in land speculation, then just after the war during the brief boom in open-range ranching, the hill country offered a rare, perhaps the only, opportunity for quick profits if not great wealth. Then new waves of settlers brought an often disasterous era of agricultural exploitation.

Although the hills long lacked good roads, they were not inaccessible, not comparable to the remote valley of the Appalachians or the Ozarks. The people of the hills were never isolated enough to create a peculiar culture, to become a distinct people in accent or folklore. Both the urban centers of Austin and San Antonio, or at least the thriving county seats of San Marcos and New Braunfels, were within a day's horseback ride of almost all hill country ranches. A major railroad skirted the hills to the southeast; later highways bisected them. Still, the hills remained a backwater, relatively isolated part of Texas in Johnson's youth. Despite the redundant labor supply, the population remained sparse. The counties, typical of those in Texas, were so small that in less populous areas they could not provide a full array of services. Counties of three and four thousand did well to coordinate local school districts, to supervise limited road building, to maintain a flimsy courthouse. The distances meant rustic, one-room elementary schools, whose seven grades provided the extent of education for almost all hill children. High schools, in the larger towns and vil-

11

lages, catered to an elite and were often too small and understaffed to meet minimal accreditation standards. The hill people enjoyed no public health services and no public libraries.

Life in the hills was not without its rewards. Typical of people in all areas of America, including the most isolated or impoverished, the natives claimed a deep love for their region. In part, they referred to the familiar landscape, the dramatic vistas. Typically, they also cited the people and neighborliness. Lyndon Johnson, in moments of nostalgia, often quoted his father's verdict that in the hills "people know when you're sick and care when you die." Scattered, lonely, the hill people, like rural people everywhere, valued their neighbors, rejoiced in social contacts at the county seat, on Sunday in a Baptist or Disciples church, at a social at the schoolhouse. Yet, scarcity also nourished other qualities—a compensatory reverence for money and for possessions, at times an overwhelming apathy or lack of ambition, and a morbid preoccupation with making a living, with purely practical issues.

For Johnson, as much as for any other American president, the role of his home country seemed to enter into, and variously complicate, his developing identity. He was a product of the hills, and at times proudly, always a bit defensively, carried his mark, his local brand, with him to Washington. And it was a burden, added to that of being a Texan and his being perceived as a southerner. He came from an impoverished backwater area of America, yet an area too small, too unbounded, to have created or nourished a distinctive provincial culture. The hill people were part of either a distinctive but small German subculture in central Texas or the larger Anglo, evangelical mainstream. They were distinctive among these groups only by being among the poorest and least educated. The hill country was not culturally homogenous, although it was distinctive in Texas because of its rather small number of either blacks or Hispanics. Thus, the hills offered Johnson no special traditions, no unique collective identity. He never claimed such. His favored images of the hills involved such generalized traits as spaciousness or neighborliness. Likewise, the hills had produced no famous role models, no easily identified heroes. Johnson's venerated heroes included several from Texas, but few home folk. Even his father, in so many ways a powerful role model, eventually suffered a financial failure. And failure, defeat, frustration were more appropriate images in the hills than fame and fortune.

How could this hill country background affect a young Lyndon Johnson? Clearly, it helped nourish insecurities. It offered him nothing very positive. Instead of fortifying any sense of self-worth, of a consoling even if an ascribed status, it eroded his sense of who he was. After all, what could one expect of a poor kid from the banks of the Pedernales? Not much. The theme is a familiar one— what can one expect of a cracker, a hillbilly, a redneck, a Cajun, on to literally dozens of local and always pejorative labels tied more often than not to one's place of birth and upbringing, to such inescapable characteristics as dialect or accent, and not to personal qualities or achievements. In some cases, the ascribed traits that purportedly go with these labels are as arbitrary, as unfair, as full of contempt as a whole range of ethnic and racial labels. And such marks are indelible, unerasable, whatever the level of achievement. One can only compensate. LBJ did this with a vengeance.

Rebekah Johnson compensated by assuming all the outward symbols of gentility and refinement. She rose above what she saw as ignorance and crudity in her hill people neighbors. At times, her romantic fantasies seemed so out of place, so unrealistic, as to be pathetic. Lyndon compensated by achievement, by proving himself over and over again through success, by doing each task to which he really committed himself better than anyone else had ever done it before. He worked himself and his staff almost to death to be the best congressman any district ever sent to Washington, at least in the sense of serving the wishes of his constituents—and so too as Senate majority leader and as president. He accepted the odds, often with resentment, even occasional bitterness. A boy from the hills, from small and pitiful schools, from a hick college, such a boy, to get the prize, had to run twice as fast as all the golden-spooned kids from—from where? Maybe those down in Austin or up in Dallas. Later in life, clearly those from a vaguely defined North or Northeast, from Boston or New York City or really any place or no place—from wherever came socially relaxed people or confident intellectuals, people who did not have to prove or justify themselves over and over again. He was jealous of such people even as he resented them, as much drawn toward them and their easy self-confidence as he was inclined to put them down.

One strategy for dealing with an ascribed handicap or inferiority—whether tied to place, family, or physical defect—is to magnify it, to rub it in. This has psychic benefits. Johnson enjoyed those. At times, he indulged an inverse form of snobbery toward those who gained success more routinely and more easily. He loved to pull down those with refined taste or a smug sense of status. A

13

master of obscenity, he used it to demean others, to pull them down to his size. Or else he exaggerated his own crudity.

To the despair of his mother, he often painted a totally false image of his childhood, a log cabin myth highlighted by dire poverty, widespread hardship, and enormous educational and cultural deficiencies. And this after all Rebekah's pampering and tutoring and support, and despite her illusions of middle-class gentility and respectability. But such a gloomy caricature of boyhood realities, such an exaggerated way-back-in-the-sticks scenario, made Johnson's achievements all the more improbable. It magnified the distance he had traveled. In some contexts this reinforced his unending bromides about how enough effort and will could ensure success for almost anyone in America, a message of uplift he preached at every opportunity, particularly when in the presence of young people. It was a message that would have seemed corny or pathetically naive had not Johnson, in a sense, turned his own mythologized life story into all the proof he needed. Look at me. The poor old boy from the hills. If I can do it, anyone can. Thus, LBJ—the great American success story.

Biographers have sought the source of certain of Johnson's policies in his past. He provided them the needed evidence. Particularly on three key issues—civil rights, education, and antipoverty—Johnson frequently appealed to his own past. He communicated a sense of having experienced firsthand the effects of poverty and discrimination, an image based more on fantasy than on fact, but one nonetheless quite appealing. And, however exaggerated his examples or however deftly he fitted them for his political purposes, he did identify with Americans who had faced arbitrary or unjust restrictions on opportunity. As a boy from the hills, as a Texan and a southerner, he knew firsthand what it was like to have started from behind in what to him was always a terribly competitive game of life. A person given to sentimentality at the drop of a tear, he added to issues involving discrimination and exploitation an authentic sympathy or feeling that complemented even if it never transcended his sheer political artistry, his compelling bent for great achievement.

But one must not take this line of argument too far, claim too much for the heritage of place. Above all, one must not suggest easy or simple explanations for his personality or for his policies. Some of his personality traits seemed present even when he was a very young child, suggesting the controlling role of genetic endowment. And many aspects of his personality, including the sense of insecurity, the desperate, lifelong battle for justifying achievement and self-worth, seemed rooted in the dynamics, possibly the pathology, of his immediate family. At the very least, one must look carefully to his youth, to all the hazards of growing up in a particular family and community, to begin to decipher, always by reflection from a very opaque mirror, the unyielding secrets of LBJ.

2

LEGENDS OF
YOUNG LYNDON

The childhood and youth of Lyndon Johnson remain buried under a plethora of opaque memories. Most of the evidence remains either suspect or very circumstantial. Johnson's own memories were varied and, often, amazingly inconsistent with known facts. The much later memories of family and friends are suspect on several counts—the distance of forty or more years from events remembered, the distorting impact of Johnson's later fame, the biases created by intense political loyalties or animosities, and the subtle impact of local legends that eventually gained all the solidity, and persuasiveness, of firsthand experience. All that is reasonably clear is the external biography, a chronology of major events. Everything else is subject to varied interpretations. Perhaps the largest impediment to understanding is the legendary larger-than-life images created by both apologists and detractors. For, behind the legends, an extraordinary Lyndon enjoyed a quite ordinary childhood.

Lyndon Johnson was born on 27 August 1908 in Sam and Rebekah Johnson's comfortable farmhouse on the Pedernales. During the summer, Rebekah's mother and sister came to live at the farm in order to relieve Rebekah of much of the housework. Because of the distance and a rare summer flood on the river, a summoned physician arrived after the birth, which was attended by the grandmother and a local midwife. Later Rebekah was loath to admit such a humble beginning for her beloved firstborn, who naturally from birth on was the pride and joy of adoring parents. And not only of parents: Lyndon happened to be the first grandson on the maternal side and thus was from the beginning the center of attention in a vast extended family. Letters and gifts flowed from all sides. From the beginning, Lyndon was an indulged child. He received all the affection and attention that normally support a strong sense of self-worth. His parents bubbled over with pride and almost smothered him with tactile stimulation. His was a hugging and kissing family, one given over to exuberant expressions of sentiment and affection. In December 1909, Rebekah composed a Christmas letter as if in Lyndon's own words, and perhaps well expressed the parents' somewhat divergent expectations for their son. Sam already identified Lyndon as an aspiring orator and translated his babble into political axioms. Rebekah saw in him the studious looks of a professor.

From all the evidence, Lyndon was a precocious child, healthy, active, and happy. His parents and several relatives quickly identified the infant as especially gifted. Of course, parents are inclined to exaggerate in such cases. But maybe they had a point. Grandmother Baines described Lyndon as an "extraordinary" boy. Rebekah perceived him as the brightest, jolliest, best baby ever. When Rebekah took him to San Marcos to stay a few days with Grandmother Baines, a lonely Sam wrote that "I do know he is the sweetest, prettiest, and smartest baby in the world." The claims had some basis in fact. Even early photographs reveal a baby exceptionally personable, one who seemed to love people, to want to reach out to them, to woo and win their affection. He basked in the attention and seemed to have been born a charmer, a natural leader. These traits gave some substance to a prediction of Grandfather Johnson, made before Lyndon was three, that he would some day be a United States senator. But he was also the obverse of this—a spoiled child, at times petulant and demanding.

Lyndon soon became merely the oldest child. Two sisters (Rebekah and Josefa), a brother (Sam Houston), and then a final sister (Lucia) soon competed for the time and attention of busy parents. Lyndon thus fell heir to the often heavy expectations and responsibilities of the oldest child and also those of an oldest son, one who happened, by genetic accident, to be remarkably similar to his father in both looks and personality. But he was never starved for attention or human contact. His grandparents Johnson lived just across a field in the next, quite visible house, upriver toward Stonewall. And just beyond them, in what is today the LBJ ranch, lived his aunt Frank and uncle Clarence Martin. The river road was well traveled. Visible just across the river was a Lutheran church, supported primarily by German families in the area. In no sense did the Sam Johnson place resemble the typically remote, isolated ranches of the more distant hills.

The records allow no detailed reconstruction of Johnson's first five years, the only years he lived at his birthplace on the Pedernales. Much later, in confidential reminiscences with Doris Kearns, Lyndon talked of an unhappy childhood, but it is not clear that these impressions were either sincere or accurate, and in any case they could not have been based on any but a few episodic memories of these farm years. Although Sam, characteristically, was already in debt because of losses on cotton he had bought for export in 1906, the family remained stable and the farm prospered, at least by the standards of the hill country. No troubling outside events intruded into the expanding family, although Rebekah undoubtedly felt a bit trapped and must have struggled with all the work and emotional demands created by babies. Young Lyndon, according to later memories, was restless, curious, and a bit wild, given to running away or hiding or other attention-getting ploys, just what one would expect from a pampered first child after the birth of siblings.

In September of 1913, as Johnson turned five, the family moved downriver to the village of Johnson City, the county seat of neighboring Blanco County. Schooling for Lyndon provided one excuse, new real estate ventures by Sam a second, and, one suspects, the aspirations of Rebekah a third. Note that Johnson City was quite familiar to Sam. The grandparents Johnson had lived there periodically in order to provide a better education for their children, and several relatives lived in the area. The move, although for a then considerable fifteen miles, never broke the ties to the old home place. Visits to paternal grandparents were frequent, and in summer months Lyndon spent extended periods back on the Pedernales.

In the year before the move, a four-year-old Lyndon began his education. The circumstances later took on national significance. Location is part of the story. Lyndon's birthplace and first home, set back about a hundred yards from the Pedernales, was not more

18

than two hundred yards upriver from a road junction and a ford (in water volume the Pedernales, except in the spring or when in flood, was closer to a creek than to what most people mean by a river). At this junction, the county had built a one-room school, appropriately referred to as Junction School, the easternmost such school in Gillespie County. It accommodated, in walking distance, the thirty or so elementary students who lived too far east of Stonewall (three miles) to walk to the larger school in that village. It was quite typical of the one-room, one-teacher schools that still dotted rural America. Unfortunately for Rebekah, who had two new babies to care for, the school play area was temptingly close to her backyard, or just across a small field. A gregarious Lyndon could see and hear the children at recess, even as he could barely be restrained from joining the children who walked by his house each morning. Given the temptation, and no restraining fence, young Lyndon kept running away to the play yard, to the despair of Rebekah, who feared that poisonous snakes might lurk in the intervening field.

As a solution to this problem, sometime in the fall of 1912 Rebekah asked the teenage teacher, Kathryn (Kate) Deadrich, to allow Lyndon to attend her school. A warmhearted Kate, despite her impossible teaching burden, consented and secured the needed permission from the school board. From then on Lyndon walked the short distance with a cousin, or Rebekah took a few minutes to escort her son to school. For Rebekah the arrangement was a blessing, a covert form of child care, the only such available in a rural area. Thousands, if not millions, of other parents in rural America made similar arrangements, usually when a second or third child eagerly sought to accompany siblings to school. Lyndon was exceptional only in being a first child.

In no full sense did Lyndon begin his schoolwork at Junction. He would enter the first grade in Johnson City the next year. The Junction experience was his kindergarten. An always solicitous and eager Rebekah had already taught Lyndon the alphabet and how to spell some words. Thus, at Junction he probably worked at what rural schools still designated the primer, or a simple reader that often took up half of one's first year at school (slow students completed only the primer in one year). Although eager for the social contact, and academically precocious, Lyndon was otherwise too immature for school. He still used baby talk (Grandmother Baines was still "Dan Mama" when he was in the first grade) and insisted on sitting on Kate's lap for reading. She remembered him as exceptionally personable—friendly and loving although petulantly demanding and egotistic. With the sentimentality and sense of showmanship so characteristic of the adult LBJ, he later invited Kate to his inaugural. He then brought the aged and retired teacher from her California home to join him in front of the old Junction School for the signing of the Elementary and Secondary Education Act of 1965. She not only received his well-publicized praise and the pen but enjoyed a brief flurry of national attention, including an appearance on one major television show.

His first schooling revealed another, often overlooked aspect of Johnson's youth. His cousin took him under her wing and escorted him to the one-room school. That was typical. Half of his neighbors were relatives—paternal grandparents, uncles, aunts, or cousins. Frequent visits and shared work kept the larger family together. Grandmother Baines spent several summers with Lyndon's parents. Clearly, many of the chores of child rearing devolved on these relatives. Even later, as branches of the family moved out of the hills, LBJ's life still moved, almost entirely, within the purview of this extended clan. Until he came to Washington as a congressional aide in 1931, he had never lived beyond the protective reach of his own kin. This support was all-important. He gained his early jobs at least in part through the influence of family members. He also learned, in this familial context, a very personal style of politics. One gained goals by bestowing and receiving favors, by building extended networks of trust or mutual dependence, by attending to the whole range of personal concerns or idiosyncracies of other people. This mode of relating and decision making bypasses formal rules, bureaucratic procedures, defined and objective criteria. It reinforced Johnson's lifelong yearning for the approval or affection of others, for concrete, often sentiment-filled gauges of achievement. Although young Lyndon sometimes rebelled against all the care and concern and close scrutiny, what is suggested by the record is a child very dependent upon his extended family. He became lonely and insecure whenever he moved out of its protective circle.

The 1913 move to Johnson City opened a prosperous seven-year interlude for the Johnson family, an interlude that ended with a move back to the farm in 1920. In these years Sam sold real estate from a small downtown office and managed several investment properties. His earnings never matched his aspirations, but he gained enough to provide all available opportunities for his five children. In 1917, blessed with a degree of financial security, Sam ran for, and in a special election regained, his seat in the Texas House, retaining it until financial misfortune and poor health induced him to retire from politics in 1924. He never lost an election. And in this second tour at Austin he added to his earlier support of economic legislation that favored the farmers of his district a spirited defense of his many German constituents against repressive legislation during World War I.

For these golden years, the skimpy records provide occasional glimpses into a close, talkative, argumentive, vibrant family, the most cosmopolitan and best informed in Johnson City. Sam controlled his penchant for alcohol and, in what later became an item of banter, even voted for statewide prohibition. Rebekah, although still yearning for a real city and more cultural opportunities, enjoyed a large and lovely Victorian home, hired help for the numerous household chores, and a large fund of respect from her neighbors, respect both for her exceptional education and refinement and for her generosity and piety. She remained somewhat aloof. She did not assume an active role even in the Baptist church. But she briefly edited a weekly newspaper, did some reporting for out-of-town newspapers, and took on a continuing but unpaid job as a teacher of elocution and dancing, both at the high school and in her home. She also tried, with an indomitable will and a toughness far beyond Sam's, to control and form her five children in her own image of Victorian propriety and vocational ambition. The children played, competed, and performed well in school. Lyndon spent the happiest years of his childhood in this, his first of two Johnson City interludes. Just before it ended, he most enjoyed campaigning with his father or rare trips to visit him at the capitol in Austin.

The move to Johnson City marked no abrupt change in the family's way of life. The small county seat, which appears drab and dusty in old photographs, served as a minor marketing center for surrounding farmers. The only buildings of any size were the courthouse and the two-story combined elementary and high school. The village had a few retail outlets, three churches, at times a restaurant, a rooming house, and until Prohibition a saloon, a cause of considerable distress for Rebekah. Even after World War I the town had only a part-time electrical generator, and this only for lights. In the twenties homes had to rely on mantle lamps, gasoline-driven washing machines, battery-powered radios, and iceboxes. The city had no water or sewage system. Thus, life in Johnson City combined aspects of city and country, with the country mode dominant. The three hundred residents lived, for the most part, in block-sized lots, which blended gradually into surrounding farms. The Johnsons, typically, pastured a milk cow,

21

built a small barn to house cow and horses, grew a vegetable garden, and had recourse to an outdoor privy. They used a hand pump to raise water to the kitchen sink. But town life did mean a clustering of people, a pool of youngsters for sport or play, and all without the problems of cities. Since everyone knew everyone else, the same neighborliness prevailed as back on the Pedernales farm.

Lyndon enrolled in the elementary section of the Johnson City school, still only a tender five years old. He averaged a year younger than most classmates. No matter. He did exceptionally well in these years. He was prodded by an eager and firmly dominating mother. His report cards for the middle years (third and fourth grades) vindicate her efforts. In the third grade he made almost all As and an A+ in spelling and writing. In the fourth, he made all As except in geography and deportment. Yet he was an indifferent student, not particularly challenged by books or by academic subjects, but able to coast along because of a sharp mind and his mother's prodding or, at times, her completion of his homework assignments. He already used his abundant skills in flattery and persuasion to woo his teachers. Classmates, in later memory, recalled a boy gifted with leadership skills and preternaturally addicted to politics. He passed out campaign literature as early as the first grade and eagerly absorbed every shred of political gossip from his father and visiting cronies. A gregarious Sam delighted in talk and in company, making the Johnson City home a way station for traveling politicians, and thus all the more exciting for the children.

In 1917, Lyndon's paternal grandmother, Eliza Bunton Johnson, died. Her death followed that of Sam, Sr., by two years, and also followed several years of invalidism. Her death left the family farm on the Pedernales to her eight children. A proud Sam decided, in 1919, to buy out the other heirs and thus kept the farm together. His brother Tom owned nearby land. The two brothers tried to turn their properties into a successful farming operation. Their timing proved disasterous, as it did for anyone who bought land in 1919. The high land values of the immediate, inflated postwar era were artificial, as were the alluringly high prices for cotton and other crops. To buy the land, and to make even more expensive improvements, Sam sold all his other holdings save the now mortgaged house in Johnson City. Eventually, he went into debt by an estimated thirty thousand dollars and then tried the impossible— to pay it off through farm earnings. He suffered from periodic droughts and floods, but even more from a disastrous plunge in

22

farm prices and land values in the early 1920s. He could not make the required payments by 1922, eventually sold the ranch for half what he paid for it, and in 1922 moved his family back to the Johnson City home, now burdened by debts that he would never be able to pay off. He endlessly refinanced them through new loans. Back in Johnson City, Sam suffered from obvious depression, drank more frequently and was often in bed. Sheer economic and physical necessity forced him to give up his legislative seat in 1924. His failure at farming, and his near bankruptcy, which recapitulated the earlier experiences of both Sam's and Rebekah's parents, also proved a terrible blow to Rebekah's pride. It mocked all her pretensions of gentility, reinforced her tendency to retreat into romantic fantasy, and often left her incapacitated for homework. This economic failure, following that of two grandparents, may have contributed to Lyndon's later, omnipresent sense of impending failure, a fear that haunted him until his death.

The Johnsons made the move back to the Pedernales farm in 1920, this time moving into the former home of Lyndon's grandparents. Although plain and unpretentious, the house was larger than the old homestead where Sam and Rebekah began their married life. Of all interludes in Lyndon's childhood, this is the least documented. Sam struggled to make a living as a farmer. The children had to do their part. Thus, a surviving neighbor remembered, or thought he remembered, Lyndon plowing fields behind a team of horses. No doubt he wielded the hoe in summer and possibly joined in late fall cotton picking. But knowing Rebekah, Lyndon never had to work to the detriment of his schooling. In the fall of 1920 a tall and gangling Lyndon, still only twelve, began eighth grade (in the Texas eleven-year system this was the first year of high school) at Stonewall, riding the three miles on a mule. He took violin lessons (but had no aptitude or sustained interest in music), excelled in declamation (a first prize), and made excellent but never outstanding grades. His report card, from the pretentiously named Stonewall High School, showed As in languages, spelling, and deportment, but only Bs or an occasional C in history, composition, and algebra. By then his confessed weakness was in math, probably because of a lack of interest and of application. Lyndon did best in subjects that allowed him to coast along on the basis of his natural cleverness, worst in courses that required sustained study or memorization.

Even though he easily passed all his courses, Lyndon now had to suffer the inadequacies of rural schools. In a letter to his grandmother Baines he referred to his one teacher at Stonewall, suggesting the continued elementary form of instruction. The academic deficiencies only multiplied in his ninth grade, which he took at Albert, a tiny community approximately five miles south of the Johnson farm. No grade reports survive, but it is unlikely that Lyndon had problems with the academic work in what was the final year of instruction at this small, heavily German school. Thus, by the summer of 1922 Lyndon was half through high school but had not yet faced any challenging courses offered by teachers with specialized competence.

At this point Sam and Rebekah made a costly, even a sacrificial, decision. Though they faced the loss of their farm and desperately needed Lyndon's labor that summer, they sent him to San Marcos to take summer enrichment courses at the high-quality demonstration school attached to Southwest Texas State Teachers College. He stayed in a boarding house, not with his grandmother Baines. His landlady remembered him as unusually friendly, but perhaps also very dependent. He treated her like a mother. One of his Albert teachers (possibly his only teacher) taught German that summer in the demonstration school and tried to help a struggling Lyndon. Rebekah wrote to enlist her support. Rebekah wanted Lyndon to be better prepared for the more rigorous work at Johnson City High. Lyndon was not mature enough for the challenge. Of course, he was in a familiar environment, but still away from a protective mother, and for the first time in his life, he faced academically rigorous courses. He overspent his allowance and lacked self-discipline in his studies.

The return of the Johnson family to Johnson City in 1922 could not be a happy homecoming. As Lyndon later lamented, his daddy had "gone bust." It could have been worse. It usually was for farmers who faced foreclosure. The critical difference for Sam once again involved the larger clan and his extensive network of political cronies. His two brothers cosigned notes that allowed him to retain the Johnson City house. In the following years, as Sam struggled with debts, uncles and cousins always stood ready to help the children. Because of this support, the plight of the Johnson family was never so perilous as Lyndon later pictured it. He suffered no childhood poverty, at least not in living standards. The family continued to occupy one of the best houses in Johnson City. An expansive Sam refused to live like a poor man; the family always had an automobile, a mark of affluence in the hills of the twenties. And, until 1924, Sam retained his seat in the legislature. He still had the respect of half the leading politicians of the state.

Because of his many political favors to his constituents during the years, he long enjoyed an exceptional degree of indulgence both in borrowing money and in postponing repayment. Thus Sam was able to live above his means for over a decade. Technically, his liabilities undoubtedly exceeded his assets from 1922 on, but in terms of consumption, of living standards, of communal standing or social status, the family continued to rank among the top in Johnson City. Much later Lyndon would slowly pay off many of his father's old debts.

No doubt the financial strain exacted its penalties. Sam degenerated in both health and morale. He drank too much. Especially when drinking, he could not control his explosive temper and often lashed out at the children. He vacillated between indulgence and overly harsh discipline. He and Rebekah grew more apart, until they led parallel but separate lives in the same house. Rebekah became more reclusive, suffered some loss of hearing, and often escaped into her romantic fantasies. The always chaotic and exciting household almost broke apart, with a father now almost pathetic because of financial distress and now all too apparent weaknesses.

It is impossible to gauge the effects of this family pathology on the children. They suffered no social stigma in Johnson City and retained their close friendships in the community. Most families have problems. Most families in the Johnson City area faced financial difficulties. Most lived with less luxuries than the Johnsons. But the Johnson children had to face up to the faults of their father, and a degree of fear and estrangement replaced the earlier camaraderie. Lyndon no longer had reason to idolize his father. Sam's absences, or his withdrawal from family responsibilities, forced Lyndon to take on more parental responsibilities. This led to the resentment of his siblings, to a more competitive relationship with his father, and to justifiable charges that he bossed and manipulated his brothers and sisters. What is not so well known is how much Lyndon would continue the role of a father throughout his life. He continued to look out for his mother and to give advice and financial support to his siblings. In many ways he was an overprotective father to his able but weak brother Sam Houston, whose escapades, drinking bouts, and unpaid debts haunted LBJ during his presidency.

In connection with this troubled period of Johnson's youth, one might ask: What about religion? Did he have the support of a church community? These questions, like so many others, allow no simple answer. Religious beliefs and behavior make up one of the most elusive, but also fascinating, facets of LBJ's career. The story must begin at the beginning.

Most of Johnson's paternal and maternal ancestors were Baptists. In the nineteenth-century South, this meant that they were Missionary Baptists, or what became the present Southern Baptist Convention. Few if any took the extreme, exaggerated Calvinist option of Antimission or Primitive Baptists, the denomination that claimed Sam Rayburn. The Missionary Baptists combined a moderate Reformed or Calvinist position with an evangelical style—that is, an emphasis upon religious experience or feeling, upon the centrality of the rebirth experience, and upon an active proselytizing of converts. The Baines family helped establish the strength of Baptism in Texas. Rebekah Johnson retained at least her nominal membership in the Baptist church, and Lyndon's sisters grew up in the Baptist Sunday schools of Johnson City. Because of this family heritage, Lyndon always acknowledged his Baptist roots and continued family involvement, and at times he used this connection for political purposes. Most of his best friends were Baptists, in part because this was, by far, the most popular Protestant denomination in central Texas, where even the most wealthy or prominent families were most likely Baptists. But LBJ never joined a Baptist church and, insofar as doctrinal issues ever made any sense to him, he rejected Baptist beliefs. Nor did he favor either the plain style of worship or the born-again emphasis of Baptists or other evangelical denominations.

Sam Early Johnson, Sr., Lyndon's grandfather, broke from family traditions and left the Baptist church. He did so in order to enlist in a very distinctive sect, the Brethren in Christ or Christadelphians. This small American movement, which coalesced by the time of the Civil War, remained tiny in spite of dedicated mission efforts. It gained a few widely scattered congregations in central Texas. Its radically independent congregations shared some common doctrines and practices with the earlier, and related, Restoration Movement launched by Barton Stone and Alexander Campbell. Like their Christian or Disciples cousins, Christadelphian congregations accepted an Arminian or radically free-will position, eschewed denominational labels, and made the Lord's Supper a central focus of their weekly worship. But unlike the Disciples, the Christadelphians adhered to the separatism of the early Brethren or Anabaptists of the Reformation era (the present Mennonites, Amish, and Church of the Brethren). They believed in a pure church separated from a sinful world and thus were pacifists and would not vote or hold public office. Finally, and most distinctive, the Brethren in Christ adopted the tenets of nineteenth-century Adventism. They accepted a Jewish and corporealist view of reality, believed in the imminent return of the Christ to establish his earthly kingdom, and rejected any doctrine of immortality. They believed death complete, with no survival, but also looked forward to a literal Resurrection. They believed the wages of sin would be a second and final death, not some eternal torment, or hell. Given their apocalyptic outlook, Christadelphians lived lives of simple purity and devotion, all the time preparing themselves for the Second Coming.

Sam Early Johnson became virtually a lay minister for this sect, its most persuasive advocate in the Stonewall and Johnson City areas. He was a close friend of a leading Christadelphian minister and welcomed him frequently to the Pedernales farm. He took his own family to the Christadelphian church in Gillespie County. When, during Lyndon's first five years, Sam and Rebekah joined the old folks for a family trip to church, this is the congregation they attended. But Sam, Jr., never adhered to his father's narrow faith. When he grew up he was too fun loving, too willing to party and dance. Also, he was politically active and held office, sins that excluded one from the pure and undefiled church by Christadelphian standards. One older Christadelphian friend of Sam, Sr., much later denied that the grandfather could ever have predicted that Lyndon would be a senator, for such an anticipation contravened his religious commitments. Yet, one senses that some of the lingering influences of the Christadelphian faith lingered on in Sam, Jr. Notably, when the family moved to Johnson City, Sam passed up the Baptist and Methodist churches and attended, although not very often, the Christian church, or the church whose beliefs and practices came closest to what he knew as a boy. What is not clear is how much, if any, Christadelphian doctrines directly influenced young Lyndon. Nothing is his career, except possibly a distaste for violence or war, revealed any detailed knowledge about, or sympathy for, the Christadelphians. In most respects his active political life was an affront to this sect. Besides, Lyndon would never delve deeply into doctrinal issues, and on the more intellectual aspects of religion he remained as simplistic and conventional as a child. From this doctrinal innocence or indifference sprang, in part, his later, much remarked ecumenical openness.

As a youth in Johnson City, Lyndon could not be aloof from the three small local congregations. They provided the major social outlet for the village. Most families adhered to one of them. In theory, the three churches offered quite distinct and conflicting versions of Christian doctrine—the Reformed doctrines of the Baptists, the Arminian and evangelical approach of the Methodists, and the calmly rational and nonevangelical free-will position of the Christians or Disciples. In fact, as in so many small towns, the doctrinal differences blurred considerably in practice, and the three congregations, each of which struggled to find and pay for at least a part-time minister, often joined in cooperative services and youth activities. When one congregation invited outside preachers to hold special summer services or revivals, the members of the other churches attended, in what served as a major social event in rural churches throughout America. In the summer of 1923, when fourteen-year-old Lyndon had completed his junior year in high school, the Christian church sponsored such a revival. Several young people, LBJ among them, made the proper confessions and submitted themselves for baptism. The Disciples did not believe in an explosive rebirth experience, but made a straightforward appeal for belief in the New Testament revelation, for repentance of one's actual transgressions, and for public confession of one's belief or faith. Upon such confession, one became a candidate for baptism by immersion and for remission of the penalty owed for past sins. Such baptism admitted one, in proper purity, into the Church of Christ. Along with a cousin, LBJ was baptized and thus became a member of the local Christian church. He retained this often nominal church affiliation throughout the rest of his life.

Such barren facts leave all the important questions unanswered. One does not know anything about the actual experiences of an adolescent in the distant summer of 1923, about the influences that lay behind his choices, about his own comprehension and understanding of the religious issues at stake. In fact, even the surface details are far from clear, and these led much later to an almost comical controversy. Since, for Disciples, baptism is the final, climactic step in the drama of salvation, they were most concerned to establish the facts about Lyndon's baptism. When Lyndon became president, Disciples nationally rejoiced at his church affiliation; except for James A. Garfield, he was the only president from their movement. Thus, in 1966 the Texas Commission on Disciples History and the Texas Association of Christian Churches decided to place an expensive bronze plaque at the site of his baptism.

Unfortunately, LBJ could not remember any of the details, frequently claiming conversion at age twelve. The local congregation had no clear records. But a few interviews easily established the correct summer, and all the local residents could point out the deep pool in the Pedernales long used for baptisms. But, just before completion of the marker, Lyndon's cousin, Ava Johnson Cox, wrote a disturbing letter to church officials at Texas Christian University. In the summer of 1923, as she remembered it, the Pedernales was all but dry. Thus, the congregation had moved the baptisms to Flat Creek, a move attested to by other participants. Ava noted the relative inaccessibility of the spot and suggested that the churches go ahead with their marker on the Pedernales, a plaque that was to read: "Lyndon Baines Johnson was baptized, summer 1923, Pedernales River." Since this site was on a paved road, she apparently did not believe a little lie would hurt anyone. Not all the church officials were so sanguine, and the marker issue devolved into a year-long controversy, one that occupied an enormous amount of staff time in the White House.

Did any continuities tie LBJ's later public religiosity to his youthful experiences? Perhaps. His choice of the Christian church may have some significance. It gave Lyndon a moderate and reasonable yet acceptable alternative to the conventional Baptist and Methodist born-again Christianity, which predominated in Texas. The Disciples also rejected the humility and self-denial that accompanied the Reformed doctrine of undeserved grace. They replaced this with a very voluntaristic religion, one that placed primary emphasis upon individual choice and continued effort (closer to a religion of good works). Lyndon understood this. Although plain and simple in their worship services, the Disciples did place a stylized Communion service at the center. Throughout his adult life Johnson seemed more at home in formal or liturgical services and caused later controversy by his penchant for taking communion in churches of various denominations. In these small ways his boyhood experience may have helped shape the adult and the politician. In the very variety of his youthful religious contacts one can find a clue to his broad tolerance and his respect for so many varieties of Christianity (and also for non-Christian religions insofar as he understood them). But the continuities are tenuous. And except in the most general and attenuated form, Christian doctrines seemed to have little to do with Johnson's career. He was not only tolerant but undiscriminating. Religion, however defined, seemed good, like motherhood. Johnson thus endorsed it, at times indulged a little of it, but one feels that he never began to understand what all the doctrines and forms meant to the devout. Serious dogmas, as much as philosophical theology, passed him by, as much unrecognized as unappreciated.

In the fall of 1922 Lyndon began the tenth grade at the Johnson City High School. At that time the three high school grades (nine through eleven) occupied the top floor of the old stone building (it later burned). A photograph shows only twenty-four students in these three grades in 1924, or too few for any student choice in courses taken. But at least the three or four teachers were specialized as to discipline, and most seemed dedicated. In Blanco County only Johnson City and Blanco had high schools, and the two competed in sports and for academic excellence. Lyndon continued his earlier pattern of performance—largely As and Bs. He finished second in his class of six and excelled in all areas of leadership. He was senior class president. Unusual for so small a school, it sponsored a debate team. LBJ and his partner participated in regional meets but never won enough to advance to state finals. The principal of the school reinforced Lyndon's interest in politics and current events. The debate team ordered materials on the League of Nations from the University of Texas, and one year it debated the issue of U.S. Marines in Nicaragua. Someone also contributed the *Congressional Record* to the school library. By his senior year, Lyndon at least assumed the pose of big man on campus, dressed more nattily than classmates, entered enthusiastically into all activities except sports (he played some summer baseball but without any noted success), and gave everyone the impression that he was going to do big things with his life. Although boastful and arrogant at times, he was so personable and charming as to win enduring friendships, some that lasted until his death. For his 1924 graduation, he was brash enough to send an invitation to the governor of Texas and because of the governor's respect for Sam, received a handwritten note of declination and congratulations. Of course, Lyndon gave the student oration at the exercises.

By high school graduation Lyndon was only fifteen going on sixteen. He looked older, because he was already over six-feet tall, beanpole thin, but mature in face and in behavior. He stood out from the crowd because of his supercharged energy, his diversity of interests, and his intense involvement with events in the outside world. His personal magnetism proved appealing to his female classmates. Two girls felt themselves special and both helped him with his homework. One, Louise Casparis, who had helped Rebekah with housework, lent her class ring to Lyndon and then had a hard time getting it back. It was clear she was infatuated with him. But she sensed, probably correctly, that the Johnson family considered itself too good for the Casparises, a family that had earlier owned a saloon.

Lyndon soon had eyes only for another classmate, Kitty Clyde Ross. Both girls had known Lyndon since age five, and both had frequently played at the Johnson house. Kitty Clyde was an exceptionally gifted young woman of sixteen, valedictorian of her class, and destined for a successful career as teacher and school administrator. The Ross and Johnson families were close. As a local merchant, the father was affluent for the area. Thus, Kitty Clyde might have met even Rebekah's high standards and seemed almost good enough for Lyndon. During their senior year she and Lyndon became very close. They "went together" but not steadily. They talked and talked. They shared their life dreams. They held hands. They never kissed. Already close friends, they were now drawn to each other, yet frightened and awed, by budding sexual feelings. Lyndon was shy, caught up in the sweet and romantic images of love bequeathed to him by Rebekah and her favorite poet, Robert Browning. Normally, Lyndon's youthful puppy love would be an unnoticed aspect of a boy's adolescence. But for Lyndon no human relationship ever really ended. He held on to all of them. The courtship of Kitty, if such it was, did not last long. Her parents, of course, opposed any steady relationship for a daughter so young. In the fall of 1922 Kitty matriculated at the University of Texas. Shortly thereafter, Lyndon ran off to California. Had their college careers coincided, the infatuation of sixteen might have matured into something enduring. Even in the perspective of forty years, Kitty retained a bit of the glow of a romantic teenager. And Lyndon retained a special tenderness toward Kitty. She married while at the University of Texas, but returned to Blanco County, eventually serving as superintendent of schools. On trips back home or on vacation, Lyndon was able to maintain the friendship. He seemed to treasure all his old friends in Johnson City all the more as he moved on to national fame. They felt honored that he even remembered them, were awed by his high offices, and seemed, in their relaxed acceptance and praise, to allow him a welcome respite from the games he had to play in Washington. Lyndon saw to it that his staff kept up all the appropriate contacts—letters at times of death, birth, or marriage.

For Kitty Clyde, Lyndon's attentions went beyond such courtesies. He visited Kitty when her mother died. He often invited her and her husband to his ranch. He gave a graduation address at the Johnson City School when she was superintendent. As president he attended high school graduation at Johnson City and of course gave some remarks. The complicated security and communications arrangements almost wrecked the ceremony. In January

31

1965, Johnson extended to Kitty and her husband a special invitation to his inaugural, flew them to Washington on Air Force One, and then to the White House in a presidential helicopter. As vice president, Lyndon even brought his famous Pakistani camel driver to visit Kitty and her school. He saw her for the last time at the dedication of the LBJ library.

Graduation from high school initiated a troubled interlude in Lyndon's life. Even in the summer of 1924 his life took on a frightening pattern, including unruly escapades with older boys and surreptitious drinking. After stealing away his father's car and wrecking it, he fled to a cousin's house in Robstown, down near the Gulf, and found some demanding work in a cotton gin (an interlude remembered, and its importance exaggerated, when LBJ became president). His parents forgave him and begged him to come home.

Then came a major disappointment. Alone among his high school classmates, Lyndon had to postpone college. Not only did Kitty Clyde Ross enroll in the University of Texas, but his four other classmates all attended Southwest Texas. But they could not matriculate immediately. As graduates of an unaccredited high school, they had to pass entrance exams in three "nonaffiliated" courses, including math. These exams usually followed at least six weeks of intensive subcollegiate instruction. Lyndon enrolled in these subcollegiate courses, possibly in August (six weeks before the fall quarter), probably in September, 1924. When he filled out registration forms at Southwest Texas in 1927, he listed this earlier attendance. He did not successfully complete this remedial work. He either dropped or was forced out of these courses because of poor performance, or, less likely, completed the six weeks and then failed one or more of the entrance exams. In later years he ruefully referred to being "kicked out" of Southwest Texas. In any case, a disappointed Johnson was unable to matriculate with his classmates.

After this galling failure, Lyndon returned home to Johnson City, dropped all immediate plans for college, and very shortly took off for California. He could have repeated his work in the subcollegiate courses during the next quarter, and possibly have passed the required exams. But then he would have been behind his Johnson City classmates. As so often in life, he chose to retreat. Also, and characteristically, he soon tried to cover up, or deny, this failure. With the cooperation of his family, particularly his brother Sam Houston, he eliminated this frustrating interlude from a carefully cultivated LBJ legend. In compensation, he substituted exaggerated accounts of a "daring" adventure in California.

Obviously, Rebekah was bitterly disappointed at Lyndon's academic failure. It threatened her romantic and soaring hopes for a great career for her firstborn. Thus, she struggled for over two years to get Lyndon back to San Marcos. Why did he rebuff her? Why did he give up so quickly? Obviously, he now had realistic doubts about his academic ability and preparation. For him to have remained longer in the subcollegiate courses would have been very embarrassing, an assault on his huge but still vulnerable ego. He lacked the needed maturity and academic self-discipline. He was abnormally young for college work. A pampered child, he remained very dependent on his immediate family, unprepared to function far beyond its protective circle. Finally, the financial plight of his father might have deterred him. Sam would have borrowed the needed funds, but not without additional hardship. Lyndon's lackluster academic prospects scarcely justified such a sacrifice.

Lyndon Johnson's California sojourn became the stuff of legend. It is impossible to get all the details straight. In the early fall of 1924, four other young men in Johnson City, those not in college, determined to seek their fortunes in a booming California. The main architects of the plan were two brothers, Walter and Otto Crider, from a Johnson City family that had been close friends of the Johnsons for three generations. An older brother, Ben, and one of the most selfless and loyal friends LBJ ever knew, had already moved to California, there to find employment in a cement factory at Tehachapi, a small town in the mountains that mark the southern end of the fertile San Joaquin Valley. Ben promised to help his brothers find jobs. Two friends wanted to go along. Lyndon, although younger, decided to join them after failing his subcollegiate work at Southwest Texas. He needed to get away. The five left in November, in a Model T Ford owned by one of the Crider boys, and took five days to go by way of El Paso and Blyth, California. Lyndon's baby brother, Sam Houston, later reported opposition from Lyndon's parents, which forced the boys to leave while Sam was out of town. Purportedly, Sam returned and called Texas Rangers along their route in a futile effort to capture Lyndon and bring him home. The story smacks of exaggeration if not pure invention.

Even more exaggerated were the stories LBJ later invented about the trip and his stay in California. In his accounts, the escapade became an early version of *The Grapes of Wrath* with thrilling incidents along the way and a vagabond life after arrival. In some accounts he stayed two years, struggled to make a living, went hungry at times, and picked grapes, washed dishes, and did migratory work. Actually, he did none of this. According to Otto Crider, LBJ accompanied the other four only as far as San Bernardino. Upon arrival there, Lyndon telephoned his cousin, Tom Martin, who grew up in the house that is today the LBJ ranch. In fact, knowing the pattern of clan support in the Johnson family, either Lyndon or his parents had already alerted Martin, who gladly met the boys and took Lyndon home with him. The other four went on to Tehachapi. Two found work in the cement factory; the other two worked at odd jobs. Sometime later, Tom Martin and Lyndon drove up to Tehachapi to visit their hometown friends and to regale Ben Crider, whom Lyndon had not yet seen, with ever wilder stories of the automobile trip. Lyndon was clearly the most imaginative raconteur of the group. Tom and Lyndon brought one of the younger boys, John F. Koeniger, back to San Bernardino. As far as the records show, Lyndon never lived anywhere except in the home of his cousin, once again demonstrating how reluctant he was to break from the protective family circle.

Tom Martin was a brilliant but unstable lawyer who had fled to California after he lost his job as police chief in San Antonio because of a nasty scandal. Married, with a child, he had established a profitable practice in San Bernardino and at least liked to boast to his admiring young friends about movie star clients. Tom proved an affable host, providing LBJ and Koeniger with room, board, and new clothes, but with no regular salary. In return, they worked in his law office as de facto secretaries and clerks. According to Koeniger, Martin held out vague promises that the two could in this way learn the law and possibly even qualify for the law board exam in an indulgent Nevada, a pipe dream that should have been transparent even to two boys from the hill country of Texas. According to Koeniger, Lyndon threw himself into the work with an energy and sense of purpose never exhibited in school. In short, the two boys practically took over the office, with LBJ soon rivaling Martin in his ability to deal with clients over the phone. In addition, LBJ also took a part-time job as elevator operator in the same office building (a job commemorated by a plaque during his presidency). For Lyndon, this law office experience became his equivalent of college—a breaking away from home and parents, intense involvement in a new enterprise, and the acquisition of insight not only into the challenges of office management but into his own superb skills in dealing with clients.

The challenging interlude proved all too brief. Life with Tom Martin was not at all the lark it first seemed. Martin had problems. When, in the summer of 1925, his wife brought their son to visit relatives back in the hill country, a reckless Tom began to indulge his two favorite weaknesses—wine and women. He openly flaunted his mistress, allegedly a divorced wife of Jack Dempsey, and launched on what amounted to a two-month binge. The two boys, now as appalled as formerly charmed by Tom, had to try to keep his law practice going. Soon they ran out of office funds and skirted criminality by offering legal advice on the phone. When they heard that the wife was on the way home, they helped Tom clean up his house and made plans to leave. Koeniger found a local job. Lyndon came home. His uncle Clarence Martin had driven the wife and grandchild back to San Bernardino and, perhaps by prior arrangement with Lyndon's parents, brought the boy home in his Buick in September 1925. He had been away for only ten months.

Of course, Rebekah assumed that he returned to enter college. Not so. Lyndon was still unwilling to face the challenge. Meanwhile, Sam had left the legislature and, after part-time work as a game warden, had gained through political connections a job as foreman on a road building crew working west of Johnson City. He now hired Lyndon, who remained on this job from September 1925 to January or February 1927. He drove the old open trucks and used horses to scoop out the cuts for the highway. Later, on job applications, he noted a promotion to some sort of supervisor, a claim impossible to verify. This road work was unfulfilling and made up a very unhappy interlude in his life. He once again ran with older and wilder boys. He joined cronies in minor thievery, in exaggerated pranks, and in the drinking of moonshine whiskey. He seemed volatile, quick to quarrel, given to exaggerated posturing and poses to please girls. It was almost as if Lyndon wanted to defy his parents or to embarrass them by his behavior.

Fortunately, Lyndon's holding pattern in Johnson City came to an end in early 1927. A new administration in Austin cost Sam his foreman's job. This meant no more road work for Lyndon. Impending unemployment joined with some climactic pranks, a nasty fistfight, and an arrest. Out of this came self-examination. For whatever reasons, Lyndon decided to go to college. The battle of wills with his parents came to an end. He would no longer waste his talents. Still a bit defiant, but with overwhelming seriousness, he begged a ride to San Marcos on 8 February 1927. He left behind his home, the beloved Pedernales. Except for vacations, or even shorter visits, he would not live here again until he retired from the presidency in 1969.

What assets did Lyndon bring with him out of the hills? Not many. He had no great achievement to boost his ego, no academic success, no athletic prowess, no special talent or aptitude, not even any clear beliefs or goals. He was not inquisitive, philosophical, or deep in that sort of way. On most moral and political issues he seemed, at best, conventional, at worst, without firm opinions of any sort. Thus, he had little in the way of intellectual resources, of mature convictions, to anchor or to guide him. His identity seemed to rest, to an astonishing degree, on the reflected perceptions of other people, on human relationships, on his ties to family and friends. His major asset was a capacity to relate, to win friends, to persuade people. The only subject that seemed to fascinate him, the one he had absorbed at his father's side, was party politics, the process of winning elections and gaining and solidifying a type of influence over others.

TOP: The Sam Ealy Johnson family in about 1895, in front of their home.
BOTTOM: The house in which Lyndon Johnson was born, in the period before modern restoration.

Lyndon at six months.
Already a politician.

Lyndon, age four or five,
and sister Rebekah.

The Johnson family home in Johnson City, about 1915.

The five Johnson children, back on the farm near Stonewall.

TOP: Lyndon in California, 1925, with cousin Tom Martin at left.
BOTTOM: Mr. Johnson with students, Cotulla, Texas, 1929.

Lyndon and college debate team, with Professor Howard M. Green (center), 1927–28.

LBJ with two debate teams at Sam Houston High.

A newly married LBJ and Lady Bird return to Washington, 1934.

3

THE
BUSINESS OF
EDUCATION

Lyndon B. Johnson pursued only two careers—the first in education, the second in government. He spent less than five years in education, including his teacher training and three brief teaching jobs. Even as he began his first career, he retained his boyhood fascination with party politics. As he studied and then taught he accumulated the political experience, and began cultivating the needed contacts, that later offered him the opportunity for political success. His career shift did not mean that he in any way became disillusioned with education. Just the opposite. He left this first mistress during the glow of an early and exhilarating romance, before the onset of any disillusionment. He retained an idealistic, almost romantic image of teaching that he earlier absorbed from Rebekah and that he further cultivated at Southwest Texas State Teachers College. A faith in the wondrous benefits of education, plus support of any measures designed to improve American schools and colleges, made up one of the few continuities in LBJ's career.

When eighteen-year-old Johnson caught a ride over to San Marcos on 8 February 1927, he came well aware of the challenge that faced him. He had to qualify by examination in three subjects, including geometry. A break of two and a half years from high school made the task even more intimidating. Since he came to San Marcos in the middle of the winter quarter, he had only six weeks to work in the subcollegiate program if he were to matriculate, as he planned, for the spring quarter. He first met with the professor in charge of admissions, and made a lasting impression by his maturity and by his detailed plans for college and career. He seemed to have it all worked out. He took the subcollegiate work and, aided by Rebekah's support and last-minute tutoring, barely passed all exams. In March he began his first quarter of college work.

Johnson's college career has supported even more legends than his youth up in the hills. No historian will ever be able, confidently, to sort out the mythic and the factual in these legends, many of which LBJ later absorbed and, typically, embellished. What the legends obscure are the prosaic details of Johnson's college experience. He came with compelling career goals—to gain his teaching credentials and a fulfilling job. He did not come as a student, in the sense of one who loves the life of the mind, who gains deep personal satisfaction from reading and learning. He viewed his courses, and his labored and unexciting study, in instrumental terms, save possibly for those courses that related directly to politics. College was a way station, a means to get ahead, a way to escape road work back in the hills. And it would work out as he expected. His college achievements opened the needed doors, launched him on an exciting career. This success helped shape his later, almost magical view of education as a tool that could enable people from the poorest or humblest background to realize their fullest potential, even to become president of the United States.

No wonder Johnson was so serious about his choice to attend college. He knew how much was at stake. This was his second chance, given his failure in 1924. He had to succeed or risk failure in life. The high risk factor had made the choice a difficult one, had helped defer the final decision. Back of the choice were lofty family expectations, a burden he carried with him always. But it had another side. Lyndon's choice mobilized the larger clan. His effort at San Marcos was a joint enterprise. Several uncles and aunts gave or lent him money to pay his way. His parents could not bear the full burden, particularly since his sister Rebekah would enter college the next fall. His mother virtually went to college with him, so deeply and emotionally was she involved with his every step. She wrote him almost daily, tutored him on weekends, even continued to help with his term papers. The circle of support extended to San Marcos, where a female cousin was already in college and where several relatives and family friends lived. Many of his closest Johnson City friends were already at Southwest Texas. It was a rare weekend that Lyndon either did not come home or entertain some member of his immediate family in San Marcos. Not so clear on the record, but possibly more important, was a broader, statewide network of friends developed over a political lifetime by Sam Johnson. For example, the parents already knew Cecil E. Evans, the president of the college, and telephoned him about Lyndon before the young man arrived on campus. They enlisted Evans's help in what became a broad cooperative effort to get Lyndon through college and launched into a promising career.

Why did Lyndon select Southwest Texas? Given his poor preparation and lack of scholarly interest, he had no other realistic choice. Nothing suggests any consideration of other options. Even his admission at the equally accessible University of Texas in Austin was questionable; its scholarly standards were high enough to frighten away a less than academically confident LBJ. Plenty of small denominational colleges would have admitted him; some would have imposed even less of an intellectual challenge, but none was as close or nearly as inexpensive. His college choice, when related to his later career, made him distinctive. No other American president had graduated from a comparable normal school or teachers' college. Those with degrees had attended either major universities or small liberal arts colleges. He was also distinctive, but not unique, in moving from public school teaching into politics without a law degree.

For LBJ, a familiar Southwest Texas proved to be an excellent choice. It demanded as much, academically, as he was then able or willing to tackle and provided a small, congenial context for the further development of his leadership skills. In a relatively small pond, he could develop confidence and gain a small measure of recognition. And despite all the later legends about glorious achievements or his unbridled quest for power, he achieved a less than average record in scholarship and just above average in extracurricular attainments. Also contrary to all the later myths, he never became the "big" man on campus.

In 1927, Southwest Texas fulfilled the same regional role as hundreds of normal schools all across America. In a roughly parallel development, these slowly evolved from teacher-training institutes, with academic standards at a high school level, to teachers colleges, with academic credentials barely adequate to

39

meet regional accreditation standards, and finally to the broad-purpose state colleges and universities of today. In the twenties, before the widespread development of community colleges, these public institutions constituted the lowest and broadest base of American higher education. Because of their flexible academic standards, low cost, and wide dispersion, they eventually made a college education available to millions of young people whose parents had never even thought of attending college. They made higher education possible for the ablest sons and daughters of farmers and artisans, for those of middling if not low income, and even for some of the children of affluent parents, those without the academic or social skills needed at prestigious universities. But, because of their selective appeal, such state colleges rarely trained Americans who gained other than local fame or eminence. And until after World War II the great majority of their graduates, more female than male, ended up as public school teachers.

In 1927, Southwest Texas was at least average in quality among teachers colleges. It had opened as a pre-college-level normal school in 1903 and had expanded to full college status in 1917; in 1919 the state gave it the name of Southwest Texas State Teachers College at San Marcos. The first and even to this day most spectacular building was what is now affectionately known as Old Main, an imposing brick castle atop the eastern crest of the ridge that marks the Balcones Fault. Its spires and red roof are visible for up to ten miles across the coastal plain. It literally backs against the hills to the north and west and looks out over the coastal plain to the south and east. At the base of the hill flows the sparkling clear and cold San Marcos River, less than a mile from one of the largest springs in the United States. The spring, the beautiful meadow, a refreshing swimming hole on the edge of the campus, and a large fish hatchery all had a distinctive appeal for students. Slowly, with growth, the campus expanded west along the crest of the ridge from the still-dominant Old Main. When LBJ matriculated, approximately nine hundred students (more in the summer quarter) took classes and studied in Old Main and in four additional brick buildings. A gym and several smaller buildings completed a campus still without dormitories. Commuting students joined the boarders, most from a fifty-mile radius of hill country and coastal plain. They lived in private houses in the residential area that blended into the commercial buildings on the square that surrounded the rather imposing Hays County courthouse.

The faculty at Southwest Texas matched the caliber of the college. Of fifty-six faculty members in 1927, only one, German professor and academic dean Alfred H.Nolle, possessed the then rare Ph.D. Shortly after Lyndon matriculated, the second Ph.D., M. L. Arnold, joined the faculty as head of Lyndon's major department, history. But all the faculty, except a few instructors, had at least a master's degree, and many had some additional work toward a Ph.D. Except for the booming summer quarter, faculty-student ratios were low, with classes averaging only sixteen students. In the late twenties the college was still expanding, faculty morale was high, and most professors tried to do well in the classroom. Of course, with weekly teaching loads of fifteen hours or more, few if any pursued any active research. None was expected. The small library, with only twenty-seven thousand volumes, scarcely matched those of large urban high schools.

Although not isolated, and blessed by frequent outside lecturers and cultural events, Southwest Texas remained an undistinguished provincial college. By necessity, most teaching scarcely rose above the level of textbooks, and by comparison to major research universities or even prestigious liberal arts colleges, the content had to be either oversimplified or considerably out of date. However conscientious or inspiring the classroom presentations, students simply could not receive a rigorous education, particularly in their more advanced courses. But for local students, most from farms or small towns, out of small and inadequate high schools, the college must have seemed a cultural and intellectual oasis. The fountain was not large or deep, but its content perfectly matched their uncultivated taste. The ablest students gained enough skills and intellectual sophistication to move on to professional or graduate schools. The vast majority gained the needed tools for successful public school teaching or for other careers back in their home communities.

Lyndon Johnson prepared himself for teaching in both elementary and high schools. He majored in history and minored in English and social studies. He took no languages and only the bare minimum of courses in mathematics and the sciences. He, like so many San Marcos students, found most memorable his government courses with Howard M. Greene, a bit of a maverick at the college. Greene also coached Lyndon in debate and formed with him a lifelong friendship. Greene lacked a Ph.D., was eccentric, used Socratic techniques in his courses, and loved to confront unbearably conventional and ideologically naive Texas students with his iconoclasm and political populism. But he respected and listened to the views of his students, and he won praise even from those who found his beliefs dangerously radical. He became a beloved institution on the campus. No other professor had as profound, or lasting, an impact on Johnson.

As always in a hurry, LBJ took his first six quarters (two academic years) of work without a break. By taking summer quarters in 1927 and again in 1928, he caught up with most students who had entered the college in September 1926. As a student, he struggled, even came close to failure. In his first, spring quarter he made a D in English, flunked physical education, and added to this only two Cs and a B. In the summer he seemed to gain confidence, or possibly enjoyed the lower standards that so often typified the booming summer program at all teachers colleges. He made his first two As in education and history, and his lowest grade was a single C. But in a disasterous fall quarter he completed only three of a normal five courses, and these with all C grades. In both the winter and spring quarters he completed only twelve hours and suffered a second D to balance out two more As. Then, dead set on the sophomore standing required for a temporary teaching certificate, he completed eighteen hours in the summer of 1928, but suffered two more Ds (in an English and an education course). He barely gained enough hours, and high enough grades, to get his sophomore standing.

The scant evidence suggests that Lyndon was insecure and often unhappy in this first interlude at Southwest Texas. He was out of his element. The academic work did not inspire him; in fact it usually bored him. He lacked the discipline for sustained study or for completing long written assignments. His mother, or friends, often had to come to his rescue. Clearly, he yearned for a different sort of challenge, for a more active life, for one in which he could assume leadership and gain mastery. Being a student—deferential, subordinate—warred against his expansive, take-charge personality. But, and this proved a lifelong trait, he accepted the lowly student role. He never in his life rebelled against authority. He honored his professors, flattered them, deferred to them. Some fellow students saw this as brownnosing, as a tactic to gain favors and better grades. It certainly was this, but, knowing Johnson, it was more. The respect was sincere, the deference only what he always gave to anyone older than himself or in a position of authority. He never ended the relationships he developed with teachers or with older persons; he kept them going for a lifetime.

During his college career, Johnson rented rooms in several houses in San Marcos, at times buying his meals in separate boarding houses. Much later, when college officials decided to honor LBJ by marking and setting aside his campus residence, they had a difficult time determining which house to select. But, apparently (reminiscences vary), he first moved into three rooms over President Evans's garage. Another Johnson (no kin), Alfred T., or "Boody" as everyone knew him, had visited Johnson City before LBJ decided to go to college. He had dated a cousin, met Lyndon, and urged him to come back to Southwest Texas. He even promised to share his room. Lyndon, short on funds, forced the good-natured Boody, football hero and big man on campus, to honor that commitment. It is not clear how long he remained in the garage apartment. According to later legends, he and Boody painted it more than once in order to earn needed money. Although unrecorded, the more likely reason Lyndon occupied the garage was telephone arrangements with Evans by Rebekah and Sam. It is possible that such arrangements took place unknown to Lyndon.

Since he never gained distinction in scholarship, Johnson tried to attain a leadership role through extracurricular activities. He faced major hurdles even here. He entered college in the spring, was never clearly a member of any one class, and at eighteen was approximately a year older than most entering students. Short on money, working long hours, he had little time for frivolity. His gift of gab, his intense but overwhelming personality, which served him so well in political persuasion and in winning the help and trust of older people, often failed to impress fellow students. His ability to relate to others was limited to deferential and paternal roles; he had few fraternal skills. Johnson seemed to sense this and to try too hard. He was not yet at ease with women, still self-conscious about his height and appearance, and totally inept in athletics, the one clear path to respect and popularity at San Marcos. In compensation he turned to his old tricks—wild claims and boastful exaggerations, which soon gained him the nickname of "Bull." Behind the bluster he was often lonely. Thus, as always, he turned to his family, in weekends back in Johnson City and in long letters to his mother that were full of self-pity or half-concealed pleas for reassurance and emotional support.

The college records suggest that LBJ, during his first six quarters, was not very well known on campus, which is not unusual for freshmen and sophomores. Fellow students, in much later interviews, could recall few details. In labored responses to leading questions, they proved that Lyndon left few indelible impressions. He tried to become a member of the one, unrecognized, social fraternity at San Marcos—Beta Sigma, or as it was informally known, the Black Stars. Boody was a member along with the other athletes that dominated it. The members made up a campus elite holding most of the almost meaningless student offices. Boody believed LBJ could benefit the club because he soon had a job in President Evans's office, but at least some members disagreed and blackballed him. After all, he had few other credentials, was a mere freshman, not well known, and much too pushy. Whether this rejection crushed an ambitious LBJ or was a minor incident remains unclear. According to a later legend, and it is little more than that, his rejection led him to retaliate, to form a new, secret organization and through it to take over the campus politically. In Lyndon's version, and that of his supporters, he rose up as a great white knight to win campus power away from monopolistic athletes and to gain it for academically abler students. In other words, he effected a minor political and social revolution. According to Johnson's detractors, including some fellow students, he unmercifully plotted his revenge on the Black Stars and built his own political machine in order to gain dictatorial power for himself. The problem with both versions is that few facts support either. During the first year and a half at San Marcos, when he failed to get into the Black Stars, he never clearly took any political role at all let alone led any student rebellion.

By choice, Johnson first concentrated his extracurricular energies on debate and journalism. In the fall of the 1927–28 school year, one of two full academic years he spent on campus, he went out for debate and made one of the second-level teams. In letters home, and to financial benefactors, he exaggerated this achievement. Back in Blanco County his mother publicized this minor honor in local weekly newspapers and by such news camouflaged Lyndon's difficult and frustrating first two years at college. He debated only one year. At the same time he volunteered for the staffs of the newspaper, the *College Star*, and the yearbook, the *Pedagogue*. The newspaper gave him his most valuable source of recognition and also a small income during the summer of 1927 and again in 1929. He became a leading editorial writer in his first quarter (largely a matter of his own initiative, not of peer selection), and apparently in the absence of any competition became editor-in-chief for the summer of 1927. Typically, he had his mother write the first editorial. In fact, she probably had a hand in several of his signed columns. At least most of them echoed the noble sentiments, and even the florid style, of Rebekah.

Under his byline, Johnson eventually wrote cliché-ridden columns on a wide variety of subjects. These included the American Constitution, patriotism on Armistice Day, Thanksgiving, the Battle of San Jacinto, bravery, the heroic Lindbergh, duty, vision, thrift, sincerity, and the evils of cynicism. Not surprisingly, he wrote frequently about his greatest hero, Benjamin Franklin. His language was full of superlatives. He always led the cheers for Southwest Texas, commended his professors, endlessly flattered Evans, and gave full blessings to mothers on Mother's Day and fathers on Father's Day. Behind the flabby generalities and the conventional values, it is difficult to locate any clear point of view, to glimpse any developing intellectual identity at all, save possibly a naive faith that a strong will and hard work, industry, and thrift would always win success. And before one reads too much into this youthful outpouring, one has to recognize the probable role of Rebekah and the later role of student assistants. Even this early LBJ preferred to give writing assignments to others and then work over their product.

Johnson's other extracurricular activities seemed less important to him. He took the lead in forming a club for students from Blanco County. Such clubs rarely met, but LBJ gained credit for first convening the group. He was never one to conceal or minimize his achievements. He joined, along with half the students, a club for future teachers. During at least one quarter he represented the freshman class on the Student Welfare Council. Nothing suggests any determined effort to compete in student politics, which very few students took seriously. What most limited his activities and crimped his style was a lack of money. Johnson shared with his father an expansive, generous personality. However much he tried, he could not lead a penurious life. By personality he was a big spender. He loved to become the center of a party, to make an impression. These proclivities always warred with necessity and with a sincere commitment to economy, to saving money and spending it only when absolutely necessary. In his own terms, he tried to get by on as little as possible, and in small areas he could be stingy with his money. But usually he was pinched for funds and steadily although not recklessly extended his personal debts. Had it not been for the help of President Evans, his financial plight might have terminated his college career by the end of the first year.

If Johnson brought any finely honed skill to San Marcos, it was an exceptional ability to relate to older people. By deference, by flattery, or possibly because of sincere respect, he could win their love and aid. Dozens of older men became second fathers (he so referred to them), and dozens of older women related to him as surrogate mothers. Unlike so many young people, he neither feared nor resented his elders. Although appropriately deferential, he gladly presumed on their time and knew deep down that they could be lonely, that they craved the attention and respect of youth even when they held high position. Combined with this was a political lesson well learned from his father—go to the top, to the person in power. Do not waste time on underlings. Thus, wherever LBJ went, whatever position he held, he cultivated those with power and authority. Jealous competitors resented his presumption or saw in his tactics the immorality of a selfish power seeker. And, clearly, such tactics always served him well. But, as always, the explanation is not as simple as all that. Johnson, not uniquely, always had great difficulty relating to social equals. A dutiful, even obsequious follower, an often magnanimous leader, he was never a good solid member of any club. He had to lead, to dominate, to be the great benefactor or the center of attention, else he usually dropped out. Thus, when he could not be a student leader, he cultivated his elders—his professors and, above all, his president, soon his friend, Cecil Evans.

An important point is that these relationships were not hypocritical. The older benefactors were not just objects that Lyndon used along his road to power. Of course, in a sense, he seduced these older people, even as he tried to seduce half the people he ever met. He pulled them into his growing circle of intimates. But he gave as well as received. He had a remarkable ability to do both. At San Marcos, as on so many occasions in his life, he began building another family, a network of love, affection, and reciprocal obligations. He valued these families, could not, in fact, function effectively outside them. They were amazingly enduring. Had he merely used President Evans, or Dean Nolle, or Professor Greene, then he would have had no reason to continue the ties beyond college graduation and his first job. Instead, he held on to them, as he did all his friends or his conquests. He took the initiative even when he became famous, even when his former professors were old, ill, or impoverished. He continued to treat these terribly ill-paid, hard-working, long-suffering professors in the more lowly provinces of academe as if they were eminent scholars. He corresponded with Evans until the old man died. He continued to flatter him as flagrantly as when a student. In return, Evans sent him the *Pedagogue* and other publications. In 1956, when Evans was near death, LBJ gave him a television set and hired him as a critic of programs on the Johnson-owned television station, as a kind way of getting the old man to accept needed gifts. When Dean Nolle retired after forty years, Johnson gave him special recognition in the Senate. And it is worth noting that he did not cultivate only the powerful elderly; he became a lifelong friend of the college janitor.

Sam Johnson provided Lyndon the entrée he needed with President Evans. Sam had been only a state representative, not a highly honored office even in Texas, but he had become part of a very complicated political system, with most of the operative rules unwritten. Evans, a guarded figure on campus, a symbol of austere authority to most students, was never a scholar or an intellectual. He was, appropriately, a crafty politician, or at least he tried to operate as such. A brother of his headed the Ku Klux Klan in Texas, but President Evans avoided the political extremes and generally concealed his own political beliefs. He had worked hard to get state appropriations in order to build an accredited, four-year college. He cultivated as much political support as possible in the central counties of Texas, where Sam was still well known. The fence building was a never-ending chore, for the hazards to any state educational institution were always great in Texas. Evans found in young Lyndon a rare asset, a person who almost intuitively seemed to comprehend the intricacies of Texas politics, much better than any of his professors, and who, in a relaxed, nonthreatening, confidential context, could talk to Evans about political tactics.

Of course, Evans might never have understood this had Lyndon not pushed himself forward. Evans had promised a campus job for Lyndon to Sam and Rebekah. Thus even in the subcollegiate courses, Lyndon began picking up trash on campus at fifteen dollars a week. He very quickly asked Evans for a better job and briefly moved to janitorial work in the science building. Within a month or two he had persuaded Evans to take him on as an assistant in the president's office. Officially, he ran errands and did minor clerical work. Unofficially, he became Evans's political adviser. According to the memory of some professors, he even helped Evans compose letters to politicians, helped prepare official reports, and lobbied with him in Austin. He was Evans's Bobby Baker. Even more critical, LBJ was a perfect seismic instrument, a source of the best possible intelligence and gossip about both state and national politics, subjects that LBJ read about and talked about all the time. In this one area he was the expert on campus.

By Johnson's politically attuned standards, he did well in his first year at San Marcos. His special relationship to Evans proved this, as did his remarkable rapport with professors. He had quickly moved to the center of power, however small the power in such a college. His seemingly calculated courtship of his elders provoked jealousy, resentment, even a sense of class treason among fellow students. This Johnson failed to comprehend, even as he did not master the prerequisites of student preferment as symbolized by his failure to get into the Black Stars. But as he knew, in the longer perspective of his life, the high regard of faculty and administrators could make all the difference in gaining future job opportunities.

With almost as much calculation, Johnson came close to choosing and winning a wife. During his difficult 1927–28 academic year he began to court Carol Davis, a San Marcos woman who had already graduated from Southwest Texas. Eventually, he failed in this courtship, which had to be a severe blow, a second assault on the still flimsy fortifications of an enormous ego, comparable to his failure to qualify for college back in 1924. Carol, two years older than Lyndon, had assets he needed. She had been an honor student, was deeply committed to teaching as a career, serious in outlook, talented in music. Not unimportant for Johnson, who was already so deeply in debt that he would have to interrupt his college work after the summer of 1928, Carol was a daughter of a prosperous, eminent wholesale merchant and former mayor of San Marcos, A. L. Davis. She had all the conveniences of wealth, including an automobile, then rare among campus students. As photographs still attest, Carol was attractive, comparable to the campus beauty queens. But shy, reserved, busy, carefully protected by her family, and part of a campus made up of almost three-fourths women, she had not dated extensively or had a serious suitor. She was flattered by Johnson's interest and quickly won over by his persuasive courtship. Before the academic year ended they were in love and practically engaged.

The circumstances of Johnson's courtship of Carol Davis invite the same cynical judgment as his wooing of President Evans. He needed Carol. She could provide him financial security, help write his term papers, and bring to his career the almost motherly support that Rebekah had heretofore provided. Conceivably, such considerations guided LBJ in his original decision to ask Carol for a date. But, quickly, the relationship rested on deep affection. Johnson fell in love, more so perhaps than did Carol. He was more dependent, more sentimental, probably more vulnerable. Eventually, she was the one who made most of the rational decisions. Already a whiz kid on political issues, Lyndon was an inexperienced, probably inept lover. After his high school infatuation with Kitty Clyde Ross, he had at best only fleeting, casual ties to women. He had dated an office secretary in California, had escorted local girls to dances back in the hill country, but, insofar as records suggest or memories recall, none of these ties became the least bit serious. And, until he began dating Carol, he had no girlfriends at San Marcos. Both professors and fellow students, in later interviews, attested to this, pointing out that he was too busy, and perhaps too impoverished, to play the field. There are hints of sexual conquest, including some typical Johnson boasting among his cronies, but little to support the rumors. In any case, such casual encounters had nothing to do with love and marriage, which he always viewed through the romantic images of Rebekah.

If anyone still takes seriously the outdated theories of Freud, then one might read oedipal content into this first serious Johnson courtship. It shared much with his second, which led to his marriage to Claudia Taylor. Carol had several similarities with Rebekah. And the whirlwind courtship by Lyndon, with his gift of gab and great dreams about the future, but his precarious financial situation, reminds one of Sam Johnson's wooing of Rebekah. The same sharp differences of personality plagued each relationship—with literacy and refinement and emotional stability on one side, narrowed political artistry and a volatile personality on the other. One circumstance was different—and telling. Carol's father, unlike an earlier Rebekah's, was very much alive and at least at first opposed the courtship. This was inevitable, given Lyndon's youth, his sophomore standing in college, and his unclear vocational future. On the other side, LBJ's parents seemed happy with Carol. She visited them at least twice in Johnson City, and soon the mother-son correspondence contained such routine references to Carol as to suggest she was already part of the family.

LBJ and Carol seemed close to formal engagement by the summer of 1928. Even the Davis family seemed resigned. In that summer, Lyndon used his father's political connections to finagle three seats at the Democratic National Convention in Houston, the one that nominated Al Smith. He took Carol and her parents, and used excerpts from his campus newspaper to persuade officials to admit him as a reporter. This was a big moment in his life, the source of embellished stories back on campus. But Carol was apparently bored by all the protracted political wrangling in the midst of the sweltering heat. Johnson further befriended the family and Carol during that summer. While in Austin, possibly at the behest of Evans, he visited a man just assuming the job of superintendent of schools in Frio County, southwest of San Antonio. Using all his ingratiating techniques, including flattery, he persuaded this school administrator to hire Carol to teach the next year in the county seat of Pearsall. Thus, Lyndon helped secure her first job. Later in the summer, Lyndon gained a temporary teaching job at Cotulla, just thirty-three miles on down federal hghway 81 toward Laredo, close enough to Pearsall for at least weekly visits with Carol.

During this busy teaching year of 1928–29, the unlikely pair slowly grew apart. Carol, in particular, recognized how divergent were their interests, how little they shared. She also acquired another suitor, one apparently more acceptable to her family. By the end of the school year she was engaged to Lyndon's rival. The full story obviously cannot be told. In such affairs records are never adequate. Lyndon apparently made a formal proposal of marriage, which Carol rejected. It is not clear how much parental opposition influenced her decision, although once she was so inclined it naturally became a justification. Notably, her father's concern had not prevented an extended courtship or led her to reject Lyndon's help in getting her job.

Carol's rejection must have hurt. Lyndon could never bear to lose the love and support of anyone, and he often went to great lengths to hold on to the loyalty and affection of employees. By the end of his year in Cotulla, Johnson was miserable, desperately hanging on to consoling letters from Rebekah. He came back to San Marcos or to Johnson City on as many weekends as possible, a journey made sad by the fact that soon Carol did not accompany him.

Out of Lyndon's hurt and pride, he eventually concocted a fantasy about his relationship to Carol. Perhaps he even came to believe it, although it contained scarcely a shred of truth. Sam Houston Johnson first published a version of the story; then, in his last years, Johnson added new details in his reminiscences for Doris Kearns. In this fantasy, Carol's father was a prominent member of the Ku Klux Klan (actually he had opposed it), who hated all "liberal" or "populist" reformers such as Sam Johnson. Thus, Lyndon outfitted the affair with anachronistic political labels that were in no way appropriate to a nonideological student back in the 1920s. In the same vein, Lyndon explained his rejection by Carol's father in family and class terms, since the "reactionary" father had purportedly condemned the whole shiftless Johnson family and what they stood for. When Johnson had visited in Carol's home, her father had allegedly slandered Lyndon's grandfather and condemned Sam Johnson's political views. When Carol repeated her father's views, a proud Lyndon purportedly told her: "to hell with your daddy," and "I wouldn't marry you or anyone in your whole damn family." According to a completely unreliable Sam Houston,

Lyndon even told her to tell her father that he would someday be president of the United States. According to LBJ, the day after the stormy session at her home Carol came to his room (where is not at all clear) crying, and announced her decision to marry him against her father's wishes. But Lyndon then cruelly refused her offer, purportedly because of pride and family honor. According to Sam Houston, she would not turn loose of the relationship and came to see Lyndon in Washington when he was a congressional secretary. By Lyndon's account, he never saw her again until seven years later when he ran for Congress and her father backed a rival. She attended one of his speeches, looking pale and sad. He saw her again, a few weeks later and for the last time, in a hospital room after the appendectomy that concluded the campaign. She announced her vote for him and her joy in his election. Johnson then "knew" that she was still in love with him.

While he misplayed the mating game, Johnson won universal plaudits for his achievements in his first teaching job. By the summer of 1928 he knew he would have to interrupt his college career. His debts had multiplied, perhaps to over a thousand dollars. Some bank loans could not be extended. He had resorted to embarrassing strategies to get this far. In February 1928, he had written a very effective plea to his congressman, stressing both his early achievements in San Marcos and his desperate financial situation. The congressman obliged with a loan. His good friend Ben Crider, now back in California, received a sad letter from Lyndon, a concealed plea for help. LBJ lamented his financial plight, talked of plans of quitting college, and asked Ben to find him a job. Meanwhile, Sam and Rebekah had written Ben, enlisting his help to keep Lyndon in college. Ben first found the job and then decided instead to send all his savings to Lyndon (nearly a hundred dollars). Such desperate measures could not continue. Johnson had told his congressman he would get a teaching position, if possible, for 1928–29, since completion of the sophomore year qualified him for a temporary elementary teaching certificate.

Such teaching positions were not easy to come by. Lyndon applied for any jobs available. He also went further in debt to buy a Model A Ford, probably in anticipation of a job. He finally secured a position, this one apparently without any intervention by his parents (a first for him), but with the critical support of his new "father," President Evans. During the campus summer quarter, he met, and won a job from, the superintendent of schools from Cotulla, the county seat of sparsely populated, dry, hot LaSalle County. His assignment—to teach the seventh and eighth grades in an

51

all-Hispanic school, one blessed by a new building. Otherwise, this was as unenviable a teaching job as one could imagine. Since Johnson talked a great line, was enthusiastic (remember that this job placed him close to Carol), and was male, the superintendent not only hired him but made him principal, superivising the five housewives who taught the other grades.

Lyndon's achievment in one nine-month period at Cotulla has become a valued part of his legend and one that has withstood all the onslaughts of critics. He gave himself completely to the task. He wanted, almost desperately, to do a great job in order to get enthusiastic letters of endorsement from the superintendent. Future and better jobs depended on this. As always, his engagement in a task unleashed an overwhelming fund of sheer energy. He scarcely ate or slept when caught up in something that captured his enthusiasm. At Cotulla he seemed never to stop. He successfully completed eighteen hours of credits through correspondence, volunteered for coaching duties in the nearby high school, courted Carol, and still put more effort into his school than anyone in Cotulla had ever imagined possible. The school fit his talent and his personality. In Cotulla, a dry, dusty, monotonous town, the "Mexican" majority lived on the wrong side of the tracks. They took the place of Negroes in much of the South as exploited workers and recipients of separate but never quite equal services. Lyndon, so threatened by people his equal, always responded with sensitivity and compassion to lowly people, to those who knew a poverty more dire than he had ever glimpsed in what seemed, from the Cotulla perspective, the lush hill country. He identified with boys and girls who came to school without breakfast, and he always wanted to help them, to uplift them, to be a big daddy to them. In another sense, such lowly people, so trusting and so grateful, helped build up his own sense of worth. Thus, no sooner did he begin working in Cotulla in September than he began to transform the school.

Johnson treated his students as if they were important, as if they counted for something. He cared about them, wanted them to learn and through education to realize their capabilities. Through repetition, he turned this hope into some of his favorite clichés, but he meant them, and briefly, he inspired his students to believe them. Because he took them seriously, he demanded much more of his students than had previous teachers. Typical of his treatment of later staff members, he drove them relentlessly, whether in assigned academic work, in endless drills on their English, or in specially arranged declamations, debates, and athletic contests. His energy, his will to succeed, his determination that his students—the clay for this artistry—should excel in all areas brought a pride and self-respect they had never before known. They never forgot Mr. Johnson. He forced his other teachers to supervise games at recess and to join in other extracurricular activities. Complaining a little, they fell in line, perhaps in sheer amazement that anyone would do so much for mere "Mexicans." Characteristically, he wrote to ask Rebekah to send two hundred tubes of toothpaste for his children, plus selections that the children could memorize for public recitations. He also tutored the janitor in English. He spent such long hours at work, he wrote his mother, that by Sunday he was often so tired he slept all day (hard to believe for LBJ). By the end of the year, he had a superb letter from the superintendent, the devotion of his students, and the grateful thanks of the parents, who for the first time had been pulled into school activities. The verdict from all sides—no one could have done a better job.

What the praise concealed was the cost, the pain. Only twenty, LBJ had endured a desperate, lonely, unhappy year at Cotulla. Only his work gave satisfaction. Outwardly so full of enthusiasm and energy, he was now outside any family network, working for and with strangers, all the while pushing himself toward complete exhaustion. The pressures were intense, his self-discipline awesome.

As he gladly moved back to San Marcos to resume college in the summer of 1929, Johnson was no longer the apprehensive, unsure youngster of 1927. He had suffered a failed love affair, proved himself as a teacher, gained confidence in his administrative skills. He no longer had to boost his ego by inflated stories or boasting. He simply wanted, as quickly as possible, to finish his B.S. in education, get his permanent teaching certificate, and resume his career as a teacher at better schools than Cotulla. Of course, he had loftier ambitions. His fascination with politics grew. He took every opportunity to get involved. Surely, at one point or another, he would run for office. But one could not predict such eventualities. Even if he remained in education, he would be able to move quickly up the administrative career ladder. He had all the requirements for an administrative position, either as county superintendent or as a state-level bureaucrat—conventional and thus safe values, a commitment to improvement or reform, soaring ambition, an unparalleled ability to persuade others, and an awesome capacity for concentration and hard work.

Johnson spent only one more full academic year at Southwest Texas, a year bracketed by two summers. His achievements, or purported achievements, during that fifteen months fathered perhaps the best known legend of his youth. According to this legend, LBJ practically took over the college. He politicized the student body, formed his own dominant political machine, gained dictatorial control over the allocation of student jobs and awards, and gained such influence over President Evans as to intimidate even professors. Notably, the legend matured only after LBJ became famous. Characteristically, Johnson loved the legend, endorsed it, and probably came to believe it. At least he did all he could to embellish it, particularly in his numerous visits back to the campus. With a different emphasis, both his apologists and his critics have accepted it because, at the least, it departs from some facts and embraces some half-truths. But it remains an unsubstantiated legend and, by the most direct and simple reading of the evidence, one clearly full of exaggerations.

In many ways, Johnson simply resumed college where he left off. He came back as a second-quarter junior, again assisted President Evans, and again served as editor of the *College Star* in the summer of 1929 (a job with an attached and badly needed stipend). He was still in debt. Unfortunately for his finances, he lost out in his bid to be full-time editor of the *Star* for 1929–30. His carefully budgeted Cotulla salary ($100 a month in the fall, $125 from January on) only paid off his unpostponable debts (to banks and for his automobile), leaving unpaid several personal loans or near gifts (LBJ would later repay all of these). He remained an underachiever as a student. By now he worked frantically to complete enough hours to graduate at the end of the summer of 1930. He took more than a full load most quarters, and in the spring of 1930 a backbreaking twenty-one hours (he had to complete one course in the summer, along with eighteen regular hours). His grades were erratic but at or above average, which is probably about all he expected or desired. Notably, he suffered only one final D and gained as many As as Cs, or what amounted to a B average. He graduated with minimal hours and with a grade point average of almost 2.5, or a C+ for his three years of work. By now he knew the system and benefited from work largely in his areas of academic strength. Perhaps because of time constraints, he did not rejoin the debating club. Nor did he find a new girlfriend. By his final summer quarter in 1930 he was actively seeking a teaching job, engaging in state politics, and largely orienting his life toward the future. He was already turning loose of college, simply going through the motions as a student.

While Johnson was still at Cotulla, a few students at San Marcos formed an ultrasecret club or fraternity. They soon used the label White Stars, since they organized to compete with the Black Stars, but such were the pledges of secrecy, and the elaborate precautions to conceal meetings and the names of members, that few nonparticipating students even knew of the organization during its first year. Somehow, a returning Lyndon Johnson learned about the new club and asked to be a member. As the two founders remember it, he was at first refused and then accepted, presumably during the fall quarter of 1929. He was not a founder of the White Stars, was never one of its more prominent members on campus, and was active in the group for no more than two or at best three quarters. The group continued and matured after Johnson left college, and eventually it became famous for the caliber of its alumni (these still hold reunions). Johnson's only unique contribution to the club was his political artistry.

The legend of a politically ruthless LBJ who took control of the whole campus rests upon only one well-documented incident—his role in the student elections for the winter quarter of 1930. The White Stars decided to run a slate of candidates. Perhaps Johnson, with his avid interest in politics, thirsty to try out electioneering techniques, persuaded the others to enter the dull, normally apathetic elections held each quarter in order to allow more students the dubious honor of officeholding (such achievements at least adorned the yearbook and carried some weight with parents or future employers). The White Stars, at Johnson's urging, selected one of his lifelong, ever loyal friends, Willard Deason, as candidate for senior class president to oppose a very popular Black Star candidate. Johnson apparently (the evidence is thin) became the political strategist for this election. He and the others decided to focus on an issue—the distribution of student activity fees—and use it to stigmatize the Black Stars. Most of the fee had gone to athletic teams. The White Stars pushed brains over brawn and advocated the use of fees for drama, debate, and other nonsports activities. They successfully solicited votes from the nonathletes on campus, including a large number of women.

Despite a good issue, the White Stars still faced an able candidate and on election eve had all but conceded defeat. Johnson, now deeply involved in the campaign, refused to give up and spent much of the night out buttonholing surprised but often amenable students. Johnson thus gained valuable political experience. Deason won, only to enjoy the office for a brief fifteen weeks. In April the White Stars ran another surprise candidate and again won. In that election, Johnson regained an earlier position on the Student

Academic Council. So that they might win, the White Stars apparently took advantage of the very informal election process and in effect packed the class elections with their own members.

That is about the extent of Johnson's campus politics. No doubt, in at least two quarterly elections, he was involved and probably had a major role in determining White Star tactics. He clearly gained a campus reputation as a political manipulator, a schemer, and for this he faced resentment from many students. He gained more sharp barbs and ridicule in that year's *Pedagogue* than perhaps any other student on campus. To suggest more than this—that he carefully plotted every move, that he gained effective control over his White Star brethren, that he carried out a great conspiracy in order to gain secret power for himself—is to go far beyond the evidence or even common sense. Such an account also suggests both superhuman cleverness on the part of Johnson and a damning degree of passivity on the part of all the other students.

Nevertheless, Johnson's involvement with the White Stars had enduring significance for his career. During this one busy year he began accumulating a retinue of loyal admirers, such as the ever-dutiful Deason. If one wants to use the image, LBJ began building his Texas political machine—a network of fanatically loyal friends, willing later to serve on his staff or practically kill themselves in his political campaigns. This was to be another familylike circle, governed by all the informal rules of the family, with loyalty the highest obligation. Also, as a member of an organized political faction, Johnson now gained his long-sought status and power on campus. A bit of an outsider earlier, he was now an insider, and as always he enjoyed the heady returns. His rapport with faculty and administrators now took on greater significance for students. He had pull. His admission to the White Stars probably rested on his ties to President Evans. Now, as the White Stars gained the more important student offices, they also worked through Johnson to get political patronage from the president's office. The White Stars ended up with all the best campus jobs. To some extent, Johnson became a minor power broker. It is easy, however, to exaggerate his influence. Evans, for example, was a cagey politician, and was not about to surrender his authority to any student. But by being in a position to consult with Evans and to recommend candidates, Johnson no doubt served his White Stars well. Whether he was responsible for jobs or not, Johnson gladly gave this impression and basked in the appreciation of those who believed him their patron. A master of self-promotion, he always made the most of even small achievements—he advertised them.

Johnson completed his required courses in the summer of 1930 just as America slowly slid into the Great Depression. His parents were gratified by his success and rejoiced in the special commendation that Evans gave LBJ during the graduation ceremony in August. Evans predicted great success for Johnson in the future, basing his judgment on the energy, careful thought, and determination he had displayed at San Marcos. But in that bleak summer of 1930 his future seemed clouded in uncertainty. New college graduates faced a dearth of jobs, and none suffered more than new teachers. As always, Johnson turned to his family. His paternal uncle George taught history and headed his division at Sam Houston High in Houston, one of the largest and best high schools in Texas. He was prepared to welcome Lyndon into his home and tried his best to find him a job, but no vacancies developed by September 1930. Thus, Lyndon finally secured a not very enviable job in a now familiar school system. The same superintendent whom Lyndon had persuaded to hire Carol Davis in 1928 now hired him for a Pearsall school, as a teacher and vice-principal at $1,530 a year. Since Lyndon had been a frequent visitor in Pearsall, the superintendent knew him well. Once again, he gained a job not through competition but through knowing the right person. Yet, he had all the needed talents. He merited the job. His Cotulla recommendations were superlative, and it seemed all his professors at San Marcos wrote letters in his behalf. The strongest came from President Evans. But history professor H. M. Greene, Dean Nolle, even the dean of women gave him hearty recommendations. Except for Evans, these supporters were not effusive. They noted Johnson's good but not excellent grades and emphasized his personality, his leadership skills, his versatility, and his promise as a teacher.

Johnson taught at Pearsall for only a month, just enough to justify newspaper reminiscences and local claims upon him when he became president. But even in that month he threw himself into the work in a repetition of Cotulla. In October 1930 the eagerly awaited opening finally developed at Sam Houston High, not in history but in speech. Uncle George telephoned the news. Johnson decided to seek a release from his contract at Pearsall and was so persuasive as not only to get the release from his superintendent but to talk him into hiring his sister Rebekah as a replacement. In late October he moved in with his uncle and aunt and lived there for just over a year, joined the next summer by his brother, Sam Houston, who came to attend a junior college. Thus, in a sense, LBJ made up part of another close family, or what amounted to a Johnson colony in Houston. His aunt mothered him and freed him for the almost frenetic work he expended on his first real, professional opportunity, one that paid $1,600, a wondrous beginning salary in the deepening depression. He took over difficult teaching assignments in the middle of the term—primarily in public speaking but also in commercial geography and arithmetic.

Once again, Johnson threw his enormous energies and talents into his work, leaving little time for any social life. To earn extra money, he taught a Dale Carnegie–type course for businessmen in the evening. He now had older high school students, but he pushed and prodded them as he had his little Mexicans down in Cotulla. Most of his efforts went into his public speaking classes, an unexpected teaching assignment but, as it turned out, a happy one. He had absorbed from Rebekah a fascination with public declamation, and at Cotulla he had found speech and drama a perfect vehicle for student growth, for giving students a sense of mastery and self-confidence. Poise, pride, and the ability to communicate were more critical to young people than even academic attainment. Thus, Johnson became the demanding audience and critic for student efforts. From the students he screened the best for forensic competition and coached both the boys' and the girls' debating teams. Always one to exploit opportunities, he gave all his infectious enthusiasm to his young debaters, transfusing them with his energy and pushing and driving them to the limit of their ability. He organized practice debates all over the state, traveling in his car and lodging with the numerous family friends that dotted the state or his own relatives or those of the student debaters. And, the first year, his male team won every match until the state finals and lost there only on a split vote. His ablest male debaters—Gene Latimer and Luther E. Jones—became lifelong friends; both would later work for him in Washington. He had a knack for publicizing the team's success, solicited local prize money, and turned debating into a popular sport at Sam Houston High. In less than one academic year, his team had made him a hero in the school and had given him recognition in the city. He received a rare raise and a contract for another year.

Johnson began his second year at Sam Houston in the fall of 1931. By now the economy had moved from a recession into the agonies of a worldwide depression. Johnson was fortunate to have a job. He still needed the money not only to pay debts but to help his brothers and sisters. In the spring of 1931, Sam and Rebekah left their Johnson City home and moved into a rented house in San Marcos, Sam with great reluctance, Rebekah gladly. She never appreciated the hills and welcomed the cultural advantages of a college town. They moved for two reasons—to provide free room and board for their remaining two daughters at Southwest Texas, and to situate Sam better for his patronage job as a state bus inspector, a job that required him to travel. Already Sam looked older than his age; he would live only six more years, the last two back in his beloved home in Johnson City. Behind all LBJ's frantic efforts to succeed in life, and to do it quickly, were compelling family needs. It was already apparent that he would be increasingly responsible for his mother and siblings. He remained close to his mother, wrote her continually, and dutifully came home on as many weekends as possible. Successful as he was at Sam Houston High, he already looked about for new opportunities, political ones if such miraculously opened for him.

He knew miracles were undependable. He punctuated all his speeches with clichés about the role of effort and will. One has to work and create opportunities. In direct, calculating ways, LBJ had been hard at work preparing for his miracle. In the summer of 1930, while in his last quarter at San Marcos, he gave almost half his time to local politics. In that summer, Welly Hopkins, an Austin lawyer and state representative, ran for state senator in the district that encompassed Blanco County. He asked for Sam Johnson's help. Thus, when home in Johnson City, LBJ went with Sam to a political rally in Henley to listen to the usual array of speakers. Hopkins spoke. So did other local candidates. But the scheduled star, Patrick Neff, former governor, renowned orator, and now state railroad commissioner running for reelection, never arrived, and thus only silence followed the call for him from the speaking platform. Lyndon knew and admired Neff. It was he, as governor, who graciously had declined Lyndon's invitation to his high school graduation, and it was he who gave Sam his bus inspector's job. What followed the call for Neff may well have reflected the prompting of Sam, who was now unwilling to mount the platform and was anxious to give Lyndon exposure. In any case, Lyndon stepped forward and gave an impromptu but appropriate talk in behalf of Neff.

Knowing Lyndon, one can assume the speech was full of generalities. Hopkins perceived it as effective and was astounded at the maturity and gall of such a young man. On the spot, he asked Lyndon to help in his six-county campaign, with primary responsibility for Hays (San Marcos was the county seat) and Blanco counties. In the time he could spare from college, Lyndon organized support groups in those two home counties, printed campaign material at the college, spent weekends in direct persuasion among local farmers and ranchers, and somehow finagled the usually neutral Evans to allow, and even attend, the final, elaborately planned, preelection rally on campus. An astounded, and grateful, Hopkins won the two counties and the election that August, and took LBJ on a vacation trip to Mexico as soon as he graduated. As a result of this campaign, Hopkins spread the word in Austin about a wonder boy down at San Marcos. Lyndon had also created a large political debt, one gladly repaid in 1931.

On 6 November 1931, the only Republican congressman from Texas, Harry Wurzbach, died. A special election on 24 November determined his successor for the populous Fourteenth District, which included San Antonio, part of the hill country, and rich farming counties all the way south to the Gulf and as far as the famous King ranch. The national Democratic party, which had barely gained a majority in the U.S. House of Representatives, badly wanted to win this seat to help assure organizing control. Thus, the party in Texas supported a polished but rather diffident Richard Kleberg, then one of the owners and a manager of the vast King ranch. His name and reputation helped assure his election, now that the depression had so badly dimmed the chances of Republicans. He conducted a campaign without clear issues, entertained audiences, bought the expected Mexican votes in San Antonio, and easily won.

Lyndon Johnson, now completely absorbed in his teaching at Houston, took no part in the campaign. Sam worked for the party in Blanco County. On 25 November, the day after the election, Welly Hopkins wrote a letter to Roy Miller, the former mayor of Corpus Christi, a polished and much-respected lobbyist for Texas Gulf Sulphur Corporation, and a close friend and adviser to Kleberg. In it he recounted the achievements of LBJ in his 1930 campaign, stressed how well Lyndon knew Kleberg's constituents in four counties, noted his unusual gifts for meeting and greeting the public, and thus recommended him as Kleberg's congressional secretary. Apparently he sent a similar letter directly to Kleberg. Miller also passed on the recommendation.

Kleberg was obviously impressed. In the next few days he called Lyndon at the high school and asked him to come down as soon as possible for an interview at his office in Corpus Christi. Notably, for this interview, the most important so far in his life, Lyndon again turned to his family for support. His father accompanied him. Kleberg was duly impressed and offered the job to Lyndon. He even telephoned Lyndon's high school principal to explain his need for Lyndon and request for him a leave of absence. The flattered principal of course obliged, granting a year's leave and later extending it year after year. Sam Houston High never finally terminated Lyndon's contract. Thus, Johnson would later joke about reclaiming his old job. But as he surely sensed and as friends suspected, his teaching career was now over. Politics would henceforth claim all, literally all, of his interests and talents. In fact, no American ever committed himself more completely to politics than did LBJ.

4

POLITICAL
APPRENTICESHIP

Lyndon Johnson arrived in Washington, D.C., on 7 December 1931. He traveled from Texas by train with Congressman-elect Kleberg, riding in his first Pullman car. He spent his first night with the wealthy Kleberg in an expensive hotel room, the last luxury he would know for the next several months. He soon settled in a small, inexpensive room in the lower basement of the Dodge Hotel. This elegant hotel accommodated affluent or influential guests in its regular rooms and lowly government clerks in its two segregated basement floors. Here Johnson would live a Spartan, almost monastic life for the next three years. But these were vital years in his development, critical for his later career as a politician. He could not know it at the time, but Washington would be his primary home and place of employment for most of the next thirty-seven years. No one ever grew to fit the city better, to master the intricacies of the federal bureaucracy more completely. As one of his later staff members so aptly remarked, Johnson became one of the most provincial of Americans, a provincial not from Texas but from the nation's capital. He was ill adapted outside its hothouse political environment. He loved his home state and did what he needed to build and maintain support in Texas, but he never held a state office and, as the years passed, he slowly emancipated himself from its distinctive political culture.

Johnson's first three years as a congressional secretary took the place of graduate or professional training. It was his substitute for law school, but three times more intense, absorbing, and demanding than even the best law schools. No student ever gave more single-minded attention to the subject matter or worked any harder at mastery. Johnson had never been versatile in interest or skills. But in college and in his teaching, he had to attend to several subjects or disciplines, although even then his first love had remained the political process. Now, as is typical of most types of professional training, he could specialize in the field of government and politics. He excluded all other subjects, narrowed his focus, even for a while gave up on any social life, and more than ever before he cut himself off from his supportive family back in Texas. He had to learn how the government in Washington actually worked, answers scarcely hinted at in his government courses back at Southwest Texas. He wanted to know who had power and influence, how they gained it, how they used it. He wanted to grasp the complex process that lay behind successful legislation and to discover how one pried the maximum benefits from a now expanding federal bureaucracy. He was in a hurry. He learned quickly, in part because of an unusual capacity for almost hypnotic concentration and for sustained work. At the end of three years, when he finally relaxed a little, even took time for a hasty courtship and then marriage, LBJ knew Washington as well as most senior congressmen.

Genius takes many forms. It can find outlet in a compelling curiosity about almost any subject and, insofar as time permits, a high degree of mastery in many disciplines or occupations. This Renaissance model was alien to Johnson. He typified the genius that finds outlet in an astonishing level of artistry in one field. He devoted his enormous energy, knowledge, and creativity to practical politics within the American federal, congressional, two-party system. Because he came to understand this system so well, not abstractly or theoretically but as it actually operated at any one time, he was able to make it work for his chosen goals, which, of course, he easily persuaded himself were also the goals most appropriate for the American public. He mastered the art of politics, not moral philosophy or the science of government, academic subjects about which he remained naive or simpleminded. Even if one did not accept his goals or endorse his means, one had to acknowledge the artistry, the efficiency of his methods, and the extent of his accomplishments. He became the most accomplished legislative strategist in American history. Typical of one who masters a system, he came to love it. He particularly loved the Congress. He used it and in subtle ways altered it, but only in his mind to perfect it, not in any basic way to change it. He adapted too well to feel any sense of alienation. He gained so much from the American political system that any deep questions about it, any challenges to it, would have threatened his own identity, his ever-fragile and precarious sense of self-worth.

This suggests a darker side to single-minded artistry. It deforms. It leads to unbearably one-sided or myopic people, those incapable of functioning at all in subjects or occupations far removed from their specialty. Politics, fortunately, is a complex art. Anyone who would master the American political process has to be open to a wide, even in principle almost unlimited range of knowledge in several disciplines. Thus, it is unfair to refer to LBJ as one-dimensional. When his political agenda included subjects as disparate as space exploration or the intricate regulation of the economy, he quickly mastered the knowledge involved, even down to some technical details. Thus, at one time or another, but always in conjunction with the political process, he at least read about or dabbled in most disciplines. In this sense he became broadly knowledgeable, so much so as to impress a varying array of academic advisers. And because the subject matter of politics is usually people, Johnson had to become an expert practical psychologist, acute in judging character and predicting behavior. The sidelight of this preoccupation with people, with what made them tick, was a normal addiction to gossip. Gossip is rarely dull. Thus, Johnson became an accomplished raconteur and mimic. He could be irresistibly charming and entertaining.

Then what does it mean to say his single-minded commitment to politics deformed him? In one sense the question is valuative. "Deformed" is in the eye of the beholder. The deformation is only the obverse of a specialized development of certain skills. For a weight lifter, bulging biceps are beautiful, not evidence of any distortion. For a politician, the use of one's brain to store an enormous range of names and minute details about people, or to contrive detailed strategies to win a few votes here or there, is not to waste talent but to use it most effectively. After all, no mortal has the capacity to excel except in a very few fields, and such achievement almost always demands a single-minded concentration, as close observation of any master artist in any medium will demonstrate. In this sense, genius, by definition, is distortion, the unequal and exaggerated development of just certain abilities. Such a single-minded absorption often leaves the artist vulnerable, incapable of even minimal competence in areas far removed from his specialty. LBJ had few interests beyond politics, and even these tended to be unrefined or even crude. He was either lost or quickly bored in most discussions of other subjects. In fact, unless he could see its relevance to public policy, almost any subject bored him. In areas of typical human fascination—religion, fine arts, the varied natural environment—Johnson was either ill informed or uninvolved. He was all but incapable of reading a book for pleasure, sitting through a play or a movie, or joining, say, a bird-watching expedition. His level of taste in these subjects was scarcely above that of a child. This underdevelopment also made him vulnerable. When his one mistress threatened to desert him—when he faced political defeat or retirement—he was lost. He was then no one.

Johnson began at the bottom. He came to Washington without governmental experience. The city was strange, awe inspiring, intimidating. His position had possibilities, but he had to discover and develop them through time. The subsequent distortion and devaluation of the word *secretary* helps conceal his expected role. He was secretary in the sense of second in command, as in secretary of state. He headed Kleberg's congressional staff, even though for a junior congressman this at first consisted only of LBJ and one office clerk who moved up from Kleberg's Corpus Christi office. Johnson could not type, nor had he ever dictated letters. But the two asistants dug into the accumulated stacks of mail and for weeks practically lived in a small congressional suite assigned Kleberg. They had all the paperwork to do. Kleberg defined his role primarily as voting on legislation and attending meetings of his one congressional committee. He enjoyed the Washington social world, was often on the golf course, and did not worry about, or personally attend to, the unending demands of his constituents. He did not come to Washington as an agent or lobbyist for the home folk who needed something from the federal government. Perhaps he was too proud to assume such a role, or perhaps he was simply too lazy. In any case, Johnson quickly assumed a range of tasks unusual for a congressional secretary. He answered most telephone calls and almost all the mail, often signing Kleberg's name. He did almost all the lobbying or soliciting in federal agencies. He carefully cultivated political support for Kleberg back in the district. And as he became more adept at his work, he offered increasingly valuable policy suggestions to Kleberg. In his capacity as the people's advocate in Washington, Johnson became the congressman from the Fourteenth District.

Given the huge responsibilities, Johnson had to learn quickly. He plied fellow secretaries at the Dodge Hotel with questions about procedures. With his now notorius charm, he wooed the goodwill of the older, more experienced women clerks in other congressional offices. He observed everyone and picked up clues quickly. He developed allies in government offices and soon had as easy access as did congressmen. Although young, inexperienced, green, he acted as if he were older and completely self-assured. He was still pushing, in a hurry, given to boasting. He acted like someone important, had limitless gall, shamelessly flattered people in power, and took every occasion to magnify and advertise his considerable achievements. In an endless pattern, he pushed his body toward the breaking point, but he was so enthused about his job, so absorbed in his surroundings, that he hardly seemed to notice. He was also more alone than ever before. He had no family in the area. His mother worried about him. He took the time, often late at night, to write letters home or to his former students at Sam Houston High. He seemed desperate to keep contact, to get their letters, to bask briefly in the glow of appreciation, support, and love. His mother began an early, later embarrassing pattern—a special delivery letter almost every day. Eventually, his staff wrote and typed most of Johnson's affectionate but stereotyped replies. Meanwhile, he often wrote personal letters for Kleberg, even to his mother. This led to an unusual situation—Kleberg played golf, and LBJ wrote his purportedly personal letters while one of Johnson's assistants wrote his letters back home to Rebekah.

Johnson's isolation ended in June 1932. When his typist returned to Texas, Kleberg was eventually able to make two staff replacements, one ostensibly to work in the House post office, but actually to spend most of his time helping LBJ. Johnson turned to his high school debating team from Sam Houston, appointing Gene Latimer and, in the same year, Luther E. Jones. The boys moved into his room at the Dodge, helped pay the rent, and created a miniature family. Johnson now became the demanding father and the boys his subservient and dutiful sons. Latimer took the post office job and would remain in Johnson's debt, usually in his employment, and always at his beck and call for the rest of his life. He almost worshipped Johnson. Jones, who combined long hours of office work with part-time law school, kept more distance, more detachment, and went on to his own successful career as a lawyer. Typically, Johnson almost worked the boys to death, forcing them to keep his long hours, but was somehow able to communicate to them his own sense of purpose. He freely used both stick and carrot, ridiculing and berating them one moment, showering them with attention or praise the next. With their help, Johnson was able to create an almost perfect congressional office. The three answered all mail promptly, spared no energy in doing work requested by constituents, scanned Texas newspapers to keep abreast of local events, and sent personalized letters, under Kleberg's name, to thousands of surprised and delighted constituents, including all high school graduates.

Jones, in line with his career goals, and despite the intensity of his work for Johnson, eventually enrolled for law courses at Georgetown University Law School. Later, he would complete his law degree at the University of Texas. Jones finally persuaded Johnson to join him in the law course in the fall of 1934. A law degree made sense for an aspiring politician. In fact, by his observation in Washington, Johnson might have concluded that legal training was becoming a necessity for a political career. But it was not for Johnson. The dull drudgery and sheer memorization required in the first year of legal training, the endless cases that students had to read, bored him to death. As Jones remembers it, he attended for only about two weeks. But from then on, in vitae and campaign biographies, he always listed his attendance at Georgetown Law School as if he had completed a portion of the degree requirements. This listing, beyond Johnson's normal penchant for exaggeration and zealous self-promotion, hinted at a lingering sense of academic inferiority, of his not having the proper credentials.

Even in his lowly job, Johnson was able to win some crucial political capital. He took every opportunity to identify himself and to gain recognition from those he helped, including even Texans outside the Fourteenth District. He developed numerous friendly contacts in the bureaucracy and particularly impressed older people. Most spectacularly, he found one small outlet for his overt political skills, this time not as a stand-in for Kleberg. He learned of a moribund organization for congressional staff members, one somewhat facetiously called the "Little Congress." By early 1933

Johnson acted like a senior staff member. He decided to challenge the existing seniority system within the Little Congress, one that elevated older, but often uninterested congressional assistants to the various offices, including the office of speaker. He launched his own covert campaign for the speakership, thus briefly politicizing the organization. He won over the new congressional staff, those who came to Washington after the Democratic landslide of 1932, and recruited members from among the mailmen, policemen, and elevator operators. He depended upon the poor attendance of old-timers. The strategy worked. He won. At age twenty-four, with great fanfare, he proclaimed another New Deal, this for the Little Congress. He invigorated the organization with weekly meetings and debates by prominent politicians (this gave him an occasion to meet famous people). He arranged policy debates on legislation before Congress, took all members on a highly publicized junket to New York City, and presided as a junior version of the newly elected speaker of the real House—John Nance Garner of Texas, who formally presented Lyndon with a gavel. He learned House rules, improved his knowledge of procedure, and at least broadened the circle of people who were now familiar with Lyndon Johnson. He sent brief news releases and photographs back to San Marcos and Johnson City, where his minor successes seemed much more important than they did in Washington. Finally, after the election of 1932, Johnson began cultivating the now powerful Texas delegation in Congress. He attended all meetings of the Texas Club, buttered up the elderly wives of senators and congressmen, and was a model of respect and deference toward his elders, one of whom was the new majority whip, Sam Rayburn.

Lyndon learned his way around Washington during a troubled, confused, but fascinating period. He arrived just as a troubling recession turned into the worst international depression in history. Throughout 1932, as LBJ struggled to keep up with escalating constituency demands, the Congress, and particularly the now Democratic House, wrestling with President Hoover over appropriate relief and recovery legislation. From the struggle emerged an unprecedented array of antidepression legislation, although in scope and in extent not nearly as dramatic as what Congress would enact in 1933. This Hoover recovery program included the Reconstruction Finance Corporation, the Home Loan Bank, emergency relief expenditures, and the first peacetime public works and public housing projects. What did Johnson think about these emergency measures? The record is not clear. Like many Democrats, he expressed a partisan concern about costs, about escalating government debts, as one of many strategies for indicting the Hoover administration. Otherwise, Johnson either had no clear position on controversial legislation or, if he had, rarely voiced it. He had two interactive goals that were in conflict with partisan advocacy. He wanted both to run an exemplary congressional office and to boost his own career. These goals required good working relationships with bureaucrats of various political persuasions. Thus, Johnson tried to appear open, amiable, and grateful to everyone. His perspective on new legislation tended to be entirely practical—what did it offer the people of the Fourteenth District? And how could he procure the largest possible share of new benefits for the people back home?

In March 1933, a victorious Democratic party took over the White House and dominated both houses of Congress. Franklin D. Roosevelt, aided by the suffering of the Great Depression, engineered the landslide victory, quickly helped energize Congress, and presided over a virtual avalanche of important new legislation. Both his political and his legislative victories excited and inspired Johnson. He always admired power and success. This does not mean that he understood, let alone endorsed, every new bill or executive action. No one could. The New Deal lacked coherence or policy consistency. The legislation, in total, conformed to no clear program, let alone any ideology. Back of the resulting legislation lay contradictory goals and interests. Some new programs suggested corporate nationalism, even a mild form of fascism, whereas other legislation suggested milder forms of socialism. But some trends soon became clear. In response to a sick economy, Congress extended the range and degree of federal economic regulation and embraced new ways of directly aiding financially beleaguered and unemployed Americans, ranging from new forms of credit through direct relief payments to expanded public works. How did Johnson react to all this? Not ideologically. Rather, his correspondence suggests he spent almost all is time trying to relate the new programs to his district, to get district farmers to sign up for the new AAA payments or to get home owners to apply for mortgage relief. Now that the federal government had so dramatically increased its patronage, Johnson tried to ensure that his constituents received more than their share of benefits. His orientation, a lifelong one, was always primarily upon government as a servant. He was there to help people.

The heady excitement of 1933 could only postpone LBJ's developing restlessness. Given all the new appropriations, his task was now more fulfilling than ever before. But his work, which at first had offered a great challenge, had become a settled routine. He now knew his job perfectly. It was time to graduate. At times, he had become the alter ego of Kleberg. He increasingly took responsibility, and credit, for his own work. He lobbied, or helped secure jobs, for a growing number of friends or influential people back in Texas. In the summer of 1934 he took leave from Kleberg's staff to help a well-named Maury Maverick, a radical to most Texans, win election in a new congressional district, one that included San Antonio. At times he seemed to be laying the political foundation for a challenge to Kleberg, although his apparent expectation was that Kleberg might gain and accept an ambassadorial appointment. But Kleberg won no such appointment and seemed unlikely to retire any time soon. Thus, an elective office seemed an unlikely possibility by 1934.

At the same time, Johnson's monasticlike personal life had settled into a rut—a dull rooming house, restaurant meals, and few enduring personal relationships. He was lonely. He had worked so hard, had been so involved, that he had almost no time to meet young women. Latimer and Jones stress how peripheral sex was in his life. They report only episodic, casual encounters, as when LBJ picked up a waitress and stayed out all night. By the summer of 1934, as he did campaign work in San Antonio, he seemed to reach the rational decision that it was time to marry. He was open to any likely prospect. And, if his earlier courtship of Carol Davis set a precedent, he would seek as a wife, not the glittering women that he charmed on occasion and whom he always liked to have around his office as a type of adornment, but someone of ability, character, refinement, and, possibly, wealth.

At another critical juncture in Lyndon's life, Sam Johnson again played a role, although this time a minor one. Sometime, probably in the summer of 1934, LBJ visited his father at the Texas Railroad Commission office in Austin, where Sam reported as Texas bus inspector. Sam introduced Lyndon to an attractive office secretary, Eugenia Boehringer, who had moved to Austin from rural Harrison County in east Texas. In September 1934, as Lyndon headed back toward Washington, he asked Eugenia, whom he had tried unsuccessfully to date, to get him a blind date. She did so, lining up another office secretary. When Johnson came to the office to meet his date, Eugenia introduced him to her closest friend, Claudia Alta Taylor, a high school classmate from the small town of Karnack.

70

Lyndon had heard about Claudia and probably had wanted to meet her. Crudely put, he knew her credentials. Perhaps he had already cataloged her name among his repertoire of potential mates. This seems likely, for at this brief meeting he asked her to meet him for breakfast next morning at the Driskill Hotel. She apparently nodded agreement but remembered later that she did not intend to honor the promise. The next morning, as she passed the hotel, she saw a solitary Lyndon at a table, almost frantically waving for her to come in. She did, and, almost immediately, the conversation became intense and personal. He took her for a drive, shared with her all his dreams. By her memory, he proposed marriage before the day was out. The following day he took her to San Marcos to meet his parents and then drove all the way to the King ranch so that she could meet Kleberg's mother, who, typically, had long since become a devoted admirer of an always agreeable and flattering LBJ. Finally, at the end of a week, as Lyndon and a friend drove to Washington, Claudia invited them to visit her girlhood home in Karnack and meet her father. He liked Lyndon. The whirlwind courtship continued through almost daily letters and frequent phone calls between Texas and Washington.

Claudia Taylor, although a Texan, had her roots in the Old South. Her father—Thomas Jefferson Taylor—had moved to Harrison County in east Texas as a young man, having left behind his role as a tenant farmer in Alabama. In the small village of Karnack he soon opened a general store and eventually expanded his enterprises to include several cotton gins, numerous farms, and a large number of black sharecroppers. In his own way, he had the same energy and proclivity for hard work as did LBJ. He returned to Alabama to marry his first love, Winnie Lee Patillo, a woman of genteel birth and aristocratic habits, and thus well above the social status of Taylor. Claudia was a late child, born in 1912 (thus four years LBJ's junior). Her two brothers were much older. Her mother died when Claudia was aged five. By then, the shy Claudia was already known as Lady Bird, an affectionate title given her by a nanny. Lyndon always called her Bird and later emphasized the shared initials of LBJ. A motherless Claudia spent some time in Alabama with an aunt, Effie Patillo, who then moved to Karnack and became Claudia's substitute mother. After attending the local one-room elementary school, Lady Bird moved with her aunt to the county seat of Marshall for high school. She finished third in her class. After two years of junior college in Dallas, she completed a B.A. in education at the University of Texas. But instead of pursuing a planned career in teaching, she completed a bachelor's in journalism in 1934. Just as Sam Johnson had met and then married a fledgling journalist, so now LBJ would repeat the family tradition.

Claudia was a jewel of great value, but in 1934 one hidden by a plain exterior. Like Lyndon's first serious girlfriend, Carol Davis, Lady Bird was painfully shy, conscientious to a fault, and gracious to the point of stereotype. Because of her reserved manner and understated dress, she did little to compensate for rather sharp features. In no sense was she a beauty, but she was attractive, more so as one came to know her. She lacked social self-confidence and on first appearance seemed submissive and deferential. Appearances were misleading. As everyone who knew her well soon found out, the hardest steel lay just behind the shy surface. She had fully as much self-discipline as Lyndon, but unlike him she never claimed the privilege of blowing off steam, of letting her feelings show. She never relaxed her outward calm, never gave in to negative feelings, never publicly complained, never fought back. Kind, generous, supportive, she had none of Lyndon's bent for putting down people. Self-conscious about any weakness, she was continually involved in self-improvement, in reading and learning and growing. In time she gained mastery at almost any task she undertook, and in a pattern reminiscent of Eleanor Roosevelt, she eventually developed the self-confidence needed to build an identity and a career quite distinct from that of her egotistic and demanding husband. In a sense her greatest achievement was to stay with Lyndon, to suffer and rebound from his childish temper tantrums, his occasional crudeness and obscenity, his overbearing impositions, his ego boosting at her expense. She not only stayed with him but gained his gratitude, his respect, even his dependence. She basked finally in his political success, shared his enormous power and used some of it to further her own goals, and enjoyed his exuberance and his overwhelming acts of kindness and affection.

Even in courtship, Lyndon was in a hurry. In November 1934, or just two months after he met Lady Bird, he drove, speeding without a break, back to Karnack, ostensibly to decide if the couple would announce their engagement. Lyndon pushed for an immediate marriage. The two drove to Austin, and he bought her an engagement ring. She would not agree to an early marriage until she talked to her Aunt Effie back in Alabama. She took the trip, and of course Aunt Effie urged delay. Lyndon worked at Kleberg's office in Corpus Christi until she returned. He then forced the issue and had the support of Claudia's father. She finally capitulated.

They drove to San Antonio on 17 November. Dan Quill, a political crony whom Lyndon had cultivated during the Maverick campaign in the summer, bypassed rules to get an immediate marriage license. He also engaged a reluctant Episcopal minister (Lady Bird's denomination) to conduct an informal service. Back in San Marcos, Rebekah was hurt at not being included, but in a warm letter she gave her blessings upon the match and welcomed Lady Bird into the family. The couple took a brief honeymoon trip into Mexico and then returned to Washington, where they rented a small, one-bedroom apartment on Kalorama Road. For Lyndon, after the years in the basement of the Dodge Hotel, this must have seemed like heaven.

Lady Bird became a vital member of Johnson's developing political team. She rarely joined in the office work, but she pampered Lyndon, took care of all his physical needs, with some difficulty learned the arts of cooking and housekeeping, used extreme frugality in managing their finances, and, most critical, became the accommodating and warm hostess for the guests Lyndon began entertaining, often without prior notice. Despite premarriage promises, he never took the time from his work to escort Lady Bird to the sights of Washington, and in contrast to her he never developed much interest in Washington's cultural events. Her adjustments had to be as difficult, in a quite different setting, as Rebekah's back on the Pedernales in 1907. But she coped wonderfully. She made guests feel at ease. Thus, she helped cultivate the friendships Lyndon had formed and needed for his career. The newlyweds entertained other Texas congressmen and friendly reporters as well as bureaucrats or office staff. They deepened a friendship with Maury Maverick and his wife. Their apartment became a second home to a lonely Sam Rayburn. As a bachelor, he soon adopted Lady Bird and Lyndon as if they were his own children. Lyndon had long cultivated Rayburn, but obvious elements of self-interest, of political opportunism, warred with sincerity. Not so in the more familial context of the apartment. Later, LBJ and Rayburn would have moments of disagreement and tension. Their friendship suffered strains. But nothing diminished Rayburn's fatherly concern for Lady Bird or her deep and unselfish affection for him. No one was closer to the later speaker of the House.

In 1935, Rayburn's friendship proved invaluable in boosting Johnson's career. In June Johnson welcomed a long-awaited opportunity to escape from Kleberg's office. No congressional secretary had ever assumed more responsibility, found so many avenues of self-publicity and self-advancement, or accumulated so many uncollected political debts. Elected office seemed out of the question, and Johnson's age (only twenty-six) made unlikely his consideration for the head of any major executive agency or program. But, as one of the ways of using the huge, almost $5 billion emergency appropriation of 1935, Roosevelt established by executive order a new work relief program, which replaced the earlier, more decentralized Federal Emergency Relief Administration (FERA). The largest new relief agency would be the Works Progress Administration (WPA), headed by Harry Hopkins. Several people, including Eleanor Roosevelt, wanted to be sure such relief funds served the needs of children and youth. Thus, as a subsidiary to the WPA, Roosevelt ordered the creation of a subordinate National Youth Administration (NYA) to be headed by Aubrey Williams, an Alabama editor and, for the South, somewhat of a radical, particularly on racial issues. The WPA, following the pattern of the early FERA, continued to administer its programs from state offices and under state relief administrators. Williams, in organizing the much smaller youth program, followed the same administrative plan. This meant, for each state, an NYA director, one who became, in a sense, the junior partner of the WPA administrator. For this position, as LBJ quickly perceived, his youth would be less of a handicap. As soon as Roosevelt issued the executive order, Johnson asked his Texas supporters, headed by Sam Rayburn, to nominate and support him as Texas director. Such early and powerful support did not at first win him the position. Only the direct intervention of Rayburn persuaded Roosevelt to reverse an earlier decision and announce Lyndon's appointment on 25 July 1935. Characteristically, Johnson then persuaded Kleberg to give his brother, Sam Houston, his old job as congressional secretary.

The NYA remained a minor New Deal alphabetical agency. The small Washington staff prepared the needed forms and guidelines, at first with a great deal of confusion. The ill-staffed state offices approved the various work programs for youth, funding them from work relief funds allocated to each state. This required a close and continuous coordination of WPA and NYA projects. In fact, one primary duty of NYA directors was to ensure that youth received a proportionate share of jobs on WPA projects and to keep records of all such employment. In addition to youth advocacy the NYA directly administered three major programs for young people—work projects for youth not in school (usually forty-six hours per month for eight dollars), work study jobs for youth in high schools and colleges, and various job training and apprenticeship programs, which included some summer youth camps.

By the summer of 1938, the NYA, in its own projects or through the WPA, offered some type of employment to approximately 500,000 youth. The NYA, from the top down, reflected a great deal of moral idealism and, because of its aid to children, never invited as much criticism or derision as its parent WPA. In fact, most communities, and most parents, appreciated NYA projects, which rivaled in popularity those of the earlier and continuing Civilian Conservation Corps. The few critics cited fear of regimentation or of subtle and covert indoctrination (this was the decade of tightly disciplined fascist and communist youth organizations in Europe). NYA wages remained pitifully low. Work projects could not compete with private employment, and thus a few tended to be trivial. The work-study funds for high school and college youngsters never began to meet the need. For example, stringent requirements (parents often had to be a relief client for their children to qualify) kept the eligibility list to less than 15 percent of all college students. But even this, given the fifteen-dollar monthly stipend, kept many young people in schools and colleges and off unemployment lists. The funds also freed up other scholarship funds. The college grants kept some campuses from closing, helped maintain jobs for professors, and even helped spur an increase in college enrollments by the mid-thirties.

LBJ and Lady Bird rented one side of a duplex on Happy Hollow Lane in Austin. This city would be their Texas residence until they bought the ranch on the Pedernales in 1951, although during these years Johnson continued to pay his poll taxes back in Johnson City and to vote there on election day. The house on Happy Hollow Lane became the late night offices of the NYA. The spare bedroom became a rooming house for young staff members. Lyndon turned to friends and old classmates to build his small administrative staff (by 1936, he had only five administrative assistants in the Austin office, plus four secretaries and seven stenographers). In the start-up period, L. E. Jones briefly lent a hand, but then returned to law school. Johnson selected Jesse Kellam as his second in command. The wiry, serious, administratively able Kellam had graduated from Southwest Texas just before Johnson enrolled. He had subsequently met and impressed Johnson, who used all his leverage with Kleberg and friendly lobbyists to get him an administrative post in the State Department of Education. He now collected on his debt in order to recruit him for a lower-paying job. In 1937, Kellam would succeed Johnson as director of the Texas NYA. Johnson also persuaded his old White Star crony from San Marcos days, Willard Deason, to leave a legal position with the Federal Land Bank to assume control over the job training and apprenticeship program. To head the work projects, Johnson turned to a boyhood playmate, Sherman Birdwell. For the four secretarial posts, for regional directors or local project supervisors, Johnson employed a dozen other former White Stars or hill country friends, including even Ben Crider. But the one older, more established administrative employee was soon also the most indispensable. Through the influence of Maury Maverick, he was able to hire Herbert Henderson to manage the Austin office and to direct all public relations efforts. Henderson's wife also assumed a secretarial position. Henderson was a journalist by profession, having worked for newspapers in Ohio and New Mexico before coming to Texas and working briefly with the FERA. Gifted, an intellectual, but plagued by alcoholism, he became Johnson's first and, well into his congressional career, only speech writer.

Once again, Johnson excelled. He quickly mastered his new position. Partly because of his ability, hard work, and solid achievements, partly because of his knack for self-promotion, partly because of Henderson's superb journalistic skills, Johnson soon gained the reputation as a youthful bureaucratic genius, as the ablest NYA director in the country (he was also the youngest). Aubrey Williams came close to saying this, and endlessly applauded Johnson's work. Eleanor Roosevelt visited his offices in Austin and added her commendations. Within Texas, Johnson cultivated all the right people, both for lending credence to his NYA program and for building political assets for himself. He sold the NYA idea, won support throughout the state, and helped local communities plan appropriate projects. For example, he selected as chairman of his State Advisory Committee an influential Austin public utilities lawyer and former state senator, Alvin J. Wirtz. Johnson had already met and befriended Wirtz in his role as congressional secretary. Now, back in Austin, he cultivated the able, crafty, powerful Wirtz as a family friend, one who had his law office in the same building as the state NYA offices. Wirtz, who had no son of his own, practically adopted LBJ and more than anyone else would mastermind his subsequent entrée into elective politics.

As an administrator, Johnson worked tirelessly. He traveled continuously around the huge state and drove his staff with the same relentless intensity he had displayed back in Washington. The productivity of his staff had to rival, if not exceed, that of any government operation in American history. Brains and muscle could not do more. From the beginning, he tried to be on top of all the rules, worked hard to complete, ahead of time if possible, all the required reports, and proved his genius in thinking up new initiatives. He overwhelmed Washington with the length of some of his reports, sent NYA news releases to every prominent person he knew, and assiduously cultivated newspaper editors all over the state. He was pushy, always dreaming up new projects or pressuring the Washington office for more funds. He asked for higher staff salaries. Yet, in what became a pattern throughout his life, he loved to come in under budget, to wring new efficiencies from his personnel. During his two years as director he always achieved surpluses in his modest administrative budget. In 1936, the total budget for the Texas offices of the NYA was only $90,000; in 1937, the year he left, an expanded staff in the field increased the allocation to $133,000.

The administrative budget made up only a small percentage of NYA expenditures. Its varied projects soon entailed several million dollars of relief funds. And here, in the actual payoff for all the organization, Johnson faced an early problem, not of saving money but of finding quick ways to spend it. That was what the relief program was all about. But this mandate soon warred against the growing rules, the strict eligibility requirments, the elaborate project proposals, the multiple application forms that soon drove Johnson's administrative staff close to insanity. As he began work in July 1935, he had two major challenges—to plan and initiate work projects that would offer part-time employment to approximately thirty-five thousand unemployed youth in Texas, and to sign up and orient high school principals and college administrators who would, come September, administer the work-study grants. By September 1935, Johnson and Birdwell could finally announce approval or pending approval for four major work projects, costing about $1.5 million. Since the boys and, less frequently, girls could not do competitive work or take jobs away from the private economy, the work had to be largely unskilled, involving no more than 25 percent of costs for materials, yet still be significant and of lasting benefit to the state. This was a hard assignment, to say the least. The largest early project involved playground improvement at schools, a project that potentially could provide jobs in all 256 Texas counties. Eventually, about fifteen thousand youngsters gained employment. Another smaller project involved youthful work crews making improvements in state parks or constructing shoulders on state highways. But the first, most imaginative, and only unique project gave the Texas NYA national recognition. In the early brainstorming over how to employ Texas youngsters, someone (not LBJ or he would have claimed the credit) conceived the idea of roadside parks. The first approved NYA project involved funding for 250 small parks, with pull-off space and picnic tables, all built with the cooperation and partial funding of the Texas Highway Department. Soon other states imitated the program, but Texas had a head start, and the state even yet is inordinately proud of its roadside park system.

Under Johnson, the Texas NYA carried out its work-study program with exemplary finesse and success. By 1936, Deason was able to provide work-study grants to 8,139 white and 887 black high school students, 5,360 white and 473 black college students, and 44 white graduate students. In 1937 this number rose to a total of over 11,000 in high school and over 7,000 in college. Johnson met with three college executives before he launched the aid program, had all the programs approved by the fall semester of 1935 (a near miracle), and quickly processed all student applications, protesting all the while the stringent eligibility restrictions. At the suggestion of President Evans of Southwest Texas State Teachers College, the Texas NYA also established and paid for textbooks and college instructors for freshman college centers, which offered credit courses, usually in high schools, for young people who could not enroll in college, another innovation copied in other states. Other educational programs involved on-the-job training, some at newly created residence training centers. In the summer the Texas NYA also conducted a few special camps for unemployed or culturally deprived youth. These camps, prophetic of the later Job Corps, taught not only job skills but hygiene, English, and fine arts. Many graduates were able to get jobs after such training.

LBJ faced, and brilliantly surmounted, the one greatest hazard to a popular NYA program in Texas—race. To an extent rivaled by few other New Deal agencies, the national NYA tried to offer fully equal opportunities to blacks. In the first hectic months, the national office urged state directors to enlist blacks on the state advisory boards. Johnson believed this would wreck his carefully orchestrated effort to win a broad base of support in Texas. He argued that if he made such an unprecedented appointment, his white board members would resign. Then he would have to resign because of the controversy or, from the Texas perspective, the scandal. He believed Texas blacks wanted progress, not friction, and that they would not cooperate in an integrated program. The NYA capitulated, as it did throughout the South. But implicit in the negotiations was a mandate, one almost never followed before in the South—to treat blacks equally even when separate.

As far as the record discloses, Johnson tried to live up to this mandate. At least he persuaded black leaders that he had done so, leaving a legacy of goodwill among Texas blacks that paid off in his subsequent campaigns. He appointed a black advisory board (these boards, both black and white, served largely as a public relations gesture, not as policy-making bodies). He included all black colleges in the student aid program. Even though blacks did not receive grants in proportion to their numbers in the state population, a much higher percentage of black college students qualified for and gained aid (24 percent, compared to 13 percent for whites). Black youngsters faced the same eligibility requirements as whites on work projects and often joined whites on road improvement jobs, usually working in separate crews. This does not mean that in all areas they shared equally. Johnson stressed local customs and all the obstacles. Even as he publicized white projects he tried to keep all news of black projects out of white newspapers. Neither did he publicize his visits to black campuses or his conferences with black college officials. In a sense, he pleased Washington by his positive steps but without in any way harming his reputation in Texas, a strategy that he used over and over again on issues concerning race.

On 23 February 1937, while escorting the director of the Kansas NYA on a tour in Houston, Johnson glimpsed the headlines of the *Houston Post.* Congressman James P. Buchanan of the Tenth Congressional District had died. His district included both Johnson's home in Austin and his boyhood home in Johnson City. Johnson immediately realized that this was his long-awaited chance at an important elective office. He rushed back to Austin. The following sequence of events is not clear; remembrances vary. But certainly he consulted early and extensively with Alvin Wirtz. As Lyndon later recalled, Wirtz at first discouraged his long-shot candidacy. Several likely aspirants were much better known in the district, and both Buchanan's widow and his campaign manager were likely candidates. Johnson, at twenty-eight, was also embarrassingly young. Apparently Wirtz did not take much persuading. As head of the Lower Colorado River Authority, he had compelling personal reasons to want an able, persuasive, friendly congressman in Washington. The fate of a large dam on the nearby Colorado River depended upon special appropriations and the waiving of existing laws. The second key consultant was Lady Bird, who had immediate access to ten thousand dollars held by her father, but part of a bequest from her mother. After agonizing appraisals of their slim chance of victory, and with support from Wirtz, she made the telephone call to her father and committed the whole sum to the campaign. L. E. Jones, who worked in Wirtz's office, recalls one decisive interview with Wirtz, an interview that committed LBJ to candidacy. To Jones's amazement, Lyndon walked out of the building and stuck his hand out to the first passerby, announcing "I'm Lyndon Johnson. I'm running for Congress." He had accosted forty people before reaching his car.

This chronology is probably a bit confused. Out of courtesy, Johnson had to wait until after Buchanan's funeral on 26 February to declare his candidacy. By then he was intimidated by the prospect of a sentimental candidacy by the widow, and thus at first joined other interested prospects in awaiting her decision. She promised an announcement on Monday, 29 February, which suggested her likely candidacy. According to Sam Houston Johnson, a despondent LBJ drove to Johnson City for the weekend, there to consult with his father. An ill Sam, only a few months from death, urged Johnson to declare his candidacy before the scheduled announcement by the widow. This might bluff her out. In any case, he could later withdraw. Johnson announced his candidacy back in Austin on Sunday evening. On Monday, Mrs. Buchanan announced her decision not to run, just as Sam had anticipated. Thus, if one can credit this story, Lyndon's father once again, and for the last time, played a crucial role in his son's career. Lyndon returned to Johnson City to give his first campaign speech, from the porch of the family home. Sam introduced him. In Johnson City this was big news. A hometown boy, from the poorest and least populous county in the district, was a candidate for Congress.

Johnson eventually won the election, and with a sizable plurality. Luck and some unique peculiarities of Texas election laws helped account for the victory of the youthful underdog. The election on 10 April did not require a runoff. The candidate with the most votes would go to Congress. Since eight candidates filed, six of them serious and roughly comparable competitors, the election result could be decided by a small minority of voters—less than 20 percent. Such a special election, with no other offices or issues at stake, also meant a small turnout. Thus, Johnson cold win if he could seize on a compelling and distinctive issue, even one that appealed to only a targeted minority of voters. Also, with each vote so critical, the election favored candidates who could, on a one-to-one basis, win over voters. Much more than in regular primaries or elections, the voters in sparsely populated hill counties, such as Blanco, could make a difference, particularly if most of them favored one candidate. Johnson capitalized on this unusual advantage for underdogs. He soon laid claim to a mobilizing issue and outworked any competitors in personal campaigning. He also enjoyed ample financial support, which helped him maximize the effectiveness of his campaign.

Alvin Wirtz, as a coldly calculating bit of advice, suggested what turned out to be Johnson's winning platform—complete support of a locally popular Roosevelt. In the spring of 1937, this meant above all else support of Roosevelt's controversial so-called Court-packing plan. FDR, frustrated by adverse court decisions on the constitutionality of major, but often poorly drafted, early administration legislation, asked Congress, in a surprise move at the beginning of his second term, to approve a new retirement system for Supreme Court justices and to permit up to five additional appointments to parallel those of justices who chose to stay on the Court beyond age seventy. This was clearly a legislative measure designed to change, more quickly than through normal appointments or constitutional amendments, the dominant philosophy on the Court, particularly as it affected the extent of permissible federal economic regulation. If the measure had set a precedent, it might have meant a permanent shift of governmental power toward the executive and legislative branches and away from the federal courts. It seemed to entail a federal government more directly responsive to electoral majorities and less circumscribed by constitutional restraints. This court bill raised a storm of protest, frightened almost everyone concerned about civil liberties, and soon faced determined and, in the end, overwhelming opposition in the Senate. Roosevelt not only lost on this issue but would never again be able to reconstruct the willing, at times almost abject, support he had enjoyed in Congress. Thus, for him, the effort amounted to a colossal political mistake. The issues were complex, involving preferences about the form and structure of American government. The debate engaged fundamental issues, but how fully the larger public understood them is impossible to know. Those who hated Roosevelt enjoyed a field day. Many who had supported most of his congressional proposals now deserted him.

81

Johnson eagerly embraced the Roosevelt position. He laid claim to this issue before his competitors, and by endless repetition and his enthusiasm, he convinced voters that he was more pro-Roosevelt, more pro–New Deal, than anyone else in the race. What Johnson personally thought about the constitutional questions remains unclear. Perhaps, typically, he did not get involved in the more theoretical issues. Much like Roosevelt, he saw the measure as a short-term tactic in an ongoing policy conflict over the extent of federal power. On 11 March 1937, he gave his opening radio address in the campaign. In an able, almost scholarly lecture, one carefully written by Henderson, he endorsed what he believed to be the key New Deal policies—opposition to entrenched wealth and privilege, and a commitment to the welfare of farmers, workers, teachers, and small businessmen. He applauded flood relief, aid to farmers, Social Security, utility regulation, and public power projects, with special emphasis on the uncompleted lower Colorado project. Then, in an extended analysis, he tried to clarify the Court issue, drawing upon the best arguments developed by the administration, with the final plea being that people were above even the Court. Changes in the Supreme Court, if consistent with the intent of the founding fathers, were critical to the preservation of vital legislation, such as the new National Labor Relations Act of 1935. Johnson soon gave up on such serious speeches, which he could never read effectively on radio. On 18 March he tried a new radio style—folksy and simple. He openly modeled his delivery on FDR's fireside chats, tried to associate himself with Roosevelt's programs, and kept up his attack on his opponents for either deserting Roosevelt or dragging their feet when the going got tough. To counter challenges to his youth, he emphasized his congressional and NYA work. He said he was a man who got things done, which became a formula in his later campaigns.

An appealing issue was not enough to win in the Tenth District, however. Johnson faced four candidates much better known than himself, and his youth was a handicap. But he compensated for these disabilities by a typically energetic, eighteen-hour-a-day effort. His youthful disciples all flocked to the cause from the NYA, from their own legal careers, or all the way from Washington. Deason, Latimer, Birdwell, L. E. Jones, and Henderson all helped out. The ten thousand dollars from Lady Bird paid the opening expenses. With funds raised with the help of Wirtz and another crafty Austin lawyer and long-term business adviser, Edward Clark, he paid for a steady barrage of radio messages by key personalities in the district, for posters, for local barbecues, and for well-planted newspaper articles. The funds also helped pay for an experienced campaign manager, Claude Wild, who had formerly worked for the governor of the state. But the crucial factor was Lyndon himself, his willingness to go anywhere, including the farthest ranch house, and his persuasive ability in any one-to-one or small-group encounter. Few voters could resist his direct appeal, or what later would be known as the Johnson treatment—riveted concentration on the other person, an intensity of voice, abject flattery, physical contact, and superb argumentative skills. The same magic worked with small groups in intimate, informal talks in country stores or courthouse squares. In such direct campaigning Johnson easily outclassed his other opponents. Because he was an underdog, not taken seriously at first, he was able to launch an earlier campaign and to gain a head start over opponents who were not able to work as hard (no one was).

Johnson missed the campaign's climax. During the last few days of campaigning, he was increasingly wracked by stomach pains. He had driven his body to its limit. He had slept little, worked incessantly, steadily lost weight, but still had not let up. He was already laying the foundation for an early death. He even made speeches while almost doubled over in pain. But on Thursday, 8 April, just two days before the Saturday election, Johnson collapsed in the midst of an evening speech in Austin and then pulled himself back up to complete it. In the aftermath his friends, who suspected appendicitis, took him to a nearby hospital for an emergency operation on what physcians reported as a near bursting appendix. Thus, Johnson lay abed during the last day of campaigning and the election. Claude Wild, his campaign manager, read his final radio address, perhaps to Lyndon's benefit since Wild was a much more polished radio speaker. Obviously this last-minute dramatic illness created suspicions among Johnson's opponents. Maybe he staged the collapse, made himself ill as a near martyr in the elusive cause of FDR. But, in light of the final tally, any votes gained by illness would not have changed the final outcome. Johnson won 8,280 votes, or 3,000 more than his nearest competitor. Fortunately, five of these opponents rather evenly divided up another 21,000 votes. The district was small, the turnout low. And Johnson's total vote (3 percent of the district's population) was surely among the lowest ever compiled by a winning congressional candidate in twentieth-century America. Even then he did not win solely by block votes from the hill counties, although he carried

Blanco by 688 to 82 for his nearest opponent. He also won in the most populous county of Travis, which included the city of Austin. He ran second or third in most of the counties that he lost. Thus, as much as any victor, he could claim to be the authentic choice of his congressional district.

Johnson exulted in his success. Congratulatory letters and telegrams flooded his hospital room. Magnanimous as always in victory, he warmly congratulated his opponents and began the task of winning their friendship and subsequent support. Johnson could not abide political enemies or unhappy constituents. He wanted everybody to be happy and supportive. He wanted to please, to serve. Even the exaggerated polemics of political campaigns always proved uncongenial to him, for he wanted to abate, not exacerbate, conflict, to find points of agreement and bases of compromise. Unfortunately, his recuperation proved more difficult than expected. When he tried serious work while still in the hospital, he had a relapse, something close to nervous prostration. This probably reflected the body's rebellion against the eight weeks of abuse in the campaign, and the brain's rebellion against the emotional intensity and mental concentration that had enabled him to win. He did not leave the hospital for over two weeks and then had to rest at home for two more weeks.

What seemed to pull him out of his postelection letdown or depression was a chance to meet Roosevelt. FDR had taken notice of the special election. Nationally, newspapers had billed it as a test of Roosevelt's popularity and of his Court plan. Obviously, in a period when the president enjoyed little enthusiastic support or unqualified approval, he rejoiced in Johnson's victory and asked to meet him. The governor of Texas, an undeclared Johnson supporter, arranged a meeting for 12 May, when a vacationing Roosevelt put ashore at Galveston. The three posed for the expected photographs (the critical need of young politicians). One of these showing LBJ shaking hands with FDR, and with the governor between them, became a famous prop in Johnson's 1941 campaign for the Senate (by then the governor had been airbrushed out of the picture). Equally flattering to Johnson was Roosevelt's invitation to accompany him in his special railroad car on the first leg of a trip back to Washington. They were together for a day, all the way to Fort Worth, and thus able to talk in private. Out of these meetings Johnson won a prized congressional committee post and gained entrée into a circle of Roosevelt's advisers.

Lyndon and Lady Bird also traveled to Washington, although not on the president's train. They arrived on 13 May so that he could assume his duties as a specially elected congressman. The leave-taking in Austin had been bittersweet. His family proudly saw him off. Rebekah gained more satisfaction from the victory than had LBJ. In a moving letter she offered her blessings, her thanks for such a successful son, and her sense that LBJ could now vindicate her father, who had lost a similar bid for national office. But Sam, who had helped plot the victory, was now ill and close to death. Two years earlier, in 1935, heart attacks had forced him to retire from his bus inspector's job. From then on Lyndon tried to save money from his salary in order to help his parents. In 1935 Rebekah and Sam had moved back to the Johnson City home place, which Sam loved so much. He thus spent his final two years in the familiar hills near the Pedernales, among the cronies of his childhood, peaceful, vindicated by his son's fame, but still in debt. He watched Lyndon leave Austin for Washington. LBJ kissed his father good-bye, perhaps with the realization that he might never talk to him again.

Johnson's first, highly successful weeks as a congressman must have boosted his confidence, pulled him completely away from the weakness and depression that had followed his election. But the news from home was depressing. Sam's health steadily deteriorated. In June, Lyndon addressed a handwritten Father's day letter to "My dearest Dad," in all probability the last letter he sent to his father. In it he expressed his desire to be in Johnson City. He wished Sam were nearby so he could talk over issues with him. But never again would he receive advice from his father. Sam suffered a major heart attack in less than a month, and entered the Scott and White Clinic in Temple. He had no prospects of full recovery. In September, when a congressional recess allowed Lyndon and Lady Bird to return to their Austin home, Sam begged them to take him back to Johnson City. Instead, Lyndon brought him to his house on Happy Hollow Lane in Austin, where he died on 23 October.

The family took Sam's body back to the old place, near Stonewall. Here he was buried in the family cemetery on the banks of the Pedernales, just across the road from the house to which Sam's parents had brought him as a ten-year-old boy, the house to which he brought his bride in 1907, the house in which Lyndon was born in 1908. Rebekah, who after Sam's death tended to elevate him to a noble perch he neither deserved nor would have appreciated, lived only briefly in her Johnson City home until Lyndon was able to help her buy a small, simple house in Austin. With Sam's death, one political career ended just as the son's reached its first milestone. From now on, Sam's son would have to go it alone, without a father's cagey advice or timely interventions.

5

CONGRESSMAN JOHNSON

From the perspective of people in the Tenth District of Texas, Lyndon Johnson proved an ideal congressman. No one ever served constituents more assiduously or with greater success. He quickly became the willing servant, lobbyist, agent, and ombudsman of everyone who asked for his help, whether rich or poor. And, by the natural order of things, people of wealth and influence most often needed and used his talents. But because of his intense commitment to his district, because of the enormous time he devoted to constituent demands, and because of ambitions to move up to the Senate, he was rarely involved with major national issues, had limited time to devote to committee and legislative tasks, and usually tried to avoid highly partisan or controversial positions

After the early glow of success, Johnson did not find his job on the House all that fulfilling. In a sense, he continued the job he had under Kleberg, only now with the title and the deserved salary. Working as a dutiful servant of constituents, however grateful they were, never provided LBJ the ego boosting he needed. He wanted power and national recognition. At first, as a junior representative from Texas, the third youngest in age in the seniority-conscious House, he had precious little power. He was a small fish in a large pond, with no audience ready to notice his tricks except for a few people back in his district, and they noticed only because Johnson overwhelmed them with exaggerated advertisements of his achievements.

Without a leadership role and no prospect of such short of at least two decades of service, Johnson at first assumed the same demeanor he always displayed when he largely had to follow other people—quiet, retiring, deferential, often bored. He was one of numerous, almost invisible representatives, one who ran an almost perfect office, but one who almost never spoke on the House floor, who enlisted in no crusades or causes, and who rarely attended debates. Only his votes on bills, or his sponsorship of local legislation, made the *Congressional Record*. Within two years he was almost desperately seeking new strategies to gain recognition and leverage. In 1941 he leaped at an opportunity to run for the Senate, but narrowly lost. He had to wait until 1948 to try again, and then barely won. But from as early as 1940 on, his highest political goal was undoubtedly a Senate seat, since the two Texas senators were old men, sure to die or retire in the next several years. He was intelligent enough to know that he had almost no chance of ever being a viable presidential candidate.

Johnson had job security. Except for a few swing districts, those evenly balanced between two parties, or for surprise congressmen elected from minority parties in presidential landslides such as that of 1936, only completely inept incumbents lose their seats in the House. In fact, such a seat carries more job security than most positions in the private sector. Given the overwhelming Democratic majority in his district and his unsurpassed skills in cultivating his constituents, Johnson had a lifetime job, as did almost all Texas and southern congressmen. He already knew all the tricks, the numerous ways of contacting and flattering voters, such as frequent radio reports, mailings to district newspapers, carefully rigged questionnaires, a prompt response to all incoming mail, and the ability to magnify and thus focus attention on his every achievement in Washington. Numerous institutional arrangements facilitated this agent role for a congressman, including the cooperation of the executive branch in routing through them announcements of local appointments or special appropriations. The system works against only one type of incumbent—the maverick or true believer, the person of deep convictions who opposes the wishes of constituents, or congressmen who, horror of horrors, refuse to act as agents for constituents or refuse to blow their own horns. If they do not publicize their own role in Washington, certainly no one else will.

Johnson disliked partisan advocacy. He always tried to harmonize conflicting viewpoints and felt more secure with moderate or middling positions between political extremes. This meant that he never joined the more active or outspoken supporters of Roosevelt, even though his campaign platform led to this expectation. Instead, without fanfare, he simply cast proadministration votes on almost all issues. He voted for the Federal Fair Labor Standards Act of 1938, for new work relief appropriations to relieve the panic of 1937–38, for continued conservation appropriations, for tax reform, for agricultural price supports, and for all public power proposals. After 1938 he consistently supported the administration on foreign policy and defense issues—the lowering of neutrality restrictions, money for preparedness, and by 1940 a new selective service system. But he was open to compromise on most issues and when necessary would bow to the demands of his Texas constituents.

Throughout his career in Congress, Johnson revealed a few consistent voting patterns. He always expressed a keen concern for frugality and a balanced budget and thus always voted for greater efficiency or economy in government operations. He had a special sentimental commitment to public power and to various relief or welfare measures. He reflected a simple, almost instinctive patriotism. He thus always voted for greater preparedness or defense expenditures and usually for security or antisubversive legislation. He voted against early civil rights proposals, justifying this stand by solicitude for state rights even as he denied any personal prejudice. His positions on labor issues were more fluid and complex. Consistently, he supported Social Security increases and minimum wage laws, or any government patronage designed, through regulation or redistribution, to help improve the life of ordinary people. This did not mean he had any special solicitude for labor unions. Expediency or constituent pressures guided his votes on union-related legislation. He was equally ambiguous or ambivalent on federal economic regulation. He had absorbed from childhood a fear and resentment of large corporate power, and particularly of the exploitative role that northern capital had played in Texas. Thus, not only in his first congressional campaign but at times throughout his political career he expressed a bit of class resentment against large, externally owned firms, such as banks and at times even the major oil companies in Texas. But his class resentments became more muted over time, and, in any case, they did not extend to all forms of wealth and power. He identified with independent local entrepreneurs and often joined small or local businessmen in their opposition to government regulations and controls.

Some of these tensions in his economic preferences emerged in his first glorious achievement as the new congressman from the Tenth District. Al Wirtz, a brilliant lawyer, the most feared power broker in Austin, and longtime lobbyist for oil and utility firms, had helped elect Johnson for a purpose—to salvage a half-completed dam under construction by the Lower Colorado River Authority (LCRA), or what amounted to a small TVA for a river that flowed through, and all too often flooded, Austin. Wirtz, after the collapse of the Insull empire in 1932 (he had lobbied for these utilities), had helped gain a state-chartered LCRA, served for years as its extravagantly paid counsel (his ninety thousand dollars in fees became a minor scandal), and helped secure Public Works Administration (PWA) funds to continue construction of uncompleted dams. Such funds financed the first large dam—the George Hamilton (later the James P. Buchanan), about sixty miles upriver from Austin in the rugged, sparsely populated hill county. As its later name indicates, Congressman Buchanan (Lyndon's predecessor) and chairman of the crucial House Appropriations Committee helped secure the funds to complete it. Since it had limited flood control potential, however, Congress approved other dams on the river, including a second one at Marshall Ford, only a dozen miles up in the hills from Austin (the present Mansfield Dam and the basis of Lake Travis).

In 1936 the Bureau of Reclamation (BOR) began construction of this dam at a projected cost of $10 million. But in the personal and often confused way President Roosevelt operated, he had given his approval of the dam to Buchanan before the BOR obtained congressional authorization. Buchanan had successfully prevailed upon the Office of the Comptroller General to release the first $5 million pending the expected appropriation by Congress in 1937. To further complicate matters, the BOR eventually learned that it was prohibited by law from building the dam, which was on land not owned by the federal government. In the unique case of Texas, ownership of public land and streams had been vested in the state by the terms of its admission to the Union. Thus, by the spring of 1937 the completion of the dam depended not only upon a congressional appropriation (since Buchanan was chairman of the Appropriations Committee, his support virtually guaranteed this) but upon a special bill to authorize the existing construction contracts already entered into by the BOR. Just when he was most needed, Buchanan died and was replaced by a brash Lyndon B. Johnson, who had neither congressional seniority nor membership on the Appropriations Committee.

Johnson had other assets, however. His election platform and his meeting with Roosevelt in Galveston ensured early administrative recognition and support. Roosevelt owed him one. And, quickly, LBJ was able to cultivate and consolidate friendships with key members of the White House staff, particularly Thomas (Tommy the Cork) Corcoran and James (Jim) Rowe. To get approval and funding for the Marshall Ford dam, Johnson took full advantage of this temporary clout within the administration.

His role may have been critical. No one can know for sure. Of course, Johnson believed it crucial and took full credit for success. His first role was indirect. He had already entertained Wirtz in Washington in early New Deal days and as Kleberg's secretary had facilitated Wirtz's lobbying in behalf of the LCRA, a minor role that allowed Johnson later to talk as if he were the father of the LCRA. Now, upon arriving in Washington, he used letters to inform Wirtz and the dam contractors of developing events in the capital. He also suggested the best time for them to visit, acted as their host, and helped smooth their access to key congressmen or executive officials. The critical bill, which legitimated the project and existing contracts, was largely the handiwork of Texas representative Joseph J. Mansfield, for whom the dam would subsequently be named. What Johnson gained, apparently, was early Roosevelt support for the legislation, which he procured by working through Corcoran. Knowledge of presidential support elicited both congressional votes and the cooperation of the Comptroller General's office and the Bureau of the Budget, although the bill would in all likelihood have made it through Congress even without Johnson's help. But in July Johnson again brought the Texas backers to Washington to consult with Corcoran, and through him gained White House backing for the additional $5 million of relief funds needed to complete the dam as originally planned. For this Johnson could indeed claim credit, for he was at the center of a successful lobbying effort, even as he probably cashed in on some of the last credit he had with Roosevelt because of his pro-Court-packing campaign. Johnson was almost ecstatic over his success and briefly enjoyed all the plaudits from back home. This was, incidentally, a brief golden interlude in his congressional career, since it preceded his father's death in the fall and the periods of doubt and depression that haunted him in the more routine months of 1938.

Johnson's successful effort in behalf of the Marshall Ford dam gained him two enduring friends and benefactors, Herman and George Brown. The brothers headed a relatively small but profitable central Texas construction company—Brown and Root—which, in a daring effort to move up to the big time, had submitted the winning bid for construction of the dam. They also shared with LCRA the legal services of Alvin Wirtz. The Browns had not supported Johnson's election. In fact they knew him only slightly, but with his election they had an enormous stake in his success. By the time they knew of the acute problems of authorization and further funding, they had already invested $1.5 million in early construction, and much of this was for equipment and cable useful only at the dam site. They faced not only the loss of eventual profits but so many unrecoverable costs as to endanger their firm's survival.

Johnson not only helped win a reprieve for the dam but graciously entertained the Browns when they lobbied in Washington. He also continued to serve as their Washington agent in securing dozens of changes and added appropriations. In November 1937 the Brown brothers orchestrated local requests for another $17 million to heighten the dam by seventy-eight feet and thus make it effective in flood control (the official purpose of the original dam, which was actually developed largely for electrical generation). Johnson, at first miffed at such tactics by self-interested contractors, ultimately helped persuade Secretary of the Interior Harold Ickes to approve the addition. A brilliant young Memphis lawyer who had served as Ickes's chief legal officer on the PWA, Abe Fortas, worked out the ingenious legal arrangements in part out of a newly developed friendship with Johnson. This did not end the favors. Throughout the construction, Johnson carefully guided change orders through the bureaucracy and at every step helped increase Brown and Root's profits even as he helped create jobs for the people of Texas. As quickly as Johnson became a vital resource for Brown and Root, he became a close personal friend of the Brown brothers, a friendship that lasted until Johnson's death. Herman and George Brown joined Wirtz and lawyer Ed Clark as

Johnson's closest and most powerful Texas friends and supporters. Soon the favors flowed in all directions.

The Brown brothers opened wondrous possibilities for Johnson even as they posed tantalizing but dangerous temptations. Johnson had never known great wealth. He both envied and distrusted those who had it. Even as a congressman, with what would seem in late depression America a munificent salary of ten thousand dollars, Johnson remained hard put to meet his ever-growing financial responsibilities. He was still the principal support of an extended family. He helped buy his mother's house in Austin, found a job for his sister Josefa in the NYA, tried to keep Sam Houston sober enough to hold down a job, and still made payments on old family debts contracted by either his father or himself. In addition, he bore the costs of an apartment in Washington, his duplex in Austin, and two or more automobile trips between the two cities each year. He could never catch up, could never escape the time and effort he had to devote to family finances. But now, all of a sudden as congressman, he had enough clout in Washington to attract a cluster of wealthy clients and would-be benefactors, people who wanted favors and who expected, in some form, to repay them. Given his needs, Johnson was unusually circumspect in accepting financial help. This circumspection involved pride, a prudent awareness of political risk, and conventional moral standards. Thus, he collected his early debts in the form of political favors, such as campaign contributions, and never in the form of personal wealth. He remained a relatively poor man until World War II and then accumulated wealth through the indirect, not the direct, patronage of well-placed friends.

Johnson's relationship with Herman and George Brown soon transcended mutual need. The three families became close. In different ways, both George and Herman enjoyed Lyndon's company, and both became fond of him despite sharply divergent political beliefs. As always, Johnson tried to find commonalities, to so shape and present his own rather slippery views as to minimize differences and to be accommodating. Thus, his friendship with Herman Brown matured even as he cultivated other friends at the opposite political extreme, such as Maury Maverick and Henry A. Wallace. Both sides thought Johnson shared more of their views than he ever really did.

No ideological trimming could bridge Johnson's differences with Herman Brown. They argued politics endlessly and soon enjoyed the game. George Brown was closer to Johnson in personality—

open, expansive, flexible—and like him, he was never a true believer, never hung up on any political philosophy. But Herman was
a near-caricature of a Texas type, one that Johnson, in most contexts, struggled against throughout his career. Herman had come
up the hard way, through work, tenacity, a stubborn integrity. He
had slowly built his construction company largely through small
road contracts. His political views verged on a unique form of Texas anarchy. He distrusted most government programs that went
beyond police and defense. He wanted almost no government
regulations, he hated taxes, and he feared the dire effects of re-
distributive welfare. He glorified rugged, entrepreneurial individ-
ualism, hated labor unions, had grotesque images of socialism and
communism, and early fell into a conspiratorial rage when confronted with modern trends in every area of belief and behavior.
In most contexts he professed a distaste for politicians. Such labels
as reactionary do not do him justice. Since Johnson had a positive
image of government, was himself a career politician, and most
easily supported government programs in such areas as health, education, and welfare, he had to view Herman as a quaint anach-
ronism. But there were a few points of convergence—a mutual
distrust of bureaucratic waste, a shared respect for practical accomplishments, for getting things done, and a distrust of intellectual abstractions.

Consistently, Herman found the admirable or bearable side to
Johnson and insisted to friends that Johnson was really a practical
and basically conservative politician, whatever that label meant.
Johnson came to despise the large number of political crazies
down in Texas, those who made his life miserable and who, over
and over again, denounced even moderate policies as dangerously
radical. The political center in Texas was way over in right field.
But in Herman Brown, who joined or helped finance numerous
right-wing crusades, Johnson confronted the devil up close and
found a person of integrity and even a type of gentility behind the
ideological mask. Johnson, more than anyone else, helped make
Brown a multimillionaire. And Brown, more than anyone else,
helped pay for Johnson's success as a politician. The ironies are all
too obvious. Brown, who hated big government, fattened on its
patronage, a patronage gained not only by hard work but by the
political finesse of politicians such as LBJ. Brown, who celebrated
a nation of independent and self-sufficient entrepreneurs, ended up
as an executive in a large, highly collectivized corporate empire.
Johnson, who retained a bit of his populist resentment of concen-

trated and entrenched wealth and privilege, ended up as the obliging servant of new wealth. His support of Brown and Root's dam building was only a beginning. The big payoff came later during the defense buildup of 1940 and then in World War II. Johnson remained Brown and Root's congresssman and then senator, a constant source of vital intelligence, always ready to use whatever influences he had to smooth the way for their winning bids or gaining negotiated contracts. If they had not had Johnson, they would have had to buy themselves a congressman.

But in fairness to Johnson, one has to emphasize that he worked just as hard for other clients or constituents. What made one a beneficiary of his favors? Just asking. And beyond the demands that came to him, Johnson took the initiative back home. He solicited requests for grants or other government favors. He was determined that his district get a disproportionate share of federal spending. An avid supporter of the new United States Housing Authority, established in 1937 as the first large-scale, subsidized public housing program in American history, Johnson came to Austin and literally lobbied local officials to get them to submit one of the first three applications from a municipal housing authority, and then rejoiced when Austin was able to complete the first units. He put even more time into guiding the distribution and use of the LCRA electrical power than he did lobbying for the dams. He eventually toured the rural counties, particularly the hill counties, pleading the wonders of a new electrical age and prodding reluctant farmers to sign up in REA cooperatives. He had to use his limited influence with Roosevelt to get the REA to waive population density requirements and approve what became in 1939 the Pedernales Electric Cooperative, headquartered in Johnson City. Brown and Root won the contract to build many of the power lines. Johnson helped bring the lights to the hills and, as farmers gained the needed funds, the wondrous new appliances that slowly relieved some of the drudgery of both field and housework. No congressman ever worked harder, or with greater skill, to bring new federal aid down to the actual recipients. From these recipients he wanted nothing more than respect, appreciation, even love, and, of course, a vote every two years. Whether they loved him or not, they obliged on the vote. They appreciated his political artistry. He was, beyond any doubt, a congressman who fulfilled his campaign slogan—he got things done. He remained a whiz kid.

Johnson was well positioned to help Brown and Root because of his membership on the House Naval Affairs Committee. He owed this committee assignment to the direct influence of Roosevelt. On their first meeting in Galveston, Roosevelt was much taken with the eager, personable Johnson, and talked to him about his favorite subject—naval affairs. To his pleasant surprise (but no surprise to anyone who knew how Johnson operated), Johnson expressed such an intense interest in the navy that Roosevelt agreed to talk about Johnson to Carl Vinson of Georgia, the committee chairman. Of course he received this assignment, a choice one for a junior congressman but one strangely inconsistent with Johnson's district and with any earlier interest of his in the navy. Later, he used his position to help procure naval projects for Texas, although not for his own district. As a junior member of the committee, Johnson had limited influence, but he was perfectly situated to learn of likely naval construction, and this proved an invaluable source of intelligence for the Brown brothers, who in 1940 won what turned out to be a huge and very lucrative contract to build the Corpus Christi Naval Air Station. Also, as war erupted in Europe, Johnson's committee rose in importance, since it matured defense bills relating to the navy. But Johnson usually played a deferential muted role on the committee. He sponsored his first committee bill only in 1943, and because of procedural problems this effort to draft absentee defense workers never made it to a vote. He never defended even his committee's bills on the House floor, and seemed to have an aversion to floor speeches. Uninterested in formal public debate, he never developed the needed skills for it.

As a congressman, Johnson faced not only the lures of self-seeking men of money and power but other more personal temptations. Young, tall, and striking in appearance, irresistibly friendly, a superb raconteur, and idealistic in his expressed hopes and dreams, Johnson soon joined several interesting social circles, some at a level of fashion and glitter foreign to his earlier experience. As in the past, he cultivated as many human relationships as possible. He then securely held on to every one, until the Johnson circle numbered in the thousands. The ties, in most cases, were relatively casual, the contacts infrequent, but Johnson used every opportunity to deepen the relationships, and by crass flattery he persuaded most of those acquaintances that he valued them, thought often about them, and above all needed their respect and love. Like a magnet of limitless power, he seemed at times to want to pull everyone into his orbit, to establish a personal bond of some type with all of them. Even the logistics of such friendship—the Christmas cards, the thousands of small gifts, the condolences and regrets—soon took up half of his staff time. He loved to give gifts, from annual Thanksgiving Texas turkeys to a few favored or well-placed friends all the way down to small tokens, such as autographed portraits, to thousands of more casual friends or even visitors.

Johnson's social life alternated among several circles. These included the lawyers and businessmen whom he joined on all-male drinking or hunting trips, the large array of old Johnson City classmates and friends he still courted in infrequent visits back to the hills, the former White Stars and other Southwest Texas classmates, the "boys" he recruited for the NYA or for his own staff, the network of local Texas journalists and Democratic party functionaries who made up a developing political organization, the widening circle of adoring women who served him as secretaries and, in some cases, fell in love with him, and a rather diverse group of influential journalists, White House staffers, or high-level bureaucrats who made up his closest cronies in the Washington cocktail circuit. Notably, he did not form close social ties to many congressional colleagues, but continued to cultivate new versions of the father-son relationship with elderly House members.

The heady social glitter of his life in Washington inevitably placed strains on Johnson's marriage. In the years just before World War II, Lady Bird remained in the background. Early miscarriages frustrated the couple's hope for children. Lady Bird helped entertain friends but remained quiet and retiring. Not a beauty, not fashionable, she never became an adornment for Johnson to display, as he was wont to display his increasingly fashionable clothes or late-model automobiles. Maybe he had regrets about his choice. Maybe the couple quarreled. No records attest to their personal relationship in these difficult years. At least they must have been difficult for Lady Bird, who had to entertain in crowded apartments and each year faced the formidable task of moving even kitchen utensils back and forth between Washington and Austin. She did it all on tight budgets. Johnson was very demanding of her as well as of his staff. By some evidence he was also unfaithful. At least he was given, in certain circles, to rather explicit boasting about sexual conquests. But given his penchant for exaggeration and earthy talk, one simply does not know how to interpret his words or what to make of his often-noted flirtations with women on his office staff. One possibility is that all the boasting concealed inadequacies as a lover. Or perhaps he nourished a lingering resentment against women and used his power and physical prowess as a tool to seduce and, in a sense, exploit simple and often trusting women who invested so much in these one-sided relationships. Only in one case did he seem to become emotionally entangled with another women over an extended period of time. But the evidence is not conclusive on the depth of his involvement or on the fact of sexual intimacy.

Without doubt, an important woman in his life was one Alice Glass. When Johnson first met her, she was the live-in mistress of Charles E. Marsh, the owner of two Austin newspapers, the *American* and the *Statesman* (on Sunday the *American-Statesman*). Marsh, an enormous egotist, headstrong, but wealthy, backed Johnson in his 1937 congressional campaign and tried to make Johnson one of his protégés. Marsh had pretensions as an intellectual and a politically astute adviser. He was neither. But Johnson needed him, flattered him, listened to him, and used him. When Johnson moved to Washington as a congressman he soon enjoyed the hospitality of several of his wealthier friends or patrons. Right off, he received invitations to Marsh's Virginia estate, Longlea, which included a great house modeled after an English country home, a house designed for his admired mistress, Alice Glass. Her photographs reveal a tall, rather elegant, attractive although not beautiful woman. She, too, had some misplaced affectations of taste and intelligence, as she tried to create her own salon at the mansion in the beautiful Virginia countryside. For the first time in his life, Johnson experienced a new world of wealth and glitter, manor houses, horses and hounds, and each weekend a horde of eminent guests. Johnson was both awed and seduced by it all. He did not have the taste or the brilliance needed to separate what was mere glitter, what was artificial and frivolous (most of it), from the authentic. He felt flattered by being included.

Very quickly Johnson was at least infatuated with Glass. Since she was drawn to tall and powerful men, fancied herself a patron of political reformers, and seemed to enjoy the excitement of dangerous love affairs, she soon had eyes only for him. According to her later and probably exaggerated reports, this grew into the most serious love affair of her life. How serious was it? The evidence is inconclusive. Johnson, in his correspondence with Marsh, almost casually referred to Alice, but otherwise his personal papers are silent on the issue. Robert Caro, who interviewed Glass's sister and cousin, gained in this indirect way full assurance that the couple had an extended love affair. Other visitors at Longlea knew of the infatuation and gossiped about secret meetings of LBJ and Glass. But one has to interpret this evidence carefully. Glass, who apparently had several lovers in her lifetime, had compelling reasons to boast of a conquest of someone who subsequently became president of the United States. If Johnson deceived Lady Bird and cuckolded Marsh, he did it all with amazing guile and without a hint of guilt, which was very uncharacteristic behavior for one who continued to affirm romantic Victorian views of marriage. He never suspended his ties to Marsh, continued to accept gifts and favors, and in letters acted as an affectionate friend. The purported affair would also have involved an almost unbelievable amount of duplicity on the part of Alice, who owed her home and social position entirely to Marsh. One bit of evidence is Johnson's continued friendship with Alice, long after any possible love affair had almost certainly cooled and after she had married Marsh. Both Lady Bird and Lyndon visited Alice's home during one of her subsequent marriages. Alice wrote to LBJ even during his retirement. Her letters suggest a very special and enduring friendship, not any more than this. Intense affairs of passion rarely wind down so smoothly.

In 1940 Johnson's political fortunes began to improve. In the complex maneuvering for the Democratic nomination in 1940, Lyndon was able to disassociate himself from the candidacy of Vice-president Garner and to become the unofficial leader of the Roosevelt faction in the Texas Democratic party. This endeared him to Roosevelt, gave him easier access to the White House, and added immensely to his patronage role in Texas, both in appointments and in the awarding of government contracts (Brown and Root gained from this). In 1938, Vice-president Garner's early bid for the presidency was in its ascendancy. Johnson apparently made an early and astute choice—to bet on Roosevelt's third term and to distance himself as much as possible from the candidacy of Garner, who remained immensely popular in his home state. In late July, United Mine Workers chief John L. Lewis denounced Garner in pungent language, branding him a "labor-baiting, poker-playing, whiskey-drinking, evil old man." The Texas delegation felt burdened to defend their colleague and, for some, friend and patron. In an early draft of a statement they denied that Garner was a heavy drinker or opposed to labor. Johnson, acording to a subsequent report to Harold Ickes, alone refused to sign it, since the allegations were in part true, and thus forced his colleagues to draft a more restrained substitute, one that denounced only Lewis's unwarranted and unjustified verbal assault. Johnson signed it.

As always, Johnson undoubtedly embellished his account to

Roosevelt's friends. He expanded some dickerings over language into a courageous confrontation. He thus posed as a hero for the Roosevelt cause despite the fact that he had signed a statement that defended Garner. Other congressmen remembered no standoff and were often unaware of Johnson's role. Subsequently, after Garner's candidacy had completely folded, in extended efforts to find a face-saving formula to allow Texas delegates to support Garner as a favorite son, Johnson worked to dramatize the disloyalty toward Roosevelt revealed by Garner's Texas supporters, including even Sam Rayburn. By these maneuvers, he was able to become Roosevelt's man in Texas and to join Rayburn in arranging a final, by then noncontroversial compromise that allowed Texans to offer a first-round vote for Garner and then switch to FDR on the second ballot. These Johnson-orchestrated maneuvers helped create enduring tensions between Roosevelt and Rayburn, and left Rayburn with some lingering hard feelings toward Johnson.

During the 1940 election Johnson finally began to build a power base among his congressional colleagues. Typically, Johnson faced no opposition for his own seat. Yet, he had numerous political credits to collect among men of wealth, such as the Brown brothers or a few rising independent oil producers or other affluent constituents whom he had befriended. The Browns were most blessed, and therefore most appreciative. So far they had been frustrated in their efforts to repay Johnson. They swamped him with expensive gifts (he reciprocated with less expensive but carefully chosen tokens of his affection), helped him buy new automobiles at or below cost, and elaborately entertained Lyndon and Lady Bird at their numerous estates, but all this was peanuts compared to the millions they made on government contracts. In the fall of 1940, Johnson gave them their opportunity. After several abortive efforts to play some formal role in the national campaign, Johnson was able to gain, from Roosevelt a rather vague assignment to assist the Democratic Congressional Campaign Committee, a committee with almost no funds and heretofore a very limited role in aiding beleaguered congressional candidates.

Johnson saw his opportunity. In a typical frenzy of activity, he solicited large sums of money from his benefactors, successfully exploited the political leverage of Rayburn, and even helped mobilize the fund-raising skills of the White House staff. In a week, he had over forty-five thousand dollars. And he used it well. He and his staff carefully evaluated the chances of congressmen, and reserved the committee's funds for elections in which candidates had a chance of victory, but needed campaign funds to ensure it. Typically, Johnson did all he could to advertise his personal role in the collecting and allocating of money and in offering other advice and assistance, such as gaining key administrative speakers or early approval of appropriations at critical moments in a campaign. For the election, some modest but financially desperate candidates received more funds than they had asked for or dreamed of receiving. Johnson's efforts probably made the difference between victory and defeat in at least a dozen key contests. Instead of the expected loss of several seats to the Republicans, the Democrats gained eight in the House and lost an unexpectedly small three in the Senate. An appreciative Roosevelt telephoned his thanks. Journalists took note and began, often for the first time, to distinguish Johnson as an especially talented and promising congressman.

More quickly than he thought likely, Johnson needed not only Roosevelt's thanks but his active support. On 9 April 1941, Senator Morris Sheppard died unexpectedly. This was great news for Johnson. One of the old men was out of the way. He had the first of only two likely lifelong chances to be a senator from Texas. This time he needed no urging, no consultations. He would run. Fortunately, the risks were low. Unlike in a regular election, when he would have had to give up his House seat to run for the Senate (he could not be a candidate for two offices at once), he could retain his seat and still compete in another special election. His chances were low, but no more so than in 1937. By 1941 he was only beginning to gain national recognition. Even in Texas he was not widely known outside his own district. Only his two years on the NYA had drawn him into contact with state and local officials. Yet he had a network of young supporters, plenty of financial support from his wealthy patrons, and the usual fund of energy.

Once again, Johnson needed a special identification with Roosevelt, and he quickly established just this. He worked through friends to get Roosevelt's informal support. One of these friends was Al Wirtz, undersecretary of the interior, who would shortly resign his position to help Lyndon in his campaign. Roosevelt, burned by his attempted purge of "conservatives" in 1938, would no longer endorse any one of competing Democrats in state contests, but he came as close as possible to backing Johnson. He arranged a White House visit by LBJ on 22 April just before a planned press conference. The reporters saw Johnson emerging from the Oval Office and heard him announce his candidacy, "under the banner of Roosevelt," of course. In subsequent questioning,

Roosevelt referred to Johnson as a "very old, old friend," which was enough for reporters to picture Johnson as one of Roosevelt's anointed candidates.

Johnson officially opened his campaign on 3 May 1941 with a rally and radio speech from San Marcos. He displayed then, and throughout his campaign, a huge, blown-up, modified photograph of himself shaking hands with Roosevelt at Galveston in 1937. As in the 1937 campaign, he began with a rather formal, reasoned speech. He had able writers in his campaign, not only the volatile Herbert Henderson but newspaperman Marsh. He gathered all his now experienced boys from the 1937 campaign and had the invaluable help of two members of a re-formed office staff—Walter Jenkins, a young, completely loyal University of Texas graduate who replaced an ill and overworked Latimer as his congressional secretary in 1939, and John Connally, a bright, less subservient, ambitious assistant who helped mastermind the 1941 campaign. In his opening speeches, Johnson stressed his all-out support for Roosevelt, a support now predicated largely on an interventionist foreign policy and a defense buildup, both nationalist issues with wide appeal in Texas. In his first speech, Johnson promised that, if he had to vote to send a Texas boy "to the trenches, that day Lyndon Johnson will leave the Senate seat to go with him."

On social issues, he stressed farm parity, electricity to all homes, new water projects, and retirement benefits at age sixty. As the campaign developed, he tried to exploit local sentiment against labor unions by condemning strikes in a time of pending war but, in less publicized language, also balanced this by attacks on selfish capitalists who often tried to shove their social philosophy down the throats of workers. For all labor-management disputes, he wanted to interpose the strong arm of the federal government. Again, pandering to local opinion, he campaigned for continued depreciation allowances for petroleum producers, against "isms" of all types, and against "socialized medicine." In his opening speech, he even tried, with small success, to emulate the speaking style of Winston Churchill (one of Johnson's heroes), crassly using the line about "blood, sweat, and tears." But, as in 1937, such a careful, almost decorous opening proved a short-lived strategy. Johnson remained a poor public speaker, at his weakest before a microphone and large audiences. At the state level he could not utilize the face-to-face, personal politics that worked so well in 1937. Above all, he had to change tactics to meet the challenge of a new competitor.

When Johnson first declared his candidacy, only two of over twenty candidates posed a serious challenge to him. Statewide polls showed both far ahead of him as the campaign opened. The best-known opponent, at least nationally, was Martin Dies, a red-baiting congressman from east Texas, and first chairman of the House Committee on Un-American Activities. Dies made anticommunism his principle plank, proved lazy and ineffective as a campaigner, and did little to expand a minority who supported him on this one issue. Dies appealed to an emerging segment of the Democratic party in Texas, one extremely nationalistic and chauvinistic in outlook and hostile to most regulatory and welfare legislation. Fear of Dies's election helped procure the firm support of FDR for Johnson's effort. The third major candidate was an able, young (thirty-four to Johnson's thirty-one) Texas attorney general, Gerald Mann. A former football hero and principled and consumer-oriented attorney general, who was close to Johnson in political leanings and a person of acknowledged honesty and integrity, Mann helped raise the early campaign to a lofty level for one in Texas. The eventual choice seemed certain to lie between a more voluble, aggressive, competitive Johnson, the early underdog, and a less personable but equally intense and hard-driving Mann. No one can say how this race would have ended. Mann had a broader statewide constituency but, as time proved, less campaign funds. The lack of Roosevelt administration support also hurt, more so as the campaign climaxed. But the confrontation between two purportedly "liberal" young men very quickly ran aground on the slightly belated candidacy of the popular demagogic governor of Texas, W. Lee ("pass the biscuits") O'Daniel. He had, at first, denied any intention of running, otherwise both Mann and Johnson might have had second thoughts.

O'Daniel had no talents to recommend him as senator or, for that matter, any political office. A former flour manufacturer in Fort Worth, O'Daniel became famous as a radio personality, combining his soothing homilies with country music, at first as a means of selling flour. But soon his sentimental and pious poems and lyrics, his Bible quotations, and his simplistic wisdom gained a following in Texas. In 1938, in the face of expert ridicule, he ran for governor on a demagogic and populistic platform, promising to clean out the professional politicians in Austin and to provide everyone in Texas over sixty-five with a thirty-dollar-a-month pension, or his version of the earlier Townsend plan. Of course, he never fulfilled this expensive promise and proved an inept and passive governor. But he remained popular in Texas, and no one in America, save possibly an earlier Father Coughlin, could so exploit radio. O'Daniel's candidacy seemed to doom that of Johnson's. In the old pattern, he fell ill, took to a hospital bed, and suffered from a week of depression and indecision, manifested as nervous exhaustion. But, again typically, he responded to the pleas of his supporters and came back to fight O'Daniel on his own terms.

By June 1941, not only Texans but Americans as a whole marveled at one of the corniest and zaniest campaigns in history. Fortunately for Johnson, the state legislature, coached by Wirtz and other Johnson supporters, kept postponing adjournment, leaving O'Daniel little time for campaigning. To counter O'Daniel's hillbilly bands and circuslike entertainment, Johnson organized his own musicians, staged well-publicized "patriotic rallies," and even offered, at each rally, war bonds or stamps to lucky ticket holders in a type of lottery. He soon subordinated his speeches to the entertainment and pulled back from the serious analysis of issues that marked his early campaign. He easily outworked O'Daniel and resorted to some sheer demagoguery against Mann (this involved jabs at his German-sounding name), but above all he steadily gained on both opponents because of an inexhaustible campaign chest and because of the clout exerted in his behalf by the Roosevelt administration. Over and over again, Roosevelt endorsed and sent telegrams, all carefully prepared by Johnson's staff, that seemed to make Johnson an indispensable ally of the president. New Deal staffers raised northern funds to aid the campaign. In Texas, the critical factor proved to be Johnson's able young staff, the veterans of the NYA and 1937, and beyond that the financial support of his wealthy friends, especially that of the Brown brothers.

Johnson's campaign was probably the most expensive in Texas history. Estimated costs soared as high as $1 million (his official campaign report to the Texas secretary of state showed gifts of only $29,619). Johnson had all the needed funds for staff, radio time, endless newspaper ads or solicited editorials, and purchased votes in San Antonio or in the boss-controlled counties of south Texas. Much of this support angered Mann, who ended his campaign denouncing all the spending, the false cover of patriotism, and the sheer political muscle of the Roosevelt administration. And, as Johnson must have known, a large share of his financial support represented illegal campaign donations by Brown and Root. Later Internal Revenue Service investigators discovered at least

$150,000 of laundered funds that passed from Brown and Root by way of honorariums or ersatz fees to the Johnson campaign. By strenuous effort, and the final intervention of Roosevelt, Wirtz and Johnson barely prevented criminal indictments against Brown and Root officials, and in 1943 the company did have to pay heavy penalties on funds illegitimately diverted from taxable income. At high risk, the Brown brothers were finally able to repay Johnson. Yet, he did not win, at least not by the final, highly suspect count of Texas election officials.

Johnson seemed to win. For over a day, journalists assumed he had won. The first reasonably complete tally on election day, Saturday, 28 June, showed him abut thirteen thousand votes ahead of O'Daniel, in what had turned out to be one of the closest statewide elections in Texas history. Johnson ran strongest in central, south, and parts of west Texas, weakest in the panhandle, north Texas, and east Texas. He and his staff celebrated the come-from-behind victory. Congratulations poured in from Washington, D.C. Even a day later, on Sunday, Johnson remained ahead. It seemed unlikely that the remaining few thousand votes could reverse the verdict, since most of these were from rural east Texas counties, the heart of Dies's support and an area at least as unresponsive to O'Daniel as to LBJ.

At this point Johnson's luck ran out. O'Daniel supporters stole the election from him. The primitive, notoriously corrupt election process in Texas allowed, even invited, such chicanery. LBJ knew the system. He used it, particularly in his bargaining for the bloc votes, mostly Hispanic, controlled by south Texas bosses. But, this time, he did not leave any maneuvering room. His backers had all reported their final tallies by Sunday. Not so several east Texas counties, which had telephoned preliminary counts but had not yet certified the final results. Such procrastination simply reflected the lack of integrity in state election rules or laxness in enforcing them. Candidates were largely responsible for monitoring the local polls and the subsequent count. O'Daniel supporters took advantage of the corrupt system and arranged expanded vote totals in several counties. They were sure of victory before the amended returns reached Austin. Methodically, in a clear pattern, the amended returns all added to O'Daniel's total. By Monday, Johnson realized that his victory has been stolen from him. He had little recourse. Inquiries would have revealed irregularities in his own campaign and might have risked an early exposure of Brown and Root. Johnson, rather typically, withdrew rather than fight back.

105

He still had his House seat. Roosevelt had never loved him as much. And, in 1942, he would be able to run once again for O'Daniel's regular Senate seat. Next time he knew he would not lose by trickery. He might win by it. But 1942 would not be the year. Pearl Harbor altered all his plans.

War came quickly. Johnson, in a sense, welcomed it. He had become deeply, emotionally committed to the Allied cause. He had long supported a military buildup, particularly for the navy. He also made personal preparations. He was now on record—if war came, he had to enlist to maintain his foolish campaign promises. Using his influence as a congressman and as a key member of the House Naval Affairs Committee, he had applied for and received a commission as lieutenant commander in the Naval Reserve. On 8 December, the day after Pearl Harbor, he requested active duty. On 11 December he asked for and received a leave of absence from the House and began duty in the offices of the undersecretary of the navy. From then on he boasted that he had been the first congressman to enter active duty, although he had not yet spent even a day in training. Politically, he had to enlist since his future career might depend on such a gesture. But otherwise, his brief naval career proved a rather useless diversion from his political life. Had he left the Congress in order to serve for the duration, the commitment would have been much more than a gesture. But Johnson always tried to minimize risk. He was not about to give up the security of his congressional seat. So off he went to war, to play sailor, but yet not to play by the normal rules. Naval officers had to try to find a role for him, an officer without military training or aptitude who was nonetheless still a congressional overseer of the navy. Such military politicians are more trouble than they are worth, and it was soon clear the navy had to go to unusual efforts and expense to keep Johnson busy and entertained. Wherever he went he received all the deference of an admiral.

Johnson wanted action. He needed to do well in the navy, make a reputation. But, at first, he was stuck in Washington, D.C., doing routine staff work. John Connally also entered the navy and served for a time as Johnson's secretary. Nothing much had changed. Finally, by March, Johnson gained an assignment in San Francisco, helping train navy employers for war production. In May, after personal lobbying back in Washington, he received his wanted chance to get at least near the fighting. He became a part of a three-member, relatively low-level military team, one charged with evaluating the military effort in the South Pacific. Johnson came west by Austin, there filed for reelection to the House (finally ending friends' efforts to get him to challenge O'Daniel for the Senate), and then traveled by air all the way to Australia. Treated more like a congressman than a middle-level naval officer, Johnson met and interviewed Douglas MacArthur in Melbourne, toured military bases in Australia, and flew north all the way to New Guinea.

Finally, Johnson was able to enjoy his brief moment of glory. Against MacArthur's advice and in spite of discouraging pleas from local commanders, in June Johnson insisted on joining with his two coinvestigators (one was a pilot) on a bombing mission over Lae, a Japanese base on the north shore of New Guinea. They flew on B-26 medium bombers from near Port Moresby. Johnson boarded one plane, left it to urinate (perhaps a sign of carefully concealed nervousness), and was replaced on this plane by a colleague. Later the plane went down, killing his friend. Johnson flew on the *Heckling Hare*, using a parachute lent by one of the crew. By the later memories of crew members, Johnson plied them with questions, showed intense interest about all the details, and then remained perfectly calm during the bombing approach. On the approach to Lae, the twelve bombers met about two dozen defending Zero fighters, enough practically to abort the bombing mission. Just short of Lae, Johnson's plane lost power in one engine, had to jettison its bombs, and turned back toward its home base. But, as a struggling plane, it was vulnerable to several Zero attacks (the number of attacking planes tended to go up in each later account). By evasive maneuvers and a skillful dive, the pilot avoided critical damage, although bullets penetrated the fuselage before the fighters turned away to engage the remaining bombers. Johnson's plane landed safely, and his one taste of combat was over. He walked from the plane as though nothing had happened and shortly thereafter visited the wounded in a hospital, as always looking for men from Texas.

The rest of Johnson's military career proved anticlimactic, though not uneventful. On a return flight to Melbourne, a storm-tossed B-17 had to make an emergency landing in the Australian outback. Johnson, typically, met and talked politics with local Aussies. On 1 July Roosevelt first called back to Washington all congressmen who remained on active duty, an order made effective as of 16 July. Sam Rayburn and other friends of Johnson apparently lobbied for such an order. It did not mean that congressmen had to leave military units, for they had the choice of resigning their seats (four did). Johnson apparently never considered this. Thus, as he flew back to the states he knew he would return to Congress. But before his homecoming he met MacArthur once again. He then learned that his dead friend would receive a Distinguished Service Cross and that Johnson and the other surviving investigator would both receive Silver Stars (the crew on Johnson's plane received no medals for the flight). The Silver Star vindicated Johnson's determination to see combat. He asked for a signed copy of the commendation for his files and ever after wore the ribbon that went with the medal. On the long flight home he suffered from intestinal problems and lay in a hospital for five days in Fiji, learning first-hand some of the problems of the wounded. He reported in person to Admiral Chester Nimitz in Hawaii and then flew on to San Francisco and Washington to resume his duties in Congress.

Johnson's war record soon became a matter of controversy. Opponents lambasted his V.I.P. status and his one useless and bothersome mission. Even as late as his presidency, Johnson's staff worked to establish the exact sequence of events and to vindicate Johnson. As for all other dramatic events in his life, he could not resist subsequent embellishments. With every telling, the number of attacking Zeros multiplied, the damages to his plane grew, and the courage and bravery of the crew increased. No doubt, his two months in the South Pacific remained as vivid as any in his career. For the only time in his life he kept a diary. In it he recorded his detailed impressions of MacArthur (more favorable after visiting with him), of other commanders, of Australians, of the then-lagging American war effort in the Pacific. He lamented the morale problems of the troops, noted excessive gambling, seemed inordinately concerned about sex and venereal disease, made slighting comments about lazy natives whom he compared to American Negroes, and referred several times to a mysterious Miss Jesus. If his trip had any positive role, it was that of any touring congressman—to keep the military on their toes. He also rendered some possibly useful reports to FDR.

Lyndon's four months away from Washington proved a mixed blessing for Lady Bird. She was lonely and swamped by work. But she gained a new self-confidence and would never again be a dutiful, retiring wife. In Johnson's absence, she took over his congressional office and in a sense served as congresswoman. Always open to self-improvement, she signed up for business courses in the evening and tried to do all the work with constituents that Johnson kept assigning her in letters and almost daily phone calls. Sam

Rayburn served as her protector and dearest friend. When Johnson returned, Lady Bird insisted that they purchase a house in Washington. She was tired of apartment living. Johnson capitulated, and before 1942 ended they moved into a handsome, two-story house near Connecticut Avenue in fashionable northwest Washington. Here, in this comfortable home, Lady Bird finally was able to carry a child for a full pregnancy. On 19 March 1944, she gave birth to a healthy Lynda. Three years later Luci would follow. Perhaps Lyndon missed a son, but he doted on his two much-pampered daughters. Sam Rayburn became their de facto godfather and found in them the delights of children he never had. Outwardly, the remaining war years were peaceful and happy for the Johnson family. LBJ gained a new appreciation for Lady Bird's multiple talents, and the new parents seemed closer than ever before.

In Congress, Johnson settled down to a now familiar routine. He continued to serve his constituents well. Brown and Root, aided at the minimum by Johnson's superb intelligence, gained military contracts arond the world. LBJ had, by now, cemented a friendly if not intimate relationship with Roosevelt and moved easily in and out of the White House. After his years in Washington he knew the key people and was adept at winning favors. But, despite his effort, he never gained a major leadership role or attracted much national attention. He tried. In imitation of Harry Truman's much publicized Senate Oversight Committee, Johnson headed a Naval Affairs Subcommittee that monitored naval contracts, but with scant publicity. Despite all his achievements, he still lacked the fame and popularity he so craved. Once again, he was in a rut, a bit bored, and in need of new challenges.

During the war, Johnson maintained his pro-Roosevelt posture. He gladly endorsed all administrative military policies, always voted in favor of wartime controls, and took second place to no one in his flag-waving patriotism. But he was also a sensitive politician, aware of the shifting moods of his constituents. In the war years Roosevelt muted his earlier class rhetoric. So did Johnson. But on issues affecting organized labor, now more unpopular than ever in Texas, Johnson broke with the administration in several speeches. His first, and unsuccessful, major bill would have drafted striking workers in war industries. He continued his earlier advocacy of public power and conservation measures and in an act of courage voted against special favors for oil producers. But he already understood that, if he wanted statewide office, he could not continue to oppose the large oil companies. In the election of

1944, Johnson backed Roosevelt's fourth term and somewhat uneasily became a partisan on the so-called liberal side in a nasty growing split among Texas Democrats. He feared such divisions and hated to be securely linked to either side. But, in the strange world of Texas politics, he now had an enduring identity as a "liberal," a label with little precise content. Johnson publicly denied the label along with all others and tried to find a precarious middle way. Generally, he remained loyal to welfare programs and to wartime and post–World War II economic regulations, but balanced these by an exaggerated emphasis on government economy and on the evils of too much bureaucracy. He easily assumed, and exploited, anticommunist sympathies and continued to use labor union leaders as whipping boys.

Johnson's verbal retreat from some earlier New Deal enthusiasms joined his own rise from near-poverty to near wealth. This story also dates from his 1942 return from the navy. But the background is important. Johnson struggled with family finances through 1941. The demands from his extended as well as his immediate family were unrelenting. He could never get ahead. Yet, he easily exaggerated his plight and perhaps unfairly forced too much austerity on Lady Bird. By 1942, Lady Bird had in hand at least $36,000 from an inheritance and sought investment opportunities. Meanwhile, LBJ's wealthy benefactors tried to help him gain financial security. Consistently, Johnson refused outright gifts. According to George Brown in a much later interview, Marsh even tried to give Johnson a personal fortune, no strings attached. Brown may have been mistaken on this point, but it is clear that Marsh often gave investment tips to Lyndon and to Lady Bird. So did the Browns. Thus, all that LBJ needed was enough funds to take advantage of such valuable intelligence. During the war, for example, Marsh identified some lakeside lots near Austin that were sure to appreciate in value. For $8,000 the Johnsons purchased three lots that they later sold for $330,000. Marsh's most critical advice involved a nearly bankrupt radio station, KTBC. By 1942, he believed Lady Bird could best use her inheritance in this area, and he helped make possible the eventual purchase early in 1943. Since this purchase would become one of the most questioned, and best-documented, aspects of LBJ's private career, it deserves a rather detailed description.

Hanging over the story of KTBC are numerous accusations of impropriety or undue influence. Because of complex but openly fraudulent funding plans, the owners of KTBC lost their license in

1940, just as they completed a sale. The owners, rather than losing all their investment, and in order to get the Federal Communication Commission (FCC) to allow the station to reopen, negotiated a new and unchallengeable contract for $20,000 (the earlier price had been $50,000). Before this sale was consummated or finally approved by the FCC, the new purchaser died, leaving his purchase option to two heirs, one a son, the other a wealthy Austin businessman. By personal negotiation, either Johnson or his immediate friends persuaded the two who held purchase options to surrender them. Both persuasion and personal favors oiled these delicate negotiations, although nothing illegal seemed to be involved. One should note that such was the near-bankrupt condition of the station that the options by now had no clear monetary value. They just blocked other interested purchasers.

Lady Bird was now eligible, along with others, to place bids on the station, bids subject to eventual FCC approval. She offered the owners $17,500, which they accepted. It is possible that they accepted because they had no doubt of Lady Bird's ability to win subsequent FCC approval. Others have suggested that just as critical was their belief that Lyndon could so influence the FCC as to get it to block any other purchaser, a perception tied to reasonable expectations but never submitted to an actual test. LBJ was a congressman who not only helped exercise oversight of the FCC but also had a very close personal friend on the commission. This certainly did not hurt Lady Bird's chances of approval. Neither did the fact that Alvin Wirtz, in the last stages of his career, and powerful Judge Roy Hofheinz of Houston both served as her counsel. But she negotiated directly and openly with the FCC, as do most applicants for stations. And, by the case presented, Lady Bird must have seemed well prepared to run a legitimate high-quality station. She had her degree in journalism. More important, she spent only half of her funds in buying the station; she thus had the means and the desire to rebuild it. And, as the wife of a congressman and a person of unimpeachable integrity, she seemed an ideal owner. It is hard to see how the FCC could resist such a compelling case. In fact, one suspects a bit of overkill in the Johnson effort.

Shortly after purchasing KTBC, the Johnsons hired a Houston advertising expert, Harfield Weedin, to manage it. He had orchestrated the entertainment features of Johnson's 1941 Senate campaign. He found a run-down, ill-equipped station. Lady Bird spared no funds in rehabilitating it. She moved the station into new quarters in the Brown Building (owned by George and Her-

111

man), acquired new equipment, gained FCC approval for full-time thousand-watt broadcasting at a new and better frequency, and gained CBS affiliation. In all this Lyndon played a vital role. He, or his staff, effectively processed a series of FCC applications, and Lyndon directly lobbied officials at CBS. He, as always, became fully, intensely involved in the station. He wanted it to be the best and attended even to such details as its daily programming. He "hired" his mother and elderly retired President Evans of Southwest Texas State Teachers College as program critics, a concealed way of giving them a sense of involvement. Even in the first, expensive year, the station broke even. By the second, it made profits. After the war, it became an extremely successful enterprise, even as its value soared into the millions. The Johnsons gambled early on television and secured the one VHF channel awarded to Austin.

Lyndon's most vital role in broadcasting, beyond the paperwork in Washington, involved advertising. He recommended clients, personally contacted some, and orchestrated the developmental work carried on by the station staff. His position certainly helped. In soliciting ads, the station manager did not need to note their ties to Congressman Johnson. Whether correctly or not, those who wanted political favors from Johnson deemed it helpful to advertise on KTBC. Within two years, Johnson's financial problems were all in the past. He now bought a new, elaborate duplex on Dillan Avenue in Austin, one with the facade of a great mansion. This would be his primary residence until he bought the Martin ranch in 1951. Profits from the radio station, plus dividends on capital gains from a number of new investments in land and in banks, not only made possible the later purchase of the ranch but the stream of improvements that turned it into the retreat of a new millionaire.

By 1947, Johnson had served a decade in the House. This did not make him a true veteran. He remained in the middle ranks in terms of tenure and influence. Real power, as reflected in a major committee chairmanship, still lay at least a decade ahead. Despite all his efforts, Johnson had not found any distinctive role in the House, any enduring outlet for his energy and leadership abilities. The House was too large, the seniority system too rigid. Johnson, never the maverick, always one to respect and play by the rules, could find no quick path to power. Yet he was too ambitious, too impatient, to await his turn, to become one of the old men with power. Besides, he might die too soon. Johnson was haunted by the heart attacks and relatively youthful deaths of both his father and his Uncle George. His genes seemed stacked against old age. His habits did not help. He abused his body—in frenzied periods of activity, by heavy smoking, by frequent bouts of drinking, and at times by overeating and a lack of exercise. In 1949 he would be forty years old. He often looked older, particularly when fatigued. As early as 1943, not long after his dashing appearance in a naval uniform, one could already note the bulging belly and the dark circles under his eyes. He was no longer the boy wonder.

More disturbing to Johnson, he seemed unable to gain the type of mature respect he always sought. Everyone acknowledged his political skills. Journalists had already identified him as an able congressman. But he had gone nowhere. And behind all the acknowledgments lurked an element of disrespect. Johnson had been such a transparent power seeker, so eager to gain publicity for himself, so much the smooth operator, that colleagues had difficulty taking him seriously. He seemed a superficial, shallow, albeit friendly fellow. One is reminded of similar comments about Franklin D. Roosevelt in 1932. Johnson was painfully aware of these evaluations and lamented their unfairness in letters to his mother, but he seemed helpless to do anything about them. In a sense, this issue became the critical motif in his 1946 campaign for reelection to the House.

As congressman, Johnson never came close to losing his post. In many years he faced only token opposition or none at all in the all-important Democratic primary. But in 1946 a brash opponent—Hardy Hollers—although with no real chance of winning, was still effective enough to worry Johnson and to stimulate a significant campaign effort. Hollers, a "true" veteran, a corporate lawyer, a prosecutor in the Nuremberg trials, and a determined antiunion agitator, hit Johnson where it hurt most. In the unique Texas ideological perspective, Johnson was the liberal candidate—he preached conservation and welfare, backed larger old-age pensions, expressed deep concerns about the atomic bomb, supported international control of atomic energy, generally supported the United Nations, and still balanced his defensive antiunion posture by criticism of large corporations. But these issues were not central to the campaign; Johnson's congressional and personal record was.

Hollars found all Johnson's vulnerable points. He showed how much puffery had accompanied Johnson's congressional career, how often he had claimed exaggerated credit for federal programs in Texas. Hollers ridiculed Johnson's war record, his "few months'

113

sight-seeing tour of the Pacific with a camera in one hand and leading his publicity agent in the other." He itemized all Johnson's ties
to Brown and Root and to other wealthy or powerful backers. He
alleged, without proof, all manner of bribery and influence peddling that had helped enrich Johnson personally and that created
such an alliance of wealth and power as to constitute an almost
unbeatable Johnson political machine. He claimed that Johnson
had endlessly abused his office in procuring and operating KTBC,
that he had sold advertisements to government contractors seeking his influence, and that he and Lady Bird, drawing on funds
from wealthy benefactors, had funded and in part owned a purportedly competitive radio station, KVET, one owned by several of
Johnson's friends or staff members, including John Connally. He
even implicated Lady Bird by charges of special favoritism given
her father in defense purchases during World War II. Finally, in a
charge later echoed by Robert Caro and other biographers, Hollers
argued that LBJ had failed as a legislator, that in his whole career
he had not written or sponsored a single bill of national importance, that he had been only a part-time congressman, skipping
major debates and rarely speaking or debating on the House floor.
The fact that Johnson refused to debate Hollers, or directly address
many of these charges, undoubtedly made them seem more credi-
ble to Texans.

Hollers at least placed Johnson on the defensive. Many charges
were old ones—his ties to Brown and Root, for example. But, for
the first time, an opponent aired charges of personal gain through
illegitimate political favors. Johnson's newly won personal wealth
invited such charges. He was in an increasingly poor position to
maintain his earlier image of personal integrity, of sharing an identity with ordinary Texans. Johnson never lived down his reputation as a skillful, self-serving operator out to gain power and
wealth for himself. Of course, the effectiveness of Holler's campaign lay in his exploitation of half-truths. Johnson dramatically
laid packets of Lady Bird's business records on the table and invited critics to discover any illegality. He itemized his and Lady
Bird's personal wealth, his two homes, his mother's bungalow, her
KTBC, and what he somewhat loosely referred to as some residential lots. He insisted it all came from his salary or his wife's inher-
itance. He proved the quite separate ownership of KVET. But such
tactics left unsettled the charges of influence peddling or unfair
collusion. To counter charges of representing only his wealthy
friends, he emphasized the whole spectrum of benefits he had pro-

cured for his district and proved that he had spread his goodness all around, that he believed in special privileges for everyone.

Johnson had a more difficult task defending his role in Congress. It hardly helped his case that he was able to identify only three sponsored bills of national significance, all related to naval affairs. He could only try to clarify the way the House operated. Major bills all came from committees. Only those who chaired committees or subcommittees usually sponsored legislation that had any chance of success. Perhaps his strongest defense was, as always, what he had done for his own district. Johnson easily won the election, but by that achievement seemed to document Hollers's charge that, as an incumbent, he had built an unbeatable machine in his district. The legacy of this campaign would hurt him in 1948 when he again ran for the Senate.

In 1948 Johnson faced a critical decision. Pappy O'Daniel decided to quit the Senate. But a popular Texas governor, Coke Stevenson, planned to run in the decisive Democratic primary and was obviously favored over any conceivable candidate. As so often in the past, Johnson agonized over a decision and, for a time, decided not to run. Maybe he used this as a technique for gaining support among staff and close friends. They rallied behind him, for their careers were at stake. He filed at the deadline in May. This time he could not take advantage of a special election. To run, he had to give up his House seat. Apparently this was not a major deterrent. He had contemplated a career in business, was clearly tired of his job in the House, and had recently given a large share of his time and interest to KTBC. As usual, he gave his all to what became another long, frenzied campaign. In addition to Stevenson, he faced one other serious candidate, Houston lawyer George Peddy. Peddy's candidacy, plus that of several minor contenders, almost assured a runoff election, since in this primary a candidate had to have a majority to win. And, indeed, in the first election no one gained a majority. Stevenson led Johnson by seventy-two thousand votes. Peddy was eliminated, a distant third. Johnson had to make up this lead and used every conceivable tactic to do it. He did win, but in such a manner as permanently to blemish the subsequent political career of "Landslide" Lyndon.

Johnson had to walk a tightrope in this campaign. He still had the support of the so-called liberal faction of the Texas Democratic party. He dared not lose this, not only because of its role in his campaign but because as a senator he needed to maintain ties with at least the dominant center of his own party. Should he become

115

fully identified with the regular, or state rights, or "conservative" wing of the Texas party, he would isolate himself nationally. Yet, to win in Texas he had to woo a portion of the regular Democrats, a clear majority in Texas. Thus, in a clever but an always opportunistic campaign, he seemed to waffle, to take both sides on most issues. He sensed, correctly as it turned out, that large numbers of Texas voters still identified with certain earlier New Deal policies, even though in 1948 the label New Deal had become a bit sinister to many Texans. LBJ continued to lay claim to the clear benefits gained by Texans—Social Security, support prices for farmers, and REA power. He tried to keep his identification with the ordinary voters by the mildest possible class appeal. He easily, and sincerely, continued his prodefense policy, and enthusiastically supported an unpopular Truman on Cold War policies. But he deliberately repudiated Truman's policies toward organized labor, civil rights, and more extreme welfare measures, such as universal health insurance. He particularly emphasized his vote for the Taft-Hartley Act and against Truman's veto of it. He fell into line on all issues affecting Texas, such as state control over tideland oil or continued favorable tax treatment for oil producers. He summarized these cautious commitments by his bland slogan of peace, prosperity, and progress, and ran a campaign that soon degenerated into generalities and inflated accusations.

Johnson shamelessly exploited two issues against Stevenson— labor union support and the ascendant issue of communism in government. Stevenson retaliated in kind. By the end of the election, Johnson had disillusioned his former liberal allies, although private assurances persuaded several that his campaign posture concealed continued orthodoxy. State conservatives remained suspicious of his seeming conversion and never really trusted him. Thus, by his balancing act he was able to avoid alignment with any ideological camp but at the same time did not have the firm support of either. In fact, Johnson, despite his many personal friends, was never able to develop a well-defined political faction in his home state.

The campaign climaxed in August 1948. The run-off election was on Saturday, 29 August. Polls showed Lyndon slowly gaining on Stevenson. He had an excellent staff, led by John Connally. He had plenty of funds and spent them freely. The Brown brothers, Marsh, and independent oilman Sid Richardson led in support. And he still had plenty of energy. He had not improved as a platform speaker, but this time he wowed the voters by technology. He hired a helicopter and thus was able to whirl into as many as ten county seats each day. The excitement, the campaign slogans, and a brief speech all maximized his assets. But, once again, at the climax of a campaign Johnson fell ill. Kidney stones racked him with pain, forced him into a hospital, and accompanied despondency and depression. With only three weeks to go and his illness publicly known, he seemed bent on withdrawing. But he passed the stones and resumed the campaign as if nothing had happened.

The vote turned out to be even closer than in 1941. On election evening, Stevenson led by only 8,000 votes out of over 750,000. The next day, Sunday, this lead fell to a minuscule 8 votes out of 976,000. At that point, a crucial addition of 429 votes in the totals from Duval County put Johnson ahead. Out of the new votes, Johnson won 427 to 2 for Stevenson. But this soon-to-be-famous switch in Duval was not clearly decisive for over a week. On Monday, Johnson was ahead by 119 votes; by Wednesday Stevenson led by 349, a lead that dropped slowly to 255 by Friday. On Saturday, a week after the election, Johnson finally regained the lead by 17 votes, and on Sunday he led by 162. When the State Democratic Executive Committee certified the final results on 14 September, in a hotly contested vote of 29 to 28, Johnson led by only 87 votes.

Stevenson challenged the results. He charged fraud in three south Texas counties. Such had clearly occurred. In fact, in post-election inquiries, both sides uncovered dozens of apparent irregularities. Lax state election laws once again led to all manner of vote buying and boss-dominated bloc voting in Hispanic areas, and to numerous manipulations of the count after the election. So flagrant were the abuses that Texas finally reformed its laws. Most of the irregularities remained only unproved charges. Because of a legal charge of election fraud initiated by Stevenson, an almost unbelievable laxness in Jim Wells, Zapata, and Duval counties became part of the public record. In these counties election officials carried ballot boxes home, left official tallies at a school or in unlocked rooms, and eventually, before the legal deadline, even destroyed the ballots. Much later, and after numerous inquiries, journalists were able to locate the responsible election official in Duval county and to document the names, some of dead people, that he added to the voting rolls in that county. No one ever found evidence of any direct Johnson involvement in this switch, so reminiscent of the tactics that had stolen the election from him in 1941. But Johnson had cultivated the bosses in south Texas and in a typical pattern gained almost all the votes in such controlled counties. But note that any emphasis upon the bogus votes in Duval County obscures the larger pattern of voting chicanery as well as the crucial returns that came in long after Duval had reported. Even if Johnson knew about the switch in Duval or even ordered it, he could not know for over a week whether this switch would be decisive in the outcome.

When hauled before a court, county election officials were vague or could not remember major details from only a month earlier. Thus, at first, Stevenson seemed sure to overturn the results. A judge in Fort Worth, friendly to Stevenson's wing of the party, found so much prima facie evidence of fraud that he issued on 28 September an injunction to keep Johnson's name off the regular election ballot on 3 November. A desperate Johnson knew this would cost him a Senate seat. Thus his friends and very able lawyers, led by Abe Fortas, quickly appealed unsuccessfully to a federal district court, and then successfully to the Supreme Court. Justice Hugo Black, without determining any of the substantive issues, revoked the injunction, which on the basis of allegations would have had the effect of deciding an election outcome.

This did not end the inquiries. Stevenson, on the unusual basis of Article 4, Section 4 (this guarantees a republican form of government in each state), appealed the election to the Senate, which eventually carried out its own investigation. But the Democrats won in 1948, while Johnson and his able allies lobbied very effectively. The Senate postponed two election inquiries until the new Congress. A then-friendly committee finally affirmed Johnson's election, citing no clear proof of fraud but plenty of charges of such on both sides. Since this was a state party primary, not an official election, the Senate was not about to intrude. Long before this, Johnson easily won the regular election against a weak Republican opponent, but one who received more than usual support because of switches by several of Stevenson's supporters. Johnson had finally achieved a long-term goal. Although the victory was not sweet, the fruits of victory would prove sweet indeed. This close, contested, corrupt election proved the most important turning point in Johnson's political career.

Lyndon and Lady Bird off to Congress, 1937.

A fond and possibly final
farewell to Dad, now near death.

A proud young congressman in his House office, 1940.

Opening of Johnson's first Senate campaign, San Marcos, 1941.

A whirly stop in Johnson's Senate campaign of 1948.

The new senator from Texas with Lady Bird, Lynda (right) and Luci, 1948.

TOP: With Sam Rayburn and Adlai Stevenson, LBJ Ranch, 1955.
BOTTOM: With Grace Tully and Estes Kefauver, 1955.

Vice President Johnson "campaigning" in South Vietnam, 1961.

Presidential oath of office on board Air Force One, 22 November 1963.

6

MASTER
OF THE
SENATE

Lyndon B. Johnson moved from the House to the Senate in January 1949. He became Senate majority whip in January 1951, Senate minority leader in 1953, and, with a shift in party dominance, majority leader in 1955. Never had a senator risen so rapidly to such high leadership posts. And never would a leader so dominate the Senate as did Lyndon Johnson during the next five years. He shifted from a relatively unknown congressman to one of the most powerful and best known politicians in America. By 1956 he was widely considered to be a likely presidential candidate. As always, the achievement involved not only luck but ambition, focused goals, intense dedication, and an impossible work load. A heart attack in 1955 may have marked one cost of such superhuman effort.

As so often in his life, the move to the Senate provided a new challenge. Johnson had bogged down in the House. Frustrated in his quest for power and national recognition, he had tended to drift along during his last term. Roosevelt had died. His close friends in that administration now lacked clout. He admired, related well to, but never established a close personal relationship with Truman. The earlier intensity, the drive, now seemed lacking. Thus, Johnson talked of quitting politics, and, clearly, in the immediate postwar years he invested as much imagination and energy in the family radio station and in other investments as he did in his job in Washington. That all changed in January 1949. As in 1931, and 1937, he once again responded to the new challenge in Washington. He had to prove—to himself, to the Texas electorate that had barely endorsed him, to Americans everywhere—that he could be the best senator in Washington.

Johnson had no early opportunity to win any large prizes for Texas. He could not begin with an immediate success, such as his victories in behalf of the LCRA. As "Landslide" Lyndon, he had to build home support or face defeat in 1954 in a Texas continually racked by internal splits among Democrats. This need reinforced his lifelong bent as a politician—to relate to an identified constituency, to assess its wants and needs, and then to try his best to please, to serve. This goal dictated caution, correct voting on issues of state interest, a careful cultivation of Senate insiders, and his usual intense efforts to learn all he could about an institution and about those who controlled it. But, at least as early as 1952, a second, often conflicting goal—to gain a national reputation and, possibly, to qualify as a viable vice-presidential if not a presidential candidate—complicated his Senate role. He now had to serve two masters and, at the very least, never irretrievably alienate either. This required a political artistry, a balancing of competing pressures, that taxed even the ability of LBJ.

Still a relatively young forty, Johnson first had to determine his role in the Senate. In light of his past career, this was predictable. He would accept the existing rules, defer to Senate elders, and try to build a power base through ability and hard work. He came to the Senate with a talented group of entering Democrats, the soon-to-be-famous class of 1948. It included such able people as Hubert Humphrey of Minnesota, Estes Kefauver of Tennessee, Paul Douglas of Illinois, Clinton Anderson of New Mexico, Russell Long of Louisiana, and Robert Kerr of Oklahoma. Douglas and Kefauver were not team players; Johnson respected Douglas's intellect and integrity but believed him to be an ineffective and at times obstructionist legislator. He considered Kefauver a posturing maverick, out to gain a national reputation, not to play a serious role in the Senate. Johnson would work well with Long but was never close to him. He carefully, and soon successfully, wooed Hubert Humphrey and both used him and helped him gain membership and power in the ruling inner circles of the Senate. He became close friends of both Anderson and Kerr. He shared with them a penchant for middle-of-the-road legislation, an affection for the Southwest, and a common fascination with gentlemanly ranching. They talked the same language, enjoyed the same rough and ready humor. Along with Richard Russell of Georgia, the most powerful Democrat in the Senate, they made up an inner circle that Johnson always turned to her for advice and support.

Because of his eleven years in the House, Johnson gained what amounted to seniority over most entering senators. His legislative experience on the House Armed Services Committee (so renamed in 1946) helped. He sought, and gained, a position on the prestigious Senate Armed Services Committee, chaired by a reserved, formal, conscientious, and gifted Russell. In addition, Johnson took his seat on the Committee on Interstate and Foreign Commerce. He rejoiced that neither committee appointment seemed likely to engage him in controversy. He began a slow but eventually successful courtship of Russell, much as he had with Sam Rayburn earlier. Lyndon and Lady Bird pulled Russell within their social circle and once again gave a lonely bachelor the comforts of family and home. Russell, so different in personality from the egotistic, vain, ambitious LBJ, eventually became an admirer of Johnson's talents, a patron who supported his national political ambitions, and a cagey legislative adviser. Johnson became a dutiful pupil and servant. He was willing to do the hard work and put in the long hours needed to build winning coalitions in the Senate. He deferred to Russell and long kept up the fiction that Russell and his cronies made all the basic decisions, after which Johnson simply carried out their wishes. Through Russell, Johnson soon developed a close working relationship with from ten to twelve Democratic senators, most from the South and West, who held the key committee posts and who could largely determine party patronage and policy. In a pattern stretching back to Southwest Texas, Johnson identified the people who had clout, those who were respected and effective, and quickly made himself so valuable to them, even so indispensable, that he came to share in and then orchestrate their power. The kid moved in, gained admission to the gang, and before anyone quite recognized it had taken charge.

Despite prestigious committee assignments, Johnson remained

almost invisible during his first two years in the Senate. He worked quietly and was uncharacteristically subdued, as if he wanted to assume the dignity appropriate to his position. He retained most of his former staff, a staff more loyal than talented. Walter Jenkins still served as his secretary or administrative assistant. As Johnson subsequently assumed leadership roles and accumulated a second office and staff, the dutiful Jenkins practically ran the old office and took charge of constituency issues. Almost all those involving Texas remained in his hands. John Connally stayed in Texas after the election of 1948 as a lawyer, an employee of oilman Sid Richardson, and later as a successful politician. Johnson never found as able a replacement. He hired, and then in a sense drove away, several assistants during his Senate career. After 1952, his ablest staff members, led by former journalist George Reedy, worked in conjunction with his party leadership post. Even here, he had difficulty recruiting and retaining able, nonsacrificial assistants. He demanded too much, was too arbitrary in both rewards and frequent abuse, to retain those with a strong ego or alternative opportunities. Thus, as Senate leader, by far his ablest ally would be a Senate employee and assistant to the leader, Bobby Baker, a bright, brash, greedy South Carolinian. For outside influence, he continued to rely upon old cronies, such as James Rowe, Clark Clifford, Abe Fortas, Ben Cohen, and Tommy Corcoran.

Johnson's move to the Senate roughly paralleled some lasting changes in his personal life. Most critical, he was now financially secure. He could forget all the earlier incessant worries about debts and tight budgets. By 1949, Lady Bird's Texas Broadcasting Company, now with television as well as radio, had matured into a secure, increasingly valuable, steadily growing enterprise, one abetted by its monopoly of the only VHF channel in Austin. Other investments—in scattered lots, in land, and in bank stock—began a rapid appreciation in value in the postwar years. The family income from such investments had reached at least fifty thousand dollars annually, and as early as 1948 Johnson estimated the market value of all of his and Lady Bird's assets at close to $1 million.

Until 1952, Austin would remain Johnson's home, his destination when he came to Texas. His mother and sister still lived there. He had his own house, plus the broadcasting facilities. But, gradually, the ties to Austin loosened. A competent staff ran the station, and he and Lady Bird devoted less and less time to its operations. In 1951, the closest of his Austin friends and mentors, Al Wirtz, died. No one could replace him. More and more, Johnson identified with the beloved hill country, with the familiar scenes of childhood, although he and Lady Bird would always maintain an apartment in Austin. Shortly after 1948, they began scouting ranches for sale in the Johnson City and Stonewall areas. Clearly, Johnson yearned to be back on the Pedernales.

In 1951, Johnson acquired what he would quickly dub the LBJ Ranch. Perhaps the scheming went back to 1948. In that year, his aunt Frank Martin, sister to Lyndon's father, widow of former judge Clarence Martin, mother of the Tom Martin who hosted a teenage LBJ in California, used legal means to regain full title to the family ranch. Her son Tom, at times a political rival of LBJ after he moved back to Texas, had just died. By then, Tom and his wife had acquired title to the ranch, conditional on a lifetime possession by the mother for whose care they took responsibility. But, with Tom's death, Aunt Frank decided to challenge the rights of the daughter-in-law and won her case in court. Neighbors later suspected that LBJ prompted this legal effort, that he and his aunt had already plotted a complicated transaction completed in 1951. Apparently, the daughter-in-law received compensation for the loss of her claim. In any event, in 1951 Johnson worked out an arrangement with his aunt, by all indications a fair arrangement from her perspective. He gained title to the ranch, and in return he gave his aunt a lifetime right to the old Johnson home in Johnson City. Apparently he also paid her, not cash, but a type of lifetime annuity, giving her a desired security for her old age. Incidentally, the now run-down ranch would not have provided her a decent income.

The Martin ranch was just up the river from the old Sam Early Johnson place, less than a half mile from Johnson's birthplace. As a boy, he had frequently visited his uncle and aunt in what had been one of the most comfortable and spacious houses along the river. The house, although in poor repair, was still imposing in size. The land, although in need of rehabilitation, gently sloped back from the river and could, and soon would, become one of the lushest ranches in the county. Johnson loved the prospects. This was a joyous homecoming for him. He and Lady Bird began the continuing stream of ranch expenditures that never ended until his death. They poured money into the ranch, with tax benefits and psychic satisfactions in return. A full refurbishing of the house allowed the family to move their Austin furnishings by 1952. Expansions of the house, a swimming pool in 1955, a guest house by 1956, a landing strip, endless barns and outbuildings joined an ever more elaborate ranching operation—purebred and prize Herefords, irrigated pastures, costly fences, and expanded acreage. Very early, Johnson dammed the Pedernales, creating a permanent deep pool in front of this house and easy access to the highway across the river. A grove of live oaks in front of the house and on the river, not far upstream from the family graveyard, became the familiar site of Texas-sized barbecues. By 1953, Johnson was already treating a parade of famous guests to his own overwhelming style of Texas hospitality. He basked in the limelight.

It would be impossible to overestimate the place of the ranch in Johnson's self-concept, its crucial role in his later life. He loved it. When he bought it he knew next to nothing about ranching. Even his father had farmed, not ranched, the adjoining acres. But, almost at once, Johnson took on the identity of a western rancher, down to the expensive boots and cowboy hats. The ranch became his only real toy, his one avocation. In the midst of his busy, often frustrating life in Washington, he could always escape, at least in fantasy, to the ranch. Endlessly he plotted the improvements. He knew every field, counted every cow, rode or drove across the land in reckless abandon, hunted deer and turkey in the fall, and in periods of depression yearned to be back at the ranch. It symbolized peace, simplicity, honest friendship, a manageable world, one colored by nostalgia and embellished by romantic sentiments. Of course, despite his effort to make it all profitable, the ranch was an indulgence, one open only to people of wealth. He did not have to earn a living by raising cattle. No one could earn more than a meager return from even a ranch as large as his soon became. Only later, when he added several other, larger ranches to his holdings, did he broach the scale conducive to profits. In a pattern stretching back to George Washington, Johnson established his roots in the soil, acquired his plantation, his country home. The Brown brothers and Marsh had set the example. His cronies in the Senate—Russell, Anderson, Everett Dirkson, Kerr, Wayne Morse—all had farms or ranches. Thus, the boys gathered in Senate cloakrooms, temporarily forgot their political differences, compared notes about ranching, and on occasion swapped real bulls.

In his first two years in the Senate Johnson sponsored no major legislation. He continued his pattern in the House, but with a difference already apparent. In the smaller Senate he would no longer restrict most of his energies to direct services to constituents or to purely local legislation. He was now determined to help shape national policies, and soon he was more involved in the details of bills and in strategies for gaining their passage than any other senator. Even in his first two years, he sponsored relatively minor naval appropriations, an addition to REA funding, and small increases in veterans' benefits, all quite safe and largely unnoticed initiatives. But he became best known for his very active support of a bill, pushed in part from conviction, in part out of self-interest, by his much more controversial crony, Robert Kerr of Oklahoma. This was a bill to deregulate the original or producer price of natural gas (not the prices charged by pipeline companies). By his stand, Johnson clearly, even rashly, bid for support back in Texas. Heretofore, he had had, at best, only an uneasy tie to major oil and gas firms. This had hurt him in 1948. He now tried to make amends, do what any statewide candidate in Texas had to do—support the most important local industry. But, to the embarrassment of friends, perhaps to his own later regret, he waded in more than he needed to and ended up with some lasting obstacles to national leadership. The damage came not from support of the Kerr bill (it passed in Congress only to succumb to a Truman veto) but from his aggressive, unnecessary assault on Leland Olds, a nominee of Truman for a continuing term on the Federal Power Commission (FPC).

The history of the Olds affair is complex. Olds had a colorful background—an Amherst B.A. in 1912, graduate work at Harvard and Columbia, politically radical journalism in the twenties, chairman of the New York State Power Authority in the thirties, an original appointment to the FPC in 1939, and chairman of the commission from 1940 through 1946. A technical expert and author in the field of regulation and resource policy, he had come to symbolize tough government regulation, although apparently he was at times a bit of a maverick on the commission. His appointment in 1944 had occasioned an extended hearing. His reappointment became a bitter public controversy because of a Supreme Court decision. The Natural Gas Act of 1938, which gave the FPC regulatory powers over the price charged for natural gas, had not, by clear wording or the apparent intent of Congress, included the regulation of prices charged at the wellhead by small producers. But the Supreme Court, in 1947, so interpreted the language of the act as to extend regulatory power to these prices. The Kerr bill would have exempted producers and thus have restored what Kerr believed to be the congressional intent in 1938.

At first, the FPC tried to appease fearful congressmen; it agreed not to extend its regulation. Olds seemed at first to concur. But, by 1948, he publicly favored extended FPC regulation, a stand that put him at the center of a storm. A diverse group of old New Dealers, labor union spokesmen, consumer advocates, and northeastern congressmen not only applauded Olds but quickly elevated him to the position of a hero in what they described as a "progressive" or "liberal" cause, even as they pictured his opponents as toadies of special economic interests. In Congress, a majority clearly opposed Olds and rejected his court-validated interpretation of the 1938 statute. Some, such as Kerr and Johnson, did so in deference to local interests. Others, and Johnson would make much of this, opposed Olds because he seemed deliberately to be defying the expressed intent of Congress. Finally, as a matter of principle, many Republicans and a few Democrats opposed extended federal regulation in almost any area. Clearly, a majority coalition in the Senate would block his confirmation.

Johnson, abetted by Kerr, turned the confirmation hearings into a demagogic assault on Olds. Johnson chaired the hearing before a subcommittee of his Commerce Committee. He allowed the questions to stray beyond the technical issues and in particular to Olds's radical activities back in the twenties, when he wrote articles for a labor-oriented press service. The tactics sometimes resembled those in the later investigations of Senator Joseph McCarthy. Not only did Johnson permit such ad hominem evidence in the hearing; but in a rare speech before the Senate he offered his own, rough-handed indictment of Olds. In part, he presented a detailed summary of the technical issues, stressed his own earlier battles with large oil companies, and tried to detach the issue of Olds—his partisanship, his alleged disrespect for fellow commissioners, his recent shift in policies—from the larger issue of federal regulatory policy. But even he played on Olds's irresponsible radicalism and extremism. Johnson's subcommittee voted unanimously against the appointment, and in the larger committee only two voted for Olds. The Senate as a whole easily voted to reject him. In this sense, Johnson won. He pleased Texans. He developed his ties to Kerr, joined cause with Russell, and thus possibly helped entrench himself in the Senate inner circle. He did their dirty work. In 1951, he would deliver another rare speech, this in behalf of high oil depletion allowances, winning by it the lasting admiration of Texas oilmen.

In the Olds affair, more than ever before, a cautious Johnson waded into ideologically loaded conflict. He took sides. This was uncharacteristic. In the elusive labels of the day, it marked him as a "conservative," and thus as an enemy of a group of identified, at times self-identified, Senate "liberals." For the rest of his political career, Johnson would try to cope with, relate to, or explain himself to such liberals. Anger, despair, even an almost paranoid bitterness marked his largely unsuccessful efforts. Over and over again he rejected any label at all, but to no avail. Not surprisingly, the labels varied with the perspective of observers. In Texas, he still suffered from his continuing image as a liberal, at least deep down if not always on the surface. And, indeed, his own flexibility, his ability to accommodate the views of widely different people, led various friends to project their beliefs and values upon Johnson, to claim him as their own. Thus, in a sense, he often suffered as a frustrated chameleon in a den of ideological protagonists. His typical reaction—to minimize differences and seek areas of commonality.

In large part, the labeling issue was always one of style or method as much as content. Johnson could not understand, in fact tended always to belittle, people who made a point of their principles or who were consistent in their commitments. In this, he equally condemned those who called themselves either liberals or conservatives. Both were inflexible, at times arrogant, unwilling to bargain or compromise. They always tried to make a point or to fight futile battles over abstractions, and were thus impractical, unable to get anything accomplished. Paul Douglas and a later Barry Goldwater seemed perfect examples. Such a stance might fit some situations—a college classroom, a church, a debate—but in his view it was always inappropriate in a legislative body. In fact, principled or idealistic or ideologically committed congressmen turned out most often to be obstructionists, perennial impediments to any legislative achievement at all.

Behind the babble of labels lay certain differences in policy. By most programmatic definitions, Johnson had always been somewhere in the middle, yet always willing to move right or left to accommodate a constituency or to get something passed. More than any other senator, he approached even legislation with a body count mentality—the more bills the better, even if some had to be compromised to the point of emasculation. To Johnson, even a small program, or an opening engagement of some critical issue, was better than no action at all.

Clearly, the meaning of *liberal*, as most people used the unhelpful label, changed through time. In the late thirties, a period when economic issues dominated congressional debates, Johnson gained the label largely through support of relief and welfare policies, public power, and an interventionist foreign policy. He had straddled such issues as support for organized labor or extensive economic regulation. In 1949, support for such welfare extension as group health insurance, or for the policies of labor unions, remained critical in the journalistic use of the label. Pressures from Texas forced Johnson to back away from open support of almost any legislation in these areas. His vote for the Taft-Hartley Act made possible his contested election in 1948. By then, other issues were becoming even more definitive of liberalism—support for civil rights, at least foot-dragging on subversive and loyalty legislation, and support for extended economic regulation in several areas, including the extractive industries. Johnson, as a national politician, would later come to terms with each of these policies, generally on the side dubbed liberal. But in 1949 these issues had a clear sectional base—the North and Northeast. They were anathema in the South.

Johnson worked throughout his Senate career to find issues that bridged the sections, that maintained a national party coalition that could win elections. He knew that constituent pressures forced senators from the North to take a stand on such an explosive issue as civil rights, even as they had to vote against the Kerr bill or the later tidelands oil bill out of deference to their own consumers. Thus, stands on these inescapable issues were divisive only when and if they became a test of party loyalty. So long as self-styled liberals supported them because of regional pressures, Johnson understood their stand. But he wanted reciprocity. He thought such liberals should understand his opposition to civil rights bills or to legislation aimed directly at Texas or southern economic interests. To expect him to do otherwise was the equivalent of asking a Michigan congressman to vote sanctions against the automobile industry or to condemn the United Automobile Workers. To him, the few good liberals granted such a reciprocity, remained flexible and accommodating, even as they used opportune times to make all the required genuflections to liberal fashions or to their own sincere convictions. In time, Hubert Humphrey learned to be such a good liberal. Paul Douglas and Estes Kefauver never did. Even more reflexive and therefore worse were self-identified liberals outside Congress, as those who controlled Americans for Democratic Action or the Democratic National Committee. Johnson had the same distrust and fears of self-proclaimed and ideologically rigid conservatives. A dogmatic Strom Thurmond was as difficult to bargain with as a Douglas, but a Dick Russell, behind the public stand he had to make out of either honesty or deference to his Georgia constituents, remained flexible, accommodating, and thus helpful in making the legislative process really work.

As Johnson assumed his leadership role in the Senate, and despite an early reputation as a legislative magician, he continued to suffer from the labeling game. He fought back only once, and ineffectively, in 1958. An assistant, Horace Busby, ghosted an article for the *Texas Quarterly* entitled "My Political Philosophy." Johnson edited it, and the final product well reflected his own views. To his mother, he lamented his popular image as a shrewd operator, lacking in depth, imagination, or moral principles. He hoped the article would make clear that his actions did not "stem solely from motives of expediency." In the article, he classified himself, in order, as a free man, American, United States senator, Democrat, liberal, conservative, Texan, taxpayer, rancher, businessman, consumer, parent, and voter. No label, he argued, was exclusive. He could not define any political philosophy or demonstrate it by any label or dogma. He resented questions that demanded such reductionist answers, summings up of all his life experiences. Yet, after such a persuasive response, he turned around and listed, in clichés, the tenets of his political life: that everyone has something to say, that a national answer exists for every national problem, that the highest purpose of government is to help Americans realize the fullest potential of their physical and human resources, and that waste of these resources is the major enemy of our society. As such loose and appealing words attest, his efforts at self-definition failed. As always when he wanted to talk seriously, he soon fell into vague or moralistic bromides, which he sincerely believed. This was his lifelong affliction. Fortunately, after this article, he stopped trying to explain himself philosophically.

Adversity for the Democratic party greased the road to national prominence for LBJ. By the 1950 election, the Truman administration was already bogged down in Korea. An array of civil rights and welfare proposals—the Fair Deal—was dead in Congress, victim of a working coalition of Republicans and largely southern and western Democrats. Incumbent Democrats were vulnerable in several states. Thus, both Democratic leaders in the Senate, Scott Lucas of Illinois (majority leader) and Francis Myers of Pennsylvania (whip) lost in 1950. Given the dismal legislative prospects over the next two years, no experienced and able senators really wanted leadership posts. Even appeals from President Truman failed to persuade Russell to take over as majority leader. He knew that too close an identification with the administration would doom his slight chances for the presidential nomination in 1952. Eventually, Russell persuaded an ineffectual Ernest McFarland of Arizona to take the majority post, a "recognition" that helped assure his defeat in 1952 by Barry Goldwater. Even less appealing was the almost honorific job of whip. It provided little real power and no rewards, but could require longer hours of work. For once the likely candidate almost had to be a junior senator, preferably one not up for reelection in 1952 and one willing to assume a thankless task. Clinton Anderson turned down invitations to stand for the job. In this context, Bob Kerr began pushing for his friend and recent ally, Johnson, who made clear that he was willing, even eager, "to serve." Another southwesterner, either Anderson or Johnson, made no political sense. Russell demurred. But Johnson was the ablest among very few contenders. He easily won in a caucus election that received little national publicity.

In most respects, his job as whip turned out as everyone expected. In no sense was it an avenue to power. Johnson, although much more able than McFarland, could not take over the majority leader's job without causing hurt and resentment. Thus, he dutifully deferred to McFarland and assumed no major responsibilities in what turned out to be an endlessly frustrating two years for Democrats. But nonetheless the whip position became critical in his career. It gave him a formal position, a claim on future preferment. Back in Texas it documented once again Johnson's amazing talents. More critical, but more subtle, it slowly shifted his constituency. Without a focused private agenda, he had always conceived of himself largely as an agent of those Texans he directly represented. Now, in a minor way, he assumed responsibility for Senate Democrats, for the party as a whole, and for the successful functioning of the Senate as an institution. At the time, this commitment could not translate into any effective action. He could not rally divided Senate Democrats around any realizable legislative program and, except on such basics as appropriations, he did not waste energy supporting Truman administration proposals. But his focus, his orientation, began to shift away from Texas and toward national priorities. Even the nature of the Senate encouraged this. The formal role reinforced it. He now had a new master to serve, and as always he tried to serve it well.

Since the whip position provided few outlets for his abundant energy, Johnson focused his effort in 1951 and 1952 on the Armed Services Committee. Here, once again, party misfortunes had benefited his career. Millard Tydings of Maryland, who had hoped to chair a special watchdog subcommittee on preparedness, would not fight to gain the position and in 1950 had to give up the opportunity because of a tough campaign in Maryland. Hounded by Senator Joseph McCarthy, he eventually lost to a Republican in the election. Johnson, who badly wanted the chairmanship and actually competed for it, won it almost by default. The post gave him a staff (Horace Busby headed it) and led to a series of unsensational but important hearings during the Korean War. Johnson supported an expanded draft, with minor qualifications backed Truman's proposals for universal military service, and helped push the military buildup necessitated by the Korean War. In 1952 he conducted a major, superbly controlled inquiry into American air power. He unearthed few major scandals, but gained some national publicity and was able both to humble the military brass in hearings and yet almost always to support their requests for additional appropriations for a war he considered in all ways necessary to check an almost mythic communism and to prevent another Munich-like capitulation to force. This subcommittee would remain central to Johnson's Senate career, a small fief under his direct control. As a result of it, no congressman in Washington had a more thorough and technical understanding of defense issues.

In 1952 the Democrats lost decisively. Eisenhower won the presidency in a minor landslide, and the Republicans, by a one-vote margin, gained control of the Senate. Disaster again meant opportunity for LBJ. Since McFarland lost, the post of minority leader was now open. As Johnson knew, Russell was the key to his chances for gaining this job, still not an enviable one but one that offered significant opportunities for leadership and achievement, perhaps more so under a Republican president than under Truman. In 1952, Russell lost his bid for a presidential nomination. Johnson had given him full support. In return, Russell had tried to get Johnson in the running as a vice-presidential possibility, but with little success. Almost as soon as the election was over, Johnson began a typical barrage of phone calls from his newly refurbished ranch. Of course, he urged Russell to take the leadership post, which was his for the asking. As he expected, Russell declined and then agreed to support Johnson. By key calls, often through indirect conversations, he lined up a clear majority of Democrats. For example, a congratulatory call to newly elected John F. Kennedy of Massachusetts did the trick. Russell's support and Johnson's existing position as whip proved decisive. A small band of liberals tried to block the caucus election. Hubert Humphrey joined the rebellion, but in the embarrassing showdown he was left dangling among only three or four anti-Johnson voters. He then moved a unanimous ballot.

More than ever before, Johnson's abilities now matched his challenge. No one ever had a greater talent for organizing and focusing the energies of small groups of people. The context, in 1953, did not allow major legislative achievements. But Johnson had an opportunity to mold an effective Democratic opposition and to use his skills to defeat or to pass the bills that originated in the new Eisenhower administration. Except for a few of the liberals, the Democratic senators made up a pliant group, very receptive to skillful management by their minority leader. By default, they turned over to Johnson an immense amount of authority. Within a year he directed a meek and cooperative Democratic Policy Committee, which determined overall legislative strategy. Johnson's cronies—Russell and Kerr—served on the committee. Soon Johnson largely determined its membership, but could do so because he at least gave appointments to each faction, including the liberals, who, by most counts, made up no more than a third of the Democrats. He also, again by deference from his colleagues, effectively controlled the Steering Committee, which largely limited itself to making committee assignments. In a sense, Johnson soon exercised the power of a near-dictator, but such power rested on consent. That in turn depended on his pleasing a vast majority of his Democratic colleagues. He tried to carry out his job, as he always put it, in a "responsible" and "reasonable" way, the two labels that became his almost reflexive defense of all his policies in the Senate. For eight years, not without some interim criticism from a few independent-minded or equally egotistic Democrats, he persuaded the dominant majority that he did not only a responsible job but the best job in the whole history of the Senate. In the glowing terms of aide George Reedy, he made the Senate work.

How did he do it? In hundreds of pages of prose, both journalists and historians have probed the answer to that question. Circumstances proved critical. Since a Republican Eisenhower was president and his administration was primarily responsible for developing legislative initiatives, the Senate Democrats had the luxury and the unifying pressures of opposition. The Democratic majority had been divided and ineffective during the Truman years. It seemed impossible to unite such a disparate group of individualists, even when they were in an opposition role. But their position as the opposition helped Johnson. It gave him his opportunity to rally the Democrats on selected and carefully outfitted issues and to create at least the appearance of legislative cohesion and success. This made individual senators look better back home.

Republican divisions also helped. Because Eisenhower was immensely popular, Johnson rarely attacked him directly or personally. Instead, he made targets of right-wing Republicans, often posing as a defender of moderate and responsible administrative policies against the saboteurs within Eisenhower's own party. For critical legislation, he was able, over and over again, to build a shifting but winning coalition made up of a majority of his own Democrats and at least a minority of moderate Republicans. He thus played a careful balancing role, using his superb persuasive abilities to win over the few critical senators needed to enact the bills he, and his policy committee, decided to support as party priorities. Johnson rarely backed legislation until he was confident he could build a winning combination, at least after a series of concessions and compromises.

Johnson brought several personal assets to his leadership role. His ideological flexibility was critical. Unpredictable on issues, he had enormous maneuvering room. He often held back. He waited until the prospects were clear before committing himself. Thus, he almost always emerged on the winning side. While he waited, he kept his own thinking to himself. Those who wanted his support, those who actively sought it, helped shape his eventual, always well-timed, public response.

Johnson knew his fellow senators. This was not primarily a matter of intuitive insight, but rather of constant, unrelenting work. The task was manageable only for one of Johnson's intellect and high energy levels. He typically spent fifteen hours a day in the Senate chambers, cloakrooms, and offices during sessions. He took every moment available to talk to his colleagues, to give direct, intense attention to them, to their concerns, moral commitments, fears, and political needs. He liked people, still tried to pull them all into the magical circle of his enveloping personality. He flattered everyone by attention even to small matters. He grieved with them in time of death, complimented them on successes, and flattered them with gifts and endless telephone calls. Like a computer,

his brain absorbed, sorted, filed, and at a moment's notice re-
trieved hundreds of even petty details about other senators. In a
sense, he knew most of them even better than they knew themselves. He knew the best tactics to use in persuading them. He
often failed, but he brought to the task more data, and better skills,
than any former leader.

As far back as his college days, LBJ had learned the art of self-
promotion. As majority leader, he gained immense power. He virtually controlled committee assignments. One of his first innovations as majority leader was an overhaul of the committee system.
He persuaded senior colleagues to support an expansion of the
number of senators on each committee, and thus made it possible
for each junior or beginning senator to have one important committee assignment. Of course, in distributing these new prizes,
Johnson managed to take full credit for each gift. He stressed, often
exaggerated, his involvement and his own power. Always attentive
to image, he tried to dress to fit his role, and eventually he turned
a newly outfitted majority leader's office—the "Taj Mahal"—into
an exclusive lair of the powerful. Because of his control over the
Policy and Steering committees, he became virtually a one-person
arbiter of which bills went to which committee and when each was
scheduled for floor debate. This meant a form of powerful patronage, which Johnson used as part of his system of rewards and pun-
ishments. Those immune to his persuasive powers, the
few mavericks who resented his subtle but full control, suffered
the penalties—poor committee assignments and stagnating bills.
Johnson never liked to use the whip. He preferred positive rein-
forcements. He kept trying to win over even his enemies. In private, he could nourish old wounds. But in public he was usually
forgiving and magnanimous, particularly when he won. He still
wanted to please everyone and was never happy until everyone
was on his bandwagon, singing their appreciation of his, and their,
glorious achievements.

A critical aspect of Johnson's leadership was legislative intelligence. He had to know, day by day, how senators most likely would
vote. Here Bobby Baker, technically assistant secretary to the minority leader but in reality Johnson's key personal assistant,
proved a near genius. Together, he and Johnson could compile
amazingly accurate head counts. This abetted the superb timing
displayed by Johnson—when to bring a bill to the floor, when to
schedule a vote, when to ensure that key senators were in town or
safely off on a much appreciated junket abroad. Even the final

strategy on the floor depended on intelligence. Johnson always had some uncollected debts. He could sway a few last-minute votes by direct pressure or personal appeals, as he moved busily about the Senate chamber. But these were ultimate weapons, quickly used up. By correct head counts Johnson could avoid wasting his resources. He lost even on a few major issues. In his last two years as majority leader (1959–60) his earlier magic ebbed. But almost never did Johnson lose because of mistaken assumptions about how his fellow senators would vote, and thus because of any failure to use every bit of leverage he had.

Johnson subtly changed the legislative process in the Senate. He minimized the role of floor debate and almost never gave speeches himself. If possible, he used prior agreement to cut off all but token debate. He had little sympathy for those who wanted to air points of view, to use speeches as a vehicle of public education. Debate tended to sharpen differences or allowed senators to posture for audiences back home. He gauged success by the number of bills passed, by output. Success required a masking of issues, not sharpening them through debate. Major legislation always reflects years, even decades, of advocacy and of bill writing. The major bills that emerge from Congress almost always contain sections written to appeal to a variety of constituencies. In a sense, every congressman votes for a different bill, because each focuses attention upon the parts that have appeal to his or her supporters. Elements of deceit are built into the legislative process. Bills pass because of selective emphasis and selective concealment.

Johnson appreciated these realities. He worked behind the scenes, through informal personal techniques and numerous small caucuses, to build the temporary alliances necessary to pass a bill. These alliances were often years in the making, were tied to numerous small revisions or excisions in ever more complex bills, and in the end reflected numerous bargains or trade-offs among senators. Johnson was a master at bringing this complex process to a final climax at the exact time he had the majority required for victory. This meant success for ordinary bills. For very controversial or innovative legislation, that marking a major shift in federal policy, he was not content with simple majorities. In these cases he would wait until he could assure something closer to a full consensus.

In the first legislative showdowns, Johnson occasionally gained the deciding few votes largely through force of personality and persuasion. This led to the much-remarked Johnson treatment, to endless analyses of how he used voice, gesture, touch, or even the largest repertoire of obscenity in Washington to breach the defenses of determined opponents. No doubt, he was adept at one-to-one argument; his admirers found him overwhelming, irresistible. But forensic skill or personal magnetism were no substitutes for information. Johnson persuaded people when he knew them well, when he could so focus issues as to involve their values or fears, and when he could draw upon a detailed knowledge of pending legislation.

Despite Johnson's success in guiding and forcing the work of Senate Democrats, he was not able to claim credit for much watershed legislation. New social legislation that formed the heart of his later Great Society proposals—federal aid to education, medical care for the elderly, various programs to aid cities and depressed areas, and broad or effective civil rights bills—floundered in the Congress for a variety of reasons and, in the case of federal aid and civil rights, despite administration support. Johnson did have a critical role in a few legislative breakthroughs. He supported the 1956 highway bill (the basis of our interstate system), although he alienated pro-union senators by early support of provisions to exempt contractors from prevailing wages. Throughout the decade he tried to evade stands on legislation touching upon union labor. In 1958, as he maneuvered for national support, he voted against the Landrum-Griffin Labor Reform Act, a bill loaded with amendments hated by unions. But even here he had waffled on the issues and used purported civil rights threats to justify his vote in the South. He usually supported extended welfare programs, including several increases in the scope and level of benefits in Social Security, climaxing in a major 1956 reform, and sponsored a major omnibus housing bill in 1957. Much of Johnson's time had to go into annual battles over budgets and appropriations or over foreign aid and defense spending. Here, in relatively safe areas, he often indulged in more open, at times more demagogic, partisanship, as in the largely symbolic battle of the budget in 1958 (Johnson engineered extensive cuts embarrassing to the Eisenhower administration, only to guide the Senate in more than restoring such cuts during the next year). In these areas, as in the politically motivated Senate refusal to confirm Lewis L. Strauss as secretary of commerce in 1958, Johnson dropped the pose of impartiality and gladly helped his party develop campaign issues.

Johnson always believed in strong presidential leadership, even for domestic issues. He saw the role of Congress as largely reactive. It had to debate, revise, or reject administrative proposals. Only when an administration rejected its legislative responsibilities should the Congress step in with its own agenda. Johnson's deference to the Eisenhower administration did not endear him to the Democratic National Committee or to a few senators anxious to create more direct confrontations. In a rare departure from form, LBJ proposed in 1956 an agenda for Senate Democrats, or what he called a "program with a heart." Typical of Johnson products, it amounted to a loose, open-ended, thirteen-point legislative grab bag, one loosely tied to almost every pending bill supported by major blocs in the Democratic party. It included lower taxes, Social Security expansion, subsidies for hospital construction and medical research, aid for school construction, the federal highway program, higher farm price supports, expanded public housing, new water resource projects, aid to depressed areas, and an anti-poll tax amendment. It ended with a proposal to deregulate natural gas, the only lingering echo of his former regionally focused outlook. Again, in 1959, with Senate liberals on the prowl and his presidential ambitions at a peak, Johnson opened the new congressional session with several welfare-oriented demands. But in neither of these two cases did he pursue anything close to a structured agenda.

In Johnson's later memories of his Senate leadership, three triumphs stood out above all others. First was his opening achievement as minority leader—the mobilization and successful guidance of senators on the explosive issue of Joseph McCarthy. Next was the Civil Rights Act of 1957. Finally was his role in developing a new space program. Each of these deserves a fuller description, for they stand as test cases of Johnson's leadership.

In no way did Johnson take the lead in opposing Senator Joseph McCarthy. Throughout his career in Congress, he always supported anticommunist legislation. In part, this reflected a deference to continuous pressures from all the political crazies down in Texas, in part an expression of his own conventional fears of Soviet power, and in part his reluctance at any time in his career to take a stand against policies on which he was sure to lose. Johnson always invested his political capital carefully in order better to benefit constituents and to further his own career. Until 1954, he never recorded a vote against loyalty or subversion legislation. He, like most of his Democratic colleagues, voted for the infamous Mc-

Carran Act of 1950 and supported the notorious amendment that allowed the internment of unconvicted citizens in case of invasion or insurrection. But, privately, Johnson was too sophisticated, too informed about the executive branch, to give credence to McCarthy's wild charges about communists in the federal government. He knew better. Loyalty to the memory of Roosevelt and of George C. Marshall, his friendship with Dean Acheson, and his allegiance to the Democratic party all made him resentful of any partisan exploitation of the loyalty issue. Finally, his firm commitment to presidential leadership prompted him to do all he could, short of a public stand, to moderate attacks on executive leeway in the conduct of foreign policy. Thus, by the time he became minority leader in 1953, Johnson was ready to play not a courageous but a vital role in censoring or controlling McCarthy, whose demagoguery he believed to be a very serious threat to the country. The virulent pro-McCarthy letters from back home only increased his fears.

After the Army-McCarthy hearings in the summer of 1954, the Senate finally voted 75–12 to appoint a select committee to investigate the behavior of McCarthy. Johnson had long supported such a committee. As minority leader, he worked with the majority leader, William F. Knowland of California, to appoint as moderate and judicious a committee as possible. He selected three Democratic senators (John Stennis, Edwin Johnson, and Sam Ervin) with judicial training and not a taint of liberalism. He wanted to avoid any appearance of the Democrats persecuting McCarthy and thus making him a martyr. Then, in crucial meetings of his policy committee, Johnson matured what turned out to be a brilliant strategy. On the issue of McCarthy, he knew the Democrats were united in detestation. But Johnson persuaded his colleagues not to make this a party issue. He did not so identify it to reporters, and he did not work openly to deliver votes. Formally, each Democratic senator was to vote his conscience. Such a strategy disarmed wavering Republicans and hurt McCarthy. In the showdown, every Democratic senator voted for a motion of censure, a rare example of party unity in the Senate and, by most judgments, the first demonstration of Johnson's newly won mastery over the Senate. Incidentally, the McCarthy issue provoked the first open discussions of LBJ's presidential possibilities. His old New Deal friend, James Rowe, wrote to warn him that concessions to Texas pressures, reflected in a vote against censure, would identify him as a sectional leader and damn any presidential hopes for at least six years.

Rowe noted, correctly, that the liberals, a minority of no more than a third in the Senate, made up the largest single bloc at Democratic conventions, a bloc capable of vetoing any candidate for president or vice president.

Johnson established his leadership capabilities in 1954. He put them to the severest test in the continuing Senate debates over civil rights legislation. From his subsequent perspective, the Civil Rights Act of 1957 was his single greatest legislative achievement. Johnson would have preferred to escape such a test. As never before he was in the spotlight on the most divisive and controversial issue then agitating public diaglogue. More agonizingly, he was caught between the passionate convictions of northern and liberal colleagues and those of an overwhelming popular majority in Texas and in the South as a whole. In this case, compromise seemed all but impossible. Thus, Johnson had to walk a tightrope and to some extent please both sides, or else surrender his budding dreams of a presidential candidacy in 1960. He did it. And however people reacted to the final, watered-down bill, they all had to confess their astonishment at what Johnson had wrought. His leadership clearly made the difference. No other politician in America could have constructed the required coalition needed to pass such a bill in 1957.

Before that year, Johnson had consistently voted against all civil rights bills, including a much-debated administration bill in 1956. Even in 1957, he seemed much more involved in the politics of civil rights than in the moral issues at stake. He had also continuously defended open debate (support of the filibuster) and thus the South's ultimate means of defeating civil rights legislation. But, all along, he had insisted that he was not prejudiced, that he wanted equal opportunities for blacks. He had backed this up by his NYA policies. This does not mean that he was immune to racial stereotypes or that he did not indulge crude jokes about Negroes. Conventional in most ways, he unconsciously reflected most of the views of his race and section. He had always defended his votes on civil rights as a way of upholding state rights and local autonomy. Given his Texas constituents, this stance was all but necessary for election, but he knew it could doom his chances in the national party. Thus, from 1953 on, in subtle ways, he tried to move to a moderate position somewhere between the Senate liberals and his closest southern cronies, such as Russell. Given his political aspirations, his southern allies understood his gradual defection, including his early choice not to become a member of the southern caucus, although in his early Senate career he almost always voted with it.

The civil rights bill of 1957 originated in the Eisenhower administration as an amended version of the proposed 1956 bill. Most Republicans supported it and saw it as an excellent means of splitting the Democratic party. On 18 June the bill passed in the House with a clear sectional majority behind it. The bill, at least for the times, seemed daring in some of its provisions. It provided for a new Commission on Civil Rights, and for a new attorney general to handle civil rights issues. In a controversial Part III, the bill gave the Justice Department significant new powers, including injunctions, to enforce the equal rights guaranteed by the Fourteenth Amendment and thus the power to back up efforts at school integration. Part IV gave the attorney general authority to protect black voting rights as provided by the Fifteenth Amendment. It provided for trials without a jury for those who illegally defied federal authority. While the bill was under consideration in the House, an anxious Johnson tried to find some stand that he could defend in both the North and the South. He assured constituents that he could not support the administration bill, which all the way to the end he described as punitive toward the South. At the same time he warned southerners that new civil rights legislation was now inevitable. The Senate had to act on a bill. National unity and the reputation of the Senate were at stake. If the South blocked any bill at all, then the hostility of the North would force cloture in the Senate and lead to radical civil rights legislation. This would set a fatal precedent on cloture, isolate the South, and leave it vulnerable in the future. By so identifying the issues, Johnson was now free to vote for a mild and less punitive bill, or what he began trying to work out in the Senate in a hot Washington July. His first decision was to vote against, but allow Knowland to win on, a motion to bypass the Senate Judiciary Committee headed by Senator James O. Eastland of Mississippi, where the bill would have died.

On the touchy issue of civil rights, Johnson finally had to take a very public stand. He talked endlessly about how reasonable men had to come up with a reasonable bill that could satisfy the whole country, although not all the expectations of any one group. He argued that it was reasonable to protect black voting rights, but not reasonable to deprive anyone of a jury trial on criminal charges; reasonable to help people in the South devise machinery to solve problems created by the Supreme Court's school desegregation decision of 1954, but not reasonable to enact a force bill directed at only one section of the country. He pushed for a bill that allowed the attorney general to protect voting rights and to punish overt contempt without a jury trial, but not to convict for criminal charges without a jury. This was to join a constitutional amendment to eliminate poll taxes and a new conciliation service to help mediate the integration process in the South, his substitute for a civil rights commission.

Extensive and bitter debate in the Senate led to a series of Johnson-backed amendments, which considerably emasculated the House bill. The surviving bill still provided for a civil rights commission and established a civil rights division in the Justice Department, but no longer included Part III and the enforcement powers of that section. It contained a clever compromise on the voting rights protection under Part IV. This critical compromise originated, in part, among Johnson's legal advisers, including Abe Fortas and Dean Acheson, and among western senators, with Joseph C. O'Mahoney of Wyoming its official author. It provided for jury trials in all criminal contempt actions (rare) and for all large fines or jail sentences under civil contempt, but allowed conviction by judges without juries for ordinary civil contempt (most cases). The crucial votes came on the amendments. Johnson built a strong coalition, centered in the South and West, against Part III, and even gained a begrudging capitulation from Eisenhower. This emasculation carried by fifty-two to thirty-eight. More critical was the jury trial compromise, which passed by fifty-one to forty-two.

He could not have won on these key votes had his southern allies not capitulated at an even more critical point. He persuaded Russell, the key senator, to allow cloture, the first in modern times on a civil rights issue. In a sense, southerners allowed a vote on the bill in order to avoid much stronger ones later. With the compromises all in place, a jubilant Johnson led the final, anticlimactic floor fight. The bill passed by seventy-two to eighteen; a miffed and frustrated Eisenhower reluctantly signed it. Johnson heralded it as a great step forward, good for all Americans, a solution for the problems of 1957. He knew tougher bills would come later. But he had won all his immediate goals—he kept the Democratic party together, prevented deeper sectional conflict, gained enormous publicity for this impossible accomplishment (the first civil rights bill since Reconstruction), and enhanced his chances of a presidential nomination. The bill turned out to be largely ineffective, as Johnson had probably expected. He largely conceived of it as a mild voting rights measure, the one issue that southerners had the most difficulty opposing. It proved inadequate for this goal. But the Commission on Civil Rights played an increasingly significant educational role in a slowly developing civil rights movement and was critical in the maturation of later, tougher bills. As always, Johnson stressed the fact of a bill, not its content. He knew that it opened the door, that in this sense it was more important than any subsequent civil rights legislation.

The achievement of 1957 did not end Johnson's dilemmas over civil rights. The issue would not go away. In the final Eisenhower Congress, Senate liberals joined with the administration in pushing for a stronger bill, one with the enforcement powers contained in Part III. The Eisenhower era was ending. Democrats had to build campaign themes for 1960. Johnson backed a series of educational and welfare measures (federal aid to education, medical care for the aged, a public housing bill, increased minimum wages) that faced determined Republican opposition or a certain Eisenhower veto. The old atmosphere of mutual respect between Johnson and Eisenhower evaporated. In the stalemate, no major legislation had much chance even with Johnson's wizardry. And the one issue that Eisenhower could best use to embarrass Johnson was civil rights. In 1959, Johnson tried to gain a coalition in behalf of a civil rights package stronger than the 1957 bill, yet so mild as not to throw southerners into open rebellion. He failed to get any bill at all and left his liberal colleagues ready to do battle in 1960.

In the 1960 congressional session, advocates of a strong civil rights bill rallied around another administrative version. As the debate raged in February 1960, sit-ins at southern lunch counters, the first of what became a series of civil rights confrontations, added special urgency to the issue. In the same month, Johnson's closest Senate friend, Richard Russell, began a six-week filibuster against the bill, a bill Johnson publicly supported. Johnson was never more frustrated or depressed. Eventually, his critics charged, he talked out of both sides of his mouth. He stressed the limited and defensive nature of such bills to southerners, the strength and the vital new precedents to northerners. Eventually, after amendments led to the end of the filibuster, the Senate passed the Civil Rights Act of 1960 (signed on 6 May). Primarily a voting rights bill, as Johnson preferred to call it and as he continually described it to southerners, it also suffered crippling amendments that made largely ineffective the work of the voting referees it authorized. In a strategy that backfired, Johnson gained presidential nominee John F. Kennedy's support for a rump session of Congress after the nominating conventions. Now fully committed to the Democratic platform and anxious to downplay his sectional image, Johnson supported a strong civil rights bill. He promised more civil rights legislation in the next 4 years than in the last 104 years. In the charged political context, Johnson could not negotiate the compromises necessary to pass any major legislation at all, and the session ended without achievement. But waiting for the new Kennedy-Johnson administration were various versions of civil rights bills that would merge into the momentous Civil Rights Act of 1964.

By 1960, vice-presidential candidate Johnson had moved about as far as possible from his pre-1957 opposition to any and all civil rights bills. What was still lacking, and what he would develop over the next three years, was the moral passion needed to support his campaign promises. So far, at least as indicated by the public record, he had not fully realized and had not internalized the problems of black Americans. Thus, his complex maneuverings until 1960 served other goals, such as proving the ability of the Senate to act on pressing and vital issues. Above all, he had preserved his own aspirations to become a national, not just a sectional, political leader. He was determined not to be another John Nance Garner.

On one glorious issue—space policy—Johnson avoided all the frustrations and dangers of civil rights. As chairman of the Preparedness Subcommittee, he developed an interest, shared by few, in rocket research and space exploration as early as 1949. Such issues remained secondary in defense planning and public consciousness until 4 October 1957, when a tiny Soviet satellite beeped its way around the earth. In itself militarily insignificant, the launching suggested a Soviet lead over the United States in rocketry and possibly even in science and technology. The symbolic impact was incalculable. Little Sputnik provoked an extended critical examination of American achievements in almost all areas, particularly education. It seemed to reinforce a growing crescendo of criticism of American mediocrity, of a plastic, conformist, quantity-oriented culture. No one did more than LBJ to abet, orchestrate, and politically exploit this developing critique.

Johnson's Preparedness Subcommittee, born during the Korean War, conducted major hearings on air power in 1952 and then lapsed into unpublicized routine hearings on military policies and appropriations in the mid-fifties. In 1957 the committee almost alone had the trained staff, and in Johnson the political clout, needed to investigate what was soon known as the missile gap. Johnson recognized the enormous political ramifications. In a typical burst of activity, he formed a special subcommittee on satellite and mission programs, hired Cyrus Vance as special counsel, and launched one of the largest and best conducted congressional investigations in American history. Johnson, in the glare of national publicity, called big names such as Edward Teller and questioned innumerable scientists and defense officials. In typical hyperbole, he talked of the "most serious challenge" to national security in all American history and lamented how woefully behind America was in the "weapons of tomorrow." But, also typically, he interpreted the problem as a challenge, one that Americans could meet in the next few years. Thus, he no sooner added to the cries of alarm than he tried to convert the concern into forceful action. By the end of the hearing, Joseph Alsop could predict that it was at least probable that the "huge Soviet rockets which hurled the Sputniks into the heavens may in the end also hurl Lyndon B. Johnson into the White House."

In early 1958, Johnson's subcommittee rendered its huge and, in most respects, nonpartisan report. It contained a detailed analysis of known facts compiled by the staff from all the expert witnesses. Briefly summarized, the committee report discounted any military significance in the now two Soviet satellites, but rather emphasized the Soviet lead in rocketry, its capability of launching intercontinental ballistic missiles, and its lead in gathering data on outer space. The United States, only even with the Soviet Union in conventional weapons, clearly lagged in rocketry and probably lagged overall in science and technology. The subcommittee stressed the short time the United States had to narrow the gap, and advocated certain immediate responses—a rebuilt fleet of bombers, a speeded-up timetable for the four types of rockets already in development, and a new early-warning network. At a broader level, it suggested a reorganization of the Department of Defense to end service rivalries, increased research and development programs, increased defense appropriations, higher military salaries, a new civil defense shelter program, an increased exchange of scientific intelligence with allies, new but as yet nonspecific educational programs, and, finally, a new civilian effort in outer space.

This final proposal set the stage for a bill, sponsored by Johnson, entitled the National Aeronautics and Space Act of 1958, possibly the most important legislation ever to bear Johnson's name. The act, as approved, created the National Aeronautics and Space Administration, with a board and a civilian director. The new agency, in so many ways an LBJ product, later repaid him by establishing one of its largest facilities near Houston. Meanwhile, Johnson chaired a new committee on aeronautics and space sciences. In 1958 he basked in all the publicity and proudly posed as America's foremost spokesman on space-related issues. The Eisenhower administration appointed him a special delegate to the United Nations in November 1958. There he delivered an eloquent speech, a joint effort by several people and shaped to reflect administration policies, in behalf of a ban on any military weapons in outer space. Americans, he argued, were united in favor of a peaceful use of the heavens. Here, all people could escape the legacies of distrust, fear, and ignorance. Johnson had never been in as much demand as a speaker, and he developed sections of speeches on space that he would continue to deliver all through his vice-presidential years. On this issue, unlike civil rights, he could easily pose as a voice of reason and responsibility and in 1959 and 1960 use his statesmanship on space as a vindication of his on-again, off-again presidential hopes.

As so often in his career, Johnson interspersed periods of intense engagement with low periods of retreat and withdrawal. By 1959, the glory years as majority leader had already passed. The job had soured a bit. In part, Johnson's mounting frustrations reflected the times, the politically charged last years of the Eisenhower era. A politics of display, of posturing, replaced one of achievement, and in this game Johnson was at a disadvantage. As Democrats built larger majorities in the Senate, and thirsted for a successful presidential bid in 1960, Johnson lost much of his earlier power to lead and discipline his own colleagues. Meanwhile, the increasingly beleaguered Republicans gained a new unity and discipline, befitting their defensive posture. All along, Johnson had faced a few carping but ineffectual critics, but now they were able not to challenge his leadership seriously but to squeeze him into a smaller and smaller middle between the Republicans and liberal Democrats. Even early in his job as minority leader, he had suffered the criticism of a handful of liberals and for a period suffered the bitter hostility of columnist Drew Pearson and the maverick Oregon senator, Wayne Morse. But, in his Senate heyday, Johnson eventually won over these two critics and by his sheer power and success gained the grudging cooperation of most self-identified liberals and the fast friendship of a few such as Hubert Humphrey.

No more. In the last Eisenhower Congress, his old critics—Douglas, Kefauver—became a sizable band. Albert Gore, Joseph Clark, Patrick McNamara, Edmund Muskie, and Eugene McCarthy openly defied Johnson and pressed for revised rules that would lessen his dictatorial power. By then, his most insistent critics was a former protégé and friend, William Proxmire of Wisconsin. The mavericks could not win. In a key confrontation in the annual, and increasingly pro forma, Democratic caucus, Johnson easily won a vote of confidence. But, as always, Johnson bent with the wind, and this gave more power to critics than they had any right to expect. He wanted to please everyone; in 1960 this was impossible. The earlier ego trip was about over. The job was no longer fun. Thus, in spite of his poor prospects, Johnson halfheartedly pursued his campaign for the presidential nomination. And, as in 1948, he probably contemplated some career shift; he also talked frequently about retirement in 1960. He probably meant it.

Johnson sensed that his life might be about over. He was only fifty-two in 1960. Yet fears of an early death continuously haunted him. The heart attack in July 1955 had been a somber warning, although perhaps in other ways a blessing. He suffered it on the way to Huntland, his old friend George Brown's estate in Middletown, Virginia, a frequent weekend refuge for him and Lady Bird. Tiredness and excessive irritability had presaged such a life-threatening affliction. Johnson's indulgences in frenzied work as well as food, drink, and tobacco had considerably worsened his chances of avoiding this family heritage. He nearly died as he entered Bethesda Naval Hospital. He remained there for five weeks and in most respects enjoyed a complete recovery, but not without the familiar bouts of depression and hopelessness. At home, and then at the beloved ranch in the fall, he built back toward full health. In fact, when he resumed work in the Senate in January, he seemed to have benefited from the six-month break. He quit smoking, tended to his diet, and at least briefly lowered his weight. For the rest of his life he would be frequently monitored by physicians, and at least at intervals he tried to be more responsible in his personal habits. Lady Bird remained solicitous, a watchdog who tried, often unsuccessfully, to pull him from his work at mealtime and who, with success, persuaded him to take a daily rest. What no one could do was cut down on his work pace, get him to bed on time, or prevail upon him, consistently, to sleep more than three or four hours each night.

Other intimations of his mortality came in 1958. Rebekah, the ever solicitious mother, realized that she had cancer as early as 1956. She last demonstrated her public pride in LBJ's career by a trip to the 1956 Democratic convention. She lingered for two more years. All along, Lyndon had managed her financial affairs. In sentiment, the mother and son remained close. But Lyndon had outgrown his earlier dependence. Their roles reversed. Rebekah died on 12 September 1958. The children buried her, in the beautiful falltime, beside Sam in the family graveyard along the Pedernales.

From all appearances, the Johnson family grew closer after Lyndon's heart attack. Lyndon became more dependent on Lady Bird. Lynda and Luci, as they moved through adolescence, were a constant delight. Luci, in particular, turned out to be an independent, rebellious, witty, sometimes troubled, but fascinating daughter, one never in any way intimidated by her father's position. Lynda, as befitted the older daughter, was more studious, serious, conscientious, conventional. She was a great help to her mother. Even in the Senate years, the family lived in the public arena. Privacy was at a premium. Even when at the ranch, Lady Bird and the girls had to confront and play host to an unending stream of guests. Lyndon wanted it that way. He fed his enormous ego on human relationships. Even in rare moments of potential solitude, he typically used his always present telephone to continue the political game—the enjoyable gossip, the building of support for varied and often small conspiracies, and the endless cultivation of a type of friendship or comradeship. By 1959, this old Johnson game had a new but flickering focus—to gain the Democratic nomination for president in 1960.

7

IN THE SHADOW OF JFK

They were never close friends. In personality they were almost opposites. But they shared a single-minded absorption with party politics, and in the presidential stakes each suffered a major handicap, John F. Kennedy as a Roman Catholic, Lyndon B. Johnson as a southerner. In 1960 their careers converged, first in a brief skirmish for the Democratic nomination and then in the unlikely and, by age and experience, inverted partnership of a successful presidential campaign. For the next three years, Johnson served as a dutiful, subdued vice president, while the Kennedy star alternately waxed and waned. Then came the moments of horror in Dallas in November 1963. Kennedy was dead and LBJ suddenly president.

Johnson and Kennedy began their serious political association in 1952, when the newly elected Massachusetts senator received a congratulatory telephone call from Johnson. As senator, Kennedy remained an outsider, by choice not an aspirant for the Senate inner circle. But he never joined the minority of Johnson baiters. He worked easily with Johnson and, as an appreciative apprentice, turned often to him for political advice or favors. Thus, until 1956 their political aspirations remained fully complementary.

In 1956, both Kennedy and Johnson tested their seemingly still remote presidential possibilities. For both, the most likely path had to lie through the vice presidency; as heirs apparent, they might break through the southern and Catholic barriers. Even in 1952, Johnson had briefly nourished some misplaced hopes of becoming the needed southerner to balance off the Stevenson ticket (he was too young and too little known, and had been too unreliable in supporting Truman's domestic legislation). In 1956, he had gained needed eminence and had an unparalleled record of legislative achievements, but by then he was at odds with Adlai Stevenson. Yet Johnson came to the Chicago convention as a favorite-son presidential candidate, and briefly, with all the illusions appropriate to a convention, he nourished ill-founded hopes that Stevenson might be stopped and that in a resulting scramble he might emerge as a viable presidential candidate. His leadership of the Texas delegation offered a temporary truce among the bitterly contending factions in the Texas Democratic party. As a symbol of southern opposition to Stevenson, Lyndon picked up a scattering of non-Texas endorsements. Among early supporters of this premature effort was Joseph Kennedy, John's wealthy, powerful, but controversial father. Johnson's followers at least acted as if he were a serious contender (Johnson never declared) and came to Chicago singing their silly refrain "Love that Lyndon."

Stevenson, after his nomination, foolishly gave to the convention the choice of the vice-presidential candidate, a strategy that provided the only thrill for an otherwise lackluster convention. Had Johnson desired, he could have enlisted a large group of southern delegates in his behalf. They resented and feared Estes Kefauver, who seemed to have a lead in the early contest. But Johnson could not win and, more important, was bidding for a spot on a ticket that could not win. Also, he needed to break away from a southern and regional identity, not reinforce it. Johnson preferred Humphrey, but could not carry his delegation for such a liberal. In a holding action, Johnson persuaded his delegates to cast their first vote for Governor Frank Clement of Tennessee. Clement then declined the honor and asked his delegates to back Tennesseean senator Albert Gore, ironically leading Johnson to support a Senate enemy. After the first role call, it was apparent that the battle was between Kefauver and Kennedy. Thus, on the second ballot, LBJ grandly cast the Texas vote for Kennedy, but to no avail. Switches by Humphrey and Gore supporters carried the issue for Kefauver on the third ballot. Viewed in retrospect, this may have been a blessing for Kennedy, who had proved his assets in the close battle but yet did not have to take any responsibility for a subsequent Democratic debacle.

In the political buildup for the campaign of 1960, almost everyone listed both Kennedy and Johnson as strong contenders, along with Humphrey, Stuart Symington of Missouri, and Stevenson. Kennedy had to defuse the Catholic issue, Johnson broaden his support beyond the South. By speaking engagements, by careful control over the expenditures of the Senate Democratic Campaign Committee, and by power plays among fellow senators, Johnson seemed to do all he could to improve his chances for the nomination. But, despite such efforts, he insisted until the last possible moment that he was not a candidate. By the early months of 1960, growing numbers of friends or potential supporters came to believe his disavowals and embraced the candidacy of Humphrey or Kennedy. As Kennedy won in primary after primary, Johnson continued to wait, yet he never decisively forbade a continuing clandestine effort in his behalf by close friends. It turned out to be a terrible year to play hard to get. Had he launched a campaign early in 1960, Johnson might have been able to rally a larger stop-Kennedy movement. Delay killed his remote chances. He refused to let his name be placed in any of the primaries, stressing his Senate duties. But he did indulge in a few politically motivated speaking trips and secretly allowed friends to recruit delegates in state caucuses. He also worked to help other Kennedy opponents. After Kennedy won almost all the major primaries, Johnson had to seek ways of preventing his first-ballot victory. Thus, he sought unlikely allies among Humphrey's and Stevenson's supporters. Finally, on 5 July, just three days before he departed for the Democratic convention in Los Angeles, he announced his candidacy.

Why the wait, the months of indecision? Johnson never gave a clear answer. Or, as so often, he gave too many unconvincing answers. As was true of most critical decisions in his career, he never fully understood why he chose as he did. Later rationalizations thus lack conviction. His formal, and politically sensible, reason for an undeclared candidacy was his duties as majority leader in the frustrating but important session in the spring and summer of 1960. Someone had to stay home and mind the store, a rationale that soon took on an anti-Kennedy ring, since Kennedy had been frequently missing for key votes in the Senate. And, indeed, Johnson's Senate position was inconsistent with the ardors of the primary circuit. What he failed to comprehend, what was not as clear to contemporaries as it is today, is how rapidly the rules for Democratic preferment were changing. Key early primary victories, and all the attendant publicity, had become critical for the success of any candidate, particularly one with apparent handicaps, such as Kennedy's Catholicism. Kennedy appreciated this reality even as he helped establish it. His well-planned, well-staffed, and well-financed campaign had practically sewed up the nomination before old-fashioned politicians, such as Johnson, began to wield influence through the party machinery. Johnson neither understood such a long, difficult, state-by-state effort nor had the staff, the time, or the skills needed to pursue it. Even had he declared early, even had he neglected his Senate duties and actively campaigned, it is still doubtful he could have won a single nonsouthern primary.

Johnson knew this. Yet, most of the time, he did want to be president. Every talented politician dreams of such recognition, yearns for such awesome power. Johnson had proven by political success and by his large supply of both talent and energy that he was of presidential caliber. From his college days on, his loyal followers had seen the potential and, in the wake of his enormous ego and personal charisma, had predicted the presidency as a climax to his career. They fed the ultimate ambition. But Johnson knew the odds. In sane moments he chanted the obstacles. In depressed moments he cited his inadequacies. Throughout his career, he shunned losing causes, however much they might appeal to his intellect or, more often, sentiments. He feared failure, at times had an almost fatalistic belief in its inevitability. One protection against failure is to disown any dangerous or fragile or remote goal.

In former campaigns, Johnson had thrown himself completely into the effort, even as he launched each new job with an avalanche of energy. But intense engagement always alternated with periods of retreat and disengagement; periods of hyperactivity with bouts of depression. When faced with possible defeat, he had backed away during each major campaign, suffered illness, tried to withdraw. It is no wonder, when he realistically surveyed his possibilities in the spring of 1960, that he held back, that he seemed immobilized by indecision. He had no proven abilities in a national campaign. The prospects of open competition without a controlling position of strength intimidated Johnson. He remained ambivalent, stymied, futile.

Then why his belated last-minute declaration? This is the hard question. For about a week the old Johnson came back to life. He took over the desperate stop-Kennedy movement. This led him, or at least his supporters, into reckless charges against Kennedy or his father. Briefly, Johnson seemed to indulge unrealistic estimates of his delegate strength and acted the part of a major candidate in Los Angeles. Did he really expect to win? Outside Los Angeles, few observers thought that he had the slightest chance. But in the strange never-never land of the convention, Johnson may momentarily have believed his own publicity. He seemed to bank on the remote possibility that enough delegates might rally around Stevenson and himself to deny Kennedy a first-ballot nomination. A rare impasse might result. After multiple ballots, the frustrated delegates might turn to such an able centrist as LBJ. His declared candidacy, his last-minute rallying of his delegates, alone made this possible. The other possibility, and one probably not as consciously explored, was to prepare a pathway to the vice presidency. Maybe Johnson, now clearly excluded from first place, was willing to settle for second and used his mock campaign, his rallying of the strongest anti-Kennedy elements, to make himself seem indispensable to an ultimate Kennedy victory.

As expected, Kennedy won on the first ballot. This seemed to end Johnson's business in Los Angeles. Although many had talked of a Kennedy-Johnson ticket, which seemed the strongest one possible, almost no one envisioned it as a realistic possibility. Johnson's last-minute effort to stop Kennedy produced reckless charges and innuendos that had infuriated Kennedy's staff. Large segments of the party considered Johnson an unacceptable conservative, whatever the label meant. His southernness and his suspect recent, possibly halfhearted conversion on the issue of civil rights did not allay the fears of blacks. More critical, almost no one believed that a proud LBJ in what seemed a moment of galling defeat would agree to second place on a Kennedy ticket. As one would expect, his staff and supporters now bitterly resented the Kennedys.

Kennedy wanted to win the upcoming election. He knew the pitfalls ahead and at that point could not foresee how ably he would finesse the religious issue. LBJ, Protestant and southern, experienced and powerful, seemed the best available insurance policy. JFK rather easily shrugged off the earlier rhetorical excesses of Johnson and his followers. His advisers pointed out all the advantages of a Kennedy-Johnson ticket, particularly in carrying Texas and a possible majority of southern states. This led Kennedy to a cold and calculating decision—to ask Johnson to consider the vice presidency. Should Johnson decline, which most of the Kennedy staff expected, then Kennedy had lost nothing and could possibly gain more wholehearted and needed Johnson support in the up-coming campaign. Should Johnson accept, then Kennedy's victory prospects in November were enhanced.

Early in the morning after the presidential ballot (on 14 July) Kennedy called LBJ and asked to come to his suite. Johnson knew what was coming and began consultations with friends even before Kennedy arrived at 10:00 A.M. to render the formal invitation. Johnson asked for time to consider it, but to Kennedy's surprise he already seemed persuaded, even eager "to serve." He won over most resistant advisers, including even Sam Rayburn, and formally accepted later in the afternoon, but not until after a confused and now famous episode involving Robert Kennedy.

The news that Johnson would be Kennedy's choice for vice president spread rapidly through the convention. In the aftermath of the heated competition for the nomination, most Kennedy delegates were shocked, some bitter and angry. A few determinedly anti-Johnson delegations, led by the ones from Michigan and the District of Columbia, tried to organize a revolt, even as they brought all possible pressure on Kennedy staffers. At least momentarily, JFK blinked. He feared a divisive climax to the convention and sent his brother to consult with Johnson. What followed is not entirely clear, although historians have scrutinized the event from every possible perspective. Even before Bobby was able to talk to Johnson, the revolt had fizzled. JFK made plans publicly to announce his selection of Johnson. Unaware of this, Bobby informed Johnson of the developing revolt, offered him an opportunity to decline the earlier offer, and clumsily promised him other positions. Johnson angrily, with a typical display of obscenity, refused to withdraw until he knew JFK's preferences. For a proud Johnson, this gesture from Bobby seemed tantamount to repudiation by the Kennedys. He was naturally incensed. So were his closest political friends. But when he finally was able to make contact with Kennedy, he learned that the plan was still on and heard from JFK the proposed announcement he would shortly make public. Needless to say, Johnson never forgave Bobby Kennedy for his inept political maneuver and never understood or accepted the fact that Bobby was only trying to do his brother's bidding.

Why did Johnson agree to be vice president? Since his decision seemed to make no sense, it has continued to puzzle historians. As always, the answers have to be speculative. The least likely explanation is that Johnson carefully weighed all his options and then made a calculated decision, one keyed either to his political ambition, with this as a possible pathway to the presidency, or to his sense of how he could best serve his party or his country. Few people so make critical and forced decisions, least of all LBJ. One unprovable theory comes closest to such calculation—that he used his belated but already foredoomed presidential bid as leverage for gaining the second prize, the only one reliably open to him. It can hardly be that simple, although Johnson surely recognized this as at least a remote possibility. The call from Kennedy was neither a complete surprise nor in any way misinterpreted by Johnson.

Other considerations make more sense. He had burned himself out in the current sessions of the Senate. He had displayed his old proclivity for withdrawal by frequent threats to resign, to return to his ranch. The frustrations of that summer seemed mild to those that probably lay ahead, either under a much-feared Richard Nixon or under a Democratic Kennedy, who would assume the key role in legislative leadership and leave Johnson with the unenviable task of supporting all administrative policies. In other words, LBJ was open to a new challenge, one quite different from those in his existing job. Every new opportunity in his life had recharged his batteries, sent him off on frenzied but always successful bouts of work and achievement. He was also always aware of issues of status. A country boy from the Pedernales could not help but be moved by the eminence, by the formal standing if not the real power, of a vice president, who is but a heartbeat from the presidency.

Equally important was another pattern in his whole career—a desire to assume a leadership role if possible, but otherwise a willingness to wait, to accept a dutiful, subservient, or apprentice role under those who enjoyed authority. He took seriously issues of loyalty and chains of command. He would have had a hard time turning down a request by any presidential nominee. His habitual response, almost by now an instinctual reflex, was to say yes, to serve. His whole life had been one of dutiful service to his various families. If anyone, either with authority over him or in his care, loved him, relied on him, trusted him, honored him, then Johnson never had the ability to say no, whether the situation required him to be a dutiful son or allowed him to be a big daddy. He did not want to sacrifice personal affection, lose close ties, destroy communities of sentiment and trust. Despite the gulf of age and experience, Johnson, as soon as Kennedy had the nomination, viewed him in a new light—as chief, boss, leader. He always honored and obeyed, whether gladly or ruefully, those in power. Kennedy's making Johnson his first choice, his coming to Johnson's room, were immensely flattering. Pleased and grateful, Johnson could not rebuff such a gesture. Thus, for one final interlude, Johnson radically shifted roles from leadership to dutiful subordination. As it turned out, the shift exacted enormous personal costs. He soon hated his new role. But he never publicly broke ranks, lapsed from his assigned role, or openly challenged the institutional arrangements that led one with so powerful an ego to have to suffer the vice presidency. This was his burden, his sacrifice, for which he expected thanks, praise, and future preferment.

As nominee of the national party, Johnson immediately made clear his wholehearted support of its platform. Flexible as always, he fully honored this commitment, and soon he meant all that he preached, even on the issue of civil rights. He had finally and fully emancipated himself from the state rights majority of Texas Democrats, from those who now hurled accusations of treason against him. Coordinating the campaign with Kennedy led to moments of tension and feelings on Johnson's part of being left out or slighted. He remained outside the already large but tight and exclusive Kennedy circle. Kennedy recognized Johnson's ego, his sensitivity, and did his best to include him and to use his unique talents. In fact, Johnson had little to offer in the development of overall campaign strategy. Here Kennedy was the expert; after an arduous primary campaign, he was much more knowledgeable than Johnson about regional and state politics. Back in Washington Johnson was the expert, but this knowledge was of little help in organizing a winning campaign. He soon realized this and often did as he was asked, although at times, in ways that had no lasting effect on the campaign, he almost petulantly asserted his independence in choosing speech sites and days. He wanted friendly crowds, seemed wary of speaking engagements in the North (the lair of all those who had opposed his selection as vice president), and thus did his most effective campaigning in the South. In a strategy that he used so often after 1963, he continually preached sermons on unity, on the commonalities that bound together North and South, black and white, liberals and conservatives, and, most important in this particular campaign, Protestants and Catholics.

The Kennedy-Johnson ticket won in a surprisingly tight race. A few voter shifts in Illinois and a loss of less than fifty thousand votes in Texas would have given the victory to Richard Nixon. The close contest lent credence to what soon became a common assumption—that Johnson's candidacy made the crucial difference, that Kennedy would have lost had he chosen any other vice president. This interpretation seems plausible enough, but is unproven and unprovable. In much of the South, Johnson was clearly more acceptable than any other of the frequently mentioned vice-presidential possibilities. As it turned out, the South was critical to the Democratic victory. But it is far from clear how much Johnson's presence helped the ticket even in Texas. Those most inclined to vote for Johnson would have voted Democratic in any case. His enemies were more bitter than ever, and the polls showed a close race to the very end. Two incidents helped—Kennedy's highly successful appearance before Protestant ministers in Houston on 12 September and a much publicized, even life-threatening harassment of LBJ and Lady Bird by right-wing fanatics in Dallas's Adolphus Hotel on 4 November. This ugly crowd, with nasty placards and continuous insults, so impeded the path of a calm Johnson and a frightened Lady Bird that it took them a half hour to cross the lobby and retreat to the second floor. The incident redeemed Johnson even among liberals, acutely embarrassed southerners, and elicited a sympathy vote that may, in itself, have accounted for the small victory margin in Texas.

Kennedy and Johnson made up an unlikely pair. Although in background and personality they were near opposites, they respected each other. Kennedy, by the fact of his position, had no reason to be jealous of Johnson and in all public forums tried to be magnanimous and generous toward a complex person whom he never quite understood. The relationship thus remained correct, formal, but never matured into a close friendship. Johnson nourished plenty of small resentments. He could not but be jealous of Kennedy's popularity, the adulation he seemed to attract by such small investments of work and achievement. Johnson literally slaved for his various publics, yet they never seemed to love him to the same extent. But, again outwardly, Johnson remained loyal and developed a quite genuine appreciation for Kennedy's skills as a politician. He won the presidency against considerable odds. Such artistry always impressed Johnson.

Despite a veneer of greater intellectual sophistication and a surface suggestion of cultural refinement, Kennedy joined Johnson in an almost single-minded devotion to political issues, to problems of policy and the means of achieving policy goals. They shared little else. Kennedy displayed an aloofness, a detachment, some said a coldness completely alien to a sentimental and effusive Johnson. This meant that Kennedy was not as full of himself, not as vulnerable, not as insecure. He was more open to self-criticism and more easily indulged wit, even of a self-deprecating variety. He knew himself better. He was more open to irony, more cynical. He came closer to developing his own coherent identity. He was not so dependent on the signals from others, not so anxious to win respect or gratitude. He could be ruthless. Not so Johnson. Kennedy could be discriminating, selective. Not so Johnson, who always wanted everything and to be loved by everyone, and who always tried to avoid exclusive choices.

Kennedy brought to the surface Johnson's deepest insecurities and sense of inferiority. Johnson fought his way up the political ladder. He had neither birth nor charisma to camouflage his political ambitions. Earlier, Roosevelt could use his patrician birth to seem, in some sense, above the political game. Kennedy had inherited wealth and good looks, and created a myth of style, polish, and taste. Compared to this, a homely LBJ, with his reputation for wheeling and dealing, with his new and possibly tainted riches, with his egotistic preening, with his hill country background, with his homely idiom and corny homilies, seemed close to a courthouse politician and possibly a crooked one at that. Johnson had few social graces, remained conventional in most areas of taste, lacked intellectual sophistication in most theoretical areas, and was given to overstatement or gaudy exhibitionism. He was thus intimidated by Kennedy and by many of Kennedy's staff. He could not talk about recent literature or current movies. Abstract issues left him cold. He was never fashionable, in dress or in cocktail chitchat. Thus, he exaggerated the intellectuality of Kennedy advisers, particularly those from Harvard, and also their purported, and again much exaggerated, cultural attainments. He conceded too much, for Camelot was more superficial than profound, more fashionable than authentic. But Johnson had none of the talents needed for such a judgment. He took it all for real and thus often felt, and then tended to exaggerate, his provincial roots.

But, as he soon realized, Johnson remained the artist, the accomplished expert, on the legislative process. He knew he was much better prepared to be president than Kennedy. Thus, even as he suffered from his sense of inferiority or lamely tried to ape the manners of the Kennedys, he often compensated by a form of arrogance. As Kennedy's legislative program floundered in Congress, Johnson came to believe that he was linked to a group of rank amateurs who were not as capable of functioning effectively in Washington as he would have been in a Harvard classroom. When he judged them in terms of practical know-how, in real achievement, these new boys, these eastern intellectuals (actually, few on Kennedy's White House staff had credentials as first-rate intellectuals) were completely incompetent. Then he tended to put them down, often unfairly. In moments of achievement, in magnanimity, he could relate well to technical experts in almost any field. But when beleaguered, frustrated, or depressed, he tended to lump experts and brilliant thinkers or creative artists together as his enemies. He thought they all had contempt for him, that they failed to appreciate his skills and thus were out to get him.

Even the wives entered into the complex Kennedy-Johnson relationship. Jacqueline Kennedy, with her beauty and a type of finishing-school refinement (language skills, artistic taste), proved a useful backdrop or adornment for Kennedy. Actually, Jackie was out of place in the White House, temperamentally averse to party politics, and in that context fully as vulnerable and insecure as LBJ was among those he called intellectuals. Poor Jackie was an ornament but otherwise rather helpless, tied down by an unlikely and emotionally unrewarding marriage, and in her unhappiness given to almost neurotic bouts of spending or lavish entertainments. Yet Johnson was jealous. Given to displays of all sorts, he would have liked to have just such an adornment, even as he tended to employ physically attractive secretaries and have them on display in his office. Lady Bird was never such an ornament, never a Jacqueline, although the two women shared a training in journalism. Lady Bird slowly gained on her own the social graces, the refinements of taste, that befit her position. Compared to Jackie, she seemed almost as dull and commonplace as did Johnson in the wake of JFK. But Lady Bird was an indispensable adviser and protector of her husband, often fully as cagey and as informed on issues as he was. She had substance, not form; strength of character, not polish; grace and compassion, not style. And, by all the evidence, the Johnson marriage, at least by 1960, was closer and more fulfilling than that of the Kennedys.

Johnson was quickly disillusioned with his role as vice president. He had hoped to upgrade the office. Most vice presidents have nourished the same illusory hopes. And, in a sense, Johnson did enlarge the duties of the vice president, even in the case of his civil rights activities in ways that stretched the constitutional definition of his office. But given his ego, his energy level, this was never enough. For the first time in his life, a new position did not lead to intense involvement and unprecedented early achievements. Apparently, he had expected to take on a rather innocuous job and so expand it as to make it critically important. But in this case institutional realities blocked his early efforts. He soon gave up and entered one of his periods of withdrawal and disengagement. He became depressed, irritable, irrational in his demands upon his staff, even as he gained weight, indulged in too much food and drink, and thus risked another heart attack.

Perhaps more than he expected, Johnson lost almost all his former power in the Senate. As vice president he had the constitutional duty of presiding over sessions and of voting in case of a tie. Because of either travel or lack of interest, he would seldom exercise this role. His former whip and protégé, Mike Mansfield took over his old job as majority leader. He graciously allowed Johnson to keep his old majority leader's office, the gaudy Taj Mahal. Mansfield also retained Bobby Baker as majority secretary. Before the adjournment of the old Congress and with Johnson's concurrence, Mansfield asked his senatorial colleagues to allow Vice President Johnson to continue to chair the Democratic caucus. This, on top of all the other continuities, seemed a clear bid by Johnson to retain at least a portion of his role as majority leader. Although the caucus had no constitutional status, this proposal threatened seriously to compromise the separation of the executive and legislative branches. Several senators pointed this out, and even close friends of Johnson joined a minority who voted against such an unprecedented arrangement. Although the vote was still in favor of Johnson, he refused to accept the now sullied honor, and with no real power and no longer part of the club, he more or less withdrew, physically and emotionally.

This meant that if he were to have any power, he had to find it within the office of the vice presidency. But, traditionally, the only role here had been formal and ceremonial. Already the jokes abounded about vice-presidential trips to attend state funerals. Johnson did play this formal role, and better than one might have expected. He and Lady Bird even sold their old home and purchased a nearby mansion (the Elms) from hostess Pearl Mesta, turning it into a small but well-staffed official mansion. They entertained more formally and more lavishly than ever before. But Johnson wanted more. He could never thrive on the mere surface glitter of power. He wanted to shape policies. And this desire, this need, ran aground on the realities of his office. As a new administration began, Johnson proposed to Kennedy an array of responsibilities that seemed to fit his talents. He wanted a free hand in these areas and hoped the White House staff would report directly to him. Kennedy knew such a plan would not work and ignored the request. The vice president could not hold a coordinate office, not without confusion over authority and a lack of accountability. Only the president could be in charge.

Johnson soon accepted this. And tempermentally ill-equipped to be an adviser without power, he once again retreated. He had his office in the White House and received at least polite treatment from the Kennedy staff, but he played almost no role in determining policy. Kennedy honored his position, tried to keep him fully informed on several foreign policy issues, frequently asked his opinion, and insisted that he attend meetings of the National Security Council. But Johnson seemed uninterested, uninvolved, even at times uninformed. He almost never joined the discussions or made independent recommendations. He was quiet, answering questions in monosyllables and mumbling when he did talk. The loudest and most aggressive politician in Washington now seemed to be a mild, ineffective subordinate. The frequent question soon became a joke: whatever happened to LBJ? In most respects, such a nonrole aided Kennedy. Johnson, in his intense, involved, aggressive mood, would have been hard to control in any administration.

In the critical area of foreign policy, Johnson had no discernible voice or impact. His contribution was almost entirely limited to his reports back from his foreign trips. He loyally defended every Kennedy initiative, and in October 1962, at the time of the Cuban missile crisis, Johnson seemed fully to support one of the most reckless and dangerous foreign policy decisions ever taken by an American president—the naval blockade of Soviet ships. As in his earlier career, he continued to fear the Soviet Union and to support policies intended to contain any Soviet expansion or, as in Cuba, to counter Soviet tactics aimed at increased prestige. He remained captive to the purported lessons of Munich and Korea. Although much less adverturesome in personality than Kennedy, reluctant to fight, averse to conflict, he always saw limited forms of deterrence as a means of preventing a third world war.

In one critical area—legislative strategy—Johnson's withdrawal proved almost disastrous. For reasons not always clear, he played almost no role at all in congressional liaison. Bill after bill floundered in Congress without a stir from an almost somnolent LBJ. The confident Kennedy staff either felt no need for Johnson's help or resented him, and thus they came to doubt his now well-hidden ability. That he was so rarely asked for help hurt him deeply. He felt an outsider, rebuffed, unappreciated. For one of his personality, for one who searched for signs of approval and recognition, such a seeming rejection prompted him to do nothing, perhaps even secretly to rejoice whenever the Kennedy crowd failed, which was frequently on major and highly controversial bills.

Subdued, a virtual nonentity in the White House, Johnson came closest to being himself in the three areas where he had primary responsibilities—in supporting the growing space program, in directing a new President's Committee on Equal Employment, and in acting as a roving ambassador abroad. Since Johnson was the legislative father of the National Aeronautics and Space Administration (NASA), Kennedy appropriately gave him full leeway in monitoring and boosting the growing space program. Johnson did this through a formal appointment as chairman of the Space Council. Here, as in few other areas, he had a right to approve all key appointees. For head of NASA, he selected James E. Webb, a protégé of his friend Bob Kerr and an executive at Kerr-McGee oil company. As his first initiative, he hired three corporate executives to make a detailed study of the space program. Out of this came new spending requests and an accelerated timetable for space exploration. Kennedy fully endorsed the recommendations, out of which came his much publicized commitment to land a man on the moon by the end of the decade. Johnson took as his responsibility the public lobbying for more support and more funds for his agency. Space was his most frequent, and preferred, topic in the many speeches he gave around the country, speeches written by Reedy or Busby in response to LBJ's directions. Unfortunately, in his subdued vice-presidential years, Johnson tended to deliver such speeches in a low monotone, with a dignity he seemed to think proper for his office. In short, he bored most audiences.

In the fullness of time, Johnson's two most remembered contributions may well involve his roles in space exploration and in civil rights. But the deeply entrenched barriers to equal rights for blacks were much harder to breach than those that had heretofore restricted man to one planet. That Johnson became the one most important architect of revolutionary civil rights legislation may appear as the supreme irony of his career, given his roots and his early determined opposition to even mild civil rights legislation. Critical to his later role, possibly indispensable to it, were his activities as vice president. When he accepted the nomination in 1960, both he and Kennedy realized that he had to defuse his image as a southerner, and also a widespread and in part justified assumption that his Senate role in promoting civil rights had been motivated either by personal ambition or by the desire to block stronger legislation. Johnson was again on the spot. But now emancipated from Texas constituents, he seemed anxious to make all the required verbal gestures. Even this did not persuade his liberal opponents. Thus, Kennedy and Johnson agreed during the campaign that Johnson would head a new President's Committee on Equal Employment (PCEE). This committee, which dealt only with federal agencies or government contractors, was established by executive order and required no congressional approval. It turned out to be the beginning of an enduring federal effort to achieve equality in job opportunities and was the predecessor of what became, after the Civil Rights Act of 1964, the Equal Employment Opportunities Commission (EEOC).

Johnson helped plan the PCEE. Various advisers, including Abe Fortas, matured the executive order that established the committee. Its membership included almost all heads of departments (Interior, Labor, Commerce, Defense) and agencies (Civil Service Commission, General Services Administration, Bureau of the Budget, NASA) that were most directly involved with large numbers of government workers or that monitored government contracts with private firms. Johnson chaired the committee. As a part-time job, the assistant secretary of labor acted as vice chairman, and under him was a full-time executive vice president or director, the person immediately responsible for staff and the routine work. The committee recommended affirmative steps to government agencies in behalf of nondiscrimination and required provisions in every government contract to prevent discrimination because of race, creed, color, or national origin. Each agency head, or contractor, was required to take affirmative action to fulfill this goal in recruitment, employment, promotions, transfers, and layoffs, and in bestowing all raises or selecting for training and apprenticeship. The committee required compliance reports from both agencies and companies, and asked government departments for frequent surveys on the use of existing employees. Government contractors were expected to use any possible means to get cooperation from unions and faced what seemed to be severe penalties for noncompliance, ranging from the cancellation of part or all of a contract to a loss of eligibility for future government contracts (the blacklist).

From the beginning of the committee, Johnson preferred persuasion to penalties. This invited criticism and complaints from those who expected Johnson to use his ultimate weapons, including the blacklist. He never used it once and never revoked a single contract, although he frequently threatened to do so. The first assistant secretary of labor and thus vice chairman of the committee, Jerry R. Holleman, was a former Texas AFL-CIO president, but not a Johnson crony, since he represented the assertive liberal faction among Texas Democrats. Holleman and an executive vice president hired from Michigan's Fair Employment Practices Commission preferred a tougher stance toward corporate contractors. Attorney General Robert Kennedy, who faced incessant demands from civil rights leaders, quickly grew impatient with Johnson's gradualist approach and with his demands for faster results increased Johnson's resentment toward him. Although the policy differences seemed to reflect a reluctance on Johnson's part to antagonize southern friends like Richard Russell, the issue was one of method, not of goals. As always, Johnson wanted to create as few enemies as possible, gradually shift people's outlook, and in the long term gain nondiscrimination without conflict. He stressed the positive, the gains achieved, the cumulative statistics on compliance.

In 1962, Johnson reorganized a quarreling PCEE staff. Holleman, tainted by a scandal involving Texas promoter Billy Sol Estes, had to resign. To replace him, Johnson hired an old friend, Hobart Taylor, Jr., who had been born in Texas. Taylor, a black lawyer already on Johnson's staff, had helped write the original executive order. Johnson and Taylor launched a veritable crusade in behalf of nondiscrimination. Johnson announced a new organization of cooperating firms, which he called the Plan for Progress. He seemed to take his cues from a fellow Texan and namesake, Hugh Johnson, and all the puffery of the early depression National Recovery Administration. By November of 1963, Johnson proudly boasted that 104 firms had joined the Plan for Progress, which meant that they had worked out a plan to fulfill all the committee guidelines. These, incidentally, did not include sex as a category of discrimination. Johnson wanted to publicize the public commitment involved in signing and to get a bandwagon going. If enough major contractors signed, then the pressures would mount for all to sign, and by a psychological ploy he might engineer a revolution in employment practices without the use of coercion. This goal was much more important than any highly publicized prosecution of violators. For them, Johnson used bribes if possible, threats when necessary, to get compliance and to correct problems. He wanted to gain, as quietly as possible, a reformed outlook and eventual compliance with the spirit as well as the letter of the law. For those who cooperated and signed on to his plan, Johnson promised favorable publicity and celebrity treatment. In January 1963, with great fanfare, he held a banquet in the White House for 250 representatives of companies that had signed the plan. Eighty-five member companies sent representatives, as did seventy-five potential members.

Seniority rules enforced by unions led to many violations. Since Johnson had no legal means to coerce unions, in the summer of 1963 he addressed a national conference of union leaders and, with obvious sincerity, tried to motivate them voluntarily to accept fair employment practices. He also developed ingenious techniques for influencing federal agencies, and in Los Angeles he brought local employers and the school board together to see if vocational education for minorities might be coordinated with local job needs.

Whether Johnson's positive strategies worked best or not, they carried a political risk. From the lunch counter sit-ins of 1960 to the freedom rides of 1961 to massive voter registration drives in 1962 to Martin Luther King's huge march on Washington in 1963, the organized civil rights movement grew exponentially year by year. It created intense pressure for public action. The Kennedy administration moved cautiously toward new federal intervention, even as it pushed unsuccessfully for a major civil rights bill in 1963. In this context, Johnson's love feast with corporate executives, his endless speeches full of moral suasion, and his aversion to tough enforcement seemed out-of-date, even politically damaging. But one charge was by now clearly unfair—that Johnson was not personally and morally committed to equal opportunity, that all his cheerleading on the committee was a public gesture merely to give an appearance of government action. From Hobart Taylor and others who listened to his sermons came one unanimous conclusion: Vice President Johnson was passionately committed to civil rights.

In part, Johnson's job created the concern. As always, when he gave himself to a task, he identified with his constituency and soon absorbed its outlook. Blacks became his primary constituents as vice president. Equally important, he worked continuously with the objects of the most blatant forms of discrimination. For the first time in his life, he looked at America from the black perspective. His corny stories about his black cook and the indignities she suffered in an automobile trip across the South were one way of personalizing the crisis. The growing demonstrations and protests, and some early violence, also affected him. Every violent repression of blacks pointed up injustices in American society. The anger of the protesters showed the bitter unhappiness of a whole class of American citizens. Deeper divisions, more violence, seemed a likely outcome. The racial issue had become the greatest challenge to the United States and to its political system. Johnson had spent a lifetime identifying and solving problems. Here was a big one, for which he had a special responsibility. Once again, as the big daddy of American politics, he had to make all his children happy. Thus, his consistent approach to the problem—gain justice, give blacks their birthright, and do it with as little conflict as possible. He tried to gain a new consensus that would bridge white and black differences.

The most critical government response included a major new civil rights bill. This gradually became a Kennedy administration priority, perhaps the highest priority by the summer of 1963. Unfortunately, Johnson was not vitally involved in the legislative effort. Once again, the inherent limitations of his office would probably have rendered him ineffective even had he been a more active strategist in the White House. He helped the cause indirectly, however. His origins as a southerner lent his numerous speeches on civil rights special impact. Even in the 1960 campaign, he had preached to southern audiences on the need for equal rights and had demanded the seating of blacks on speaking platforms. As the congressional fight heated up in the spring of 1963, Johnson traveled to Gettysburg for a special Memorial Day speech in the centennial year of that critical Civil War battle and the famous address by Lincoln that followed. His speech writers prepared an almost eloquent address, one subtly keyed to some of Lincoln's famous phrases. As always when moral passion lay behind his words, Johnson's speaking style matched the content. He began: "One hundred years ago, the slave was freed. One hundred years later, the Negro remains in bondage to the color of his skin." He stressed that Americans do not "answer those who lie beneath this soil—when we reply to the Negro by asking, 'patience.' " America would have to yield up its destiny of greatness among the civili-

165

zations of history unless white and black set about resolving the present challenge. This led to his forceful peroration: "Until justice is blind to color, until all education is unaware of race, until opportunity is unconcerned with the color of men's skins, emancipation will be a proclamation but emancipation will not be a fact."

Just after his Gettysburg speech, Johnson talked by phone with Theodore Sorensen, Kennedy's special counsel and speech writer. A cassette recording of their amazing exchange has survived. A surprised, almost overwhelmed Sorensen had no chance to talk, but only interjected an occasional "yes, sir." The subject was the pending civil rights bill. Johnson offered an informal lesson on how to get bills passed. Although directed at Sorensen, his message was for Kennedy, a message from an expert to a bumbling amateur. Johnson believed Kennedy, if he handled Congress correctly, could get a strong bill in 1963. The timing and pacing of the effort would be critical. Kennedy should first force Congress to act on other, less sensitive legislation, particularly the vital tax cut, and then hook up all the horses for civil rights. Johnson believed Kennedy should open with a good speech (he even suggested some of the wording), possibly delivered in Mississippi, one that would establish the moral issues, win over the church people, and drive the demagogues and bigots into a hole. Kennedy had to inform and inspire the nation, had to look people in the eye and state the moral and religious issues. Southerners might disagree, but they would respect his courage. Kennedy might lose the South in 1964, but so be it. He might have lost it already. And he must not play politics with this issue. He had to make clear that the government was on the side of the Negro, who was tired of piecemeal action, and persuade blacks of this commitment by dramatic and convincing action, such as support for more jobs and for new educational programs. So far, Kennedy had failed to mobilize the required coalition and to get the needed help from Republicans, nor had he used such leverage as a Lockheed contract to soften southern resistance. A high, lofty appeal could do it. After all, look how Johnson had been able to press the civil rights issue in the South. With a bit of pride showing, he recommended that Kennedy make a speech like his at Gettysburg in the South, possibly in San Antonio. Unknowingly, he had suggested the legislative strategy that he as president would use a year later in behalf of the Civil Rights Act of 1964.

In at least the two areas of space and civil rights, then, Johnson's vice presidency was unusually productive. But compared to his usual work pace and his legislative involvements of the preceding decade, these tasks required only a small share of his energies. To him, he was all but idle, relatively useless, and thus frequently bored. Trips abroad at least relieved the monotony. During his years as vice president he made eleven official trips. No previous vice president had traveled so much. With two exceptions, the trips were not of such importance as to boost Johnson's ego. His first junket to Senegal in April 1961, as part of a celebration of its independence, was all too typical. As in subsequent trips, Johnson asked to mingle with the people, visited a native village, and exchanged gifts with its chief. He went as the official representative of the United States or of the Kennedy administration. Unspoken, but clear, however, was the fact that he represented the United States whenever the occasions or the issues involved were not of sufficient importance to justify a presidential visit, or whenever Kennedy could not possibly leave the country. Even the frequency of administrative requests for Johnson to travel symbolized how marginally he was involved in major domestic and foreign policy decisions. No inconveniences followed on his being out of the country.

His longest and most important trip came early—in May 1961. This took him around the world, with official visits in the Philippines, the Republic of China, Vietnam, Thailand, India, and Pakistan. The primary reason for the trip was a deteriorating situation in Laos and South Vietnam. He tried to evaluate the U.S. position in Southeast Asia, visited with Premier Diem in Saigon, wrote a detailed report for Kennedy, and prepared a statement for his subsequent appearance before a House committee. The Saigon visit deepened his earlier, almost reflexive support for an increased American commitment in Indochina. He enjoyed his talks with Diem and came to admire his courage in resisting an insurgency backed by North Vietnam, but he believed that Diem was too aloof from the people. On the other hand, he was the most reliable leader the United States had in Vietnam, and Americans could either support him with enthusiasm or let South Vietnam fall to the Communists. He found no desire or present need for American troops, but stressed that the United States should never renounce such support as a future eventuality. His report, and his support for increased aid for Diem, played at least a small role in encouraging the Kennedy administration drastically to upgrade the level of American commitment, particularly military advisers, in South Vietnam.

In Vietnam, as in his subsequent and well-received stop in India, Johnson acted the part of a politician. He mingled with crowds of people, shaking hands as if he were a candidate for local office. In Pakistan he met and invited for an American visit a camel driver. Johnson would subsequently escort him around the United States as if he were a dignitary, all with plenty of publicity. Johnson reacted pointedly to some press criticism of his folksy style and his mingling with people. He said that Americans needed to outgrow all their nonsense about inscrutable Asians: "The only generalization that I am going to accept is that these Asians are just like you and I are, and that they share the same hopes and dreams." They desired more rice, better homes, good schools, freedom from disease, and a place of dignity under the sun. Americans could not persuade them how our free institutions would help secure such benefits, when "our representatives fly over in an air-conditioned plane, jump into an air-conditioned limousine, ride to an air-conditioned palace to talk to an air-conditioned prince, and then flit home pretending to have conquered the world." Our ambassadors had to get their homburgs dirty, walk the streets and byways, and show America as a dynamic country dedicated to change and to social justice.

Symbolically, Johnson's most important trip was to West Berlin on 19 August 1961. He came to show American solidarity just after Soviet officials had sealed off the Eastern zone and had begun erecting the infamous Berlin Wall. Kennedy could not come to Berlin at this tense and gloomy moment. He thus requested, almost begged, Johnson to do it. Surprisingly, Johnson almost refused and resented some successful arm-twisting by Robert Kennedy. But once there he performed magnificently, in what turned out to be the most fervent reception he ever encountered in all of his travels (a million people lined the streets to greet him and General Lucius Clay). His speech writers prepared a simple but eloquent statement. He pledged "our lives, our fortunes, and our sacred honor" to the defense of the freedom of West Berlin at a time of crisis reminiscent of the Berlin blockade of 1948.

Unfortunately, his other journeys lacked the drama of Berlin or the diplomatic significance of his fact-finding mission to Saigon. Eventually, he also visited Jamaica, the Dominican Republic, Lebanon, Spain, France, Britain, Italy, the Middle East (Iran was the target, but he stopped in Cyprus and Turkey), all the Scandinavian countries, and, just before Kennedy's assassination, the Benelux countries. State Department reports on the trips noted his penchant for informality, for visiting ordinary people, and for always falling behind schedule, but generally concluded that Johnson won new friends for the United States. What the official reports neglected were the sleepless nights suffered by American diplomats in arranging and guiding his visits, the constant concern of the Secret Service for his safety, and the numerous small embarrassments occasioned by his late arrivals for appointments or his capricious decisions. Generally, he best served our foreign policy goals in underdeveloped countries, where his style, somewhere between a village politician and a western cowboy, helped create a more open and inviting image of the United States. His interest, his concern about human welfare, came through quite clearly. In the sophisticated countries of Europe, particularly in Scandinavia and the Low Countries, his breakaway excursions into the often disappointingly small crowds still created a bit of bond with the ordinary people. They seemed to respond to his almost corny approach. But journalists ridiculed him, students noted the simplistic nature of his speeches, and sophisticates laughed at such gestures as a Texas barbecue he prepared for three thousand guests in Finland. Officials were often unimpressed, tending to underestimate his intelligence and ability. His European trips did not enhance his image when he became president.

For Johnson, the trips abroad were ego boosters. Temporarily, he broke free from the constraints he faced in Washington, from the daily self-discipline he had to impose on himself in the Kennedy White House. Thus, particularly in his first trips, he reverted to the old, energetic, free-wheeling LBJ and seemed to gain a new self-confidence from the large crowds. People, most of all lowly people, as in India or Pakistan, posed no threat to his ego. They were open, eager to receive his approval, grateful for small favors. Above all else, Johnson liked to give gifts; he took all types on his trips, including gilt cards with his name, which he handed out to youngsters. But his travels also brought out the worst side of his character. Frequently, he acted like a spoiled brat, angry at the smallest inconvenience, a stickler about personal details, overly sensitive to apparent slights, and impossibly demanding about private comfort (a special bed, his own large pillows, the right scotch). From the perspective of his staff, or the American officials who had to make all the local arrangements, he was an egomaniac, acting more like a petulant emperor than the simple friend of the people he projected to his audiences.

Johnson had no sooner returned from the Netherlands than he

joined in the planning of a special presidential visit to Texas. In many ways, the trip amounted to an early investment in the 1964 campaign. Ostensibly, it was part of a Democratic National Committee fund-raising effort. In fact, it represented an effort to drum up support for the administration in Texas and to get more unified support from the always divided state party. In November 1963, the Kennedy administration was in political trouble, particularly in Texas and the South. In a sense, the trip also amounted to a Kennedy vote of confidence in Johnson. Although Kennedy had always denied any hint of it, LBJ remained insecure, afraid that he might be dropped as vice-presidential candidate in 1964. This view gained more support from recent, much publicized charges against his friend and former Senate secretary, Bobby Baker. In low moments, he saw the investigation of Baker as part of the handiwork of Bobby Kennedy, and at times he imagined all manner of conspiracies against him.

The trip, on the surface, seemed to pay off, with large and surprisingly friendly crowds in Houston and San Antonio on 21 November. Kennedy first spoke at Fort Worth on the morning of 22 November and then moved on to Dallas for a midday appearance in the heart of Texas Republicanism and old guard Democracy, the site of the near assault on Johnson only three years earlier. Even here, the crowds seemed friendly as the motorcade moved toward the western edges of downtown. Johnson's limousine followed behind Kennedy's, which included Jacqueline and the host governor, John Connally, and his wife. At about 12:30, as the lead car turned a corner in front of the Texas Schoolbook Depository, came the horrible, memorable moment. Of the three rifle shots, one so shattered Kennedy's brain as to leave him legally dead. Unknown to Johnson, who was pushed to the floor of his limousine by a Secret Service agent, he inherited at that moment the duties of president of the United States. A half hour later physicians declared JFK dead. The news reached President Johnson about 1:30. At 2:40P.M., on Air Force One, with the body of Kennedy on board and in the presence of Kennedy aides and a blood-besmirched Jacqueline Kennedy, Johnson recited the oath of office before his friend, Judge Sarah Hughes.

Delayed by the oath taking, Air Force One finally flew President Johnson back to Washington. So suddenly as to be all but incomprehensible, Johnson's role had shifted once again from discipleship to leadership—not according to his ambition, not to match any earlier fantasies, but in a moment of horror. Later, Johnson tried to chart not only his actions but his thoughts during that momentous day. Such self-serving reconstructions are worthless. Above all else, he must have been numbed. Kennedy was not close. In no deep sense could Johnson have felt the loss of a friend. In some unacknowledged sense, he must have felt both the strange unwanted joy that sweeps over the survivors of a great disaster and a sense of liberation, for he had clearly resented Kennedy even as he had quietly suffered the imprisonment of the vice presidency. But a man of sentiment, of generous even if shallow affections, he was undoubtedly sincere in his expressions of grief and in his empathy for the Kennedy family and staff. He always cried at funerals. He cried now.

His sense of loss also had to involve deeper levels of commitment and affection. Johnson was a simple patriot. He loved Texas and he loved America, enough in each case to hold numerous illusions about both. The assassination besmirched both, assaulted his image of both, and for him, as for almost all Americans, it created deep doubts and confusions about American institutions. In this the worst of times he had to take responsibility for the healing, for the restoration of confidence, for some regained sense of national unity. He did not know if he could meet the challenge. Fortunately, he had so much to do, plunged so quickly back into an almost frenetic work pattern, that he could not agonize over his inabilities to meet an impossible challenge. But the experience humbled him as no earlier one had. A peceptive staff member and speech writer, Harry C. McPherson, Jr., observed Johnson at a special service at St. Mark's Episcopal Church the Sunday after the assassination. After a moving sermon, during the singing of "America," Johnson wept.

LBJ now wielded enormous power. As a dedicated "servant," he wanted to use it for good. That meant, in his case, in a way to benefit and please as many Americans as possible, and thus win their gratitude. He had been a perceptive observer and critic of presidents from FDR to JFK. He had endlessly meditated on how he would have improved upon their performance. Now was his chance. He wanted to outdo all his predecessors and, in particular, to undo Kennedy's frustration in getting critical legislation through Congress. Of course, in his language, he had to complete what Kennedy began, vindicate by solid achievement his earlier and eloquent commitments, even in a sense bring redemption out of his martyrdom. His strongest asset as president would be the constantly invoked memory of his predecessor. In this sense, the long shadow of Kennedy proved one of the necessary conditions for the legislative avalanche of 1964–65.

But in a personal sense that shadow still haunted Johnson. He was more intimidated by a dead Kennedy, by the soon mythological king of Camelot, than he had been by the living but flawed reality. He had to follow a god. However much he achieved, he could not measure up to such a standard. No one could. As Kennedy's idolaters kept reminding him, Kennedy would have done as much as Johnson and with a great deal more grace and style.

Johnson now had the power. He soon proved his artistry, his political mastery. But he never quite felt, at least in darker moments, that he had the proper mandate or gained the proper appreciation. His presidency lacked legitimacy, or at least he often believed that it did. And this fact would gnaw at a sensitive Johnson any time the going became rough. It set the stage for endless insecurities, even a degree of paranoia. Johnson never publicly acknowledged his continuing hurt, never once took a potshot at the Kennedy icon, but personally he suffered from all the comparisons. Like someone of religious faith who comes to believe her god is dead and who has to live a lifetime haunted, even in many ways controlled, by one who is not there, so Johnson had to live the rest of his life under the shadow of a dead god. This is a terrible fate for anyone, even one blessed or cursed by enormous power.

8

PRESIDENT JOHNSON

For the last time the cycle repeated itself. In his five years as president, Johnson moved from brilliant early success and from intense but fulfilling engagement to galling frustration, a sense of failure, and then to a characteristic withdrawal. Once again he focused all his enormous energies, his intellect, his persuasive abilities on a challenging new job. Once again he was determined to do it better than any predecessor, to be the perfect public servant. And once again he had the needed talent. For a time, he lived up to his high expectations. For almost two years, from November 1963 to the late summer of 1965, his presidency was an unalloyed success story. No other president, before or since, achieved as many legislative goals or seemed as fully a master of the whole spectrum of tasks that go with such an almost monarchical office.

Just as after the election of 1948, once again Johnson had to prove his legitimacy. He did it quickly, as the election of 1964 would prove. He relished the effort. He soon basked in the power and status of his office. Unlikely as it seemed, Sam Johnson's boy from down on the Pedernales had beaten all the odds and reached the top. In a thousand ways, particularly among family and friends, he indulged his pride in such an achievement. In so many ways, he had it made as president; he was constantly in the news, protected, catered to, with every need met by a staff befitting an absolute monarch. He loved the exposure, the constant attention. His delight in the position, his occasional strutting and preening, had an innocent, childlike side to it and was one of the more appealing aspects of his personality.

But Johnson could not relax and enjoy his position for long. He took his responsibilities too seriously. Deep insecurities still haunted him. He had the power. He had to use it well. The possibilities were awe inspiring but included failure as well as success. Johnson wanted to serve his national constituency. He searched continuously for signals of approval. He wanted to be liked and admired, much as Kennedy had been admired. As always, he tried to win such love by good works. He skimmed the newspapers, scanned his multiple television screens, and installed a teletype in his White House office, always looking for news about himself, always seeking evidence that the great amorphous public appreciated his dedication and his wondrous gifts. Since his very identity, his sense of well-being, was tied so closely to achievement and to the gratitude of his constituents, he could never for long gain any sense of self-acceptance or peace. He kept trying harder and harder, pushing ever more futilely toward the ever-retreating goal of respect and popularity. The high point of his life was the election of 1964. But even then almost 40 percent of the people did not vote for him. Such ingratitude was beyond his comprehension. Every hostile newspaper story or editorial, every real or imagined slight, every deprecatory remark, even the absence of expected praise—all bothered him or pulled him into a bout of self-pity.

Johnson handled the difficult, postassassination period almost to perfection. By persuasion bordering on pressure, he recruited both Chief Justice Earl Warren to head and Richard Russell to join other distinguished Americans on a high-level commission to inquire into the assassination. During its extended investigation, its very stature allayed fears. Later, its magisterial report seemed to establish beyond reasonable doubt the solitary role of a troubled Lee Harvey Oswald in the actual shooting. Despite a few puzzling later revelations, the commission's restrained verdict, which played an important political role at the time, still remains the one most consistent with the evidence. In any case, the doubts and countertheories came to the fore long after the country had come to terms with Kennedy's death.

By the time Johnson arrived back in Washington on the fateful evening of 22 November, he had established his dominant theme for the next few weeks—continuity, unity, reconciliation. Such themes came naturally to him. Consistency meant that he had to keep intact Kennedy's cabinet and White House staff. In a series of conferences, at which he was a master, he persuaded even the most loyal Kennedy staffers to stay on. This included Attorney General

174

Robert Kennedy. Coupled with this was a carefully disciplined deference to the Kennedy family. Never once, despite some nagging provocations, did Johnson publicly reveal anything but concern, sympathy, and a desire to help in all possible ways. He did not immediately occupy the Oval Office, only gradually moved his personal staff into new quarters, and postponed until 7 December the family move out of the Elms into the White House. This amounted to an overly generous gesture toward Jacqueline Kennedy, who had a difficult time turning loose of her former life. The Kennedy children continued their kindergarten in the White House until Christmas. In all this Johnson was generous and magnanimous to a fault, forgiving of several small gestures of resentment toward him. For Robert Kennedy, in particular, Johnson had to appear as a virtual interloper; at times Kennedy so acted toward him or seemed to assume the right of an heir apparent. But in the transition months, as he later admitted, he never found a single cause for complaint against Johnson.

Later, at times of low fortune, Johnson voiced some regrets over having to begin with an inherited and thus never completely loyal staff (in his low moments, no one was loyal enough to please him). But, most often, he emphasized the positive benefits of his inherited crew. Kennedy had carefully recruited both his cabinet and his key White House advisers in behalf of political balance and competence. He had developed a national political organization and had excellent contacts with academic experts, particularly those in the Northeast. Johnson had few of these assets. Had he accepted the offers of resignation from key cabinet members, he might have been able to recruit reasonably competent political replacements. He understood this game. But, in retrospect, he doubted that he would have found anyone as brilliant as Robert McNamara at defense or as competent and loyal as Dean Rusk as secretary of state.

As for the White House, Johnson simply did not have, in his own personal staff or among his close friends, the needed experts except possibly in the two areas of congressional relations and space policy. For foreign policy advice, for the Council of Economic Advisers, for legal advice, for the heavy burden of speech writing, he needed the Kennedy appointees, at least for the critical transition months. Even when he had a chance to make his own appointments, as most of the Kennedy appointees gradually left, he still turned, more often than not, to former Kennedy officials or to Ivy League professors, most conspicuously so when he appointed Kennedy's brother-in-law Sargent Shriver to head the all-important Office of Economic Opportunity (OEO). Later, both friends and critics pointed out the critical role of former Kennedy foreign policy advisers, particularly William and McGeorge Bundy and Walter Rostow, as well as Rusk and McNamara, in shaping Vietnam policies. Correctly so. They played a critical role. Johnson depended on, and generally followed, their advice. But he followed it not because they deceived him or even carefully educated him but because he shared their perspectives on the issues at stake. Had he sought out his own cronies in these foreign policy areas, he would have recruited men with a similar outlook but with much less ability. Of course, a group of bumblers might not have been able to get the United States so deeply mired in Vietnam. In this sense, less able advisers might have been a blessing. But who would suggest, as a policy, that a president seek out incompetents for his staff?

The theme of continuity, in addition to restoring popular confidence, proved a powerful tool in achieving Johnson's legislative goals. Perhaps because of his past experience, Johnson seemed to assume from the beginning that his primary domestic responsibility was to get Congress moving, to persuade it to enact a whole bundle of bills needed, in Johnson's perspective, to solve a spectrum of identified national problems. Once the bills were passed, he had the further responsibility of executing them, an administrative responsibility Johnson took very seriously. But the immediate problem, and so often with Kennedy the most intractable one, was legislative. Here Johnson was the expert. Here lay his highest priority, for by talent and interest he was our preeminent president-legislator. Johnson quickly grasped how powerfully Kennedy's death boosted the chances of legislative action. Thus, his first speech as president, by choice to the Congress on 27 November, just after Kennedy's funeral, set the recurrent theme. Americans could honor the Kennedy vision only by action, by moving ahead in the direction Kennedy had charted as early as his 1961 inaugural.

In this critically important speech, anxiously watched by a vast majority of troubled Americans, Johnson did everything right. He planned the occasion very carefully, down to the seating of visitors in the gallery. He had Theodore Sorensen, Kennedy's favorite speech writer, compose the original draft and then let Abe Fortas and others modify the style to fit Johnson's idiom. He was never an effective speaker. He always sounded a bit stilted, and the formal setting constrained him. But now, at the time, his mid-American accents, his homely appearance, his deliberately soft and modulated delivery proved tremendously reassuring. His message was vintage Johnson. He took his opening theme from Sorensen's text: "Let us continue," a deliberate and nostalgic play on Kennedy's opening "Let us begin." But the meaning was soon clear. Congress was forewarned. It now had to do its duty to a dead hero, move beyond partisan wrangling and enact all the pending legislation that Kennedy had supported. The typical Johnson imperatives were there—get moving, do your work, avoid delay, be responsible. On 8 January, in a very brief but pointed State of the Union address, Johnson further clarified what he expected of Congress—the early passage of the pending tax cut and a major civil rights bill. And this was only the beginning.

Johnson, as president, would allow no relaxation. His high energy level, his intensity, was contagious. In effect he fulfilled Kennedy's 1960 promise—to get America moving again. With only three or four hours of sleep a night, Johnson launched his administration with a frenetic tempo. He counseled with hundreds of well-placed Americans. He courted both business and labor leaders. He sought support from all sides. Meantime, he interspersed these domestic efforts with meetings with a stream of foreign heads of state and with attention to several foreign policy issues, including a chaotic situation in Vietnam. Then, as the expected Christmas break approached, he forced the House to stay in session until 24 December, when it passed a controversial foreign aid bill that allowed credits to the Soviet Union to purchase American grain. Only a Christmas party the evening before at the White House appeased the frustrated congressmen, many of whom had to rush back to Washington for the key vote. But, in only one month, Johnson had gained as complete control over the federal government as few presidents achieve in their first year.

Back to the ranch! This was the only secure element of relief in Johnson's presidency. He was so busy, took it all so seriously, that he never had much chance for relaxation in Washington. Thus, at every opportunity he and Lady Bird flew back to the hill country for over a dozen visits each year of his presidency. Even there, a busy schedule, a string of guests, hovering reporters, the glare of lights, and all the state police and Secret Service guards lent a circuslike atmosphere to what heretofore had been an almost peaceful retreat. But the ranch still symbolized home and friendship. A disciplined actor, almost always on stage, LBJ could here let his hair down and usually find a few hours for daring drives through the ranch, hunting excursions, or almost private visits with relatives or neighboring ranchers. Here at the ranch he held many critical conferences and even entertained heads of state (Chancellor Ludwig Erhart of Germany was first on 28 December 1963). The new security and communication facilities at the ranch and the frequent transfers of dozens of staff members, facilitated by a new paved runway in the backyard, cost the government millions of dollars, but no one seemed to mind. Camp David, Maryland, provided a much closer, less expensive, but never so valued retreat.

The presidency meant difficult years for Lady Bird and for Lynda and Luci. LBJ had very limited time to spend with his family. Lynda temporarily moved her college studies from the University of Texas to George Washington University; Luci, who resented and fought against the new restrictions on her, became a high school student at the National Cathedral School. In the next five years, in the glare of national publicity, they dated, became engaged, and married, with the younger Luci first. Gossip about the daughters in part compensated for the newsworthy entertainments of an earlier Jacqueline Kennedy. Given the circumstances, the talented and morally sensitive daughters fared well and kept a close relationship with their parents.

Lady Bird assumed a range of new responsibilities, making her the most active presidential spouse since Eleanor Roosevelt. She had overall responsibility for the White House staff, made the final critical judgments about formal entertainments and White House dinners (serious issues for her), made a special speaking tour to the South in the campaign of 1964, tried to symbolize humane concern by her role in publicizing various antipoverty programs, became a close political adviser to her husband, and formally chaired a new beautification committee. In the beautification programs she enjoyed the close support and advice of New York socialite Mary Lasker. She also had a very able press secretary and assistant in Elizabeth Carpenter, who played a significant role in the whole administration. Lady Bird took most seriously the work of her beautification committee. She never enjoyed public speaking, but served her cause by trips all around the country, by endless dinners, and by a series of carefully crafted speeches. At first she received a sympathetic response, but later, with the Vietnam controversies, she often bore the brunt of criticism and hostility, always with a public posture of graciousness and gentility. By almost everyone's evaluation, she was an unusually involved and successful presidential spouse, possibly the ablest ever to hold this informal, unofficial, but critical office. Publicly loyal in all respects to her husband, she could be critical in private. Always kind in public, even to the point of an almost frozen smile, she suffered immensely from all the hostility that marked the last Johnson years.

Insofar as time permitted, Johnson continued contact with his numerous relatives and with his childhood friends in the hill country. Every cousin, known or unknown, rushed forward to claim kinship. Johnson remained reasonably close to his two sisters (Josefa had died), and entertained them and their spouses either at the ranch or at the White House. He kept his now crippled brother Sam Houston in near protective custody at the White House. This helped avert new scandals over his drinking, his debts, and his bent for exaggerated statements, but it also kept nearby a cagey and usually overlooked political adviser. When back at the ranch Johnson loved to visit old cronies. They basked in his fame and to the end honored him by their friendship and support. Along with cousins and aunts and uncles, he brought as many of them as possible to the White House and provided them with escorted tours of Washington. Reporters occasionally noted the relatives, particularly those with quaint names, such as Lyndon's maternal aunt Ovilee Baines, or those who seemed, at least to urban reporters, to represent Lyndon's more rustic past. Most notable here was Oriole Keele Bailey, a second cousin on the Bunton side who lived at the old Sam Early Johnson place. Elderly, ill, lonely, and unaware of patronizing smiles, Cousin Oriole gladly received reporters in her modest home. Legally, Johnson and Lady Bird turned over their productive assets, including the broadcasting company and the ranch, to a trust, but in this case the trust was never blind. LBJ was not about to give up a role in the management of his ranch and thus kept in constant contact with his local manager, close friend, and business partner, Judge A. W. Moursund. Old friend and former employee Jesse Kellam managed the broadcasting empire.

Back in Washington in January 1964, Johnson launched his first crusade for new legislation. Out of this congressional session would come at least twenty major bills, including the most important civil rights bill in American history, the complex Economic Opportunities Act that spearheaded a new "war" on poverty, and a critical tax cut that helped ensure a growing economy over the next two years (see below). In these efforts, Johnson quickly established his administrative style. As one would expect, he was most distinguished by his constant interaction with and careful cultivation of the Congress. Not only did he insert himself more directly into the legislative process than any predecessor, but he continued to find many of his key advisers among congressmen. The interaction was continuous and went in both directions. At least on domestic issues, congressmen of both parties had every reason to feel flattered and appreciated. They were continuously wined and dined, briefed, and complimented for each important achievement.

Johnson never acted as a remote chief of staff. He had to have his say on every issue, and as much as time permitted, he tried to become informed on every bill, every agency, every foreign policy problem. He wanted not only to make the critical final decision but to shape the process. At times, he wasted precious time on small details. This degree of oversight placed impossible burdens on him. This is not to say he did not use advisers. He had to. In some cases he relied extensively upon experts. But he wanted the advice in digestible form so that he could decide. In the White House, he established no clear hierarchy, no chain of command. He liked to keep even middle-level staff aware that they worked for him, not for someone nominally over them. Thus, he personalized the system, often to the despair of staff members. He expected complete loyalty and could subject even lowly clerks to a tongue-lashing if they ever seemed too relaxed or, horror of horrors, made a mistake.

His advisers fell into at least three distinct categories. Critically important, but always in the background, were a half-dozen old friends, including Abe Fortas, Clark Clifford, James Rowe, former secretary of state Dean Acheson, fund-raiser and businessman Arthur Krim, and on occasion old New Dealers such as Tom Corcoran. These men admired Johnson's talents, but had been too able, too independent, to subject their will to him and become permanent employees. He approached them as friends and equals, and thus in an informal, relaxed way. He enjoyed them and turned to them in times of crisis or on issues of first importance. Among such close advisers only one, and this the most important, was a woman—Lady Bird. Johnson verbally embraced the cause of women's equality, took pains to improve their opportunities in civil service appointments, and dutifully appointed a few women as ambassadors, as assistant cabinet secretaries, as head of consumer affairs, and as members of the Tariff and Atomic Energy commissions. But none of these became an intimate of Johnson or had any major role in shaping administration policy.

Johnson retained a few of his established groupies. These made up his personal staff, at first headed by Walter Jenkins and including his key secretaries. Jenkins, until his arrest for a homosexual encounter in 1964, was the closest thing to a chief of staff in the White House. Later, W. Marvin Watson filled part of Jenkins's role and became known as a tough appointments secretary who was ideologically opposed to much Great Society legislation. These intimate, almost family members did not play a major role in policy-making and were so loyal as to suffer and forgive Johnson's bouts of abuse and ill temper. He used them to vent his frustrations, and as near slaves they took it. Other staff members, friends, or speech writers such as George Reedy, Horace Busby, and above all Jack Valenti (he married one of Johnson's secretaries) maintained a bit of distance from Johnson. So did young protégé Bill Moyers. But these men also were part of a group of intimate cronies, most with Texas roots, who were dutifully subordinate and willing for a time and within limits to suffer an erosion of their personal egos in order to share, or bask in, Johnson's great power. These aides, and their spouses and children, were part of an extended Johnson family in Washington. LBJ and Lady Bird frequently took meals at the Jenkins or Valenti homes and at times dropped in for a relaxing visit without any prior warning.

The final level of advisers included Johnson's cabinet and almost all the Kennedy appointees to the White House staff. Johnson had never worked extensively with such a staff and had to learn how to use it. These people were not Johnson men, had no loyalty to him as a person or even nourished private doubts about his beliefs or abilities. Culturally and temperamentally, they were often the opposite of Johnson. Most were talented and accomplished, and in their own areas they were much more knowledgeable than Johnson could ever be. Some, such as Robert McNamara, intimidated Johnson by sheer talent. Others fanned his insecurities because of academic credentials or socially secure roots. Johnson needed these advisers, had to win their support, and at times was overly concerned about how much they respected or liked him. Thus, he had to approach them as near equals, even come as a supplicant in their areas of competence. And he could not indulge, with them, his penchant for childish tantrums or abusive intimidation. He had to be on guard at all times, which meant a proper, even formal context for staff meetings. Such staff members normally matured their advice in the form of written memos and kept a large degree of personal distance from Johnson. But he expected them to be at their desks early, to work weekends on demand, and to put in up to sixty hours a week. In the staff context they were free to disagree with administration policies or to advocate new options, and many did. Publicly, they had no such freedom. Johnson demanded both confidentiality and public support for administration policies. If anyone breached these sacred rules, Johnson stripped him of power and, as soon as possible, eased him into a less critical position. Only with great travail, or in a sudden burst of anger, did he dismiss staff members. In no case would he easily let loyal staff members resign (this was close to treason), and by pressure and persuasion he kept people on board for years who really wanted to escape the Johnson pressure cooker.

One special adviser who fits no clear classification was Senator, soon vice president, Humphrey. Johnson had long admired Humphrey. Everyone liked him. Humphrey shared Johnson's vitality, his sentimentality, his openness to people, but he had few of Johnson's psychological hang-ups and little of his overpowering intensity. In the Senate, Johnson had made Humphrey a bit of a protégé. He befriended him and to some extent bought his loyalty. Behind his exuberance and talkativeness (LBJ once remarked to Lady Bird: "If I could only breed him to Calvin Coolidge"), Humphrey was an intellectual with a few scholarly credentials. This side of him, and his identification with the Senate's northern liberals, created elements of jealousy and resentment on Johnson's part. Thus, his relationship to Humphrey was complex.

Johnson often treated Humphrey like a member of his staff. He tried to dominate him and could be cruel, not that Humphrey ever became a groupie or gave up his own independence. But Johnson had a hook in him—Humphrey's presidential ambitions—and on occasions he twisted it. His cruel streak always lurked in the background, for Humphrey represented people and positions Johnson either feared or hated. By 1964 it was all but obvious that LBJ would choose Humphrey as his running mate, since both personal and political reasons suggested him. But he played the game. After conferring in a tense meeting with Robert Kennedy, who quite obviously would not be Johnson's choice, he then went public with the lame rationale that he would not turn to any cabinet member. Everyone saw through this strategy. Then, as the convention approached, Johnson deliberately kept Humphrey dangling to the point of assaulting his self-respect. He played around with other names for obvious reasons—to add excitement to the convention, to keep reporters guessing—but a display of dominance was part of the game. Despite this and other examples of seemingly deliberate humiliation, Humphrey never broke ranks or, in public, expressed any doubts about Johnson.

One critical staff task was writing Johnson's numerous speeches. Short or long, his speeches or extended statements averaged at least one a day. Most were rather innocuous, such as formal statements honoring one or another group or cause, or brief greetings to foreign visitors, or commendations to members of White House conferences or presidential commissions ("Rose Garden rubbish" was Moyers's title for all these). On trips, both at home and abroad, or in the 1964 campaign, the number of speeches could rise to five or six a day. Even routine efforts kept a stable of five or six staff members busy. The more lowly writers, most enticed away from work in journalism, vied for the honor of having some work of theirs actually incorporated into a major speech. This honor alone dignified their boring, usually unacknowledged labor for a president who rarely, if ever, knew who first coined his gems of wisdom. A major speech included any delivered before Congress or before a national television audience, or any, including even local speeches, that Johnson selected as a vehicle for the introduction of a new policy. In all such major speeches several writers typically prepared whole or partial drafts. A key staff member—at first Reedy or Richard Goodwin, then Moyers or Valenti and, toward the end, Harry McPherson—made the writing assignments, screened the often competing drafts, and merged them into a single mock up for Johnson's perusal. In the case of a State of the Union address, almost everyone could have some impact, including cabinet members, for the various components came from each area of the government. Johnson had a major hand in selecting the final content for major speeches; for routine ones, he often read the words for the first time while speaking. For critical drafts he occasionally solicited speech material from outside advisers, even at one point from novelist John Steinbeck.

Johnson had neither the time nor the ability to prepare his own speeches. No recent president has. From the beginning of his career he had depended on writers. This did not mean that he was incapable of speaking extemporaneously. Before his presidency, he had done so frequently. He was also largely on his own in facing press conferences, but even then he did better when he stuck to a text. When he went extemporaneous or ad-libbed, he tended to ramble, to talk in generalities or clichés, to go on too long, to embellish facts or tell wild stories about himself, or at times to lapse into intemperate, even vivid and pungent language. Several of his more demagogic statements about Vietnam opponents reflected departures from a text. Yet, without such detours, Johnson's speeches could be deadly, for he never relaxed as a reader and the formal language never fit his exuberant personality.

Johnson offered rather detailed guidelines for his writers. He wanted his speeches short and simple, without big words. He wanted eye-catching phrases or newsworthy announcements, so he could capture the attention of the press. He liked to appear literate and thus welcomed quotations from famous writers, usually ones he had never read. On policy issues he often was as knowledgeable as his writers, and in these cases he could dictate much of the content of a speech. From his voracious reading of newspapers, the *Congressional Record,* and staff reports, he often gathered speech material and gave marked passages to writers. Since he used so many writers, his speeches never reflected any one style, and some were distinguished by the phrasing, or even the policy priorities, of the key writers. To conceal the lack of a Johnson style, the writers typically used local-color material, such as references to Texas, the ranch, or Johnson's almost mythical boyhood experiences. Above all, Johnson wanted some good jokes. The junior writers held "joke" meetings to gather material and even tried without success to produce jokes by committee meetings.

By most judgments, Johnson was blessed overall with an able staff; it was certainly a well-trained one. Even a majority of his Texas-born advisers had Ivy League degrees. Johnson, influenced by Kennedy and anxious to imitate him, liked to boast of the academic credentials of his staff. But even such an able staff could not protect Johnson from some of his worst habits or maintain the public image and reputation he needed to gain support for all his policies. Perhaps if it had not been for the bitter fruits of the Vietnam War, his worst traits and most glaring disabilities would have remained a little-noticed sideshow of his presidency. But even early on he suffered from a lack of credibility and tended, because of certain insecurities, to dissipate the early atmosphere of good feeling and high public approval. This was most apparent in his dealings with the press and in a much less important way in his relationship to people who were, or at least claimed to be, artists and intellectuals.

Johnson loved both people and attention. He thirsted for publicity. No one was ever more attuned to the flow of news and shifts of public opinion. He tried to read the public pulse daily. His mother and his wife had been journalists. Thus, in every way, he seemed favorably predisposed toward those involved in communications, a profession he valued along with education. And in certain contexts he related well to newspeople. He liked most correspondents, loved to entertain them with gossip or mimicry, and in a relaxed, private context was often amazingly open and self-revealing. He and Lady Bird, either at the White House or at the ranch, could be unusually attentive to the physical comfort of journalists, often providing them unexpected meals and refreshments. Yet, because of an overweening ego and certain personal peculiarities, Johnson was almost always unhappy with his treatment by the press. And he often said so. By 1967 he was conducting a virtual cold war with newspeople.

Why? In part, he never understood the rules that journalists followed. Their attempts to maintain distance, to give balanced accounts, to see all sides, or in certain contexts to be extremely critical of government were foreign to Johnson's temperament, although intellectually he acknowledged, at times almost ruefully applauded, these very traits. Johnson loved to persuade, to bargain. As Senate majority leader he had been able to establish a special close relationship to the few reporters who covered congressional affairs. He entertained and informed, and generally received a favorable treatment in return. But as president, he found that such small, informal briefings no longer worked. Dozens of reporters, representing all shades of opinion, now hung on to his every word; they were too many, too unwieldy, and too pushy for Johnson. He never did well at formal staged news conferences and could not handle implied criticism with any deftness. Thus, he usually resorted to sudden, almost impromptu conferences involving only White House correspondents, a strategy that helped him gain a reputation for either secrecy or manipulation.

More critical, he tried to bargain, to buy a sympathetic press corps. He wanted to serve reporters too, to make them appreciative constituents. Thus his chummy approach. They often responded at a personal level but then tried to write professional reports on Johnson and his policies. A few seemed vindictive, returning kindness with ridicule of Johnson's corny style. Either way he felt cheated, betrayed. Even generally friendly articles bothered him if the praise was not continuous and exaggerated. The digs at him, questions about his motives, accusations of duplicity, or unanticipated stories about secret plans or policies all infuriated Johnson. He expected journalists to be like staff members, or at least loyal Americans, which to him meant a willingness to give the benefit of any doubt to the administration, particularly on foreign policy issues. Averse to conflict and confrontation, he was amazingly helpless in confronting a hostile press. As always, his inclination was to retreat, which in this case meant more secrecy, more efforts to avoid journalistic scrutiny.

Confidentiality had been part of the political game as Johnson played it. A master of careful plotting and exact timing, he had tried as a legislator to transact as much business as possible outside the public limelight. He was a schemer. He rejoiced in successful, often dramatic outcomes and basked in the praise that came his way. Secrecy along the way was essential to effective achievement. Almost playfully, he liked to conceal his purposes, to provide deliberately misleading clues as to what he was about, and then to surprise everyone. Thus, as president, Johnson was not only less than honest with reporters; he scarcely understood what that meant. He loved to mystify and shock. He was incensed at any coverage that spilled the beans too soon. Continually, and with no good excuse, he omitted details, denied facts, or avoided direct answers. At times he conspired, with a great deal of wasted time and attention, to show up the press, to prove that the more critical editors or reporters did not know what they were talking about. During the last two years of his presidency he loved to torment accompanying reporters by announcing his travel plans only at the last moment. Unfortunately, Johnson let these games influence his decisions. In a few cases he withdrew appointments prematurely leaked to the press or deliberately altered policy decisions that he had already adopted but not yet announced. These tactics, joined with his lifelong penchant for embellishment and invention, or, in brief, for lying, led reporters to conclude, and the public eventually to concede, that Johnson was not only secretive but extremely duplicitous. He could not be trusted.

With academic specialists, established literary figures or painters, and people of broad learning or developed taste, Johnson always felt insecure. He moved back and forth between harsh denunciation and unjustified deference. In part, his sense of inferiority was justified, for Johnson was not philosophical, not very thoughtful, and not appreciative of the fine arts. He had devoted his talent to other subjects and could not rest easy with his own mastery of the art of politics. As a result, he had a hard time communicating with academics and, unfortunately, often tried to fake an interest in the arts. Alternately, he played the part of the philistine and rebelled against culture by displays of vulgarity or by his well-rehearsed obscenity. Such publicized incidents as his picking up his two hound dogs by the ears and his publicly displaying the scars from a gall bladder operation reflected this temptation to amaze and shock. So did his embarrassingly well publicized and, for accompanying women reporters, frightening drive through the Texas countryside at ninety miles an hour with a beer can in hand, or his anatomically and functionally specific description, to other women reporters, of the role of his prize breeding bulls.

Actually, by the report of those intellectuals who worked with him in his administration, Johnson was broadly albeit unevenly informed on a fascinating array of topics. He was also a quick learner. On issues related to space, he picked up a smattering of highly technical knowledge and could converse with the best of scientists. He had a longtime fascination with economics and proved a very adept pupil to his economic advisers. He could talk their language. But he always refused to be pulled into highly abstract or theoretical discourse and professed contempt for all philosophical or ideological discussions. When, during the Vietnam War, a majority of academic specialists and most influential writers and critics joined in angry protest, Johnson's most paranoid fantasies about intellectuals, particularly those from the North and Northeast, seemed fully vindicated. Inversely, the academic horror over Vietnam reinforced images of Johnson as a morally insensitive, tasteless Texas cowboy.

The Kennedy myth aggravated the conflict, which was based on image more than substance. The Kennedys had projected an image of high culture, of fashion, taste, and intellect. They graced their fashionable dinners with serious music and honored major composers, painters, and writers. Actually, Jack Kennedy knew little more about such subjects than Johnson. Conversely, by diligent reading and cultivation, Lady Bird became quite knowledgeable in the arts and, without affectation or pretense, exhibited excellent taste. She was not far behind Jackie. But LBJ remained untutored and wary. Typical of the layperson, he thought the arts important and easily applauded all of them indiscriminately. He wanted those people who appreciated such "higher" attainments to be able to enjoy them. Thus, in 1965, he supported with enthusiasm the creation and first funding of the National Endowment for the

Arts, the first major federal patronage of the fine arts since the New Deal.

In a sense, Johnson came off worse when he tried to be cultured. He and Lady Bird invited both popular and classical musicians to play in the White House. The caliber of performance was as high as under Kennedy. But LBJ appreciated few of them. The Johnsons hosted all the required formal receptions for heads of state. They employed an excellent chef and did things right, but at times it did not seem natural. The huge barbecues along the Pedernales best fit Lyndon's style. Yet Lady Bird was superb in a receiving line and LBJ loved dancing with and flattering the wives. But he wanted more, to appear as a patron of the arts. He supported a new Council of the Arts and then in June 1965 held the White House Festival of the Arts. Everything went wrong. During the planning, the use of American troops and bombing in Vietnam, joined with the landing of U.S. Marines in the Dominican Republican, led to a national teach-in, to widespread academic protest, and to the opposition of several intellectuals. White House adviser and historian Eric Goldman has recounted in sordid detail his tribulations in planning the festival. Robert Lowell, the erratic and brilliant poet, turned the event into a political cause when he, by letter, and as a way of protesting administration foreign policy, retracted his earlier agreement to read his poetry at the opening session. In agreement with him, a few key participants returned their invitations, and others used the occasion to protest the war. LBJ, ever sensitive and suspicious, almost repudiated the conference, tried to control who came and what they said, and then made only a brief and rather surly appearance at the end of a day-long feast of literature, music, art exhibits, and dancing. The fallout of publicity further embittered Johnson.

Another small but embarrassing confrontation with an artist involved painter Peter Hurd, who completed an official portrait of LBJ in October 1965. Lyndon hated it—it was too large, too unflattering, with an unwanted violet background. He tried to explain his concern to Hurd, who with misgivings agreed to work at suggested changes. He never met Johnson's expectations and eventually in public statements blamed the fiasco on Johnson's lack of taste.

Ineffective speeches and poor press relations hurt Johnson's public standing after 1965 and a major Vietnam escalation, although not so much before. The polls revealed a very high approval rating, often up to 70 percent during the transition period, the election of

1964, and most of 1965. This rested on unprecedented achievements and on a correct public apprehension that Johnson wanted, desperately wanted, to succeed as president. Clearly, no one had ever worked so hard or achieved so much in so brief a time. In fact, he almost killed himself in all the work, and tied to this were his own idealistic goals—to perfect every institution, to solve all pressing problems, to eliminate glaring inequalities and injustices, to realize the old, even if opaque, dream of equal opportunity for all. In the most literal sense, he wanted reform more intensely, even passionately, than any former or subsequent president. Not revolution. Not basic structural changes in institutions. Not class conflict. But an enormous range of repairs and supplements to an existing and beloved America. And he wanted it all as quickly as possible. He would not be president long. He might not live long. He had power now. This was the golden moment. The first great opportunity came after the assassination, the second after his landslide election in 1964. Neither interlude could last long. The future of America depended on the maximum use of these rare opportunities.

The election of 1964 was the highlight of Johnson's life. As he put it, he had lived his whole life for just such a moment. His reelection was scarcely in doubt from the Republican convention on. Barry Goldwater proved the weakest possible candidate against such a centrist incumbent as Johnson. Goldwater's campaign was inept. His ideologically tinged speeches, his radicalism and extremism, and his seeming proclivity for a direct confrontation with Communist forces in Vietnam and elsewhere alienated most moderate Republicans. But even the ablest Republican could not have defeated Johnson in 1964, for he had captured the broad middle bloc of voters, representing all classes, all ages, and, except for the Deep South, all sections. So far, his administration had co-opted almost everyone, for up until this point he had been able to build broad coalitions for all his legislation—the tax cut, the Civil Rights Act of 1964, and his antipoverty program. So far, he had seemed cautious in Vietnam; yet he used the Tonkin Gulf incident to demonstrate that he would stand firm in defense of American interests and honor. Even the glow of a dead Kennedy seemed to bless his candidacy. Only southerners, alienated by his civil rights stand, and a few far-right groups bitterly opposed Johnson.

Given his prospects, Johnson did not need to campaign. Given his personality, he could not resist the opportunity. But he refused to enter into any detailed discussion of issues, would not debate

Goldwater on television, and guided the convention in adopting as bland and inoffensive a platform as possible. Only in the South did he risk controversy; there he spoke out in behalf of his civil rights bill. In September he began his campaign, crisscrossing the country, enjoying the results of an able, well-financed campaign organization, and basking in the approval, even what seemed the adoration, of cheering crowds who seemed to buy his message of unity and harmony and reasoned responsibility. He loved it all. He could hardly pull himself away from one site and all the hand-shaking to get to his next scheduled stop. Soon, his goal was not just victory but the largest mandate in history. Expert pollsters made clear that this was a possibility. Thus, Johnson directed an intense, sophisticated campaign, one based as much or more on the dangers of Goldwater as on the assets of Johnson. The carefully orchestrated campaign against Goldwater occasionally involved poor taste (particularly two television ads that suggested that Goldwater would use nuclear weapons) and the use of innuendo or spurious charges that bordered on the "dirty tricks" of Nixon's 1972 campaign. In return, Goldwater supporters tried to emphasize morality in government and to suggest a shady or corrupt side to Johnson's career. This strategy failed. Even the arrest of aide and friend Walter Jenkins in a men's room of the YMCA seemed to have little effect on voters.

The election results vindicated Johnson. He won over 61 percent of the popular vote, and the largest plurality in history, but not as high a percentage as Roosevelt won in 1936. Goldwater won only in the Deep South and barely carried Arizona. The Democrats also won thirty-seven new House seats and two in the Senate. Johnson had his mandate. If he had tried hard in 1964, he would push even harder in 1965, arguably the most critical year in American political history since the crisis of the Great Depression and World War II.

It is difficult to recapture the ferment of the early Johnson administration. Too much happened too quickly. In just over two years, Congress enacted over two hundred major bills and at least a dozen landmark measures (see chapter 9). The pace of activity, both in the White House and in the Congress, was unprecedented, as was the number of outside professors or other specialists recruited for at least temporary work or consultation. The ferment, the chaos, rivaled that of 1933, and all at a scope at least four times greater than the early New Deal. No one person could comprehend the whole. Even yet it is almost impossible to sort it all out, to find useful patterns, even adventitious ones. The only focus, the only center, was President Johnson. He somehow made the needed staff assignments, recruited the outside experts, received the results of over a hundred inquiries, approved a legislative agenda for each session, orchestrated the brilliant and unprecedentedly successful legislative effort in the Congress, and then finally set up the administrative machinery to effect all the new programs. Two questions beg an answer. How could he do so much? What vision guided all his activity?

Johnson had two well-developed work habits that were prerequisites of his presidential performance. One was his ability to give intense, almost hypnotic concentration to a task at hand. The other was his enormous energy and thus his long workday. In his Senate career, he had learned to shift mental gears many times during the day. In the White House he had to shift roles with even greater rapidity. He moved, in a typical day, from a rapid survey of newspapers and the *Congressional Record*, to several staff conferences, to ceremonial speeches, to a congressional luncheon, to a foreign policy briefing, to detailed military planning, to a formal dinner, to an evening concert and dance, and finally, to long hours of reading in bed. He gave full attention to each task, but so much happened, so rapid was his shift of interest, that he later could not remember even some major decisions. It all went by so fast as to seem almost a dream.

Johnson combined this mental agility with a sixteen-to-eighteen-hour workday. In fact, every waking moment was work time for Johnson. A five-minute break between appointments meant three or four phone calls to key congressmen. He made the telephone a virtual extension of his body. He began his reading on awakening and received staff briefings before breakfast. Meals, even visits to the bathroom, never interrupted his work. Thus he became famous for the briefings or conferences that made up his highly public toilet breaks. Even his ribald humor, perhaps appropriately, usually involved bodily functions. He did a third of his work in pajamas, while in bed, or naked, in his almost daily swim in the White House pool, again with a retinue of staff or visitors (Billy Graham, among others, was embarrassed by the obligatory nudity). The talk and the scheming never stopped. He did try to take a brief late-afternoon nap at the end of a normal workday, only to begin a second eight-hour stint that often ended in the early morning hours.

Critical to Johnson's presidency was his night reading. Before leaving work each day, his staff carefully selected items that Johnson almost had to see and left this stack for him. To get materials into the night reading became a prestige item for junior staff. With his ability to read and scan rapidly, he tried to get through the whole bundle before exhaustion and sleep ended his day. Often, this was only three or four hours before it began all over again. The frenetic pace exacted its penalties. He aged visibly, and in October 1965, after the most productive two years of his life, he entered Bethesda Naval Hospital for a gall bladder operation. He needed the break and the recuperative interlude, filled with plenty of work, back at the ranch. By then, all the fun, all the satisfaction, of such a demanding job was already draining away. He was mired in Vietnam.

What were his goals? The question allows no easy answer. Johnson in his first two years epitomized a mood that might best be called conventional utopianism. He was both vague and conventional in values. He most easily spoke of basic human needs—food, housing, jobs, health care, and education, but joined these with more elusive or luxurious attainments—art and beauty, expressive freedom, and self-fulfillment. He loved American institutions, including the congressional form of government and a mixed but still primarily private even though highly collectivized economy. He accepted, and wanted better to harmonize, the federal system, the division of government functions between national and state governments, although he came to appreciate how much local institutions could impede the implementation of idealistic federal programs. He saw government at any level as a wonderfully flexible tool to aid people in achieving their goals.

Tensions remained. He valued frugality and strove for balanced budgets even as he rapidly expanded the range of government services. He lauded individual responsibility and freedom even as he extended government patronage and control. He had an almost irenic confidence in the possibilities of peaceful compromise, of successfully bridging differences of class, race, culture, and economic interests, even as his policies contributed to some of the deepest conflict in American history. Differences, he believed, rested upon such a solid core of commonalities as to be resolvable if only people would reason together, seek out avenues of reconciliation. This turned out to be a big if, and when people failed this vision, when they indulged in bitter factionalism or resorted to violence, his explanation almost always took an environmentalist twist. Conflict testified to the bitter fruits of unjust deprivation and a lack of opportunity, and thus might be erased through reform, although not necessarily in a present generation.

This upbeat outlook, as reflected in his early administration, was full of generous sentiment, soaring romanticism, and great expectations. Johnson knew that injustice and poverty were deeply rooted, that improvements would be slow. But no problem, in principle, was uncorrectable, given time and enough effort. He had found it so in his career and generalized his experience to fit everyone and all types of problems and challenges. In the deep morass of Vietnam, he continued to search for the way out. There had to be such. And failure to find the answer to that riddle had to mean that Lyndon Johnson had failed, not that this was an example of a tragic dilemma, one in which people were trapped with no solutions at all. And in other areas, he never easily conceded that any except purely private problems did not lend themselves to a political answer. That is, government could directly or indirectly alleviate any distress. It could not enable people to be more brilliant, help them marry happily, or allow them to escape illness and death. But it could so educate everyone as to allow each to realize his or her fullest talents, provide the economic security and environmental conditions that support stable families, and assure everyone adequate health care and a decent burial. Such concrete promises typified Johnson's idealism.

But, as almost anyone will point out, Johnson was an often insufferable egotist, self-serving, and with a soaring, almost unquenchable personal ambition. Quite so. How is this consistent with such a broad idealistic reform agenda? Actually, they go together. His powerful ego, his impossible expectations, defined the breadth and extent of what he wanted to achieve. Without his ego and overweening ambition, his Great Society would be inconceivable. Heretofore, he had mastered every task. He had always pushed harder, achieved more than anyone else expected. Now, in a position of enormous power, he had quickly to gain enormous achievements, more than any previous president. Nothing else would do, not for Lyndon Johnson. He aspired in superlatives, worked in a frenzy, and, like a heavy and lurching boat, he always left behind a wake that was deep and broad even if turgid or dangerously turbulent. Great achievement and soaring idealism are not inconsistent with a powerful ego. In fact, they are all but inconceivable without it. Had Johnson been less driven, less ambitious, less preoccupied with his image, his achievement, his reputation, and his status, less paternal toward all those people who depended on his leadership, he would have been a less activist and aggressive president. And since, in his case, he armed his ambition with overwhelming political skills, he was bound to make a large impact on American history. If one shared his goals, it was wonderful to have him in charge. If one had different goals or simply wanted to keep things as they were, then Johnson was always a dangerous president.

Johnson came to know intense frustration. In his last two, beleaguered years, he often felt trapped. He kept hoping for a solution, a way out of the mess in Vietnam, some vindicating victory or negotiated settlement, some magical strategy or sustained effort that would master the problem so that he could get back to ordering an economy threatened by inflation, pass some more of his ever-developing legislative agenda, and attend more carefully to the administration of Great Society programs. These hopes proved illusory. And, in a certain sense, Johnson, so much bigger than life, confronted tragedy. But he was not open to tragic experience, to the recognition of man's relative impotence before fate, to the likelihood, even the inevitability, of dead ends, of inescapable traps, of accumulated human choices that are, in their totality and their consequences, irreversible and unredeemable. But unwilling to confront such a view of humankind, to grasp that terrible outcomes often flow from even the noblest human effort, he never felt tragic. And for anyone who knew him, from his earthy language to his frequent need to use and dominate other people, he was anything but noble. Thus, the image of Johnson in 1968, or whenever his fortunes were low, is that of a stumbling giant, still powerful enough to crush any foe, to lead some new charge, but suddenly flailing only at the unresistant air and flinging out his cosmic orders to a few ants. The power, the potency, remained, but lost was the occasion, and thus the giant seemed helpless, pathetic, but never noble or tragic. And, as for any giant, even a usually kindly giant, but one who at times had played the bully or flaunted his achievements, the less powerful multitudes were not in such a case inclined to cry over the fate of their flawed hero, but openly or secretly to rejoice at such a one brought low.

This image of President Johnson may be unfair if it suggests inordinate pride on his part. In most respects the presidency humbled him. He was always awed by the position. The best evidence of this, perhaps not surprisingly, was reflected in his personal religious stance. Overtly, he had always professed to be a Christian, whatever the label means, and had remained a nominal member

194

of the Christian or Disciples movement. But one sensed before 1963 that these professions were rather perfunctory or merely expedient. Johnson was not active in his church and would never commit himself on doctrinal issues. As soon as he inherited the presidency, he changed. To the surprise and gratification of a more devout Lady Bird, he immediately began prayers before each meal. And during his presidency he rarely missed Sunday services at some church, in some denomination. His church in Washington was the National City Christian, where he had a presidential pew, but his attendance proved intermittent. Its pastor, George R. Davis, tried to be his confidant and spiritual adviser, relished the praise Johnson gave him on his sermons, and later spoke out in defense of Johnson's Vietnam policy. But Davis tried too hard and at times intruded more than Johnson seemed to want. At the same time, Johnson seemed, in personal taste, to crave a more liturgical worship; thus he enjoyed Episcopal services in Lady Bird's St. Mark's Church and later created a bit of a controversy by taking communion in Episcopal churches. During his presidency, daughter Luci converted to Catholicism. Through her, Johnson met several Catholic priests in Washington, attended Catholic services at her small, simple, integrated St. Dominick's Church, and sought out local Catholic chapels for private prayer and meditation.

This overt ecumenicism might suggest political opportunism. No charge could be more unfair. It did reflect an eclectic approach both to creeds and to worship styles. Johnson sought in churches a type of support or consolation. Age and responsibility helped push him back toward the religious certainties of childhood, and in some sense he wanted to be able to defer to a higher power, to be able to claim a sense of cosmic righteousness for his causes, and to use prayer to find help in making critical decisions. Thus, for his private purposes, a loose and generalized version of Christian doctrine seemed sufficient. Let the theologians argue niceties of doctrine. His was a rather childlike approach. He liked to sample different churches and also enjoyed, monarchlike, the giving out of his blessings upon the cause of religion, whatever the variety. In his travels he loved to surprise and flatter a local congregation by attending services. Later, at least one courageous Episcopal minister treated him to an anti–Vietnam War sermon. But he continued to resist any final choice among all the religious options. The more evangelical forms of his Johnson City childhood retained a nostalgic appeal. Billy Graham, a frequent White House visitor and close friend, became his semiofficial chaplain and exploited this side of Johnson's religiosity. But in times of crisis he seemed to crave the more esthetic, ritualistic, and traditional worship of Catholic churches. Even at the ranch he increasingly attended St. Francis Xavier Catholic Church in Stonewall; the local priest became a close friend and spiritual adviser. His flirtation with Catholicism led to false rumors, particularly among hostile Protestants, that he had either recently converted or would soon do so. He may have considered it but was never inclined to choose sides.

In religion, as in all areas, Johnson was never given to deep, probing questions. In politics, he never came close to doubting, or agonizing over, existing arrangements. In all areas he affirmed popular, moralistic, mainstream beliefs and preferences. This meant, at one level, a very conventional presidency. He followed existing trends and fashions in both economic and foreign policy. His desire for continuity, for achieving what Kennedy began, fully reflected his own views. But inevitably these continuities have been obscured by the more dramatic and controversial aspects of his administration—the Great Society legislation and the Vietnam War. Actually, each of these reflected Johnson's commitment to continuity. Both involved quite conventional, even commonplace, beliefs. But in total impact they came to distinguish his administration, and thus each deserves an extended treatment. Unfortunately, this means, in a short book, only a cursory treatment of what took up almost half his time as president—maintaining and extending existing foreign policy commitments and managing an ever more complex economy.

In foreign policy, Johnson combined a type of idealism with an easy acceptance of traditional guidelines. Despite what might seem to be the implications of Vietnam, he was, by inclination, pacific. He wanted to lower tensions, to find reasonable bases of accommodation, particularly in those areas in which global conflict might ensue. Thus, he gladly built upon the thaw in Soviet-American relations that followed the Cuban missile crisis. He deliberately eschewed harsh, anti-Soviet rhetoric, worked hard to get congressional approval of credit-based grain sales to the Soviet Union, finally joined the Soviet Union in 1968 in signing a nuclear nonproliferation treaty, helped begin several new cultural exchanges, signed a 1967 treaty with the Soviet Union on the peaceful use of outer space, and had progressed by 1968 to the near beginnings of formal talks on a Strategic Arms Limitation Treaty (SALT). In 1967 he met for two days with Soviet Chairman Aleksei Kosygin in Glassboro, New Jersey (not a formal summit, since Kosygin came to attend a meeting of the UN), and explored with him the complications that followed the seven-day Israeli-Arab war. He also, with unclear results, used Soviet agencies to try to get North Vietnam to open peace negotiations. This does not mean that the cold war ended, but Johnson believed, apart from the aggravating issue of Vietnam, that he had worked successfully to lower the risk of a major war, and in an exuberant moment he talked about moving from a policy of "coexistence" to one of "peaceful engagement."

His idealism took another form. Some jokingly referred to an international Great Society. From his vice-presidential travels, Johnson developed a deep personal interest in the problems of underdeveloped countries. He wanted to help them. This explains his emphasis, in his memoir, *The Vantage Point*, on the Food for Peace Act of 1966, on the huge grain shipments to India during the first two years of his administration, on support for the Agency for International Development (AID), and even on his famous scheme for a TVA of the Mekong, which took tangible form in an Asian Development Bank. Yet, the problems of such countries often outpaced solutions, the cost of the Vietnam War forced cuts in foreign economic aid, and the United States, by exploiting its commercial advantages, continued to enjoy cheap commodities and resources from such countries. In other words, Johnson's sympathy never translated into great benefits.

In Latin America, Johnson continued to fund Kennedy's Alliance for Progress, but soon confronted new problems. He appointed as chief Latin American adviser a former Mexican ambassador and Texas friend Thomas Mann, who was sympathetic to private investment and who, in crisis, too easily blamed problems on communists, whatever the label might mean. Johnson idealized his youthful involvement with Hispanic Americans, gained closer ties with Mexico, and amazed delegates by his enthusiasm and goodwill when he attended an Organization of American States (OAS) conference at Punta del Este, Uruguay, in 1967. But twice he had to deal with serious crises.

Early in 1964, American high school students in the American-controlled Panama Canal Zone hoisted an American flag at their school, contrary to an earlier agreement to fly no flags at all in deference to Panamanian feeling. A protest march by Panamanian students led to a riot and in its repression to over twenty deaths among the leftists involved. This forced the Panamanian president to press again for renegotiation of the galling 1903 Canal Zone Treaty. Johnson used a telephone to talk to the Panamanian president, but to no avail. Further violence threatened and a diplomatic impasse resulted, since Johnson would not agree, under pressure in the very beginnings of his administration, to renegotiation. Anxious not to appear weak, he virtually sabotaged several agreed-upon verbal compromises and embarrassed helpful representatives of the OAS. After his hard stand and considerable ill will in Latin America, he then turned conciliatory and accepted a statement committing the United States to a "review" of the treaty. This led in 1964 to beginning efforts to renegotiate the treaty, or what Panama had requested all along. The episode showed Johnson at his worst—still insecure, anxious to have full control over an issue, fearful that anything less than a hard line would lose him domestic support, and unable effectively to use outside mediators. But typically, when he had full control and could pick his own time, when he could seem to effect a result by his own effort, he then proved magnanimous.

The second crisis—in the Dominican Republic—hurt him much more politically. In September 1963 a military coup in this small island republic displaced an elected civilian government that in 1962 had replaced the longtime dictatorship of Rafael Trujillo. The resulting right-wing government never gained popular legitimacy and, by April 1965, faced incipient revolt. It unsuccessfully begged the United States for increased aid. On 24 April an attempted coup led to civil war which, although confused, was mainly between a rightist military faction and a coalition of largely socialist parties, the rebels. An overreacting American ambassador, W. Tapley Bennett, clearly favored the military faction and claimed, as it turned out incorrectly, that the country faced an imminent takeover by communists. His increasingly hysterical telegrams painted a dire picture of bloodshed and incipient anarchy, and when the military faction seemed on the point of losing, he requested U.S. Marines, ostensibly to protect American lives, in fact to prevent the rebel faction from gaining power. Johnson, without consulting congressional leaders or even notifying the OAS representative in Washington, ordered marines in and subsequently supplemented them by airborne army troops. At first, even in briefing congressmen and in a public announcement, he disguised the political goals and made the military effort out as a protective measure. But even the military intervention itself, and the role of the marines in preventing a rebel victory, led to the first wave of criticism, most vehemently from those already critical of the recent escalation in Vietnam. It was easy to see in Johnson's action an effort to suppress popular revolution, to support elite or authoritarian or militaristic elements in Latin American, or what was in part descriptive of the effect, if not the intent, of American military intervention.

The criticism had a telling effect on a sensitive Johnson. In reaction, he tried to justify the action. His escalating rhetoric became part of a propaganda effort to win broad public approval. In the process, he seemed unclear as to American goals and at first seemed defensive about the communist issue. But as he warmed to the task, he began to magnify the alleged communist role in the Dominican Republic until the rebel cause became a communist-dominated effort to create a second Cuba. The extreme claims lacked any proof at all and soon contradicted detailed information from the Dominican Republic, making Johnson seem either a fool or a liar. To the almost unanimous concern of or repudiation by Latin American leaders was now added growing, bitter repudiation within the United States. Beleaguered and fatigued, Johnson never seemed as unsure of himself. For two weeks the fighting continued, and the United States did not even have a prospective candidate to head any new government. But in late May the OAS assumed responsibility and added peacekeeping forces to the American troops. More expert diplomatic efforts in the fall of 1965 led to stability and, after surprisingly peaceful elections in 1966, to a stable and overtly democratic government. But at home the bumbling and the false rationalizations lost Johnson a great deal of political support.

Fortunately, except for the largest one of all, Vietnam, no comparable crises plagued Johnson's last three years. He was involved, but only indirectly and at a distance, in a futile effort to dissuade Israel from its unilateral action in the Seven-Day War of 1967. During it, Israeli planes sank an American ship, the *Liberty*, in international waters off the Israeli coast, killing thirty-four Americans. Johnson was low-keyed in response and accepted apologies and payments from Israel. In 1968 he was likewise restrained when North Korea captured an American spy ship, the *Pueblo*, and kept its crew hostage for nine months. In 1968 he protested, but could do little else, when Soviet troops repressed a liberalizing government in Czechoslovakia. In these scattered crises, Johnson glimpsed much higher stakes than in either Latin American or Vietnam—direct Soviet-American conflict and the possibilities of a third world war.

Restraint and initiatives in behalf of East-West reconciliation should not conceal how fully Johnson had absorbed and accepted the rationale for American foreign policies since 1938. He lived in the long shadows of Roosevelt and, even more, Truman and Eisenhower. Munich and Korea remained vivid reference points. The United States had learned a costly lesson in the years leading up to World War II. It had to resist aggression early. And it needed to maintain an effective counter to Soviet power. This meant, for him, support for the North Atlantic Treaty Organization and a continuous concern to maintain American military strength superior to that of the Soviet Union, not only in nuclear weapons but also in conventional forces, a policy earlier pushed by John F. Kennedy. He knew that the United States did not confront any monolithic communist force. In quite detailed talks in Warsaw, American diplomats began the slow road to rapprochement with China, a process that could not advance as far as open diplomatic relations until the peace talks were underway with North Vietnam. But Johnson did view Marxist-socialist parties, wherever in power, as natural opponents of the United States, and, as in the Dominican Republic, he easily reverted to the language of the cold war. In this, he echoed Dean Rusk and most of his foreign policy advisers. Thus, in his overall foreign policy he was conventional but not rigid, idealistic but not ideological, pacific but fearful of any hint of appeasement, flexible on tactics but not open to any major redirection of policy.

Many of the same characteristics fit his approach to economic policy. He wanted to follow Kennedy's example. He hoped, by fiscal and monetary policies, to trigger sustained economic growth, to realize full employment, and yet to avoid any dangerous inflation. Obviously, almost anyone could applaud these goals. Controversies involved only the means. And for almost three years, Johnson seemed to realize those goals. It was not as clear to him, as it is today, that the achievement rested more on factors beyond government control than on any of his economic policies.

In the American economy almost everything seemed to cycle out right for the United States in 1963 and 1964. A happy coincidence of circumstances supported healthy growth and suggested at least a possibility of major affordable reforms. The Great Society legislation and the accompanying rhetoric grew out of the strengths and some of the illusions of that economy. From 1963 to 1966 the gross national product rose at an almost unprecedented peacetime rate of above 5 percent. Behind this lay often unnoticed factors. First in importance was a post–World War II boom in American agriculture, in which productivity increases approached revolutionary levels year after year. The agricultural boom meant steadily lower costs for basic subsistence and provided the major component of exports needed to retain favorable trade balances (not always a favorable balance in payments). Western Europe and Japan approached full recovery from World War II and contributed to a stable international market, but they could not yet offer dangerous competition to America. In the United States the memories of depression lingered. Demand seemed a critical concern. But the baby boom of the fifties helped create demand in several areas by the sixties, while low interest rates still encouraged an expansion of credit and a continued explosion in housing. From a later perspective, it is clear how much the economy enjoyed the short-term benefits of very low international resource costs (Arab oil discoveries were critical to continued low rents or access costs for fossil energy) and of many postponed costs of past and present growth (various forms of pollution, capital depreciation in manufacturing, and several types of urban decay).

When Johnson took office, the fashionable or orthodox approach to economic policy was, quite loosely, Keynesian. Walter Heller, the Kennedy carryover as chairman of the Council of Economic Advisers, and Johnson's 1964 appointee, Gardner Ackley, both supported countercyclical policies that, by at least a loose identification, were consistent with the earlier theories and equations of Lord Keynes. Such policies meant that the federal government tried to so determine taxing and spending choices as to maintain relatively full employment without uncontrollable inflation. For any Democratic president, who had the strong backing of wageworkers and union labor, the commitment to full employment had to be central. It remained so to Johnson. By the standards of the 1980s, he was wondrously successful. During his administration, unemployment fell from over 5 percent in 1963 to a low of about 3.5 percent when he left office, an achievement that resulted in part from the demand created by the Vietnam War. Unlike even a decade later, the targeted unemployment rate of less than 4 percent was consistent, without mandatory controls on prices and wages, with an inflation rate of less than 3 percent until at least 1966. Such goals seemed normal then, visionary to the extreme by 1986.

Several factors, most unnoticed but nonetheless helpful to Johnson, explain this favorable job-inflation ratio. In the mid-sixties, inflationary pressures built only slowly. The sources of growth in the fifties, centered in agriculture, had not reflected expansionist or daring fiscal policies. In real dollars, federal expenditures had remained stable from 1952 through 1961. Both the federal budget and the federal deficit had dropped sharply as a percentage of gross national product. In effect, the United States had been steadily retiring its debt. The government had not resorted either to increased expenditures or to tax cuts to increase demand. Both remained unused but potent weapons, and Johnson would use both. After a period of low inflation and three recessions under Eisenhower, with one overlapping the first Kennedy year, and with lingering memories of a Great Depression, nothing like an inflationary mentality (buy and borrow now and enjoy later) had taken hold. Finally, compared to the present, the economy did not have to absorb nearly as high a percentage of the potential work force as even a decade later. Beginning in the sixties, and paralleling Great Society programs, was a steady increase of middle-income women moving into the work force, often displacing low-skilled and minority male workers. By 1985 a higher proportion of potential workers were employed than in 1965, yet unemployment rates rose to the 7 to 8 percent range and, in certain categories such as young black males, were much more intractable than ever before. Thus, Johnson was lucky on the employment side.

In 1963 the economy had seemed healthy but not robust. Because of fears of a new recession and an early failure to meet his campaign commitment to more rapid economic growth, Kennedy had pushed hard for a major tax cut (over $10 billion, or almost 10 percent of the appropriated budget). Closely counseled by his economic advisers, he had chosen tax cuts, some contrived to increase business investment, rather than increased expenditures (each can stimulate the economy, although the exact nature of the cuts or increases determines the areas of the economy stimulated and the total impact). Such a cautious strategy should have appeased most business interests, but it still raised old fears of budget deficits and, with them, higher inflation. Johnson had always been deeply committed to fiscal caution and to balanced budgets. He always would be. Thus, as the new president, he had to develop his enthusiasm for the cuts. He proved an apt student of his economists. But he saw the political hazards in the Senate (the tax cut had passed in the House before the assassination), and he chose to join with the cut an even more insistent effort to cut spending (cutting off the lights in the White House became a symbol).

Fortunately, the situation in 1964 allowed significant cuts, particularly in defense spending. Secretary McNamara proved a magician in the Defense Department, introducing there new budget controls based on the types of systems analysis developed by the Rand Corporation. By 1964 Johnson was able to force such a system, with its requirement of clear goals, cost-benefit evaluation, detailed planning, and a consideration of options, upon most departments. Drawing on those techniques and pushing each agency toward the lowest possible request, he was able, almost miraculously it seemed, to keep the federal budget (exclusive of various funds) under $100 billion for the last time in American history. The tax cut would probably have passed without Johnson's magic. But given his legislative skills, it not only passed by a wide margin in the Senate (seventy-seven to twenty-one) but gained support from all sectors, including business. Thus, in his first major congressional victory, Johnson gained his perennial goal—consensus. He did it by trying to give a goodie to everyone. Even Senator Harry Bird, long the fiscal watchdog of the Congress, almost succumbed to Johnson's obvious and welcome passion for economy and, although he could never vote for the cut and impending deficits, he did not actively oppose the president.

The tax cut worked. It helped stimulate demand and increase production. Given significant cuts in defense, joined with growth, the deficit increased only slightly. In fact, for Johnson's first three years in office, the debt as a percentage of gross national product continued to decline until the mounting costs of the Vietnam War, and to a much lesser extent new transfer payments tied to Great Society programs, reversed this trend by the end of 1966. In later jargon, Johnson had proved that supply-side economic policies could sometimes work. Because of a range of factors, the economy enjoyed the largest recession-free period of growth in American history. For a decade (1960–70) the gross national product rose every year, with only a minor economic slowdown in 1967. Productivity increased at a more than 3 percent annual rate, and until 1967 inflation remained low, even by the then current standards. In that year, living costs rose by about 3 percent, or enough to frighten almost everyone. Johnson was horrified and struggled with the ogre of inflation for the last two years of his administration.

One of his problems in economic management reflected his inability to coordinate his Council of Economic Advisers and the Federal Reserve System. The supply of money rose rapidly in 1964 and 1965, exceeding the rate of growth. In mid-1966 the Fed, fearful of price inflation, used its multiple weapons to raise interest rates. It overracted, leading to a shocking credit crunch and no monetary growth at all in late 1966. Legal limits on the interest paid by banks discouraged deposits, even threatening some banks and savings and loan associations with failure. Most threatening to the public were unprecedentedly high mortgage rates (over 8 percent), which briefly almost wrecked the housing industry. In early 1967, as a delayed consequence, a recession seemed imminent as growth stopped for the first quarter. But in late 1966 the Fed had relented, even in a sense repented, and thus lowered its rediscount rate. Without the monetary crunch it had risked, and the near recession, living costs might have risen at a much higher rate than the 3 percent of 1967.

As the economy resumed growth in the spring and summer of 1967, as Vietnam costs and budget deficits rose, and as low interests pushed monetary growth to dangerous levels of over 8 percent, Johnson tried to find a means of averting impending inflation. In August, he first asked Congress for a major tax increase (a 10 percent surtax). He failed to get it. As he had long feared, the Great Society programs became hostage to the surtax. Arkansas's Wilbur Mills, chairman of the critical House Ways and Means Committee, refused to report out the tax increase without severe cuts in domestic spending, and the increase, which Johnson soon elevated to his highest legislative priority, or at times defended as one of the last hopes of Western civilization, did not pass until 1968. In the meantime, Johnson could only use persuasion, tied to wage and price guidelines that he recommended, even in some sense pushed upon, corporations and unions. He would not ask for mandatory controls. His economists did not want them. The distortions and built-up pressures might fit a normal wartime situation, one with realistic prospects of early, sharp, deflationary cuts in defense spending. No such cuts seemed likely in the future. More important, Johnson did not want to use Vietnam as an excuse. He did not want to admit its high cost or to elevate the war to the center of public attention, for this would provide an excuse for sabotaging his first and greatest love—the Great Society.

Guidelines proved a weak anti-inflation medicine. Johnson no longer had the prestige to whip employers or laborers into line, except possibly for defense-related contracts. Back in the pre-Vietnam glory days of 1964–65, he might have brought it off. In April 1964, he practically arbitrated a threatened railroad strike; he brought negotiators into the White House, placed their bargaining in the limelight, and made clear that no one would leave without a settlement. Of course, he won. Again in September 1965, he used almost the same tactics to force an end to a steel strike. But the problems were much too great for persuasion in late 1967. After Britain devalued its pound in November, the dollar rose, imports expanded, and prices seemed sure to soar. By January 1968, Johnson had to bargain with Congress and first promised $4 billion in reduced spending to buy a surtax. Eventually, he had to raise this to a $6 billion budget cut to get his surtax passed in June, and by then in a somewhat contrived, crisislike atmosphere. At best, the new taxes only slowed inflation, for by the end of 1968 living costs were up by 4.7 percent, which in 1968 seemed terribly dangerous. In part, the pressure on prices reflected developing expectations on the part of consumers. In part, it reflected continued low interest rates and excessive monetary growth, for the Fed had feared the deflationary effects of the tax cut. As yet, Johnson still believed it politically desirable and economically possible to keep unemployment at or below 4 percent. He achieved only this goal in his last year in office and retired to his ranch soul-sick over developing economic problems. He felt that he or a recalcitrant Congress had failed in economic management.

Did Johnson really fail? And if so, why? He clearly failed his own expectations, but no one could have achieved all his goals. They were impossible. By 1968, with the demand created by the Vietnam War and with total annual federal expenditures up about $50 billion over a four-year period, Johnson could not hold down inflation and keep unemployment at 3.5 percent and prime interest rates at 5 percent, at least not through persuasion. He could not continue to please all his constituents. Had Congress responded more quickly and more fully to his tax proposals, the cost of living would still have climbed, although at a slightly slower rate. The combined fiscal and monetary restraints sufficient to reverse the rise in living costs would have required a slowdown in the economy, possibly a recession. This meant political and human costs that Johnson could not accept. Had he opted for wartime controls, and had he gained public acceptance of them, he might have controlled inflation but, with the built-up pressures, would have laid an even more treacherous trap for his successor. Thus, his problems need to be kept in perspective. By later standards, the inflation even in 1968 was relatively mild. It joined with continued increases in productivity, with real growth, and with a federal debt that rose only slightly as a percentage of gross national product. In a sense, it reflected, as yet, only a somewhat deceitful but very traditional way of paying for a small share of soaring government costs. Its psychological effect was probably most critical. But the fact that these price rises turned out to be the beginnings of a major inflationary spiral in the seventies is largely explained by later unanticipated economic factors, such as soaring oil prices, not by the fiscal policies adopted by Johnson.

One frequent criticism of Johnson is that he, either deceitfully or foolishly, tried the impossible—in his own terms, to buy both guns and butter. He could not have a Great Society and fight a war in Vietnam. The charge is absurd. He not only could do both, he did. In his five years in office, defense spending rose (in 1972 dollars) from approximately $75 billion to just over $100 billion, or a 33 percent increase; payments to individuals under various social programs rose from $40 billion to $58 billion, or a 45 percent increase. Note that almost half of the social increase had nothing to do with any Great Society legislation; one-third of it reflected increases in Social Security retirement payments. But clearly the federal government did buy a lot of guns and butter under Johnson. These expenditures reflected real goods and services, consumed as produced. In this sense, he did it. And given the wealth and the talent present in America, under duress the people could have produced a third more than this. The problem, therefore, was not whether Americans could afford both. They clearly could, given a lot more hard work. But the sticky problem was how to assess the costs and distribute the rewards. Here Johnson confronted a thousand dilemmas.

If Congress had permitted, Johnson could have used taxes and tight money to dampen down rising prices. He could also have asked for controls. But one likely outcome would have been increased unemployment and more, not less, poverty and thus a need for increased welfare. Even had he targeted his high taxes entirely at the one great reservoir—middle-income Americans—he might have curtailed investment and in this way increased unemployment. More important, he might have lost a large share of always soft support for his Great Society, support predicated upon continuing economic growth and thus no higher tax rates. Given these hard realities and Johnson's political outlook, the mild but frightening inflation of 1967–68 may have been the best solution he had to mounting economic problems. It enabled him, at least to the end of his administration, to keep a reasonably coherent, middle-class consensus on the direction of domestic policies. Any other strategy, either controls or fiscal toughness, would have threatened

206

what Johnson wanted above all else to avoid—class conflict and class politics. For any other strategies that he followed would have forced Americans to confront the hard implications of income-transfer programs—one has to take from Peter to pay Paul. And in a no-growth situation, this means that Peter has to lower his living standards. With this unwanted eventuality, Johnson would have had to give up on the only game he ever wanted to play—one with no losers. With losers, his Great Society was in jeopardy. It was his great gift to Americans. To a large extent, he preserved it for them to the end of his administration. Ironically, by then fewer and fewer ungracious Americans seemed to love it.

9

THE
GREAT
SOCIETY

By choice, Lyndon Johnson sought and then worked to establish a label for his administration. After extended staff debate, he chose "Great Society," a phrase that was neither new nor very catchy. Richard Goodwin, a Kennedy carryover and most idealistic of Johnson's speech writers, incorporated the phrase in several of Johnson's speeches in the early months of 1964. No one picked up on it. Then, on 22 May, Johnson used an almost utopian commencement speech at the University of Michigan to fix the term and make it the symbol of his domestic program. In subsequent speeches, many written by Goodwin, he further filled out his dream for a future perfected America and suggested that the new legislation he would propose would move America toward such a Great Society. How far, and how quickly, was never clear.

Like the earlier New Deal and Fair Deal, the label Great Society soon stood primarily for the more innovative or welfare-oriented legislation enacted during the Johnson administration. The bills that fit such a label soon numbered at least two hundred. They still defy easy classification. From Johnson's perspective, the Great Society required civil rights for blacks, a broad war against poverty, broader educational opportunities for all youths, improved health care for the aged, several new initiatives to upgrade the quality of life in American cities, more protection for consumers, and several new conservation and environmental regulations.

In 1964 and 1965, Johnson loved to talk about his Great Society. At times he even personified the label and referred to a Great Society doing this or that. Johnson spoke as often about the quality of life, about beauty and community and dignity, as he did about basic economic needs, and as much about meaning and purpose and the intrinsic benefits of work as about wages or economic security.

The breadth of expressed concerns, the sheer number of bills and new programs, made even comprehension, let along evaluation, almost impossible. Johnson talked about a perfect America. He seemed to want to solve all its problems susceptible to political correction and to do it all quickly. It is hard to identify any one focus or find any controlling priorities because, in a sense, Johnson never adopted any save those related to political opportunities. He tried to so time the introduction of his legislation as to maximize chances of passage. Otherwise, he simply wanted it all. By 1965 his staff, quite literally, began looking for new or heretofore overlooked problems in order to prepare a legislative agenda for 1966. At a lower level, his legislative task forces also worked to find the appropriate questions, to discover problems, before going on to offer suggested solutions. Thus, more than ever before in American history, an administration moved beyond a response to pressing constituency pressures, beyond crisis-induced legislative action, to a studied, carefully calculated effort to identify problems and to create the needed constituencies to help solve them.

In all the legislative ferment, Johnson never tried to impose any blueprint on the whole. He had none. He did not believe in such. He relished the broad, open-ended, almost utopian goals of his Great Society speeches. Beyond this form of cheerleading, he saw himself primarily as the great facilitator. The suffering and unhappiness of Americans identified problems enough. In the past, a complex process of political bargaining had led to legislative proposals. Johnson wanted to improve on that process and thus talked, vaguely at first, of secretly enlisting all the great intellectuals of American into some type of super brain trust; he then in fact turned to academic experts for much of the work of his task forces. Out of the process would come the proposed answers to America's problems. Johnson could then take over and get passed as close an approximation of the proposed solution as his legislative skills allowed. Then he would get the right people at work on the implementation of such legislation.

The task force became the most original legislative tool of the Johnson administration. Neither the name nor the design was new. Kennedy had formed a few task forces. But never before had an administration appointed so many study groups or made them such a critical component of the legislative process. A rather loose, informal task force quickly developed the Economic Opportunity Act (EOA) of 1964. Subsequent to this, Johnson formalized the process. All in all, he would appoint approximately forty outside, and over ninety internal or interagency task forces. The outside committees were most crucial in 1964–65, for they matured the more innovative details of legislation passed from 1965 through 1968.

A typical outside task force included from ten to twelve members. About half of these came from the academic world; the other half represented the private sector (business, labor) and local governments, with one or two representatives of federal agencies or the White House staff. The work of each force was confidential, although not secret in the sense of defense data. The White House, except on rare occasions, did not make public the names of members or publish the final reports. Private members received all expenses and, if they wished, a small honorarium. Most refused any pay. They served gladly, in part because the administration committed itself to take their proposals seriously. With a few exceptions, they were able to see their work appear in one or more bills. Because of expert knowledge or persuasive ability, academics dominated the most important forces. The professors or heavily represented academic administrators tended to be older, at the top of their disciplines, and by this fact not as innovative or as politically radical as their younger colleagues. They rarely advocated extreme measures, but were idealistic and serious, and thus proposed a great deal more than Congress was ever willing to fund.

By far the most important outside task forces began work in 1964. These also had the ablest and most prestigious academic membership, with universities on the two coasts most heavily represented. Harvard and Berkeley led the list. A few professors served on more than one force. Don Price, a Harvard political scientist, served on three. Other multiple appointees included Ben Heineman, president of the worker-owned Chicago and North-western Railroad, and Robert Wood, a Kennedy adviser, a Harvard Ph.D., and a former professor of political science at the Massachusetts Institute of Technology. By 1965, LBJ insisted upon a greater regional diversity and attained this goal for later task forces, even as the scope of the studies tended to narrow. One task force included the president of a suddenly booming Southwest Texas State College (for unclear reasons, it seemed to profit from every new federal program).

No series of inquiries under federal sponsorship ever rivaled in scope and influence the outside task forces of 1964. Under very broad mandates, ten such forces sought out problems and solutions in areas of economic and social policy: income maintenance (a source of Medicare proposals), agriculture, health, environmental pollution, education (John Gardner chaired this critical force, which helped mature the Elementary and Secondary Education Act of 1965), metropolitan and urban problems, natural resources, the preservation of natural beauty, transportation, and the sustaining of prosperity. Five more task forces explored fiscal and structural issues: foreign economic policy, cost reduction, government reorganization (the first of two), intergovernmental fiscal cooperation, and the international competitive effectiveness of American business. From 1966 on, new outside task forces either further studied the same issues or worked on more narrowly focused aspects of general topics. New and broad studies included those on Native Americans, crime, and childhood development. After 1966 the major legislative work occurred in the interagency task forces, with the most innovative work still in the areas of health, education, and welfare. Special Assistant Joseph Califano supervised many of those search and draft missions. By 1967 he had come closer than ever before to perfecting a well-oiled legislative machine. By then, task forces had studied almost all conceivable problems and helped shape hundreds of bills or amendments to existing bills.

Of course, Johnson could not guide, or even become informed about, all the inquiries that were soon under way. He also had little to do with the writing of most legislation, although he exercised his political judgments in shaping final versions of major or controversial bills. Such a role for Johnson allowed him to facilitate passage of an unprecedented body of legislation, spawned by a mixed group of people with divergent beliefs and preferences. Collectively, the bills reflected no single coherent plan.

Such a facilitating role allowed Johnson to avoid what he nei-

211

ther liked nor could do well—clarify in terms of precise beliefs and clear values his broad moral goals. He passed the problem of values back to unclear groupings of Americans. The wants of people, at least those who could make their wants known, defined the problems of America. Their happiness defined a government's achievement. Obviously, some of the wants conflicted. Johnson knew that. Anyone would have to be blind to ignore valuative conflict. But he always tried to avoid confrontation and conflict, both of which flourish in an environment of scarcity, one in which only a few claimants can get what they want. His preferred answer was to give everyone something. Thus, if increased welfare costs worried those who might have to pay for them, the government could, in a sense, buy them off by granting one of their special requests, such as a new tax incentive. This approach means that the federal government should be open to all demands, sensitive to all needs, and, whenever possible, it should avoid decisions that entail winners and losers. In the political game, unlike competitive sports, everyone should win something. Johnson hated subtraction and division; he loved addition and multiplication. A no-losers game, of course, is more easily played in a period of economic growth, but it does not require continuous growth. It requires a very skillful and harmonizing allocation of available resources, which is easiest in an affluent society and in one with a broad base of shared beliefs and preferences. In the heady legislative harvest of 1964 and 1965, it seemed briefly that America had these prerequisites. In the factional conflict of 1967–68 and with mounting economic problems, it became apparent either that it did not or that the Johnson administration did not have the skills needed to make everyone happy.

By 1965, Congress was turning out major bills so rapidly that the government quickly faced a type of administrative overload. Johnson, who set up huge White House charts of all pending legislation and almost daily updated the progress of each, from task force investigation to final passage, almost fell into a game—the scorecard was all-important. The number of bills passed was in itself a great achievement. When legislation simply extended existing programs or utilized existing agencies and staff, this quantitative emphasis posed no great problems. But for new programs, it proved almost impossible to reap many early benefits. The complex legislation usually left open many key policy decisions; these had to be worked out in the new agencies, often with new personnel. Frustration and confusion were inevitable. Also, so much of the Great Society legislation involved unknown claims on the future, including ever-mounting monetary costs. It is no wonder that, after 1966, a major share of administrative concern shifted from new legislation to means of implementing that already passed. The most important new task forces tackled administrative and structural issues, including the relationship of federal to state and city governments.

Any list of Great Society legislation soon becomes staggering. Thus, the only practical strategy for assessing the Great Society is to focus upon a few landmark bills. No two people would rank the legislation the same way, but most would include three civil rights bills, the Economic Opportunity Act of 1964, the Elementary and Secondary Education Act of 1965, the Higher Education Act of 1965, the 1965 Medicare and Medicaid amendments to the Social Security Act, the Model Cities Act of 1966, and the Housing Act of 1968. Although not deemed that significant at the time, the Food Stamp Act of 1964 eventually became one of the most important antipoverty or welfare measures in America. And although no one bill rivaled these major acts, the cumulative effect of several environmental, consumer, and cultural programs rivaled the impact of any of these landmark bills.

The major bills all had roots in the past, some as far back as the Truman administration. Kennedy, in some form, had made every one of these part of his agenda. The most reform-oriented measures, such as the war on poverty, involved legislative efforts that predated Kennedy's administration and political priorities that had already become central to northern, urban, labor, and black factions in the Democratic party, or an agenda usually dubbed liberal for no apparent reason except journalistic convenience. But, in a quite literal sense, the major Great Society legislation did involve unprecedented federal liberality or generosity.

Each of these Great Society commitments promised benefits to a targeted and often an increasingly self-conscious interest group (blacks, the aged, the educationally deprived, the poor, the unemployed, urban ghetto dwellers, consumers, nature enthusiasts). In no case did the targeted recipients of new favors have either the political clout or the leadership to gain the legislation. But in each case their visibility or their protest helped create broader attention and concern. Passage of each major Great Society bill thus depended upon a broad coalition. Central to this, in almost every case, is what might be called a politics of moral complacency, a politics that fit the mood of the affluent and the would-be righ-

213

teous, not usually the outlook of the more alienated recipients of some of the political gifts. Johnson appealed most effectively to those Americans who felt guilty about social problems, who wanted to rest at ease in their own abundant life. He also appealed, perhaps more broadly, to enlightened self-interest, to those who saw ahead festering social problems and, in the long term, enormous costs or open violence.

The legislative avalanche of 1965 came exactly thirty years after the only other legislative session of comparable importance. The class-oriented and welfare legislation of both years admit useful comparisons, but in one respect the two efforts could not be farther apart. Roosevelt in 1935 deliberately appealed to class interest. He attacked the rich and privileged and sought support among the broad categories of Americans who had experienced duress and nourished resentments of those at the top. This meant that the recipients of New Deal favors made up effective voting blocs. Roosevelt, in a sense, appealed to poor people, but at a time when over half of Americans had suffered sharp economic reverses. His class politics was not aimed at the very bottom—at blacks in urban ghettos or at Appalachian whites—because deeply entrenched poor people have little political clout. Johnson did aim his programs at those who were at the very bottom even in a period of great prosperity. To gain the needed legislation, he had to appeal to the nonpoor. He both flattered and bribed the wealthy and the privileged. Thus, he avoided class rhetoric like the plague and either appealed to the paternal concern, the moral guilt, or the fears of nonclients, or built into welfare programs enough bribes (academics could win research grants to study poverty, contractors could grow rich building subsidized housing) to gain broad support.

The Civil Rights Act of 1964 is a good place to begin a survey of the legislative harvest. It must rank among the five most important bills ever passed by Congress. It had enormous, even revolutionary implications for, and consequences in, the South. It gave broader protections to blacks than all prior civil rights bills combined. And because of an unplanned, undebated amendment that added sex as a category to the comprehensive antidiscrimination provisions of Section VII, the bill became the most potent legal basis for women's liberation. In one sense, Johnson contributed little to the bill. It developed out of earlier unsuccessful aspects of civil rights bills stretching back to 1956 and, except for amendments, gained its final form in 1963 under the Kennedy administration. As the continuing attorney general, Robert Kennedy worked effectively to get the bill passed. Johnson was in no way involved with the key amendment involving women. His role, as always, was in directing the legislative battle, in getting such a controversial bill through the Senate. No one could have been more successful at this. As a southern president, and one long committed to a strong civil rights bill, he felt that in this case he could not compromise. As never before he wooed congressmen, so expertly courting the support of Republican minority leader Everett Dirksen as to give Dirksen a proprietary claim to the successful result. For the first time ever on this issue, the Senate voted cloture against a southern filibuster and by a consensuslike majority of seventy-one to twenty-nine. The final vote was pro forma, and for the first time ever a strong civil rights bill passed with no crippling compromises or amendments.

In almost all respects, the 1964 act justified all the effort. It was a broad antidiscrimination bill. Title I included the toughest controls yet over state voting laws and included detailed guidelines for the use of literacy tests and quick injunctive relief for discrimination in either registration or voting. Title II, under the constitutional rubric of the broadest possible definition of commerce, mandated equal access to all public accommodations; Title III did the same for all government facilities. Title IV involved school integration. It provided for several forms of assistance to local school districts, but balanced this with severe penalties for any continued discrimination. The attorney general, as in most of the titles, could seek injunctive relief with or without complaints from parents, and the federal government assumed the legal fees for those parents willing to charge discrimination. In a sense, Title VI, which forbade discrimination in any federally assisted program, only added powerful sanctions to this integration effort, for after the new federal aid provisions of 1965, local school districts dared not risk a cutoff of funds. Title V continued and expanded the powers of the Commission on Civil Rights. Finally, and in the long term most important, Title VII, one of the most complex and critical legal documents in American history, forbade all discrimination in employment and included sex as a category along with race, color, religion, and national origin. To monitor the detailed, almost definitive guidelines, it also provided for an Equal Employment Opportunities Commission (EEOC).

The tough voting provisions of the 1964 act changed little in the South, for the Justice Department could not monitor each county and ward and intimidated blacks would not use its legal remedies. Continued intimidation and an arbitrary application of literacy tests practically excluded blacks from registration throughout much of the Deep South (only 6 percent of blacks were registered in Mississippi). By the end of 1964, as revealed by still frustrated voting registration drives by civil rights activists, it was clear that only more forceful, legally unprecedented federal intrusion could quickly alter southern voting patterns. Johnson, in close contact with civil rights leaders, had his staff begin drafting a tough voting rights bill in 1964 and asked Congress for such in his January 1965 State of the Union address. He, as always, exploited circumstances. The golden opportunity came in March as a result of events in Selma, Alabama. Martin Luther King, aware of inept but rigidly segregationist officials in Selma, selected the city for a major registration drive. Such efforts provoked massive arrests, media attention, and dramatic plans for a civil rights march from Selma to the state capital in Montgomery. The first attempted march, on 7 March, ended when Alabama State Troopers beat up the leaders on a bridge leading out of Selma. On 9 March a second, larger band of marchers, some from all over the United States, confronted a similar barrier of troops and, by prior agreement, peaceably gave up. But the murder of a young white minister in Selma, coinciding with the shooting of black students at Jackson State College in Mississippi, outraged much of the country and made Selma the symbol both of southern repression and of the civil rights cause. Thousands came to Selma for the much-publicized and successful march that began on 21 March now under protection of a federalized National Guard.

But the long procession toward Montgomery was almost anticlimactic. On 15 March, in the midst of the Selma crisis, Johnson spoke before Congress and a tense national television audience. By common consent, this was one of the most moving and eloquent speeches of his career, a speech almost perfectly composed for the occasion. And, more than usual, Johnson added feeling, even passion, to his delivery. He asked Congress quickly to enact a new voting rights bill, whose tentative provisions he summarized. He climaxed his speech by a line from an old hymn that had become the slogan of the civil rights movement. "We shall overcome." Much of his audience was in tears, for he had succeeded in doing what he had asked Kennedy to do in 1963—use the presidency as a moral platform. The timing was, as always, perfect, with southern resistance more discredited than ever before. Still, he had to use his best skills to build yet another winning coalition in the Senate. The Civil Rights Act of 1965 passed on 5 August.

The voting rights act allowed an unprecedented federal intrusion into state voting procedures. Whenever a county in any state used literacy or other similar tests or failed to register 50 percent of its voting age population the Justice Department could interpret this as prima facie evidence of racial discrimination. It then could suspend literacy tests, and if this failed to end racial discrimination, it could use federal examiners to register voters in each offending county. The law worked. Most counties complied voluntarily; federal examiners took over in sixty-two counties. Just as the 1964 act ended most legalized segregation in the South, so the voting act, in only three or four years, made the franchise available to almost all southern blacks. In Mississippi, black registration rose from 6 to 44 percent in three years, even as blacks began to capture local offices in counties in which they had a majority. The act transformed southern politics. A decade later, former race baiters like George Wallace of Alabama would campaign actively for black votes and, surprisingly, often get them.

The early, nonviolent, racially mixed civil rights movement climaxed in 1965. Already, for two years, various forms of dissent had been brewing in the black community among those who spoke of black power, who mocked the nonviolent tactics of Martin Luther King, and who wanted to break free of white support. By then, the leaders of the Student Nonviolent Coordinating Committee, which at first entered the dangerous trenches in the battle for voting registration in the South, had shifted toward black power and the use of force to attain black goals, which went far beyond legal equality. After Selma, even King tried to shift his leadership away from legal and largely southern problems to economic issues, such as problems with jobs and housing in urban centers in the North. These gradual shifts among blacks paralleled the eruption of urban violence in most large cities, presaged in 1964 by several small riots, but indelibly etched in the public mind only in 1965 by what happened, just after passage of the Civil Rights Act, in Watts, a black area of Los Angeles. Such violence, almost entirely in black neighborhoods, raged each summer through 1968, with the most extreme death and destruction convulsing Detroit in 1967 and Washington, D.C., in 1968, just after the assassination of King.

Johnson could scarcely comprehend the anger and bitterness of blacks, particularly after all he had done for them. At times, he reacted in bitterness or anger. Along with the Vietnam War, and extensive campus protest against it, these urban explosions jeopardized his Great Society, for the backlash against such violence soon encompassed not only ghetto blacks but poor people as a whole. Johnson made the required gestures and supported federal aid to upgrade the training of police, but he also tried to understand the causes of such violence. In fact, his willingness to appoint commissions of inquiry, to send staff members into urban areas, and to seek legislation aimed at urban problems helped arm the rioters with power. Johnson, who wanted to serve and please all Americans, was particularly sensitive to and eager to respond to protest. And even Johnson had to admit that the first two civil rights bills, which had eliminated most forms of racial discrimination in jobs, services, public facilities, and education, had hardly touched upon the problems of the cities. The civil rights acts addressed legal disabilities, not to de facto racial separation and the deeply entrenched economic problems faced by urban blacks. They also failed to outlaw segregation in housing.

Out of Johnson's increased sensitivity to the problems of cities came several urban and housing proposals and finally another civil rights act. In 1966, King shifted his emphasis and began a drive for open housing in Chicago. After new violence in the all-white suburb of Cicero, he gained promises of fair housing procedures from city and real estate officials, but nothing changed. Even as King helped publicize the problem, Johnson once again sponsored legislation, first announced in his 1966 State of the Union address. Another civil rights bill, with sweeping open housing provisions, went to Congress in April. But Johnson, now losing support over Vietnam, was unable to build his needed coalition to overturn another southern filibuster. Dirksen and the Republicans would not buy a bill that for the first time cut deeply in the North as well as in the South. Residential segregation was the norm throughout the country and a sensitive issue for white voters. The bill fared even worse in 1967. But in 1968 Dirksen once again rescued the bill and helped push it through the Senate. In the emotional aftermath of King's assassination on 4 April, it also passed the House, although not without tough provisions aimed at urban rioters. It outlawed discrimination in housing but set up no agency to enforce its provisions. At least in form, lenders and realtors accepted its terms, but rarely so in spirit. Integration in housing came at a snail's pace. But the bill did set a moral standard and provided a legal basis of appeal for blacks who were willing to defy local conventions and demand access even to wealthy suburbs.

Whatever the limitations, or any later failures of enforcement, or the moral conundrums tied to affirmative action, or the unsuspected and often unwanted fruits of court-forced racial balancing in the schools, Johnson's three civil rights bills still seem to represent an unprecedented success story in the area of social legislation. The acts met a major problem head-on, were tough, and effected, in a short period of time, a dramatic transformation in the legal status of blacks, particularly in the South. The time was ripe. Organized protest and political agitation worked. Credit for the bills was due to millions of Americans, even to the gaudier defenders of the old order who so unwittingly helped dramatize the moral issues. But, in retrospect, one has to emphasize the political artistry of LBJ, particularly in 1964 and 1965. Given the pressures for change, strong civil rights bills were all but inevitable. Yet no president less gifted than Johnson would have achieved as much and as quickly. In this case his facilitative role was crucial.

No other major Great Society bills had the focus, the clear goals, and the unambiguous results of the civil rights acts. This is most true of Johnson's declared war on poverty. Here nothing is very clear. And, behind the obscurity, the evaluative skirmishes go on and on.

The background, as always, was complex. President Kennedy, spurred on by the civil rights movement, much influenced by the growing debate about poverty in an affluent America, and moved by socialist Michael Harrington's much-read book, *The Other America*, asked his Council of Economic Advisers in 1963 to study the problem of poverty and to mature legislation to address these problems. Even before this, Robert Kennedy became deeply, emotionally involved in the problem of urban ghetto dwellers and personally lobbied for a 1961 Juvenile Delinquency and Youth Offenses Act. Close friends of his ran a new but small grant program ($30 million over three years). In supervising local delinquency projects, they emphasized the involvement and empowerment of the poor, such as in urban gangs, and thus the need for the poor to challenge or bypass existing welfare agencies and urban political machines. From the developing program came two or three key architects of the 1964 Economic Opportunities Act. But as Johnson took office in November 1963, the plans for antipoverty legislation remained incomplete. It is not clear how rapidly Kennedy would have pushed ahead on new programs. In retrospect, it is clear that the very complexity of the problems hidden behind the elusive word *poverty* required extended research and jeopardized the success of any hasty legislative program.

Vice President Johnson knew of the Kennedy studies on poverty and had expressed his support for some as yet unclarified legislation. The topic was a natural for him, given his mythical interpretations of his childhood. He often seemed to feel that because of experience he was an expert on poverty, and he even liked to exploit a proprietary claim to the subject in his dealing with academic experts. Just after the assassination, he began talks with Walter Heller on poverty issues and encouraged an early maturation of needed bills. He mulled over the issue and had some final discussions at the ranch during the Christmas break. Out of these discussions came an early decision—to make a crusade against poverty the centerpiece of his new administration. The issue fit his conception of the presidency, since he wanted to be a patron to all lowly Americans. Thus, in his State of the Union address, he announced that his administration "here and now, declares an unconditional war on poverty in America." He stressed the length and difficulty of the struggle, but said "we shall not rest until that war is won." Unfortunately, the impersonal *we* and inflated promises suggested that the war might be won during his administration.

Various poor people, whatever the standards used to determine poverty, were prime beneficiaries of Great Society legislation. Thus, in the public mind, the phrases "war on poverty" and "Great Society" soon became almost synonymous. Even the civil rights bills had increased access to jobs for unemployed blacks. The Appalachian Regional Development Act of 1965 was a major antipoverty bill. The first and most important provision of the huge Elementary and Secondary Education Act of 1965 directly addressed the problem of poor and disadvantaged children. A whole series of bills involving housing and urban services was targeted at slums and black ghettos, thus at populations with a high proportion of the poor. Medicare catered to the age group with the highest incidence of poverty, as did the Older Americans Act of 1965. Conversely, what subsequently proved to be one of the two most costly antipoverty programs instituted by the Johnson administration—Food Stamps—received little public attention when enacted in 1964. The Food Stamp Act was a high-priority administration bill, one tied to a larger agricultural package that included higher support prices for wheat and cotton. It expanded and made permanent a three-year pilot food-assistance program developed by the Department of Agriculture, which in 1965 cost only $75 million. Today, food stamps and Medicaid join Aid for Families with Dependent Children in the holy trinity of federal welfare policy. But in the Johnson years a few relatively small (in funds) and publicized programs, all authorized by the grab-bag EOA of 1964, best came to symbolize Johnson's antipoverty crusade. And of these new programs, two administered by the new agency created by the bill—the Office of Economic Opportunity (OEO)—received the largest share of attention, not because of their scope or cost or economic significance but because of innovative and highly controversial policies.

The EOA grew up in haste. Johnson wanted to get his antipoverty programs going as soon as possible. He selected Sargent Shriver to head a task force to mature a bill. Shriver still directed the popular Peace Corps and had married one of Kennedy's sisters. He gave visibility to the effort and was full of enthusiasm, but he had no particular expertise on the elusive topic of poverty. Few people did. His somewhat informal task force heard from a series of outside experts, including Harrington, as well as some cautious officials from the departments of Labor and Agriculture. Most controversial of the planners and of Shriver's close associates was Adam Yarmolinsky, who came from the Defense Department with developed plans, backed by the Labor Department, for turning abandoned army camps into training quarters for a new Youth Conservation Corps. As the task force struggled to get a bill together, inevitable rivalries among advisers threatened to sabotage its legislative prospects. As always, the final bill included bits and pieces of most of the various schemes. Always open to multiple answers, Johnson did not try to arbitrate the controversies or to give any clear focus to the bill. He just wanted an action program to vindicate his declaration of war and to become a centerpiece of his presidential campaign. In numerous speeches and through plenty of personal pleading, he pushed for his poverty bill and won widespread support even among businessmen, but he did little to clarify the implications of what the bill actually contained.

The bill passed easily in the Senate but floundered in the House. To spur its passage, Johnson believed he had to sacrifice Yarmolinsky; false charges of disloyalty led Johnson to give up on Shriver's plan to move him from the Defense Department and make him assistant director of the new OEO. The EOA authorized a wide spectrum of relatively modest programs. The total first-year appropriation for all the projects amounted to only $800 million, and this grew to only $1.7 billion by 1968–69. Thus, as a percentage of the whole appropriated budget (less than 1 percent), the program was only a pale reminder of the nearly $5 billion relief bill of 1935, which was almost half the then total federal budget. The separate, independent OEO, headed by Shriver, supervised two major programs—the Community Action Program (CAP) and the Job Corps—plus several smaller ones. Other delegated programs had to have Shriver's approval, but were administered by existing government agencies. All the programs were, according to the preface of the bill, to commit the United States to the elimination of poverty by opening to everyone opportunities for education and training, work, and a chance to live in decency and dignity.

The daring, at points radical, CAP supported a spectrum of activities at the local level, including projects in such areas as job training, legal counseling, community health, vocational rehabilitation, housing, home management, welfare reform, and various educational programs. Beginning in 1965, a series of innovative programs, all funded under the CAP budget, but with separate budget lines and centralized rules, attained the greatest popularity. These included Legal Services, Project Head Start (a type of community-organized nursery-kindergarten program for underprivileged children), Upward Bound (a special program to enable talented but poor children to qualify for college), and Neighborhood Health Centers. Often overlooked but in the long term the most unchallengeable achievement of CAP was the funding of major academic research on poverty (up to 15 percent of its budget) and, as part of this budget, the funding of demonstration projects. Research had to begin with the elusive issue of definition and include the complex issue of causation. Whatever the accepted definition and the understanding of causes, the OEO projects were too small to do more than scratch the surface of poverty in America. Had Johnson not seemed to promise so much, had he not launched these small programs in a flood of puffery, all of them might best have functioned as local experiments to supplement the research effort.

The various CAP programs quickly became the most controversial wing of the antipoverty crusade. The idea of community action, which flourished in the mid-sixties among radical groups, came into OEO directly from the early juvenile delinquency project. From it came the leading architect of CAP, Richard Boone. He helped write this part of the act and then tried to shape the local programs. It was Boone who insisted upon what became the most tantalizing phrase in the bill—that community projects be "developed, conducted, and administered with the maximum feasible participation of residents of the areas and of the groups served." Politicians, including Johnson, did not realize the dynamite in that requirement. Boone and other idealistic directors of the program did.

The CAP was primarily a granting agency. It invited grant applications from cities willing to set up Community Action Agencies (CAA). These were to develop new services for the poor, to coordinate all federal and local programs relating to the poor, and to promote institutional changes that would help the poor. And, in each such agency, the poor had to be involved as much as possible in all the plans and programs. This meant that each CAA had to include the poor on its governing board, hire them as subprofessionals (teaching assistants, hospital aides), and help them organize into what amounted to political pressure groups. This gave a peculiarly antiestablishment slant to the early CAP, particularly in a few cities. The poor, including welfare clients, organized, at least under the tutelage of dedicated and idealistic OEO representatives. In many cities they tried to reform the police and welfare agencies and to gain more control over schools and local services. In Syracuse, a local and quite radical CAA even hired the guru of nongovernmental community action, Saul Alinsky. In several cities Legal Service lawyers became ombudsmen for the poor, often directly challenging local politicians.

The early CAP cured very little poverty. Its funds ($340 million in its first year) soon flowed into over a thousand CAAs, some of which in rural areas or on Indian reservations did little more than sponsor a Head Start program. The majority of funds went to large urban programs, welcomed by city officials, who rushed to file successful proposals. But federal guidelines, and particularly the maximum feasible participation requirement, either bypassed or directly challenged existing city agencies and the entrenched, usually Democratic political machines. In short, the CAP was subversive of the existing order. The wilder CAAs—Newark, Buffalo, Syracuse, San Francisco, Detroit, Durham, Cincinnati, Hartford—floundered in problems of organization and leadership. The money often seemed to dwindle away, funding little more than the wages of CAA employees. In a few cases, militant black activists captured the programs, leading to an ironic twist—federal funds subsidizing a virtual revolution directed at the very source of the funds. Local chaos or local radicalism, elements of a class struggle, led to effective demands for more local political control, particularly from

Mayor Richard Daley of Chicago. Johnson, himself a mild paternalist but above all a politician, almost always sided with the local politicians. The early insurgentlike activists lost control over the CAA after the first two years, and the great experiment in participatory democracy—the empowerment of the poor—had almost ended by the time Johnson left office.

In 1967 the OEO faced such severe amendments in Congress as to threaten its survival. Concentrated administration efforts salvaged even the CAP, but not without amendments that strengthened the power of local officials and downgraded the power of the poor. Already, the trend was clear—to transfer OEO programs to existing and safer federal agencies, a trend completed in the Nixon administration by the abolition of OEO. But even that late the flavor of its beginning, the zeal of a unique corps of federal bureaucrats, lingered on in such programs as Head Start, which effectively recruited parents and rallied neighborhoods, and in Legal Services, which created an enduring legal subculture in America.

The Job Corps was only the largest and most controversial of the other OEO programs. The largest job program, in numbers served, was soon called the Neighborhood Youth Corps, and after 1967 it would be administered by the Department of Labor. It provided funds for the employment of youth, particularly in cities and mostly in the summer, in public service jobs. Other programs included grants and loans to impoverished rural families or to farm development corporations and rural cooperatives, a small grants program to help local governments improve the life of migratory workers (administered by the Farmers' Home Administration), special loans to small businesses to get them to employ the long-term unemployed (administered by the Small Business Administration), funds to the Department of Housing, Education, and Welfare to expand existing manpower training programs for unemployed fathers, and a small OEO-directed domestic Peace Corps, Volunteers in Service to America (VISTA), which employed over three thousand volunteers by 1968. In addition, the Office of Economic Opportunity began a work-study program for low-income college students, a program expanded by the Higher Education Act of 1965 and transferred to the Office of Education.

The Job Corps had special appeal to Johnson because it had ties to two of his favorite New Deal programs—the Civilian Conservation Corps and the National Youth Administration. It provided funds on a contract basis to federal and local agencies or private firms willing to set up conservation and training camps for youths aged sixteen to twenty-one, with an eventual and overly optimistic target of 350,000 in training at one time (the enrollment was only 36,000 by 1968, with about a third of these in separate women's camps). The camps were to offer educational and vocational training along with actual work experience. Three federal agencies—Park Service, Forest Service, and Bureau of Land Management—established small conservation camps (100 to 200 enrollees), mostly in the West. In most cases, private firms contracted to operate the larger, more controversial "urban" camps, which housed from 1,000 to 2,000 youths, often on older and deserted military bases. The Job Corps targeted one of the most intractable problems in America—how to utilize the skills of young high school dropouts, particularly those from urban ghettos. To be eligible for the Job Corps, one had to be outside the normal schooling process and without employment. The Corps paid all travel and maintenance costs, provided thirty dollars a month allowance, and also gave a credit of fifty dollars a month to each trainee, collectible upon completing the program. If the trainee so chose, the Corps would send twenty-five dollars of that to a family member each month and match it with an additional twenty-five dollars, an updated version of the old CCC rules. If states so chose, and some did, they could get OEO grants for additional state Job Corps. The program excited idealists and had broad appeal when first proposed, but it ran into early and almost insurmountable problems.

The targeted youths were hard to deal with. Most came from inner cities; over half were ghetto-hardened blacks. Ability levels were generally low, attitudes either passive or belligerent. The skills learned almost had to be entry level, and thus, at best, the graduates had to compete in a tight and shrinking job market. Morale problems, conflict, and delinquency marked all too many early camps, with a few nasty local scandals. In the first year, half the men and women dropped out before completing the training, and, predictably, costs per student were higher even than those in an Ivy League college. Given all the pitfalls, the corps could not rescue many people from poverty; continued unemployment or low incomes typified most of its graduates. But, for the targeted youngsters, the corps, after perfecting its techniques, probably did as much as any program could. It was too bad that lingering romantic memories of the CCC, with its quite different clientele and in a very different age, created so many false expectations for the Job Corps.

The EOA reflected a relatively small scattergun approach to carefully targeted populations mired in poverty. The Elementary and Secondary Education Act of 1965 reflected a major, largely indirect, nationwide attack on the roots of joblessness and poverty. It also marked a quantum leap in federal funding for education. For Johnson, this act, joined as it was with what he counted up to be sixty other education bills, was one of three or four great achievements of his life. His pride in it sprang not only from his lifelong perception of education as the main pathway to opportunity, a theme rooted in his own experience and his earliest career choice, but also from his success in maneuvering any federal aid bill at all through the church-state mine field that had so long intimidated Congress. When supplemented by other public education measures, such as the 1967 Education Professions Development Act (this included a small Teachers' Corps), and several higher education initiatives that involved aid for prospective teachers, it easily made Johnson the most active education president in American history. No one else came close. It is hard to overestimate the pride he felt when he came back to the ranch and, in the yard in front of the old Junction School, signed his great education act on 11 April 1965. He flew his first teacher, Kate Deadrich Loney, all the way from California to participate in the signing.

The Elementary and Secondary School Act, in its all-important Title I, authorized an original appropriation of $1.06 billion to improve schools and student performances in low-income districts. As a way around the perennial issue of parochial schools, the act targeted aid on the basis of the number of deprived children in a school district and allowed several new services—media centers, mobile services, radio and television programming, even shared-time access to new classrooms—to go to private school children. It was this compromise, in a decade with less Protestant-Catholic conflict and in the wake of Kennedy's presidency, that allowed Johnson, after another typically brilliant lobbying effort with key congressmen, to get the bill enacted.

Another sacred cow in education was local control. Thus, the bill targeted the grants to local school districts to pay for the new staff, new facilities, and new equipment necessary to upgrade or equalize educational opportunities for children from poorer homes. A district qualified for such grants if it had a hundred children from

226

families with incomes of less than two thousand dollars (the defined poverty level, in 1965, was three thousand dollars for a family of four) or, in the case of small districts, had 3 percent of its children in this category. This meant about 90 percent of all school districts qualified for aid, including some in predominantly wealthy neighborhoods. The formula for aid was based on both the number of deprived children and the level of local funding (the grant for each such child would amount to one-half the average per-pupil expenditure in that state). The other, less costly titles provided grants to states for libraries and instructional supplies, for special educational centers and programs, for upgrading state educational agencies, and for special research and development laboratories. Congress took pains to defuse the religious issue (no direct grants to private schools, no salaries for private teachers, no aid for any sectarian instruction or books) and the issue of local control (nothing in the grants could in any way influence or determine the content of courses or the selection of texts).

This critical bill moved far toward federalizing the financing of public education. But since it retained full local control over educational policies, this meant local control over the expenditures of federal subsidies, which made it almost impossible to measure with any rigor the effect of the federal funds. Clearly, by tying the largest grants to the poverty of parents, the act helped equalize educational funding. Districts in some poor areas qualified for almost 50 percent federal funding, and poor states like Mississippi gained the highest percentage of support from the grants. Had the funding formula been based on average per-student expenditures nationally, the equalizing effect, and the shift of funds from affluent to poor areas, would have been even greater. But what is hard to gauge is how much state and local school districts gradually allowed federal funds to replace what they would otherwise have raised through local taxes. In other words, the targeted federal funds, after the initial boost, may have in part supplanted rather than supplemented local funding and reflected little more than a transfer of educational responsibility. Fulfillment of the stated objectives of the bill—to upgrade the education of poor children—was even more problematic. Since local districts controlled the spending of the grants, they had many strategies for evading the purposes of the law and the rather detailed guidelines worked out by the Office of Education. Districts often apportioned funds to schools with only a few deprived students, and new staff or facilities clearly spilled over to aid all students. Even new compensatory efforts, largely in reading and arithmetic, usually encompassed low achievers whether poor or not. But in any case, the federal aid began as a major financial infusion for many local school districts in the most impoverished areas of America. And, insofar as money can buy better education, the act boosted the quality of education for most American children.

Johnson also had a bag of tricks for higher education. This included funds for college improvements in the Higher Education Facilities Act of 1963, the OEO Work-Study program of 1964, the Sea Grant program in 1966 (research funds for marine investigations), and the International Education Act of 1966 (grants to expand area studies programs). But the climactic achievements was the Higher Education Act of 1965. It included, in Title I, an original $50 million to fund community service programs developed by colleges and universities, $50 million for library improvements, $15 million for the training of librarians, and $30 million in improvement grants to developing (read struggling) colleges to fund cooperative courses, professorial exchanges, and national teaching fellowships intended to lure outstanding professors for a visiting year at small colleges. But its main goal was improved educational opportunities for students, particularly those from low-income families. Thus, it authorized Educational Opportunity Grants (the federal government picked up as much as half the value of scholarships targeted at disadvantaged students), provided funds for the active recruitment of disadvantaged college applicants, and financed an insured loan program for what turned out to be largely middle-class college students. These loans ($700 million in 1966) helped boost college enrollments in the late sixties, became the backbone of college financing for many parents, and helped keep open several small private colleges. All eligible students, based on a floating scale of parents' income, could defer interest until graduation. For the neediest, the federal government paid the deferred interest and up to all but 3 percent of the continuing interest. This act also tremendously expanded the Work-Study program and added additional funds to the Higher Educational Facilities Act of 1963.

For Johnson, medical insurance for those over sixty-five was a long-delayed commitment. He made what became known as Medicare the first legislative item for 1965. The bill, which involved major amendments to the Social Security Act of 1935, became S. 1 and H.R. 1 in the 1965 postelection Congress. Like most Great Society legislation, the bill was long and complex. At the time, the only major provision seemed to be a new Section VIII, which established Medicare. It included a mandatory hospitalization plan (Plan A), based on added Social Security taxes, and a supplemental benefits program covering many physicians' costs (Plan B), paid for by deductions from Social Security retirement payments. In the short run, the bill tremendously increased the security of older Americans. It raised above the poverty line some of those struggling to survive on Social Security retirement payments and unable to afford any private health insurance. The long-term effects have been less clear. The escalating cost of health care, in part spurred by Medicare, soon undermined many of its benefits. Since Medicare never paid all bills—it never provided coverage for chronic illnesses and long-term hospitalization or for most nursing home care—the added cost may have in time canceled out most of the benefits gained by a majority of retirees. By 1986, Americans over sixty-five paid the same percentage of income for health care (15 percent) as in 1965, and by then Medicare covered less than half of all medical costs. Meantime, its cost has soared from an original $3 billion to over $70 billion. But such a pessimistic prognosis overemphasizes the role of government payments in stimulating higher medical costs and, in any case, rests not so much upon any policies adopted during the Johnson administration as upon later policy decisions, including a failure of the federal government effectively to address the spiraling medical costs of the seventies and early eighties.

Medicare was, in a sense, another important antipoverty measure. It also reflected a major step toward the socialization of medical costs in America. Clearly for many elderly people, really for most American families, the risk of major illness, or even a series of minor illnesses, gradually became unbearable. Bankruptcy loomed for the unlucky. One way of socializing such risk is insurance. Thus, the federal government, by various tax benefits, had long subsidized group health insurance, in most cases provided as a benefit by employers. American families with at least one stable worker were usually able to share risks through corporate or cooperative group insurance. Their monthly deduction or payment, in a sense, represented another form of taxation. The retired, the unemployed, and several categories of underemployed or insecurely employed workers remained largely outside this middle-income refuge. Before 1965, they either suffered inadequate care or received a mixture of free or local welfare-supported care from physicians in hospitals as part of an informal system of indigent relief.

This largely passed the burden of such care to local governments, to medical facilities, and to affluent and insured patients, who had to pay larger bills.

The legislation of 1965 shifted much of this burden to the federal government in much the same way that the educational burden shifted to Washington. Along with Medicare, Congress authorized a grants program soon called Medicaid, which in the seventies soared in cost to become one of our major welfare programs. At the time, members of Congress did not envision such an important and costly program. Medicaid originated as part of another complex addition to the Social Security Act, Section IX, entitled "State Medical Assistance Program." In intent it was, above all, a way of consolidating in one program several forms of federally subsidized medical assistance heretofore authorized by the categorical aids provisions of the 1935 Social Security Act (for the indigent aged, the blind, and children of dependent families). Henceforth, these federal funds would go to the states under a single category. The matching funds were to be based on average per-capita income in each state, with the average federal share at 55 percent and the highest share at over 80 percent. The later role of such grants was presaged in one critical new category: other people with "sufficient financial need." To determine this, states were to set up flexible and what turned out to be highly variable income tests. By 1975 the coverage had to be universal. That is, every person who met the income requirements had to have access to medical care of "high quality."

Together, Medicare and Medicaid, joined with employer insurance plans, rather completely socialized the cost of medicine in America. These insurance plans make up a typically American, mixed, ad hoc system, one that has encouraged technological improvements, helped recruit very competent young men and women for the medical professions, and provided exemplary care for the affluent and for all well-insured patients, including early Medicare recipients. But the system has invited soaring costs, placed few checks on exorbitant fees and bills, allowed many people to slip through the security net, and generally continued, or in some cases rigidified, the second-class facilities and care provided for low-income and indigent patients, including most urban Medicaid patients, who are welcome only at underfunded public or charity hospitals. From the legislation of the sixties, Americans inherited a complex, uncoordinated, largely uncentralized health care system, a system supplemented by a wide spectrum of other medical programs enacted under Johnson (Nurses Training Bill of 1964, Allied Professions Training Act of 1966, Comprehensive Health Planning and Services Act of 1966, Mental Health Centers Act of 1967, and the large Health Manpower Act of 1968). It is only fair to point out that the resulting patchwork of plans, despite the soaring costs, enabled Americans to avoid many of the problems faced by centralized, publicly financed European programs—low-paid and less able physicians, crowded clinics, long waits for noncritical care, and much less technologically sophisticated hospitals.

Throughout his administration, Johnson struggled to find answers for the problems of large cities. Dozens of bills resulted. In totality, they provided federal assistance, or matching grants, for almost every city service, including public transportation (Urban Mass Transportation Act of 1966), sewers and waste treatment (Solid Waste Disposal Act of 1966), and the training of police (both the Safe Streets Act and the Law Enforcement Assistance Act), and even efforts to control urban rats (the much ridiculed Rat Extermination Bill of 1967, a bill often referred to as the "civil rats act" or even the "Rat Patman bill"). But most integral to urban reform was the perennial problem of housing. From the thirties on, the federal government had offered a bag of tricks in this area. The most successful program had all involved mortgage insurance for those able to afford private housing. The FHA and VA programs continued and expanded under Johnson. Supplemental to this, but plagued always by problems, had been subsidized public housing programs, beginning in 1931 with temporary programs, permanently funded after 1937, and tremendously expanded in the major housing act of 1949. The effort had often led to ugly projects, and the urban renewal aspects of such programs had only begun to alleviate the problem of slums. In fact, urban renewal projects in the fifties typically displaced low-income tenants or owners with commercial development or upgraded housing for the middle classes. With this as a backdrop, and under pressures from the exploding urban violence that began in 1965, Johnson tried to find legislative answers. Two innovative strategies deserve attention—the Model Cities Act of 1966 and the huge Public Housing Bill of 1968.

The model Cities proposal emerged from another of the major problem-oriented task forces that Johnson appointed in 1965. In some ways, the bill sounded like an expanded CAP program, and in fact it was developed to complement the CAP. It was also to be the showpiece of a newly created Department of Housing and Urban Affairs (headed by Robert C. Weaver, the first black to hold a cabinet position). The major stated goal of the act was to improve the quality of urban life, or what the bill's authors described as "the most critical domestic problem" facing the United States. Its main weapon was to be comprehensive demonstration projects in slum or blighted areas, designed to improve the welfare of the people who already lived there. The act, in its idealistic language, closely resembled that which led to the CAP. The federal government offered block grants to cover 80 percent of the cost and development of such projects, which were to go beyond low- and moderate-priced housing to encompass jobs, education, health care, crime prevention, even recreation. Quite intentionally, the detailed means had to be worked out locally, and the bill stressed "flexibility" and "new and imaginative" proposals. For 1966–67, Congress authorized a considerable appropriation for such demonstrations, $412 million, rising in 1967–68 to $512 million. Supplementing this major, soon well-publicized, and controversial program were smaller grants to cities for metropolitan planning and for technical assistance.

As so often with locally administered federal grants, the new demonstration projects were difficult to evaluate. The approach was new; idealism abounded. But the program quickly ran aground on charges of political favoritism (early grants seemed to reward congressional supporters) and local mismanagement of funds. Thus, any fair evaluation of the various demonstration projects would have to be on a city-by-city basis. Model Cities suffered many of the same problems as CAP. The critical one was how to achieve rational goals in programs planned in Washington but administered at the local level. The problems of coordinating federal and local action, and the seeming impediments that entrenched local interests posed to Great Society programs, led Johnson to appoint a task force on government programs in 1967. It thoroughly explored the developing administrative problems not only in antipoverty and urban programs but also in overcoming entrenched interests in existing government departments. It ended by suggesting rather moderate structural changes, such as a proposed new office of program coordination in the White House. This office was to utilize a permanent field force to help mediate agency conflict and to work to gain presidential goals in the local administration of programs such as CAP and Model Cities. By 1968, Congress was not about to give a beleaguered Johnson such new administrative authority.

232

The Model Cities program had limited impact upon housing. Thus, in 1968, Johnson submitted the most extensive and most expensive public housing proposal in American history. Legally, it involved several amendments to the acts of 1937 and 1949. The bill had several sections, all aimed at eliminating substandard housing in the next decade through the completion of 26 million new homes or apartments. Its two major programs involved plans for up to 600,000 annual, mostly new subsidized housing units for low- and moderate-income Americans. This greatly increased America's commitment to public housing, but nothing less grandiose would have matched Johnson's aspirations. The original act authorized a total of $1.7 billion in costs over the first three years. Most older, massive public housing projects had been funded by subsidized loans and developed by local limited dividend housing authorities; their rents were set according to family income. They usually clustered the poor in what often became notorious projects, beset by crime and violence. Johnson's plan, one eagerly supported by private builders, seemed to avoid such massive projects.

In the first of two main strategies, the government heavily subsidized and also insured the mortgages for low-cost privately owned homes costing up to twenty thousand dollars. Prospective owners bought from regular builders, with the Department of Housing and Urban Development paying various proportions of the interest costs according to family income levels. Supplementing this was a special mortgage insurance program for low-income families not able to qualify under normal FHA rules. These programs led to a surge of relatively inexpensive, often shabbily built homes, and to plenty of eager applicants for the new mortgages. An even larger rental program set fewer precedents. In it, the federal government subsidized 1 percent loans to developers who passed on the interest savings to low- or moderate-income occupants. The Johnson plan so limited the profits of developers (to 6 percent) that only nonprofit or limited dividend public organizations submitted proposals. In 1969, during the Nixon administration, Congress relaxed the interest ceiling, and then many private builders successfully procured such mortgages.

These new forms of public housing promised plenty of new houses and at low cost. The Nixon administration completed over 1 million units in the next three years. Never before had lower- and moderate-income Americans faced such appealing options. But some perennial problems haunted the program. As always, the FHA screened applicants carefully. Most of those selected to purchase homes tended to be at the upper limits of eligibility (that is, most had moderate incomes). Even in the rental units, the screening again favored the ablest families, leaving the most vulnerable poor, such as single mothers with children, to compete for the older project housing. But even more damning to earlier hopes, too many local developers built shabby homes or apartment units and by hook or crook gained FHA certification. By the early seventies, complaints about the program approached a major scandal. The Nixon administration suspended it and substituted direct housing allowances for the poor, a new approach that soon nourished scandals of its own. But in cities where the government inspectors did their job, the purchase plan was very popular. It did not remove very many people from poverty, but it enabled many working-class families to enter the ranks of home owners, exactly what Johnson wanted. That the program provided profits for builders and jobs for construction workers was also what he wanted. The more goodies for the more people the better, so long as benefits for one group took nothing from another, and so long as taxpayers gained the social goals that motivated their generosity.

It is easy to confuse Johnson's Great Society with the more limited issues of poverty. He had much broader aims. His goal was never a vast redistribution of income, any heightening of class feeling, any equality in returns, but rather a harmonized, happy, generous society, one that met the needs of all classes. The greatest problems, the deepest sense of alienation, involved those at the bottom of the scale. Johnson wanted very much to help them move up, to give them new opportunities for achievement, to help make them all, in some sense of that most loaded classification, successful middle-class Americans. He always stressed how much, and in what ways, antipoverty measures helped all Americans, and not just in the cynical sense that each program had built-in benefits or profits for nonclients. True, farmers zealously supported food stamps because of surpluses awaiting markets—they benefited. But in addition to the needs of the poor, Johnson responded to needs felt almost entirely by nonpoor Americans. This he did through consumer, safety, and environmental legislation. Even more narrowly elite groups became enthusiastic about beautification programs or new federal support for the arts and humanities.

In the perspective of a century hence, the Johnson era may be most remembered for the steadily maturing space program (lunar orbits and spaceship landings) and for the first critical turnaround in attitudes toward the environment. The growing awareness of ecological interdependence and of humanity's devastating impact upon fragile environments first exerted a major impact upon public policy in the Kennedy administration and would not peak until the Nixon administration. Johnson was never a perceptive student of the environmental movement or a committed partisan in supporting new legislation. But he was responsive, and he loved to add environmental protection, along with beautification, to his array of Great Society achievements. No single all-important bill reflected these concerns. But cumulatively the new legislation exceeded by far all earlier federal efforts. A listing of bills or new agencies has to support this judgment: a new Federal Pollution Control Administration, several amendments to the Clean Air Act of 1963, an amended Federal Pollution Control Act, the Water Quality Control Act of 1965, the Water Resources Planning Act of 1965, the Clean Water Restoration Act of 1966, the Air Quality Act of 1967, the Water Pollution Bill of 1968, and new radiation controls in 1968. Closely related were Lady Bird's beautification projects, the largely ineffective (as far as billboard removal) Highway Beautification Act, a new Wild Rivers Act, and an unprecedented creation of new national parks, scenic areas, recreational sites, wildlife refuges, and wilderness areas.

Most of these measures meant new bureaucracies and new regulations, as did Johnson administration initiatives in the area of consumer and safety legislation. A partial list here might include truth-in-securities and truth-in-lending bills, controls over flammable fabrics, the Fair Packaging and Labelling Act of 1966, the Automobile Safety Act of 1966, the Meat Inspection Act of 1967, the Poultry Inspection Act of 1968, the Coal Mine Safety Act of 1968, and the very important Occupational Health and Safety Act of 1968. Johnson also convened a President's Committee on Consumer Interests (1964) and appointed the first White House Special Assistant for Consumer Affairs. Less intrusive was a whole body of cultural legislation, including a National Museum Act, the Public Broadcasting Act of 1967, various grants-in-aid for local theater and dance, and the 1965 legislation that created both the National Endowment for the Arts and the National Endowment for the Humanities.

That is it. The Great Society—in brief, summarized, and oversimplified. What is one to make of it all? Johnson loved it. His domestic triumphs alone sustained him during the darkest days of the Vietnam War. What president ever did so much for the American people? He knew the pitfalls, came to understand the administrative problems, struggled with agencies that never quite fulfilled expectations. Such frustrations are inevitable. But he never repudiated the effort, the overwhelming commitment to attend to all human needs. Difficulties, delays, frustrations—they are a part of the game, good reason to try harder, to amend bills, to pass new ones. The problems are a challenge to government, to both legislators and bureaucrats. It is the duty of both to keep their hands on the throttle, their eyes on the rail. In his four years of retirement, Johnson continued to rejoice in his Great Society legislation and to lament threats to it during the Nixon administration. It was his great bequest to his country. He died with full confidence that historians would agree with his assessment and pronounce their almost unanimous judgment: well done, good and faithful servant.

How can a historian respond to that challenge? One critical assessment is both fair and easily sustained. The legislation enacted under Johnson did not fulfill, or has not yet fulfilled, the almost utopian vision that Richard Goodwin wrote into Johnson's 1964 speeches. This failure could indicate that the legislation was ill conceived from the beginning or that later politicians and bureaucrats betrayed its earlier promise. At a more restricted level, few of the bills came close to achieving the broad purposes that, typically for the Congress, prefaced all such legislation. In either case, the discrepancy is rather easily explained and certainly was not new to the Johnson administration. Presidents, in order to rally support for legislation, typically, perhaps appropriately, indulge a type of hyperbole, particularly in talking, even if vaguely, of their long-term goals. They then speak as prophets, as visionaries, even when they realize, as Johnson often remarked about his antipoverty crusade, that the road to such goals would be long and treacherous. In other words, such idealistic language sets the directions of public policy and inspires effort and support, but cannot chart the prosaic means of getting there.

Given a normal dichotomy between ends and means, one may still fault Johnson for verbal excess, for claiming too much for the actual legislation he was able to push through Congress. Here, one may argue, his language should have been descriptive, not visionary. Over and over again, particularly at bill-signing ceremonies, he talked as if an often limited, poorly funded bill would solve a problem, literally chart the way to racial equality, to equal educational opportunities for all, to health care for the elderly, or to opportunity pathways out of poverty. Some have argued that his glowing and exuberant celebration of his new legislation helped raise unfulfilled expectations, particularly for urban blacks and the poor, and that the resulting frustrations lay behind the unprecedented urban violence from 1965 through 1968. At best, his promises made up only one of many necessary conditions for the explosion, and even this causal connection is unprovable. It is also clear that Johnson's enthusiasm for his Great Society legislation was more innocent than deceitful. Sentimental, given to verbal excess in all areas, he indulged too many superlatives. And at the moment of legislative triumph, Johnson was not given to any thoughtful appraisal of future hazards. He was never detached enough to do this, never able to distance himself from his momentary achievements. Thus, in 1964 and 1965 he clearly indulged some completely unrealistic advertisements for his Great Society.

Johnson had little sense of irony. He expected problems. At low moments, he felt that fate was against him, that he was bound to fail. But he usually personified the causes of failure. Someone was always against him—northeastern intellectuals, the press, disloyal advisers—and this accounted for any defeats. He had little sense of how even the best-laid plans go awry, of how often the consequences of human choice are the very opposite of what one intended, of how unknown complications always lurk and often doom our best-intentioned efforts. Since he could not easily accept this, he was indeed a utopian, for he saw few limits to human achievement. Over and over again he told lowly Americans, those without hope, that all levels of achievement were really open to them, given enough will and enough effort. Such a boundless sense of possibility appropriately joined a conspiratorial explanation of failure (they did it to me) or a moralistic one (they lacked the required determination) or an environmentalist one (they never had a fair chance). And these obstacles are the very ones that lend themselves to legalistic and bureaucratic remedies. No other American president has expected, and demanded, so much of our congressional government, been so oblivious to its, or humanity's, inherent limitations.

When one moves from such assessment in terms of the goals and achievements of the actual actors to evaluation, one enters the lair of ideology—of reasonably coherent systems of belief and preference. Of course, Johnson was not ideological. He never probed basic beliefs or tried to clarify operative values. But, by that very fact, he easily reflected entrenched beliefs and values. That is, he lived them, unreflectively, uncritically. This explains why he was so conventional in both his goals and his means. He was unconventional, even unprecedented, in the amount of energy he expended to attain his goals and in the intensity of effort, his haste to get there, and his egotistic desire to do it all himself.

The Great Society legislation, so diverse and unwieldy, did in the broadest sense continue a tradition. It expanded what, by 1964, was an accepted, even orthodox, American approach to the problems of a highly productive, collectivized, interdependent, and dependency-producing economy, and to a highly mobile, increasingly cosmopolitan society. Americans had all along clearly favored mild, in part decentralized, pluralistic solutions both to older insecurities and inequities and to new types spawned by collective forms of production. Throughout the twentieth century, the federal government in response to focused demands from voters had opted not for centralized governmental ownership of productive resources, not for any centralized and detailed management of the economy, and thus neither for classical socialist remedies nor for any corporatist, fascist, or supernationalist strategy. Europeans adopted, or at least flirted with, these solutions. Instead, Americans chose a limited socialization of management through modest, often indirect regulations, controls, or subsidies. That is, our government tried to influence, guide, or set outer limits to private choice, but still leave the most basic economic decisions to private individuals or firms. Americans also came to accept, often out of necessity, a limited socialization of product, a modest redistribution of income, of the final product, through various welfare measures or transfer payments. Johnson's major legislation, all prefigured by legislative proposals over the preceding two decades, simply expanded on these two strategies but at an unprecedented rate. In five years the American government approximately doubled its regulatory role and at least doubled the scope of transfer payments. Thus, policies that were orthodox and cumulative came at such a rapid pace as to seem to some almost revolutionary.

The most effective perspective for criticizing the Great Society legislation is to reject the underlying orthodoxy, to repudiate a mild, uncoordinated, loose regulatory-welfare approach. Then, even if Great Society welfare or regulatory legislation worked about as well as could be expected, given the fallible people who had to administer the programs, one could still argue that these were misdirected or inadequate remedies for deep-seated forms of injustice or irresponsibility. Or, from the other perspective, one could argue that such regulation and such welfare creates a paternalistic and overly intrusive state, distorts production, diminishes individual responsibility, threatens critical incentives to work, impedes economic growth, and even undermines the traditional family. Given the values and perspectives of such critics, they are all correct, and the Great Society indeed was either pitifully inadequate or dangerously misdirected. This is only to reiterate the obvious—Johnson was too conventional, too unperceptive, too unphilosophical to embrace either daring structural innovations or, more radical in impact, any reactionary path back toward less regulation and less welfare.

No doubt the federal government became a great deal more intrusive in the sixties. Almost any legislation, even welfare measures, involved new rules, new guidelines, that circumscribed the behavior of some Americans, at times even those who collected new subsidies. In each case, the new rules, from the perspective of Congress, served desirable, that is moral, ends. Ironically, some rules—as in the civil rights acts—limited traditional majority patterns of behavior in order to "liberate" blacks or women. Governments face a perennial problem—how to balance the ends served by regulations with other potentially harmful (from the perspective of the whole) efforts that may derive from too many of even the most noble regulations.

This is only to introduce an ongoing dialogue about Great Society legislation, a dialogue tied not only to the original legislation but to how later bureaucrats interpreted the rules. Have federal officials been too arduous or too lax in enforcing consumer, safety, and environmental regulations? Has the EEOC or the Commission on Civil Rights gone too far or not far enough in requiring affirmative action by employers? But even such questions assume that the government needs to make rules, to order behavior, in these areas. The more sweeping argument is that, in at least many cases, the federal government has embraced tasks either that no central government can do or that no government can do well. One twist on this is the old "capture" thesis—that regulatory agencies almost always become captive to the outlook of those purportedly the target of their regulations. In this sense, regulation never serves its intended purpose. And behind such a sweeping and deeply pessimistic judgment often lie beliefs about some intractable human nature. But most such sweeping indictments of government action reflect economic theories, which suggest that regulation, however humane in intent, so distorts a market as unfairly to favor certain competitors, to lower the efficiency of the overall economy, to slow or reverse economic growth, and thus to move a society toward greater scarcity and with it more poverty, suffering, and class conflict.

The other side has its own compelling arguments. Passage of the Great Society legislation paralleled, and in small ways was influenced by, the intellectual ferment of the middle and late sixties. Particularly among college students, all the older institutions and values came under severe challenge. It is hard to find any consistent ideology among the different critics. But at least widespread was a concern over greater realized equality not just in opportunity but in income and an encompassing desire for the political and economic empowerment of ordinary people, for what some called participatory democracy. These concerns most influenced the CAP, but even then in ways that confused and then forced a modification in its leadership and goals. For these goals, whether stated in the fuzzy form of New Left advocacy or dignified by a coherent and rigorous, perhaps Marxist, ideology, were not the goals of Johnson and the Congress. In the context of the continuities of domestic policy, such concerns remained largely alien and radical. And, therefore, it is not surprising that the new legislation never achieved such goals, even though one may feel passionately that federal legislation should serve such egalitarian but, by that very fact, not libertarian ends.

The antipoverty or welfare legislation exemplifies such non-achievement, given this perspective. Johnson never made any major redistribution of income an administrative goal. Whenever general revenue taxes fund welfare programs, they do redistribute the final product. Even the term *transfer payments* assumes this. The point is that Johnson's focus was on the recipients, on creating a type of safety net for the most intractable poor, on opening opportunities for as many of the poor as might be able then to make it on their own. He expected this much generosity from those who had already made it as a matter of stewardship as well as self-interest. But if the poor could become consumers, could become more productive, such welfare could in a sense pay for itself in the form of growth. Welfare would indeed require more and more tax revenue, but not necessarily higher tax rates. This was the ideal answer and also the easy one. And whatever the aggregate effect of Great Society programs on income shares in America (this is still a highly technical and debatable topic), it is obvious that Medicare, Medicaid, food stamps, and subsidized housing did provide new security for people unemployed, unemployable, or not open to employment because they have young children. And, quite inadequately, the CAP, Model Cities, and various job and retraining programs did provide a favored few with opportunities to move out of poverty and to gain employment, even if rarely decent or well-paid employment.

But the Great Society legislation did not end poverty in America, even when it altered the conditions of poverty. The safety net rarely served as a launching platform. Of course, by use of aggregate data on the number of poor or on income distribution, one can both defend and damn antipoverty programs. For example, Johnson rejoiced, by 1968, in the large number of people who had risen above the official poverty level (down from 20 to 12 percent in only five years), as if his Great Society caused it. In fact, a near-wartime economy and a 3.5 percent unemployment rate were the major causes of such a lifting at the bottom. In the 1980s critics used aggregate data on the number of impoverished families, on the percentage of single-parent families, and on illegitimacy rates among black mothers to prove that Great Society legislation had not cured, but created, grave social problems. Such exaggerated, at times dishonest, charges also ignored the much more potent effects of 8 percent unemployment, of the displacement of unskilled black males from the job force, and of the migration of labor-intensive industries away from northern cities. The point of all this is obvious—Great Society welfare measures could alleviate some of the burden of the poor, but had little impact on broad changes in the economy and on the cultural roots of poverty.

Such a general analysis of Great Society legislation may miss the point. The fairest evaluation would have to attend to the peculiarities of each bill and each agency. When looked at individually and in terms of the purpose of Congress, the Great Society legislation fared rather well. The bills, as a whole, reflected careful legal craftsmanship. Almost without exception they were sustained by court decisions or, ironically, in some cases effectively expanded by court interpretations, as in the case of civil rights. The majority of bills reflected an exceptional amount of background investigation and inquiry, and because of the times, the rush of legislation, or Johnson's artistry in the case of the most controversial bills, they passed with unusually few amendments or deletions. Even the tempo of legislation helped keep bills intact. Most legislation received a full congressional airing only in friendly committees. Other members of Congress could not be familiar with each complicated act. And, except for the major, highly publicized bills, the public remained all but oblivious to what was happening. Thus, constituency pressures were muted. Few people who lived through the mid-sixties, who were preoccupied with the Vietnam War or civil rights, can even remember the enactment of important Great Society bills. It is almost as if the greatest legislative avalanche in American history passed unnoticed. This helped Johnson and, in a sense, helped ensure more coherent, better focused bills. And in all the haste, many of the new agencies had at least a bit of leeway, for they were safe for a brief time from close congressional or public scrutiny.

Thus, the Great Society legislation, to a sweeping extent, did exactly what Johnson and his advisers and friendly congressmen wanted it to do, at least in the short term. Being problem oriented, the legislation provided typical political answers. Not full answers and, of course, never all the money wanted by activists, but all the money that Congress was willing to grant. Conventional in design and narrowly focused in intent, the vast majority of bills led to effective regulation or to lasting and growing transfer payments, many directed not only, or not even at all, at the very poor. Coerced or bribed, Americans moved in policy directions that then seemed desirable.

Of course, ironies abound. Unexpected outcomes always accrue to legislation. And, as everyone knew, any new program was most likely to create new problems. The Johnson legislation thus reflected the increasing complexity of American society, the rapid tempo of change, and an ever-growing number of problems and human concerns that cry out for political answers. That, for a few brief years, Congress responded to these problems and concerns more promptly than ever before or since, at times more responsibly and in a few cases more daringly, was in part a product of the chaotic times, but also a product of the legislative magic of Lyndon Johnson. By any number of moral perspectives, our society was not great either in 1963 or in 1968. If not great then, it probably seems even less so today. But at least briefly, in the mid-sixties, the federal government did try to be generous. Big Daddy saw to that.

Johnson and a reluctant cowboy, Vice President Humphrey, celebrate the landslide victory of 1964.

LBJ assesses a prize bull.

To win support for antipoverty legislation—at the Kentucky home of Tom Fletcher.

Signing the Elementary and Secondary Education Act of 1965 at old Junction School and with Johnson's first teacher—Kathryn Deadrich Loney.

Signing the epochal Civil Rights Act of 1964, in East Room of the White House.

TOP: A Tuesday luncheon in 1967, the setting for crucial Vietnam decisions.
BOTTOM: Selecting bombing targets in the White House Situation Room.

Agonizing over a new Vietnam policy just before the 31 March 1968
speech.

J and grandson Patrick
ndon Nugent, August 1968.

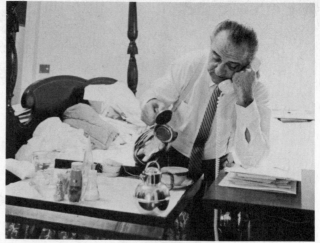

The last morning in the White House, 20 January 1969.

The last golden days, 6 November 1972.

10

VIETNAM:
INTO THE TRAP

Lyndon Johnson's presidency ran aground on Vietnam. On this, as on no other issue of his life, Johnson failed. He knew it. He suffered intensely. Here, finally, his lifelong, almost fatalistic expectation of failure found justification. Yet the failure, as he understood it, flowed from no ignorant or mean-spirited choices. He never repudiated his critical decisions about Vietnam, never. even in hindsight identified any alternative policies that, at the time of choice, seemed to make better sense or to promise better outcomes. In this sense, alone, his failure had a tragic dimension.

Johnson's Vietnam policies flowed consistently from a series of decisions made by three earlier presidents. Continuity, not new departures, marked his choices, not because of a lack of experience on his part or any incapacity for dealing with foreign powers but because of his own conventional beliefs and values. A cautious president, one as adverse to conflict and violence as any president since Hoover, LBJ made restraint a hallmark of his presidency. He was far less bellicose and adventurous than Roosevelt and Truman, let along Kennedy. He disliked confrontations. And, from the perspective of his advisers and, until 1967, by his probably accurate understanding of the most likely sources of intense political opposition within the United States, his role in the Vietnam conflict was one of moderating and restraining others, of setting very limited goals and eschewing reckless and dangerous means of attaining them. He wanted, above all else, to contain the Vietnam conflict, to prevent it from turning into the opening phases of World War III.

Yet despite all these qualifications, Johnson made a series of decisions in 1965 that took the United States virtually beyond any point of return in Vietnam. He committed American planes and then American troops to the active defense of a beleaguered South Vietnamese government. He chose war. Earlier choices by his predecessors provided a rationale for his decisions. For him to have chosen differently, for him to have permitted the collapse of the non-Communist regime in South Vietnam, would have required a new and radically different understanding of events, a new rationale for American foreign policy in Southeast Asia, and unusual political courage. Earlier precedents made other options unappealing, but options still existed. LBJ and his advisers endlessly considered them. They rejected them. Of course, they never expected all the consequences that followed, never quite realized the extent of the risk that lay behind their policies. But even had they known this, it is doubtful that their choices would have been all that different.

The Truman administration made the first critical American Indochina commitment in 1949–50. In late 1949 the Chinese Communists won in that country's civil war, with enormous psychological reverberations in the United States. The felt need to prevent further Communist gains turned Ho Chi Minh, the leader of Vietnamese anticolonial forces, into a threatening figure. In February 1950, the United States committed itself through various forms of economic and military assistance to the French cause in Indochina, a policy not only predicated upon perceived strategic realities in the Far East but also tied to an effort to win a reluctant France into a new European alliance system, one containing West Germany as a full partner. This new commitment, which was tremendously reinforced by the Korean War in June 1950, meant that the United States now began to assume responsibility for maintaining non-Communist, even anti-Communist regimes in Indochina. Such were the internal dynamics in Indochina, and most particularly in Vietnam, that political goals led the United States to side with the French, or with collaborationist elements, and thus to oppose nationalist and socialist forces. In this lay the seeds of a later Vietnam war.

The next critical policy decisions came under the Eisenhower administration in 1954. Despite American assistance of over $1 billion in 1954 alone, France suffered a galling defeat in Dien Bien Phu in May and, at a conference already convened in April in Geneva, it began bargaining for a means of granting full independence to its former Indochina colonies. The Eisenhower administration seriously considered asking for a congressional resolution permitting the use of American troops to bolster the French cause; the Joint Chiefs of Staff recommended air and naval support. Lyndon Johnson was among those who most actively opposed American intervention. Besides, the French lacked the will to continue the war, and to the despair of the United States on 21 July they agreed to a complex formula for immediately ending hostilities and for the rapid withdrawal of all French forces.

The Geneva Declaration recognized three independent states. Cambodia and Laos agreed to move to national elections and to pledge themselves to a fully neutral role in world affairs. The agreement for Vietnam was necessarily more complex because of the deep divisions among the Vietnamese people, or what already amounted to a near civil war between opposing factions. The declaration provided for two temporary regrouping zones, divided by the seventeenth parallel, to permit the peace and stability required for internationally supervised elections, scheduled for July 1956. The southern zone provided the refuge for non-Communist elements in Vietnam, including most Roman Catholics and most former French allies. The original government was nominally headed by the former French-supported puppet, the Bao Dai, but soon effectively came under the control of Premier Ngo Dinh Diem. The northern zone offered a refuge for some of the most militant nationalist elements and for disciplined and effective Vietminh troops. By provision of the declaration, the Vietnamese people were free to move to their preferred regrouping zone, and a considerable population shift occurred among those with strong political or ideological allegiances, with the largest movement of people toward the pluralistic South.

Politically, American overt and covert aid helped Diem to consolidate power in the South and by 1956 to develop a reasonably secure government. With American sufferance, Diem sabotaged the scheduled 1956 national elections. In Vietnam neither the word *free* nor the word *election* had very clear meanings, but such were the power relationships that the Ho Chi Minh government would in all likelihood have won a majority, thus unifying Vietnam as a Marxist and socialist state, one supported and supplied by the Soviet Union and, despite traditional resentments, still backed by Mao Tse Tung and the Peoples' Republic of China. In short, the Eisenhower administration, as much as it was able by the terms of the Geneva Declaration and through extensive covert activities, became the sponsor and guardian of the Diem government in South Vietnam, or what seemed the last but very vulnerable obstacle in the way of full Communist control in Indochina.

Critical to subsequent American policy was the nature of the two regimes in Vietnam. In the North, Ho Chi Minh bested, and often ruthlessly suppressed, all competing factions and as quickly as possible built a Marxist-Leninist regime. It was, in intent if not yet achievement, egalitarian and totalitarian. Ho, in past residences in Paris and Moscow, had become a committed Marxist. He returned to Vietnam during World War II with clear goals—to defeat the Japanese, to prevent the restoration of French rule, to build a modern, unified socialist state, and to align it with the international Communist movement to which he turned for economic support. He was a philosopher, an ideologue, a true believer, but also a cagey politician. After 1954 he was able to fulfill most of his ideals. He had, in his Vietminh, a core of disciplined, loyal supporters. They were able to set up a tight administrative system, establish a largely state-owned economy, launch an effective program of mass education and ideological indoctrination, reeducate or exile effective opponents, and thus move toward an ordered one-party state. The effort depended on a common belief system, one tied to the values of communal solidarity, equal returns, and disciplined work. In other words, Ho brought a form of puritan zeal to North Vietnam. In contrast to the South, he was able to impose state authority on a formerly localized, poor, largely peasant society. But, quite clearly, his regime was unlikely to gain much sympathy from the United States, not only because of its alignment with the Soviet bloc but also because Ho rejected the pluralistic institutions of the West. His regime did not brook dissent, carefully regulated and circumscribed expressive freedoms, and centered political control in a small, tight cadre of party leaders.

In the South the Diem regime remained committed to a more pluralistic, Western type of society. It included many bitterly anti-

Communist factions. Diverse religious groups, including Diem's own powerful Catholic minority, had to work together. Diem, a person of ability and considerable integrity, tried to build a modern state in the South. He only partially succeeded. He faced almost impossible problems—a highly decentralized society, a lack of qualified personnel, and a lack of ideological zeal or ruthlessness. Although himself a nationalist, he suffered the political cost of continued dependence upon the West. He would later lose support because of nepotistic family allies and his own authoritarian tactics, particularly against suspect Communists. Thus, in the brief time he had, Diem was able to build only a flawed caricature of a Western constitutional republic. His major failures were often camouflaged by the obvious ones—personalized lines of authority, undeveloped representative institutions, corrupt local officials, and seemingly harsh policies toward various Buddhist factions. But these problems diverted attention from his most critical failure—to extend effective state authority into the rural areas. He suffered, indeed, from arbitrary exercises of authority, but this only reflected the lack of a system of hierarchical and bureaucratic authority and an effective administrative and police system. Diem failed to impose law and order and discipline on the South, all goals more easily attained by the more monolithic, more ideological, more puritanical, and more ruthless regime in the North.

The next American policy shift toward Vietnam came under Kennedy, but with the full complicity of LBJ. The backdrop involved a gradual escalation of local insurgency movements in both Laos and South Vietnam. The division of Vietnam into two sections had created a perfect setting for subversion and insurgency. Thanks to the Pentagon Papers, historians have some detailed information about the wide range of clandestine, destabilizing activities, or even overt sabotage, carried out by the United States and Vietnamese agents in North Vietnam. They have no such details of clandestine activities in the South supported by North Vietnam, but one can estimate that these were much more extensive and more effective. They clearly became so after 1958, with a degree of resurgence among pro-Communist groups that had suffered severely under tough security measures attempted by Diem. The level of insurgency in the South seemed to grow exponentially in 1959 and 1960, and by then organized resistance forces controlled large areas of the countryside. These so-called Vietcong (a label for the Vietnam Communist party) also enjoyed direct support from the North, presaging a full-scale war. Thus, the new Kennedy administration found a rapidly degenerating political and military situation in South Vietnam, even as it had to adopt policies to cope with an overt civil war in Laos.

President Kennedy significantly increased American support for South Vietnam. The Eisenhower administration had stopped short of any overt violation of the Geneva Declaration. Not so Kennedy. Shortly after his inauguration, Kennedy approved the use of 400 new Special Forces troops in Vietnam, or a level of military support clearly precluded by the Geneva Declaration (this limited American personnel to the number in Vietnam at the time of the cease-fire, or to only 685). Kennedy joined this open support with a new major clandestine operation in Laos and North Vietnam. Then in November 1961, he decided to expand the number of American advisers in South Vietnam (to over 16,000 by 1963) and to use them in direct combat-support roles. In some cases he permitted them to defend themselves against the Vietcong. This meant American involvement in battles and soon a trickle of American casualties. The escalation of the American role was not primarily a reflection of Kennedy's penchant for military adventurism, but what seemed to his advisers a necessary prop for the beleaguered South Vietnam regime. Short of such support the existing government of South Vietnam would likely fall either to the Vietcong or to a nationalist coalition that would, in the long term, lead to a unified but Communist Vietnam. Joined with the perilous situation in Laos, the long-term prospect seemed an all-Communist Indochina with subsequent pressures on other Southeast Asian countries. No American president ever subscribed fully to a simplistic domino theory (that if Vietnam fell, so inevitably would other Southeast Asian countries), but they envisioned increased levels of subversion in Thailand and Malaysia if Ho won in Vietnam.

Kennedy was also concerned that Vietnam was a testing ground for wars of national liberation and other forms of insurgency. He saw the American response as critical, as a test of the American will and capacity to defeat such movements. But note that even as Kennedy upped the odds in Vietnam, he vetoed suggestions from his Joint Chiefs of Staff and key White House advisers that he commit American ground troops to Vietnam, or even more compelling pressures to begin overt bombings in Laos and North Vietnam (covert air raids were frequent in Laos and even in border areas of North Vietnam). Thus, Kennedy's policies, like so many of Johnson's, involved a minimalist or restrained approach. At the time,

248

and given the American understanding of what was at stake, no other alternative seemed tenable. This is only to say that neither JFK nor LBJ could even contemplate policies that would allow South Vietnam to become Communist.

What lay behind the opposition to a Communist South Vietnam? Both in South Vietnam and the United States, large groups of people, most fervently Christian, always viewed Marxist beliefs as fallacious, evil, and exceedingly dangerous. As true believers themselves with an alternative ideology, even one at times as broad and encompassing and thus as totalitarian as any version of Marxism, they posed their truth against alien error. In the United States such ideological anti-Communists needed no other reason to oppose North Vietnam and constituted, from beginning to end, the constituency that pressed most consistently for a full war and complete victory. Johnson did not share such an ideological commitment, but in Texas he had struggled with such religiously zealous anti-Communists throughout his career. If anything, he exaggerated their numbers and their strength, and in the early escalation of the war he always felt that they, in their willingness to risk a third world war, made up his most powerful critics. He carefully developed his policies with them in mind and thus saw himself as restrained, moderate, and responsible in his decisions.

Johnson represented a broad, complex, immensely varied American mainstream in his views of communism, which he rarely defined very carefully. Not ideological, Johnson never pictured the Communist party or leaders as evil. Misguided perhaps, but not evil. He even recognized a socialist economy as an option that newly independent peoples might choose for themselves. Thus, his stated support of South Vietnam always reflected two issues—the aggressive side to North Vietnamese subversion, which meant that unwilling South Vietnamese would be forced into a Communist system against their will, and the ties of North Vietnam to China and the Soviet Union, which meant that victory by the North in the South would have major implications in East-West relations, would threaten important if not vital American interests, and would destabilize other Southeast Asian countries vulnerable to externally funded subversion. His major advisers agreed with him in this understanding. Note that their commitment to South Vietnam rested not so much on ultimate issues of good and evil as on costs and benefits, including at times moral costs. If defense of South Vietnam meant a third world war, of course they would not defend it. If the ultimate human suffering in protecting South Viet-

nam outweighed the benefits of such a stand, then they would repudiate the effort, as many subsequently did. This practical
approach encompassed widely divergent strategic goals. It involved hard-headed realists and romantic idealists. It also included almost all those who, sometime after 1965, shifted from support
of the war to opposition.

One additional point of view complicated even the opening debates about Vietnam policy. Unlike in the Korean War, a third
group of Americans was large enough and articulate enough to influence policy. It included those people who preferred North Vietnam to South Vietnam and who even before 1965 opposed
American efforts to sustain the Diem regime. In a sense, after 1965
they wanted the United States to lose if it would not get out of
Vietnam. Those who so chose sides in the war also reflected a
broad spectrum of opinion, but almost all of it was to the left politically. Such views both caused, and then grew because of, the
policy debates about Vietnam. For a few, the outlook had roots in
the pre–World War II Communist party and in even older socialist
traditions. In any case, it fed as much, or more, on the perceived
sins of the American or the South Vietnamese government as on
any realistic appraisal of North Vietnam. But for a few college students, it also involved ideological affinities with the Marxist
North. Those students embraced solidarity and equality as primary goals, much more important than, and at times clearly in
conflict with, competitive and libertarian values. Tolerance, pluralistic accommodation, abstract bureaucratic rules, preference to
high achievement, often grouped under such labels as liberalism
or capitalism—all lost appeal. Young people yearned for a unifying
ideology and for communal solidarity, and they found models of it
not in repudiated Christian doctrines (the Christians had all sold
out to the establishment, to capitalists and imperialists) but in one
of many versions of Marxism or in other even more esoteric ideol-
ogies. They romanticized Ho Chi Minh and his people's struggle
against colonial oppression. They launched their own small cultural revolution in the United States. They cut sugar cane in Cuba,
idealized Che Guevara, and above all came to hate Lyndon Johnson. He seemed to epitomize all that they had rejected.

Kennedy's policies in Indochina had helped stimulate the first
such reactions on the Left. His policies also failed. Negotiations in
Laos led to an ostensibly neutral government, but one soon aligned
with the socialist bloc. Here, unlike in South Vietnam, the United
States supported opposing insurgents or terrorists (when these

support the American side, they are called "freedom fighters"). In South Vietnam, Diem seemed to lose support each year. Concern over Diem led to Vice President Johnson's trip to Vietnam in May 1961, a trip that, with its personal and emotional elements, reinforced Johnson's wholehearted support for Kennedy's policies in Vietnam. By late 1963, Diem's regime seemed likely to collapse without vastly increased American aid. Kennedy gave up on Diem, who had rebuffed pressures for reform, for more conciliatory policies toward Buddhist opponents, and for less arbitrary and repressive tactics. By the fall of 1963, the Vietcong seemed stronger than ever, controlled large sections of the countryside, rather cavalierly carried out nighttime raids in most areas, and were now able to field battalion-size forces. Even provincial capitals were now vulnerable, and the threat of assassination had either demoralized or effectively destroyed local government and local police. Increasingly, the often arbitrary, frequently corrupt authority of the South Vietnam government was limited largely to the cities or to daylight hours.

Had the Diem government initiated major reforms, it is possible that Kennedy would have committed extra American ground forces by early 1963. But the increased ineffectiveness of Diem made such a move hazardous at best, although military advisers then as later dramatically underestimated the level of American forces needed to defeat the Vietcong. In a sense, Kennedy used the prospect of increased support, even of a direct military role, as a bait to induce domestic reforms. Diem usually refused the bait, at least by American estimates, for he launched an overt attack against Buddhist opponents in the summer of 1963. Thus, the final phase of Kennedy's Vietnam policy in 1963 involved two interactive goals—first, to prevent further military deterioration and, second, to gain a more effective South Vietnam government. The second goal led to the reluctant decision to support a 1 November coup in Saigon, which led against American wishes to the murder of Diem and his much-hated brother, Ngo Dihn Nhu. The military situation remained perilous, but in an unjustified burst of optimism, and for political consumption at home, Kennedy even suggested an early reduction in the sixteen thousand American troops in Vietnam, an optimistic view reiterated by Lyndon Johnson just after he assumed the presidency. Kennedy's assassination, falling immediately after the coup in Vietnam, left a desperate crisis to Lyndon Johnson, what turned out to be a horrible trap.

As president, Johnson had to assume the full and awesome responsibility for Vietnam. He apparently did not realize the perils that it posed for his presidency. Heretofore, he had been at the periphery of Vietnam decision making but a personally and emotionally involved partisan. Even though he had criticized Diem, he also liked him and had opposed the American-supported coup that led to his death. With power came greater caution and restraint. On assuming the presidency, Johnson neither initiated any new internal policy review on Vietnam nor changed any of the existing policies in the field. He retained all Kennedy's military and foreign policy advisers. He did nothing to influence ongoing strategic decisions, for Johnson had no sense of any real alternatives to what Kennedy had tried to do. The well-established and consensual goals seemed clear enough—to suppress or defeat the Vietcong insurgency in the South, to use either force or bribes to get North Vietnam to discontinue its support of such insurgency, and in this way to secure an independent non-Communist state in the South. Johnson, like his predecessors, usually added some glittering ideals to dignify these goals—that South Vietnam be "free," that it be "democratic," that it have a "constitutional government," and that it offer something close to a modern welfare state to its citizens.

Such language floated far above the realities of Vietnam. In the context it had almost no operative meaning, although Johnson undoubtedly took such verbal glitter quite seriously. During his first full year as president, Johnson did not endorse any major new departures in Vietnam. His relative caution reflected personality, political considerations in an election year, intense fears of Chinese or Soviet intervention, and his primary commitment to domestic issues. From behind the often optimistic reports on Vietnam, the actual dangers of a Communist victory increased monthly. Ironically, the political instability under the new and weak premier, Nguyen Khanh, helped postpone any new military initiatives. The United States was afraid that they would only incite more Vietcong attacks, further demoralize the country, and in the short term worsen an already perilous situation. Likewise, any American bombing of North Vietnam might lead to international pressures for negotiations at a time when South Vietnam was in no position to do much beyond capitulate to some neutral coalition, or what the administration viewed, undoubtedly correctly, as an indirect path to Communist control. In this sense the United States welcomed a temporary stalemate, although its public pronouncements soon became a litany of optimistic estimates, of endless progress reports that never seemed to cumulate in any significant improvement. With every glorious South Vietnam victory the over-all plight of the region seemed to grow worse, an outcome lamely but in part correctly attributed by administration spokesmen to ever-increased infiltration from the North.

Even as Johnson postponed any new initiatives, even as he posed as an unusually moderate and restrained alternative to Barry Goldwater in the 1964 presidential campaign, his advisers worked out new and bolder military plans. This suggests nothing new and unusual. This is what a staff is for. But what turned out to be crit-ical in all the planning was a near unanimity among both military and civilian advisers. With the exception of Under Secretary of State George Ball, who developed doubts as early as 1964 about the utility of further escalation, all major White House advisers urged Johnson to commit more American air power or ground troops if such were necessary to preserve a non-Communist South Vietnam.

Ball eventually presented his fullest forebodings in a long 29 June 1965 memo to McGeorge Bundy. In brief, he argued that nei-ther bombing nor the use of conventional troops would likely win in Vietnam. And any eventual hard-won victory would be Pyrrhic, for we would have to maintain troops in Vietnam indefinitely. Next to Ball, the hardest questions came from Chester Cooper, former CIA agent and White House aide to McGeorge Bundy; Cooper would soon become deeply, personally involved in efforts to begin negotiations with North Vietnam. Among outside private advisers, Johnson received the fullest warnings from Clark Clifford, who as late as May 1965 predicted that Vietnam could become a quagmire and involve an endless commitment of American troops with no realistic hope of an ultimate victory. He noted the dissimilarities with Korea, from the political factions involved to the widely dif-ferent terrain. He proposed the best political settlement we could negotiate. Finally, in the Congress, his friend Majority Leader Mike Mansfield persistently advocated negotiation in behalf of a neutral government in the South. Most White House advisers at least con-sidered all such options, including an immediate pullout from Vietnam, but most could never seriously contemplate any backing away from a goal now certified by three previous presidents, hal-lowed by American losses, and anchored, in their understanding, by treaty commitments.

In the spring and summer of 1964, as the military situation in Vietnam worsened, the Johnson administration had to consider major new American responses. Secretary of Defense McNamara visited Vietnam in both March and May. In March he was able to recommend the detailed planning of two new initiatives—major across-the-boarder air and ground raids by South Vietnam forces into both Laos and North Vietnam in response to each guerilla attack, and sustained air attacks on North Vietnamese military targets by American piloted planes. By May, the United States had increased its clandestine air war in Laos and had begun low-altitude reconnaissance flights over North Vietnam. LBJ endorsed these initiatives but stopped short of any overt escalation. Both the weaknesses of the Khanh regime and the political risk of escalation at home discouraged any new departures, particularly those that could not be concealed from journalists. Nonetheless, advisers worked out an exact scenario to accompany eventual air strikes against the North. Also, the military began stockpiling needed supplies in South Vietnam. In late July, at a National Security Council meeting, and in response to some frantic overtures from General Khanh, the Joint Chiefs of Staff proposed air strikes by unmarked planes. The Tonkin Gulf incident arrested all such planning and led to the first overt response by American planes.

During this planning stage for what became, early in 1965, a quantum jump in the American role in Vietnam, Johnson and his advisers considered carefully the problem of congressional support. At least later, Johnson would explain how he tried to avoid Truman's dilemma in Korea—no declaration of war and no clear congressional authorization for that "police action." He believed, as Truman had, that because of treaty commitments and the constitutional prerogatives of the commander in chief, he had a legal and constitutional right to offer military assistance to South Vietnam. But he wanted more. Thus, beginning in February 1964, the administration began both to consider and, by May, to draft possible authorizing resolutions. But the nature of the developing political campaign, with Johnson the model of responsibility and restraint, almost precluded any submission of such a resolution before the November elections. Then a small, still highly controversial event in the Tonkin Gulf in early August offered the needed excuse.

The backdrop of the incident in Tonkin Gulf involved several South Vietnam initiatives. Closely supported by American equipment and advisers, it began in the spring of 1964 extensive sabotage-terrorist raids into North Vietnam, some through air drops and others by PT boats and commandos along the coast. On 30

July such naval commandos raided two North Vietnamese islands in the Gulf. On 1 August, by accident or intent, South Vietnamese planes bombed a North Vietnamese village next to the Laos border. Even as the coastal raids occurred, the U.S. destroyer *Maddox*, apparently with no knowledge of the specific raids, sailed north toward the islands on an offshore intelligence-gathering mission. On 2 August the *Maddox* twice changed course to avoid North Vietnamese torpedo boats still searching around the islands for the raiders. When the destroyer reached the end of its northern run and turned back south, at least three of these torpedo boats joined in an attack against it, perhaps in the belief that it had directed the commando raids. During the skirmish, U.S. planes from a nearby aircraft carrier damaged two of the boats; guns on the *Maddox* sank another. The *Maddox* suffered no casualties and no damage.

The next day, 3 August, President Johnson ordered a second destroyer, the *Turner Joy*, to join the *Maddox* on continued patrols along the North Vietnamese coast. The United States also warned North Vietnam of the dire consequences of any repeated attacks. On the night of 3 August, South Vietnamese PT boats resumed their sabotage raids along the North Vietnamese coast, this time with the knowledge of the two destroyers. The destroyers avoided the areas of the raids. But the next night, torpedo boats apparently attacked both destroyers. This attack remains highly controversial; the evidence for it turned out to be flimsy. Even some naval officers expressed doubt that an attack ever occurred. But the reports sufficed for the Johnson administration. In its effect, this second Tonkin Gulf incident or nonincident, which purportedly involved the ineffective firing on two U.S. destroyers by an unknown number of small PT boats, took its place as a junior version of Pearl Harbor.

The purported second PT boat attack, following the warning to North Vietnam, seemed to Johnson justification for a harsh American response, one politically acceptable, even popular in the United States. Because of prior military planning, the Joint Chiefs had a ready list of enemy targets. They selected four coastal bases and one oil depot for a devastating aerial attack. Johnson, on the same day as the alleged attack, approved the retaliatory raids, gave permission for the deployment of further strike forces in Southeast Asia, prepared a resolution for Congress, and at 11:36 P.M. (Washington time) went on television to announce a "limited and fitting reprisal."

The subsequent resolution, prepared for Congress by several

people, became the blank check for all subsequent escalation in Vietnam. Senator J. William Fulbright of Arkansas, chairman of the Senate Foreign Relations Committee, and Representative Thomas E. Morgan of Pennsylvania, chairman of the House Foreign Affairs Committee, introduced it in the appropriate houses. By it, the Congress approved and supported "the determination of the President as Commander in Chief, " to take all "necessary measures to repel armed attack against the forces of the United States and to prevent further aggression." It defined as vital to the U.S. national interest the "maintenance of international peace and security in Southeast Asia." After citing the Constitution of the United States, the United Nations Charter, and the obligations of the Southeast Asia Collective Defense Treaty, the Congress stated that the United States was prepared, "as a President determines, to take all necessary steps, including the use of armed force, to assist any member or protocol State of the Southeast Asia Collective Defense Treaty requesting assistance in defense of its freedom." It is difficult to conceive of a broader grant of authority to a president. After secret committee hearings in each House and testimonies by Secretaries Rusk and McNamara, the House approved the resolution unanimously, the Senate by a vote of eighty-eight to two, with Wayne Morse of Oregon and Ernest Gruening of Alaska the only dissenters.

The overwhelming congressional vote for the Tonkin Gulf Resolution left troubling questions. Did Johnson procure a blank check through deceit? Although the answer is not a simple one, some facts are clear. LBJ decided to turn the second Tonkin incident, minor or even imaginary as it was, into a major provocation, as if North Vietnam had launched hostilities against the United States. But this scarcely amounted to deceit. Congressmen knew the limited, almost miniscule, aspects of the attack by small PT boats against two well-armed ships. The symbolism, not the reality, determined the vote. The critical issue is how much congressmen knew about the numerous provocations that helped explain at least one reckless and hopeless North Vietnamese attack. Here the evidence is inconclusive. Certainly, Johnson in his speech to the people did not fill in this critical part of the story. But any congressman who wanted to be informed on prior events in Vietnam had a range of available information. French newspapers had carried extensive reports on South Vietnamese commando raids. In Washington, *I.F. Stone's Newsletter*, a radical but respected weekly, had carried translations or summaries of these reports. In the secret Senate hearings, Wayne Morse showed a reasonably full awareness of recent raids on the two North Vietnamese islands, based on his own searching questions to McNamara about them, and thus alerted the members of the Senate Foreign Relations Committee to what had happened. Senator George McGovern also raised the issue of the raids in the public Senate debate. Of course, McNamara, before congressmen and in news conferences, downplayed the extent of the South Vietnamese raids and denied any direct American direction over them or any detailed advance knowledge of individual raids. If not lying, he at least very carefully evaded the truth, which is not unusual in questions about covert American actions. His testimony and the statements and speeches of Johnson led few Americans to suspect the range and extent of American involvement in Vietnam or the provocative nature of covert raids against the North, let along the range of developed military plans for future action. But the launching of five successful retaliatory air raids within one day should have suggested some of this.

On balance, it seems that the majority of congressmen were not deceived into passing the Tonkin Resolution, but in that vote demonstrated their full complicity in Johnson's Vietnam policy. Had they known the full story of American covert activities, it is doubtful that more than a handful would have changed their votes. In 1964 doubts about at least the degree of American commitment so far made to South Vietnam or about the long-term implications of such a limited commitment remained the property of a few academic intellectuals, a growing network of college students, and traditional left-wing organizations. The more widely appealing criticism of Johnson's policies all came from those who wanted more aggressive U.S. involvement, the position then taken by Goldwater in the presidential campaign. The Tonkin Resolution gave those hawks a bit of what they wanted, while Democratic and Republican supporters of Johnson's Vietnam policies found in it a perfect vehicle for proving their patriotic zeal and their determination to defend the United States from any overt Communist attack. In 1964, the Tonkin Resolution reflected as near a consensus position as one could ever desire for another remote, already costly, and almost entirely unilateral American effort to halt the spread of communism in Asia. Of course, Johnson wanted it this way. Those who voted for the resolution did not fully understand the complexity of the problems in South Vietnam, did not embrace a clear set of goals, and did not foresee the enormous cost ahead. But neither did the Johnson administration. The ignorance was mutual. Ironically, the only government agency that did foresee many of the difficulties and the enormous cost was the CIA. Consistently, almost no one in the administration ever bought its pessimistic prognoses.

In the immediate aftermath of the Tonkin incident, both the new ambassador in Saigon, General Maxwell Taylor, and the Joint Chiefs of Staff tried to make the retaliatory air raid only the first of a series of carefully orchestrated air attacks on North Vietnam. Johnson held back. The election was not the only deterrent. He recognized open bombing as a new and critical threshold, one that made any disengagement short of the announced goal—a secure South Vietnam—very difficult. He understood the enormous risk, although a risk that then seemed less ominous than an early Communist victory. In a sense the administration was already trapped. No politically acceptable answers remained. In October, Johnson approved American air strikes against Laotian infiltration routes, an action that began in December. But in November, after a provocative Vietcong attack on American planes at Bien Hoa airfield and urgent military requests for major air strikes in the North, Johnson approved only retaliation within South Vietnam. He also chose not to exploit another minor attack on American ships in the Tonkin Gulf.

Out of these incidents came a new interagency analysis of policy options by an administration team headed by Assistant Secretary of State William Bundy. The team proposed three options. Each involved bombing in the North. The weakest required only reprisal raids. The strongest combined this with the possible use of American troops in the South. In December, Johnson approved, in principle, reprisal raids, but then delayed implementation until 8 February, in part because of a minor coup and near collapse of a South Vietnam government in December. The first bombing on 8 February by forty-nine carrier jets was in response to a Vietcong attack on a U.S. military advisers' compound at Pleiku. This was followed by a second reprisal raid a few days later. Then, on 13 February, Johnson upped the ante with tentative approval of sustained bombing of the North, an order not finally executed until 2 March because of a coup in Saigon and in deference to international peace efforts. Nonetheless, this was a critical decision, for it amounted to the first of two steps toward full war in Asia. The decision came without any publicity and with little widespread awareness in the United States.

Johnson was still holding to a middle course. His decision for a steady, slowly escalating bombing campaign against only military targets and targets well south of the population centers of Hanoi and Haiphong still fell far short of what the military had been demanding. The Joint Chiefs wanted a massive, rapid buildup of bombing, an option that might have led to strong international pressures for negotiations. Ironically, at this time nothing seemed as unwanted or poorly timed as a peace conference, given the weakness of the South Vietnamese regime.

What, one could ask, were the goals of the bombing? These never seemed very clear. In large part, the immediate goal seemed to involve the South more than the North. This new initiative seemed likely to improve morale in the South and to provide more American leverage for its now frustrating efforts to push the South Vietnamese government toward domestic reform and a larger, more effective military effort. Everyone hoped that the bombing might entice North Vietnam to curtail its support for the Vietcong. The opposite, in fact, occurred, and soon administrative spokesmen could claim only that the bombing increased the cost of continued infiltration, a noncontroversial claim to say the least. Only the CIA consistently pointed out the limited effect of such bombing on the decentralized economy of North Vietnam and on its highly dispersed military efforts in the South. It never made psychological sense to argue that such attacks would lower civilian morale or lessen North Vietnam's commitment to a unified socialist Vietnam. And, at the time, the bombing was in no way aimed at early negotiations of any sort, at least any that involved concessions on the part of the United States. From early 1965 on, the Johnson administration made clear that our minimal negotiating goal would be cessation of all North Vietnamese support for the Vietcong, or what would have amounted to complete capitulation on its part. The United States would not consent to any coalition government or offer any formal role for the Vietcong in negotiations.

The actual timing of the bombing reflected the near collapse of the South Vietnamese government. It seemed in early 1965 that the Vietcong might be on the verge of a complete political victory, perhaps in the form of agreement to a coalition government. But, always, the overt and official justification for bombing involved allegedly increased infiltration from the North. The numbers were not all that large—no more than thirty thousand North Vietnamese in the South. Many of these had formerly lived in the South, and most blended so well into Vietcong units as to be all but indistinguishable. By late 1964, South Vietnamese reports of North Vietnamese regular army troops in the South seemed to presage—correctly as it turned out—a more threatening form of infiltration. These infiltrators reflected an increasing North Vietnamese support for insurgency in the South, particularly since such insurgency had been so successful. How extensive, and how necessary, their support role was in early 1965 became an intense subject of controversy back in the United States, as a protest movement began to build on campuses, among intellectuals, and even among a small minority of congressmen. The other side of this question was to what extent the war in the South was a largely internal civil war or a product of external aggression. Of course, it was both.

The slowly expanding air war in the North made almost inevitable further escalation in the South. The buildup of bases and supplies to support the air war increased the need for security forces, for the South Vietnamese army was in no condition to protect American bases. The political situation in South Vietnam reached its lowest ebb in early 1965. An aborted coup in February led to the resignation and then the exile of General Khanh. Until the summer, no clear leader emerged from among the controlling and youthful and largely military junta, leading to a series of leadership changes. In this context, the Army of the Republic of Vietnam (ARVN) almost gave up on fighting the Vietcong, which, after a period of relative inactivity, launched its most vicious offensive on 11 May. By then it seemed possible that South Vietnam might go under long before the bombing ever had time to affect the outcome in the South. Even the massive bombings long urged by the Joint Chiefs of Staff could not have relieved the immediate pressures by the Vietcong, and such bombings posed a great risk of retaliation by China. The Johnson administration thus sank deeper into a trap, with no options except an unwanted pair—either give up on South Vietnam or assume responsibility for the fighting in the South. Either option was sure to arouse determined opposition within the United States, although at the time giving up the cause was sure to evoke the broadest base of criticism. No president wants to retreat or to admit failure. Nothing in the personality of LBJ inclined him to give up, to leave South Vietnam to its own resources. Few presidents, in a similar position, would have taken this option.

The crucial decisions came in rapid order from April to July. Cumulatively, they committed the United States to a major, perhaps lengthy land war in Asia. The decisions were all hesitant and all incremental, with no big moment of choice, no one critical decision. Even when Johnson seemed to move forcefully in one direction, he often backed away and hesitated in another. The first major decision came at the end of a strategy session at the White House on 1–2 April. Johnson tentatively approved an expanded role for ground forces, a role that would involve more than the defense of American bases. But the exact nature of the expanded and in some sense offensive role remained far from clear, and not until late June did American troops actually seek out and engage a large Vietcong force. Equally critical, Johnson tried to conceal from the public any changes of policy. Until July he carefully stressed the continuities of policy and only indirectly, or in ambiguous language, admitted the expanded role for American troops. Possibly until July he retained maneuvering room. He could still have defined the early ground engagements, or what would soon be called search and destroy missions, as experiments. But by July he had no reason to so equivocate. By then the actual course of the fighting in Vietnam made clear to everyone the extent of the new American commitment.

The buildup of American forces also began with the April strategy sessions. On 6 April Johnson approved up to 20,000 additional support troops (added to the 27,000 already in Vietnam), plus two new marine battalions (these came ashore equipped for offensive action). Already, the new commander, General William C. Westmoreland, wanted at least 70,000 troops. By late April Johnson had agreed to up to 82,000. Then Westmoreland's estimates of what he needed tended to soar after the largely successful Vietcong offensive in May and June. Finally, on 7 June, Westmoreland estimated that it would take 44 battalions (almost 200,000 troops) to shift a balance of power in South Vietnam by the end of 1965, and possibly many more to go on from that to a final victory. By then the South Vietnam army, so often diverted by political coups, securely controlled only a few large cities and parts of the Mekong Delta. Johnson, however reluctantly, approved whatever level of troops his commanders believed necessary to win. Thus on 28 July he agreed to a buildup to 125,000 troops as soon as possible. Two days later the Joint Chiefs of Staff requested the whole 44 battalions. By 31 December 1965, total American forces numbered 184,000, and in the new year would quickly expand to 200,000, or all Westmoreland had requested in April 1965. Such a rapid buildup, brilliantly carried out by McNamara's Defense Department, soon crossed a point of no return. July might best qualify as the watershed month. By then Johnson had committed too much for any graceful retreat. He had to win his goal in Vietnam, and winning now meant not only a cessation of overt or clandestine North Vietnam activity in the South but the defeat of the elusive Vietcong. The failure of that goal would mean a political disaster for the Johnson administration. And, as events proved, too high a cost in achieving the goal also meant grave political risks.

Newly declassified documents reveal, in great detail, the internal White House dialogue that supported the critical new initiatives in Vietnam. But still unrecorded is Johnson's personal reaction to all this. He never put it on paper. It is clear, from all witnesses, that he agonized over, and endlessly postponed, the critical decisions. In fact, his seeming evasiveness and his denial of major policy changes after American troops were engaged in search and destroy missions suggest that Johnson tried as long as possible to deny even to himself the magnitude of his commitments. He certainly did not back into a war. Nor was he led, protesting, into it by overly militant advisers. He chose it and with as full an understanding of the risks as any president ever had. After all, the hard decisions came over several months and involved thorough intelligence, an array of various options including eloquent pleas for disengagement, and, most critical, frequent and frank discussions of the grave risks either of blundering into a war with China or of the eventual collapse of the South Vietnamese government despite all the American help. Johnson agonized so much because he knew so much and because, with his penchant for fatalistic resignation, he must have sensed that Vietnam might be his undoing, that it might destroy his administration and jeopardize his Great Society.

In a press conference on 28 July 1965 in the midst of the final decisions for war, Johnson offered a sorrowful statement. Even it reflected the words of a speech writer, but it rang true. He talked of American goals in Vietnam. He referred back to Munich, to three earlier wars, to the hazards of retreat. He talked of the desire of North Vietnam to impose its system on the South, of the background support of China, of the protective shield of the United States that alone prevented Communist expansion. We were "the guardians at the gate" for a small and valiant nation. Three presidents had made the commitment. Our honor was on the line. Only terror and a horrible repression would follow our retreat. Thus, the United States would stand firm, seek help from allies in the United Nations, and work for a peaceful negotiated settlement.

Then, in a personal almost pleading vein, Johnson talked about how hard it was to send boys to their death and to think about all the weeping mothers. This led him back to his alleged childhood poverty, to his dreams of an education for every child, of equal opportunity for every Negro, of a decent home for every family, of healing for all the sick, of dignity for the elderly. These were the goals he had lived for, what he had wanted to achieve all his life. And now he saw the prospect of all that running aground in the wasteful ravages of a cruel war. He would try to avoid this terrible result. But not by backing down in Vietnam. We had to have the courage to resist those who hate and destroy. Corny? Of course. But it was in character and deeply felt. And it was also, as the anonymous speech writer must have understood, a slightly modified version of Woodrow Wilson's famous lament in 1917 about the probable costs of World War I.

11

THE
ENDLESS
WAR

Lyndon Johnson agonizingly chose a full-scale war in Vietnam. He did it in the full confidence that such a hard decision would alone uphold and fulfill the goals of his predecessors, particularly Kennedy, and that such a choice alone would uphold American honor. Consistent with his deepest forebodings, he moved into a war that he was never able to win or conclude. What he did not, could not, anticipate was the degree to which a growing number of former political friends and colleagues would eventually reject the assumptions underlying American policies in Southeast Asia. In a sense, this shift in understanding, particularly in his own Democratic party, paralleled changes in domestic outlook. LBJ finally embraced and, with a "show them" ardor, enacted the broadest possible welfare and regulatory agenda, but in the same decade large numbers of intellectuals repudiated such mild economic and social strategies and the consensual politics that made them possible.

Johnson remained clear and consistent about the American goal in Vietnam. It was all so simple and so limited: the United States had no designs on North Vietnamese territory, no desire to invade it even for temporary strategic reasons, and above all no desire to do anything threatening to China. It only wanted North Vietnam to stop all forms of support for the Vietcong in the South. Without such support, in weapons and personnel, Johnson believed that South Vietnam, with limited American help, could crush the locally based Vietcong and get back to the task of creating a constitutional government and a prosperous economy. American military intervention served only these restricted goals and would continue only until they were gained. As it had seemed to Kennedy in 1963, so in early 1965 such a limited objective seemed consistent with a reasonably small, short-term American military commitment. This helps explain Johnson's low-key approach and his expectation, up until June or July of 1965, that he could gain this goal without major costs and without alarming the American public or inducing a warlike crisis. In a sense, he wanted Vietnam to be a little-noticed, backhanded operation while he kept public attention focused on his Great Society. He did almost nothing to prepare Americans for a long and costly war.

The limited objectives in Vietnam made another form of rationalization very difficult. Why was the United States, with restricted allied support (mostly from Australia and New Zealand) and no United Nations mandate, willing to commit so many resources and risk the lives not only of its young men but of so many Vietnamese to help secure the existing non-Communist regime in Saigon? Here, Johnson was never consistent or, overall, very persuasive. In his eager, almost desperate efforts to win popular support for the war, he variously used a dozen different arguments, and whenever he departed from prepared scripts, he often seemed confused. One set of arguments involved our treaty or moral commitments to the people of South Vietnam. The treaty argument was legalistic—South Vietnam was not a member of SEATO—and seemed adventitious and contrived. The moral argument, in itself persuasive, lost force either by rhetorical overkill and exaggeration, by constant references to freedom and democracy, or by idealistic descriptions of South Vietnam contradicted almost daily by news reports and television images. Another line of argument involved earlier commitments, the investment, the lives lost, and thus the dishonor of quitting in the middle of the game. Frequently, Johnson emphasized the effect on other friendly countries if the United States reneged on its promises, if it let an ally succumb to external aggression. Versions of the domino theory usually followed—the impact of a Vietcong victory on neighboring Southeast Asian states. Finally, Johnson appealed to American interests, to the elusive theme of national security. In a sense, this was an encompassing argument that embraced all the others. Otherwise, on close examination, it seemed oddly abstract and empty. The United States had no tangible interests in Vietnam, no needed resources to procure, no likely market to exploit, and no clear strategic sites. It was thus hard to specify, apart from issues of honor, moral obligation, or ideological preference, how a Vietcong victory threatened the United States. Of course, if communism were an evil plague, then all humankind suffers when it infects any part of the world. And if the cold war were a type of football game, then the "loss" of South Vietnam would be like the Communists kicking the extra point after their touchdown in China.

As Johnson knew, all such rationalizations would lose force if the costs of victory were too high. In the summer of 1965 he had broad, albeit often soft, support for his new war. Survey data showed overwhelming public support for his policies in Vietnam joined with considerable anxiety. He still had the Congress with him, but a growing minority lacked enthusiasm and already awaited opportunities to snipe at the details of his policies. The overt opposition still came mainly from the extremes and from peace groups. This seemed manageable, although draft resistance on campuses already presaged the coming revolt.

Early administration evaluations of the war were not very hopeful. John McCone, soon to retire as head of the CIA, reflected continuing doubts in his agency. All along, the CIA furnished realistic estimates of enemy strength, noted the futility of bombing, and pointed out the difficulties faced by ground troops. McCone believed we might not win. Even in the summer of 1965, the main architects of the new strategies, including McNamara and Rusk, faced the possibilities of failure, by which they did not mean any American military defeat (that was inconceivable), but such high costs as to risk all political support and make likely an eventual withdrawal with little or nothing gained. What that threshold of effort and time might be, no one knew. But the point is that even the most avid supporters of escalation talked in terms of odds and probabilities, not certainties. McNamara was a key and in some ways a tragic figure. On the technical side, he did almost everything correctly. The buildup in Vietnam was a model of logistical planning and execution. And he, perhaps more than anyone else, had expected the bombing and American military engagement to force North Vietnam to concessions or negotiation. As early as the fall of 1965, he recognized that he had miscalculated. Horrified by the costs and the cruelty of the expanding war and swayed by the critics, he suffered from a devastating ambivalence.

One fatal miscalculation lay behind most of Johnson's choices in 1965. Relying on Westmoreland's estimates, he believed that 200,000 American troops could turn the tide in South Vietnam by the end of that year. This scenario suggested a stable if not diminishing American military involvement as early as 1966, probably joined by some type of prolonged but potentially successful negotiation that would be made possible by American military ascendancy in the South. Had it worked that way, the Vietnam War might have joined the Great Society as one of Johnson's brilliant, even though ambiguous, political achievements. In any case, his political losses would have been minimal. In actuality, the tide would finally turn, although not very conclusively, only in early 1968, after almost three years of buildup, after the employment of 500,000 troops, and after the most divisive American domestic conflict since the Civil War. Even then, after the ebbing of Vietcong power and the achievement of a reasonably stable government in Saigon, the goal of a fully secure South Vietnam still lay years ahead, years of difficult negotiation and continued fighting. Thus, because of the nature of the war in Vietnam and the tactics pursued by North Vietnam, it took Johnson over three times as long to turn the tide as it did Truman in Korea. By 1968 he was roughly where Truman had been in 1951—in a position to negotiate in behalf of an armistice that would have allowed a continuing non-Communist government in the South for so long as the United States was willing to support it by economic and military aid and by a small contingent of American troops. In 1968, this negotiated outcome might still have been a politically acceptable solution, but Johnson left office long before he could attain it.

By 1973, after the pressures of new American incursions into Cambodia and periodic renewals of bombing of population centers in North Vietnam, Richard Nixon and Henry Kissinger were able to reach a settlement in Paris. By then a continuing American military commitment was politically unacceptable. Thus, they bargained only for time, for a face-saving interlude to withdraw American troops and to rejoice in the return of American prisoners. In 1975, North Vietnam, in a conventional military action similar to that of North Korea in 1950 and now unopposed by American troops, simply overran an amazingly inept South Vietnam army. South Vietnam lost the new war in which the United States was not militarily involved. Later assertions that the United States lost a war in Vietnam are absurd: it actually came close to winning its limited objectives. By 1973 South Vietnam was free of almost all insurgency and also free from any overt North Vietnam military attacks. This is the goal that Johnson committed the United States to in 1965.

Long before the tide turned, Johnson had lost the political support he needed to conduct the war. Even in the best of circumstances, it is difficult to maintain broad public support for a sustained but limited war, and particularly one haunted by so many moral difficulties. Truman had barely kept enough support to continue his war in Korea. Except for fanatical anti-Communists, Americans were not easily persuaded that either North Vietnam or the Vietcong represented unalloyed evil. The obviously uneven struggle between the wealthiest and most powerful country in the world and a small underdeveloped North Vietnam in itself made the American cause suspect. In earlier wars presidents had worked carefully to nourish the required war psychology, a psychology abetted by moral absolutes, by sharp contrast of evil and virtue. This requires some control over news, successful propaganda efforts, and possibly a degree of ideological naïveté on the part of the public. It also requires a certain status or legitimacy on the part of the government and particularly a willingness to trust the president. Given the increased sophistication of Americans, given the role of news organizations, given the sharp ideological divisions of the sixties, and given Johnson's image as a slick salesman, a sharp trader, a manipulator, then one can doubt that any strategies available to him could have sustained support for such a costly but limited war over a long period of time, particularly a war that would provide such slight psychic benefits even if won, if anyone could clearly determine exactly when or if victory had arrived.

Johnson never used the weapons needed to gain such support. He deemphasized the seriousness of our involvement until too late, tried to camouflage the cost of the war, tried to eliminate it as an issue from public dialogue, and continued for three years to claim more progress than events ever justified. In 1965, had he wanted wholehearted support, he could have declared a state of emergency, called up reserves, narrowed the grounds of draft deferment, set up press censorship, possibly initiated price and wage controls, and in his speeches emphasized the discipline and cost of such a war. This might not have helped. Events might have revealed the crisis to be overly contrived, and unlike the situation in past wars, the opposition was already well organized, deeply suspicious, and ready to pounce on any sign of hypocrisy in Washington. In any case, Johnson could not afford to go on to a war footing, for this would have threatened his Great Society. Every doubting congressman would have had a perfect excuse—patriotism—to vote against more regulatory and welfare legislation, and thus all Johnson's hopes of being a great president would have been in ruins. So he set himself up. If he had to have an unwanted war, only a quick, easy, and victorious one fit his larger presidential ambitions. He needed a Grenada, not a Vietnam.

From a moral perspective, the Vietnam War was exceptional. Not in the sharp etchings of good and evil—these turned gray for most observers—but in the unusual degree to which American civilians had to confront the death and suffering and physical destruction of war. They experienced it through detailed, on-the-scene, uncensored reports and through vivid television images. In World War II, American censors rarely allowed even published photographs of dead American soldiers. In the Vietnam War, television viewers, if they could stand the strain, saw the most extreme atrocities. Of course, the verbal and visual images were selective, contrived, even in a few cases posed. Photographers, film crews, and above all film editors controlled the final product. Support or opposition to the war influenced the selection. Because of accessibility, the view of the war had to be from the American side, which also meant that the ugly images of the war—the napalm, agent Orange, massive bombing—all had an American brand on them. This raised issues of fairness and bias, as well as secrecy, for newsmen often unearthed or leaked information that damaged the American cause. But these issues have little to do with the uniqueness of the war—that it was so continuously visible, so much on display. Americans in an almost brutal way had to confront all the moral ambiguities or moral horrors of what their country was doing in Vietnam. No amount of praise for the South Vietnamese government or its army, which fought more battles and suffered more casualties than the Americans, could quite undo the famous photograph of the exploding brain of a captured Vietcong soldier summarily executed by a South Vietnamese officer just after Tet or another of a screaming, naked, burning girl running down a road after a napalm attack.

The war was also unique because of the intense public dialogue over its justification. Protest punctuated it from the beginning. Johnson's most appealing tactic against critics was to emphasize the humane and idealistic side to the war, a side he talked about less with each passing year. In his first major speech on Vietnam, on 7 April 1965 at Johns Hopkins University, he tried to take the high ground. Then, as later, he stressed his willingness to open negotiations (not quite true) and announced plans for a vast cooperative relief and development program for not only Vietnam but all Southeast Asia, with a beginning $1 billion to fund it. He mentioned major, TVA-like dams on the Mekong River and established an Asian Development Bank under United Nations auspices. In May he followed these gestures with a five-day bombing pause, the first of several, ostensibly as a way of enticing Hanoi to open negotiations.

Joined with such gestures were the ongoing and in time successful efforts to build a viable government in South Vietnam. The most auspicious achievement in 1966, a hard, building year for American troops, was the establishment of an enduring military-based government in Saigon under Nguyen Cao Ky and Nguyen Van Thieu. In the next year this government carried out a reasonably fair and extensive series of elections to secure a constitution, an elected assembly, and an elected president. Along with painfully slow political changes, the Agency for International Development (AID) tried, with great frustration, to work on the issues that Johnson often professed most interest in—economic aid, new schools, trained police forces, new health facilities. This was, to him, the soft, humane aspect of the war, the one continuously aborted by military setbacks. Until regions were secure from Vietcong attacks, such economic aid was ineffective. Instead of rebuilding villages, too often the American forces had to evacuate them, pack villagers off to refugee camps, and then destroy buildings and vegetation in order to get at the elusive Vietcong. Too often Americans, quite literally, had to destroy villages (not villagers) to secure them.

The two major parallel efforts in Southeast Asia were military and diplomatic. Both the fighting of the war and the frustrating efforts to open negotiations with North Vietnam are stories that deserve at least a book. Here only the briefest outline is possible. Militarily, the war involved two major American efforts—bombing in the North and extensive ground action with air support in the South. Johnson rejected to the end of his administration any massive, World War II–like bombing of cities and civilian populations. Instead, he opted for carefully selected targets, at first largely transportation and military facilities and eventually crucial economic facilities, such as oil depots and power stations. He personally approved all major new targets. In a sense, this careful strategy proved the worst possible one politically. It inflicted cruel but never backbreaking penalties on the North. It also created intense anti-American sentiment, helped Ho Chi Minh further unify his people, and helped persuade them to bear the high cost of total mobilization. Instead of persuading Hanoi to cease its efforts in the South or to come yieldingly to a conference, it had the reverse effect. Thus, militarily, the raids may have increased, not decreased, the effectiveness of the insurgency in the South, even as they tremendously increased the costs of supplying such insurgents from the North. In any case, the most intense, massive bomb drops in history never stopped the steady, often makeshift, transportation of men and supplies across the seventeenth parallel or along parallel routes in Laos and Cambodia, a maze of primitive roads often collectively, misleadingly, referred to as the Ho Chi Minh Trail. The raids also proved costly to the United States in lost planes and pilots. North Vietnamese antiaircraft guns and missiles, steadily supplied by the Soviet Union, proved deadly. The cost of the raids, in dollar terms, may have exceeded the monetary damage inflicted on a still primitive decentralized North Vietnam economy.

Politically, the nature of the bombing hurt Johnson among almost all constituencies. Hawks lamented his failure to follow persistent Joint Chiefs of Staff requests for massive bombings of key cities and the port facilities at Haiphong, the type of cruel bombing that could indeed have devastated the North and threatened its morale. More critical, the growing opposition focused continuously upon the air war. It came to symbolize the unfairness of a great technological society making war at an insulated distance upon the peasants of Asia, because they supported a Marxist government and wanted to unify their country and expel all Western influences. And, obviously, the carefully targeted raids could not always be as discriminating as Johnson desired. Bombers missed targets. Crippled planes had to drop their bombs indiscriminately. South Vietnamese pilots never observed American rules. Later, urban targets overlapped housing areas. Thus, as North Vietnam officials liked to point out to visiting journalists, the bombs often hit hospitals, schools, and civilian factories. Psychologically, the restricted bombing created the same bad taste as more extensive raids. No matter that the total civilian casualties in North Vietnam may have numbered less than those inflicted by two World War II raids—on Hamburg and Dresden. In the long run, the bombing had only one clear benefit for the Johnson administration—its destructive potential made it a powerful bargaining tool in gaining negotiations in 1968.

In the South the military effort posed a thousand problems. Here, Johnson deferred to Westmoreland and his chiefs of staff. He tried to give them what they needed in men and supplies and until 1968 never ultimately turned down any major request. Except for one disastrous effort in 1967, and again just after Tet, North Vietnam did not mass its troops in the South and engage in conventional battles. Instead, it dispersed its infiltrated troops widely and used them to strengthen, at times to control, local Vietcong units. The Vietcong forces used various strategies. In areas usually under their control, they might form battalion-sized units and these at times engaged regular American forces, the nearest approach in Vietnam to open battle. In areas at least nominally under South Vietnamese control, they constituted an underground terrorist network. Dispersed, often through extensive tunnels, they operated mainly at night or unexpectedly. American intelligence was limited to overall assessments and to predictions of major offensive action, but it was almost never able to give warning of local attacks. Vietcong soldiers easily blended into the civilian population and often had civilian support. Elusive, mobile, yet often well armed, the Vietcong constituted an elusive enemy, here today, gone tomorrow.

The American army and marines worked in conjunction with the ARVN. From 1966 on, with American help and increased political stability, it became an ever more effective force. The only possible strategy, if one chose to engage the Vietcong on their own turf, was endless search and destroy missions aimed at securing villages and regions and keeping them clear of the Vietcong. Only in such pacified areas could the United States begin rehabilitation programs, or the job of "winning the minds and hearts" of the people. But unfortunate South Vietnamese civilians, in heavily infiltrated Vietcong areas, became the real victims of the war. At best they suffered evacuation and refugee status; at worst they became casualties. The type of warfare invited, even required, atrocities on both sides. The Vietcong made terrorism one of its major weapons, its method of intimidating or eliminating local elites. American forces, by the very attempt to minimize casualties, inflicted terror by their widespread use of herbicides, as an incidental accompaniment of their massive aerial bombardment of sighted Vietcong units, and by a policy of returning fire on villages that often housed only a few Vietcong. In March 1968, in the only documented case and probably the most flagrant, American troops at the village of My Lai murdered up to four hundred civilians. Higher officers tried to conceal the facts. This was exceptional. Most Vietnamese suffering was incidental to military action, but no less painful. And for the first time in American history, such civilian suffering was in the news and on television. It proved very difficult, month after month, to justify such a war, one soon symbolized by napalm, agent orange, and exaggerated body counts. But if the United States were to win its objectives by military means, this seemed the only possible way to do it.

Given the problems, the American military effort was impressive. Because of publicity and the detailed knowledge conveyed through the media, the troops in Vietnam became notorious for low morale, for drug use, for indulging prostitution or black-market profiteering, for disobedience of orders, for using subterfuge to evade action. They probably were not all that different from troops in Korea. Americans simply knew more of the story. It was a long and unpopular war, with rather abstract objectives and an elusive or unidentifiable enemy, fought largely by draftees, a high proportion of them from low-income families mostly on a one-year tour of duty (thus over two million troops fought in Vietnam). The war allowed few psychic benefits—few major victories, few permanent gains, and no end in sight. Back home, the war steadily lost support, and out of guilt as much as moral clarity, much of the mistargeted protest was directed at the men who were so unlucky as to have to fight in Vietnam. Veterans came home full of doubts or guilt, not as heroes.

What option did Johnson have but to continue the same frustrating course? He would not give up and withdraw. The only other alternative had to be negotiation. This became the easy answer to his critics, and upon Johnson's failure to initiate negotiation rested the steady defection not of the radical youth who had sentimental ties to North Vietnam but of a majority of academic intellectuals, a growing segment of the Congress, and large numbers of business and professional classes.

Although several peace efforts preceded the full-scale war in 1965, no basis for serious negotiations developed until mid-1966. Until then the United States had no bargaining chips even close to those required to gain its one unnegotiable goal—an independent, secure, non-Communist South Vietnam. The weak vulnerable regime in the South gave the United States no basis of strength for any significant concessions. Briefly, in 1965, the administration hoped that the bombing and the early American troop deployments, possibly tied in with some economic bribes, might encourage the North to desert the Vietcong. Various informal contacts, or what Johnson would misleadingly describe as offers to negotiate, soon made clear that North Vietnam seemed firm in its one unnegotiable goal—American withdrawal and a broader coalition government in the South. Given such irreconcilable goals, each side talked about negotiations and stressed its willingness to negotiate, but neither made important concessions. Thus, the diplomatic game throughout 1965 was largely a matter of show, a bid for international support. This was true of Johnson's first bombing halt in May 1965.

The next major American gesture—the bombing halt from 5 December 1965 to 30 January 1966—was transitional, hopeful, tentative, but still largely a propaganda effort. Some American officials, including McNamara, hoped against hope that the rapid buildup of American troops might have softened the views in the North. Johnson clearly shared such hopes and probably was serious when he promised talks without preconditions. But his key advisers were unwilling to promise any clear political role for the Vietcong. Johnson launched his own peace offensive, sending envoys to capitals around the world. This too was largely for show. But even the gesture pulled in other governments, including Poland, Hungary, and the Soviet Union, and led to attempts to formulate a verbal basis of talks by a Polish representative in Hanoi. To many of those involved, the prospects seemed at least hopeful at the time Johnson finally resumed the bombing. Given the public displays, the hopes created, and the international involvement, the failure turned into a propaganda victory for the North. In Congress, waning supporters now became open critics of Johnson's conduct of the war. Chief among these was his friend, Senator Fulbright. Johnson felt betrayed, used, for Hanoi had publicly responded to his overtures with a tough, unyielding demand for American withdrawal.

By June 1966 the situation had so changed in South Vietnam as to make negotiations seem more likely from an American perspective. A relatively stable South Vietnamese regime removed one obstacle to talks. A stabilized military situation meant that, although they were not yet clearly winning, the American troops could look forward to steady gains in the war. Surely the North Vietnamese could recognize that they had nothing to gain, and much to lose, from a continuation of their insurgency in the South. The United States could stop its bombing; North Vietnam could stop infiltrating. Some role for the minority of South Vietnamese sympathetic to the Vietcong (all efforts to assess public opinion in the South showed an overwhelming majority in favor of the southern regime) would be possible in a new, fully democratic South Vietnamese government. Even by the summer of 1966 the eroding domestic support for the war, added to its soaring cost, made a negotiated settlement politically desirable for Johnson. Yet he was unable to gain such a goal until 1968.

Here, more than in any other area of policy-making about Vietnam, Johnson seemed to blunder. Negotiation did not mean a betrayal of his limited goals in Vietnam but only a more rational and humane strategy for attaining them. From 1966 on he wanted to talk. Nothing so much frustrated him as the failure to gain negotiations. But he consistently betrayed possible openings for talks and, against his own inclinations, followed the skeptical advice of his advisers, particularly those in the State Department. In fact, the skeptics may have been correct. North Vietnam probably did not really want formal talks that involved any modification of its goals in the South. It used the various contacts for propaganda purposes or at times to provide a cover for an increased buildup of its forces in the South. But what the skeptics overlooked were the compelling political benefits of even insincere negotiations. Even if these failed or if actual negotiations led to no armistice, Johnson would have gained immense political benefits. Instead, skepticism, caution, and ineptitude seemed to plague the peace process from June 1966 to early 1968. And Johnson, the one president most open to reason and reconciliation, to seeking common interests in the midst of conflict, allowed himself to be painted as an inflexible, hard-line cold warrior.

The most extensive, and in the end the most embarrassing, peace effort took place in the summer and fall of 1966. Like all the secret initiatives, it gained a code name, Marigold. The main intermediaries were Italians and Poles. In June 1966 the Italian ambassador to South Vietnam began arranging talks between the American ambassador, Henry Cabot Lodge, and a somewhat mysterious Polish member of the International Control Commission on Vietnam, one Januscz Lewandowski, who traveled back and forth between

Hanoi and Saigon. From these talks, Lewandowski developed a carefully worded, even though ambiguous, list of ten points that he hoped expressed the American conditions for negotiation. On the basis of his wording of the points, or his interpretation of them in Hanoi, he apparently gained a promise from North Vietnam to explore the possibility of formal negotiations through direct talks with Americans in Warsaw. By then, Averell Harriman and Chester Cooper made up a nonofficial, peace-seeking team representing the Johnson administration, and they, along with the American ambassador in Warsaw, took responsibility for the various talks that ensued. After months of highly secret efforts, the United States, not without verbal qualifications, seemed to accept the ten points, and this by 3 December 1966. Thus, American representatives in Warsaw waited expectantly to meet the promised North Vietnamese contacts. None ever surfaced. Subsequently, as news of the peace process leaked to newspapers, the Poles and North Vietnam argued that the United States had sabotaged the promised talks.

The weaker claim was that the United States had never unambiguously accepted the ten points. Indeed, the United States had reserved the right to interpret key language, particularly on the issue of a Vietcong role in a subsequent South Vietnamese government. The critical point committed the United States to a change in the political status quo in the South and contained the strong wording, "must be changed," whereas the Americans preferred weaker phrases, such as "would be changed." Other points committed the United States to internationally supervised elections that would include "all" groups in South Vietnam. On the critical issue of bombing; the United States was prepared to stop it in order to facilitate a peaceful solution, suggesting some proper North Vietnamese response, but to do this without requiring North Vietnam to admit infiltration of the South. Throughout, the State Department was very nervous about the language of the ten points and forced Lewandowski to make endless changes. The language did not clarify very much the sticky points that had all along impeded negotiations, but instead was cast in generalities that papered over the differences. This may be appropriate in the opening of negotiations, which after all are for the purpose of establishing the ultimate points of compromise. But American quibbling about the wording at least gave Hanoi an excuse to break off the process if it wanted to. And, clearly, by mid-December it chose to terminate Marigold.

The major North Vietnamese excuse, and one that gained it

broad international sympathy, was a series of American bombings in the Hanoi area. For Chester Cooper, who was desperately seeking a way to open talks, these raids were "disgraceful," an "obscenity." His boss, Harriman, was later more sanguine and understanding. American bombers had first hit transportation targets within five miles of the center of Hanoi in June and again in August. It did not target such sensitive areas again until 2 and 4 December. In November, partly because of weather, the bombing in general had slackened. Of course, from North Vietnam's perspective, this restraint might have seemed a gesture in support of the Marigold process. The bombings of 2 and 4 December, at a critical juncture of the Warsaw talks, could be easily interpreted as an arrogant escalation or as an attempt to force Hanoi to talk. But Lewandowski believed the peace process survived the first attacks. Not so the raids of 13–14 December, the largest yet in the Hanoi area. In this case stray bombs hit civilian populations and even damaged the Chinese and Rumanian embassies. Hanoi vehemently condemned the bombing, chose to interpret it as an act of bad faith, and not only sent no representatives to the Warsaw talks but subsequently rebuffed almost apologetic American concessions to keep Marigold alive. The United States even pledged on 24 December to suspend all bombing within ten miles of Hanoi's center, to no avail. Even this substantial gesture did not undo the earlier damage.

Johnson, it seemed, had sabotaged the one best prospect for negotiation. In fact, as far as records indicate, he did not do so deliberately. The bombings reflected only a carrying out of long-matured plans and thus were in no way tied to the secret talks. But if true, this suggested an even harsher judgment—that the Johnson administration did not take Marigold seriously enough to try to coordinate military and foreign policy. From the viewpoint of skeptics within the White House and the State Department, the whole affair was a propaganda effort by Hanoi. It probably never intended to open talks and obviously tried to use the promise of such to limit American military efforts.

The second missed "opportunity" was at a much higher level and once again revealed an inept Johnson administration. It climaxed during the 1967 Vietnam holiday, Tet, when the United States chose briefly to suspend its bombing. Already, an American Chargé d'affaires in Moscow had held a series of January meetings with his North Vietnamese counterpart, talks that led to no agreement but only to a further clarification of what had become the sticking point—the conditions under which the United States would suspend its bombing. The North Vietnamese wanted an unconditional halt. The United States consistently tied a halt to some North Vietnamese response, meaning some undefinable diminution of its role in the South. The United States, at its most yielding moments, as in the final Marigold talks, was willing to go first (phase A), given a clear promise of an acceptable Hanoi response (phase B) within a limited period of time, or a plan for mutual deescalation. But during the Moscow talks (dubbed Sunflower), as the United States prepared a personal appeal from LBJ to Ho Chi Minh, the United States backed away from phase A–phase B and, in the resulting letter (carefully worded, conciliatory in tone), asked for a promised halt in infiltration as a condition for a bombing halt, or a tougher position than during the Marigold negotiations. The letter, to the despair of Johnson, led to a militant, unyielding response from Ho. But even as the State Department matured the letter, a much higher level supplement to the Moscow talks took place in London.

On 6 February 1967 Chairman Aleksey Kosygin arrived in London for meetings with Prime Minister Harold Wilson, and this during the bombing halt. Wilson, hurt by American secrecy during Marigold, had been aware of the Sunflower talks in Moscow and very much wanted to serve as a peacemaker (hundreds of people thirsted for such a role). The United States knew of Wilson's hopes and briefed him on its conditions for negotiations in language that seemed to incorporate phase A–phase B. Kosygin, for reasons not clear, seemed very anxious to facilitate a Vietnam settlement. Thus, the two heads of state tried to act as agents of the two sides and to find a formula acceptable to both, which they wanted to issue as a joint statement in their capacity as cochairs of the Geneva Convention. In the midst of the London talks, Kosygin seemed interested in the phase A–phase B formula and asked for a written version of it that he could present to North Vietnam. Chester Cooper, our peace envoy then in London, prepared a draft consistent with the most yielding earlier American position. He submitted it to Washington for what he assumed would be routine approval. He waited and waited until the very end of Kosygin's visit. Then, at the desperate last moment, he received a revised draft that, in effect, through a change of verb tense, took the tougher position reflected in the LBJ letter to Ho (North Vietnam had to stop infiltrating as a condition of a bombing halt). Wilson felt betrayed and was enraged at a seeming reversal at such a critical moment. He used two telegrams in an unsuccessful effort to get Johnson to reverse this last-minute shift in language. Cooper was so disheartened that he soon resigned his position. On top of the tougher language, the United States had demanded an acceptance from Hanoi within one day. Kosygin doubted that he could get an answer so soon, and none was forthcoming.

Why the tougher position in Washington? During the brief bombing halt, North Vietnam had rushed supplies and troops to the South. Intelligence reports suggested that another three to four North Vietnamese divisions might move south during any continued bombing halt. Thus, the hard line reflected estimates of the military situation in Vietnam and continued State Department skepticism about the sincerity of North Vietnamese promises to open negotiations. In any case, the resumption of bombing only two days after the London debacle probably doomed this seeming, possibly illusory, opening toward peace. Once again Johnson seemed to be the devil of the piece.

Marigold and Sunflower were only the two most promising of a continuing, frustrating series of efforts to find a basis of negotiation. Even Henry Kissinger, as a private citizen, helped arrange North Vietnamese contacts in Paris. All such efforts failed, even though the United States, by September 1967, came back to its more lenient phase A–phase B position (eloquently expressed in a speech Johnson delivered in San Antonio). A modified version of this policy would be incorporated into Johnson's speech of 31 March 1968, which did lead to negotiations. Whether such a public gesture earlier would have brought Hanoi to the conference table is not clear. The San Antonio version was more generous than what Johnson offered in 1968 and it did not lead to negotiations. By the summer of 1967, Secretary McNamara had joined the few doves in the administration in recommending an indefinite, publicly unconditional bombing halt. As late as November, when McNamara presented these views in a memorandum, Johnson rejected them short of some assurance that Hanoi was ready to negotiate. Such an unlimited and unconditional halt, he argued, would signal a weakening of American will and play into the hands of congressional doves. Implicit in this was his appreciation of the high political cost of any resumed bombing. At the time, Johnson was again probably correct in his estimate of Hanoi's intentions. By then, North Vietnam had reason to believe that time was on its side, even as it built strength for the upcoming Tet offensive.

The failure to find a path to negotiations proved politically disastrous. The hard line taken at each critical point made Johnson's stated desires for peace seem hypocritical. Up until 1966, the opposition to the war came primarily from two quarters—the political left, which preferred a unified socialist Vietnam, and peace activists, often tied closely to churches, who reacted in moral horror to the cruelties of the war. Neither group was large enough to pose major political dangers for the Johnson administration. In 1966 and 1967 Johnson slowly lost a critical support group—those who had defended American policies in South Vietnam, who wanted to honor past commitments and somehow preserve a non-Communist government, but who increasingly viewed the costs of the war, moral and financial, as way out of proportion to these goals. They also believed that in light of the growing Sino-Soviet conflict even a fully Communist Vietnam posed few security threats to the United States. To such critics, a negotiated settlement was the obvious out, although given the obstacles and pitfalls, one more easily endorsed than achieved. In 1966 a large, loosely united wing of the Democratic party began to swing against the war, at least as Johnson pursued it. This included, most significantly, Robert Kennedy, and with him went a large share of northeastern urban support. Johnson was incensed. He had simply followed the earlier policies of these same Kennedy Democrats in his Vietnam effort. They had helped create the situation, get him into the trap. Now, in the crunch, they deserted him. He was bitter, and, to some extent, for good reasons. For back of the developing protest lay clear personal animosities and self-serving political ambitions. A critical stance toward costly, unpopular Vietnam policies helped prepare the way for wresting the presidency from Johnson in 1968. Events favored the critics. By 1967, as violence exploded on campuses and earlier civil rights marches on Washington gave way to equally large antiwar demonstrations, the critics could sense that, as earlier with civil rights, time was on their side. It was.

Poor Johnson. He was confused and almost helpless. By early 1967 he had traveled two years too far to turn back. By then the personal cost was almost overwhelming. He had aged ten years in only two and was now visibly an old man, shaken, ineffective, almost beleaguered in a White House surrounded daily by angry protesters. As early as February 1966, Lady Bird had noted in her diary that the glory was now all over, that no joy remained in the White House, that Johnson's presidency was already an endurance contest. In June 1966, for the first time, Johnson's approval rating fell below 50 percent in the Gallup poll. In the same month, late in the night, he told Luci he wanted to go to a church, and eventually he knelt alone, secretly, in a small Catholic chapel. By 1967 Lady Bird could talk of a "miasma of trouble" that hung over everything. By then nothing seemed to go right for Johnson. At the end of the year, the heavy blow was the pending resignation and, in effect, defection of McNamara. His private doubts went back to conversations with Johnson in November 1965. By the spring of 1967 he opposed the sending of extra troops and the bombings of Hanoi and Haiphong. But, at the time, he had to authorize each escalation and, out of his own moral doubts and hard work, he faced exhaustion and a possible mental breakdown. Johnson, sorrowfully, let him out of the Defense Department in order to take charge of the World Bank.

In a sense, the war did go better in 1967. By the summer and fall the Vietcong seemed to be in retreat. The 460,000 American troops had finally gained an ascendancy, and Johnson planned to have about 500,000 men there by the end of the year. More areas of South Vietnam were pacified than at any time since 1964. After discussions with Westmoreland in Washington in July, Johnson announced his satisfaction that the war had clearly moved beyond a stalemate, that enemy casualties and defections were up, that the ARVN was fighting the war more effectively than ever before, and that the Vietcong had won no significant victories in over a year. Yet, American casualties remained high, and the Gallup poll revealed that a bare 52 percent of the public still supported Johnson's Vietnam policy. In the late fall the news remained upbeat and, as later revelations made clear, more optimistic than justified by hard intelligence estimates. Westmoreland, in part for political reasons, pared his estimates of North Vietnam and Vietcong troop strength to a bare, probably unjustified minimum. In a November press conference, Johnson exulted at the gains in Vietnam, both political and military. For the last two years the news from Vietnam had never been so upbeat.

Then came Tet. On the Vietnam New Year (31 January 1968), with most South Vietnamese troops on holiday, the North Vietnamese and Vietcong began a long-awaited but surprise attack. After a lengthy lull in the fighting, such an attack had been expected, but not on Tet. The attack was countrywide and led to the capture and brief but destructive holding of Hue, the old imperial capital, to the capture or infiltration of several sections of Saigon, and to an embarrassing but brief intrusion by Vietcong troops into the courtyard of the American embassy. The Tet offensive succeeded only temporarily. American and South Vietnamese troops gradually regained the initiative and rescued the conquered areas during the next few months, although not without extensive casualties. Nor could they undo the devastation wreaked upon so many South Vietnam cities, the vulnerability created for American troops in the northern provinces, or the psychological damage inflicted by the extended North Vietnamese siege of Khe Sahn, a northern base so reminiscent of Dien Bien Phu. Also, the daring scope of the action, the early success of the Vietcong, seemed to give the lie to earlier administration optimism. The vivid television images of Vietcong successes cast doubt on tentative predictions that, in 1968, the United States would pass a critical turning point in the war. Ironically, Tet, as it turned out, was just this. The enormous losses sustained by the Vietcong practically ended the insurgency in several areas of the South. Once recaptured, many districts remained at least reasonably secure all the way to 1975.

Politically, Tet proved disastrous for the Johnson administration. By March his approval rating dropped to 36 percent; by then only 26 percent approved his handling of the war (the doubters included more hawks than doves). Major news media, including the *Wall Street Journal*, the *New York Post, Life, Time, Newsweek*, and for all practical purposes, CBS News, came out against the continuation of existing policies. It was as if a dam had burst all at once. Johnson, ever keyed to public opinion, had to reevaluate his policies. In retrospect, it is ironic that a near military debacle for the North had such a political effect. The explanation was simple and involved mistakes by the administration. In the immediate aftermath of the attack, it simply was unclear what the long-term results would be. No one could then know that the counteroffensive would succeed as well as it did. In a 2 February press conference statement, Johnson claimed that the attack was expected, that it was being repulsed, that all the heavy losses were on the Communist side, that extensive American losses of airplanes and helicopters would not significantly harm our military effort, and that militarily the North Vietnamese attack had been "a complete failure." But he seemed shaken, a bit unsure of himself. He admitted shock at the ferocity of the attack and noted a short-term psychological setback until Americans knew all the facts. In the next few days the administration rushed to reassess the results and to claim a major victory. In the context, such claims had a hollow ring and were further weakened when newspapers leaked a February request from General Earl G. Wheeler, chairman of the Joint Chiefs

of Staff, for over 206,000 additional troops, a request that suggested a longer and harder road still ahead. Westmoreland, who had
initiated the now embarrassing troop request, would soon relinquish his command in Vietnam to General Creighton W. Abrams.

Tet undoubtedly paved the way for opening negotiations. It is
now clear why North Vietnam in late 1967, with the Tet attacks
pending, kept rejecting American bids for negotiation. It is also
understandable why, before Tet, an increasingly confident Johnson
administration was reluctant to agree to any new concessions. It
sensed a better bargaining position with each passing month.
From a North Vietnamese perspective, Tet did two things. It destroyed the capability of a small, drastically overextended country
quickly to rebuild the Vietcong units in the South; thus it made a
negotiated settlement more attractive. At the same time, the political and psychological effects of Tet, as reflected in American opinion shifts, meant that extended negotiations probably favored
North Vietnam. It might now gain its ends by nonmilitary means.
For the United States, the rapid erosion of political support for the
war meant that Johnson had only one possible means of salvaging
his primary goals in Vietnam—an independent, secure, non-Communist South Vietnam—and this was through some negotiated
settlement. He could not fight on toward a clear military victory.
Johnson had one bargaining point left—the enormous damage he
could inflict by an expanded bombing of the North. By March he
decided to use this leverage. For the first time he decided to risk a
major unilateral initiative in behalf of peace.

The background of this shift in administrative policies in March
is complex and much controverted by participants. It is important
to note that, apart from the psychological impact, Johnson
changed his policies only slightly and in a direction that he had
almost embraced earlier. The shift, at least in part, grew out of
Johnson's need to respond to the new troop request. Only an intensive evaluation of policies could justify what would be a very unpopular decision further to escalate the war. On 1 March, Clark
Clifford, his old friend and skeptic about the opening of such a war,
but a public supporter throughout, took over as secretary of defense. He later recalled his open-minded desire to look carefully at
existing policies. Even such an openness was refreshing in the
White House. In the beleaguered months of 1967, Johnson's staff
had protected and isolated him and, in all too many cases, said
exactly what he wanted to hear. The livelier debates of 1965 had
become an unaffordable luxury.

Clifford soon identified the lack of a clear rationale for the war. It had become an impossible morass. Working closely with his own study group in the White House, he soon realized that he could not support the existing policies, a change of heart that piqued Johnson. But Clifford was not alone. The political context made every adviser question existing policies, even those most hard-nosed before Tet. Rusk has remained mute on his role; Johnson, perhaps misleadingly, later gave him major credit for the proposal he finally included in his 31 March speech. External events also influenced the reevaluation. Campus ferment reached a new peak of violence in the winter and spring of 1968. In February, Senator Eugene McCarthy, an avowed critic of Johnson's Vietnam policies, came close to outpolling Johnson in the New Hampshire primary. On 16 March, Robert Kennedy announced his candidacy. And in Congress the prospects of a new buildup led to extensive, often hostile hearings in the Senate and to a House resolution, with broad support, asking for a congressional review of policy in Southeast Asia. Confused and unsure of what to do, on 25–26 March Johnson convened a Senior Informal Advisory Group, soon dubbed the "Wise Men" and including Dean Acheson, General Omar Bradley, former adviser McGeorge Bundy, former Treasury Secretary Douglas Dillon, Abe Fortas, UN Representative Arthur J. Goldberg, Henry Cabot Lodge, General Matthew Ridgeway, Cyrus Vance, and several others. Most had been hawks. A majority were now pessimistic about any continuation of present policies. They advocated a halt in the bombing and a more active quest for negotiations, all only five days before the scheduled 31 March Johnson speech.

Even as the Wise Men debated, the White House staff worked on Johnson's speech. Between 25 and 28 March, Johnson decided to go with those urging a degree of disengagement and negotiations. He had the key text ready by the evening of 28 March, but, as he later emphasized, he could still have changed it and might have if the North Vietnamese had launched a new offensive. In this dramatic speech he announced that he had ordered a halt to all bombing of North Vietnam, except for the area near the demilitarized zone (the intended limit was to be twenty degrees north latitude, but after intense criticism of one raid that far north, it would be informally defined as nineteen degrees). He urged Hanoi to show similar restraint and to move to formal peace talks. He ended his speech with a surprise announcement that he would not be a candidate for president in 1968, but instead would devote all his time to the search for an honorable peace.

284

In one sense, so little had changed. In another sense, everything had changed. American goals in Vietnam remained the same. The means of attaining them shifted only slightly. Johnson in no way repudiated his decisions in 1965. He conceded none of the charges of his critics. In the same speech he announced a slight increase in the number of American troops in South Vietnam. But the speech elicited a response from North Vietnam on 3 April; it was now ready to send representatives to arrange formal talks. This was only the beginning of one frustration after another, with the first involving the site of the talks; only on 3 May did Hanoi agree to Paris. Elderly Averell Harriman and Cyrus Vance led the small U.S. delegation. The first informal talks began on 10 May, but the North Vietnamese were not open to any concessions and throughout the rest of the year made a complete bombing halt a precondition of any substantive bargaining. They also at first resisted any inclusion of South Vietnamese representatives in the talks. Enormously complex negotiations led on 31 October to an American agreement to halt all bombing of the North, conditioned on informal promises of military restraint by North Vietnam, inclusion of the South Vietnamese in the talks, and a new round of serious, higher-level negotiations. Even this agreement, at the last moment, was almost sabotaged by an increasingly recalcitrant South Vietnamese government, which refused to join the talks without major new concessions from the North. The United States, after an embarrassing delay, had to go it alone. Other delays and controversies over procedures delayed the opening of the new talks until 25 January, when Lyndon Johnson was no longer president.

Meanwhile, the Vietnam War continued. The bitter divisions at home intensified, and campus violence increased. The tensions came to a climax at the Democratic convention in Chicago. The fallout from those confrontations may have cost Hubert Humphrey the presidency. The war changed, but not always in ways that benefited the United States. After the suppression of the Tet offensive, the war bogged down in a type of stalemate. The fighting was more clearly concentrated in areas of North Vietnamese strength and came closer to the frustrating small gains and losses of the later phase of the Korean War. Troop morale fell. But the ARVN did slowly assume more responsibilities, and in the summer of 1968 the Johnson administration began planning for a gradual decrease in American troops, or what President Nixon would subsequently call "Vietnamization."

Johnson's policy shift in March 1968 came less than halfway

285

through the Vietnam War, a fact that would have seemed unbelievable at the time. Even the American lives lost by then (approximately twenty-five thousand by March 1968) were less than half of the eventual total of fifty-eight thousand, and the financial costs of the war, then estimated at an absurdly low $25 billion, were less than a fourth of the eventual total. Five frustrating years would pass before a final settlement. In those years the bitter fruits of the Vietnam War became ever more apparent. The most horrible consequences fell on the small country of Cambodia. Opponents of the war viewed the ravages of the Khmer Rouge as a fallout of the destabilizing effects of the Vietnam War and of later American intrusions into Cambodian territory; they thus identified the United States as in some sense responsible for the terrible bloodbath. Supporters of the war saw it as a perfect example of all the evils of communism, a somewhat ironical judgment because a Communist Vietnam, over American protests, eventually crushed the Khmer Rouge. The post-1975 fate of America's firmest allies in the South, and the bitter drama of refugees and boat people, led to further laments about American perfidy and, even among the war's most fervent critics, to a new appreciation of all the moral ambiguities that still haunt even the word *Vietnam*.

12

GENTLY
INTO THE
NIGHT

Professionally and politically, Johnson retired on 31 March 1968, not 20 January 1969. In his speech he put it bluntly: "I shall not seek, and will not accept, the nomination." He so decided, he said, because, in a time of so many challenges at home and abroad, he did not believe he should devote "an hour or a day" to personal political concerns. For the final time in his life he surrendered, disengaged, retreated. He spent another frustrating ten months as a lame duck in the White House. He struggled with the two overwhelming problems of his last year—the inflating economy and efforts to begin substantive negotiations in Paris. He was still intensely involved with such problems. He wanted, even desperately wanted, to salvage his Great Society and to gain his goals in Vietnam. But these were old issues, not new ones. His task was now concluding, winding down. His reputation, not his prospects, was at stake. For the first time since childhood he was not tugged and pulled by ambition, not challenged by some new task. And, in a sense, the Lyndon Johnson that everyone had known before, that people admired or hated, that no one could ignore, expired in 1968. But the subdued, passive LBJ who survived lived on for almost five more years.

Johnson's decision not to seek reelection surprised almost everyone. Even his closest White House aides knew about the carefully guarded secret ending of his speech only a day before he delivered it. As they knew from past experience, he had a habit of making sincere or feigned threats to resign that he either never meant or quickly repented. Possibly even Johnson himself did not finally decide whether to read that portion of his speech until it appeared on the teleprompter and he paused for a moment. Once made, the decision turned out to be irrevocable. At moments he surely regretted it. But nothing short of a massive public demand could have justified a reversal, and that never came. It surely hurt Johnson deeply that his public, for whom he had done so much, would let him go with so little protest.

In retrospect, the decision made sense. It was more consistent with Johnson's character than involvement in a divisive, hard-fought campaign for renomination. He never liked to fight. The early primaries, the Kennedy candidacy, made clear how difficult and politically costly it would be for him to gain the nomination. Then it might not be worth much, for a sharply divided Democratic party could not win in November. Whenever the odds were against him, Johnson had always preferred a graceful retreat. He could now take the high road, seemingly sacrifice his ambitions for the sake of peace and reconciliation, and leave office with regained respect. But his adamant stand in Vietnam led the public to a different view of Johnson—as an aggressive, inflexible competitor. Actually, he stayed the course in Vietnam only because he believed that American interests required it. He hated the game.

Back of the decision to retire lay two long miserable years. The job had become a burden. It no longer offered an appealing challenge. He gained no kicks from it. He had lost his capacity to achieve large goals, to serve his public, to play the role of a magnanimous big daddy. His bouts of depression became more numerous and joined with continuing health problems. Because of a heritage of heart problems, the intensity of his life, and the anguish of Vietnam, Johnson was an old man at the age of sixty. He looked it and felt it. He craved peace and quiet. He idealized the joys of retirement back at his beloved ranch. And he always insisted that he had long planned to retire at the end of his first term. Indeed, he had talked about it to friends. He had so often promised it to

Lady Bird that she accepted his sincerity. But it is hard to know what to make of his frequent promises. After all, he had talked of withdrawal in 1964 and even wrote a statement. And, with a conviction born of his ability for self-deception, he often argued that he did not want to be vice president in 1960 (almost but not quite believable) and that he never really wanted to be president (not believable at all). He even told Robert Kennedy this just before Kennedy's assassination. About all this proves is that Johnson in his low moods had indeed contemplated early retirement. It was, in this sense, a live option, one best understood and interpreted by his family and immediate staff, but rarely even suspected by the public.

To cite reasons, to know precedents, is not to explain. For such decisions never follow upon sufficient conditions. Had Johnson at the last moment decided to stay on the job, not only he but historians could easily have cited justifying reasons. Even minor eventualities might have changed his mind. Certainly, an earlier agreement by North Vietnam to open negotiations would have changed the whole context of choice, even as it would have defused the candidacies of McCarthy and Kennedy. It is also possible that the short-term triggering motives were most critical. Johnson loved to shock and surprise, to confuse the pundits. He loved all the publicity and attention that followed. And, out of the near paranoia and conspiratorial fantasies engendered by Vietnam protest and urban violence, he probably relished the feelings that go with martyrdom or even suicide. By his sincerity, magnanimity, and willingness to sacrifice a career for the cause of peace, he could make his former critics and enemies feel repentant or miserable or guilty. Withdrawal was his ultimate weapon at a time of low fortune.

His bombshell of 31 March briefly boosted Johnson's spirits. His popularity ratings soared. The bombing halt in Vietnam promised much more than materialized and therefore briefly led to euphoric hopes of early peace. Instead of jeers, Johnson confronted cheering audiences. Even Ivy League campuses welcomed him for speeches. But the euphoria was short-lived; new frustrations came almost daily. The nation endured again the shock of assassinations—Martin Luther King and then Robert Kennedy. Johnson had to suffer through the tense Democratic convention at a distance; he gained small joy from Humphrey's nomination. He felt hurt and rejected when Humphrey tried, in limited ways, to assume a more dovish position on Vietnam. Finally, Johnson had to accept a degree of personal responsibility for the victory of Nixon, for in so many ways the votes reflected disillusionment with both the war and the Great Society. Almost his only consolation, the only new challenge, was developing plans for an LBJ Library and School of Public Affairs, already abuilding on the University of Texas campus. Methodically, with none of the old spark or enthusiasm, he played out the year. He proved magnanimous toward the incoming Nixon administration, mechanically joined in the Nixon inauguration, and presided over the tearful farewells in the White House.

Back to the ranch! This time to stay. Washington had been his home, the focus of his talents and energies, since 1932, or thirty-seven years. The ranch had never really been home. It was a vacation retreat, a romantic dream, an indulgent refuge from his real world. Heretofore, he carried a part of Washington back to the ranch, made it an extension of his vocation and his identity as a national politician. Now, he came home with no job, no political role. In a sense he came home defeated and disgraced, for even he accepted the latter-day failures of his administration. He came home to be a real rancher, a formerly idealized vocation that in no way matched his talents or inclinations. He needed the continued support of people, not of cows. He came home ill prepared for retirement and a life of leisure. He had almost no hobbies, no real interests outside politics. He was not contemplative, not given to leisurely reading or reflection. He always had to be busy, to be engaged, or else he turned in on himself, brooded, became depressed.

Of course, he had plenty to do. Unfortunately, the various tasks only partly engaged his talents and energies. At times, he was intensely involved with the progress of his library at Austin. He used an Air Force helicopter for frequent flights to the library, landing on a pad on the roof. But his visits were usually brief. He never had the energy, or possibly the talent, to give the lectures or do the teaching he had contemplated in the School of Public Affairs. Later, he gained satisfaction from the opening in 1970 of a restored replica of his birthplace by the National Park Service. Subsequent to this, he often walked down the road toward the old Junction School in order to visit with the people coming to the new shrine. He even kept a careful, anxious record of the number of daily visitors, and of the receipts for admission and gift shop sales, as if he owned the enterprise or his family depended upon its returns for a living.

This left only two challenging tasks—to write his memoirs and run his business affairs. Obviously, he could not write a book, for he never had such skills. Thus, the completion of *The Vantage Point* became a large staff project. Johnson reaped the prerogatives of ex-presidents—paid office space, Secret Service protection, mailing privileges, the use of military transport. On the ranch, the unneeded Secret Service guards turned into personal servants at Johnson's beck and call. To help with the book, he called on former aides, who formed a writing task force headed by Robert Hardesty and William Jorden. Doris Kearns, one of the ghostwriters, has given a vivid account of their frustration. Since Johnson was a great raconteur, not a writer, they tried to get him to dictate sections of the book. But what came out was cold, sterile, and overly defensive. And even when they prevailed upon him to relax, to recount his stories in his pungent, earthy, conventional style, he would not let them incorporate his language into the book. It had to be dignified. Besides, he soon grew tired of the effort. What emerged was a staff product, a well-documented white paper reminiscent of Johnson's presidential speeches, with little of his personality in it. But it did give, under several topical headings, his personal view of his administration and its achievements. In factual detail it was accurate, tied to abundant sources, which included secret tapes of most White House telephone conversations. On some details he even had it checked with many of the participants, again reminiscent of the elaborate process that went into producing his State of the Union addresses. In interpretation, Johnson forced upon the book his own peculiar gloss on both people and policies, including the critical events leading up to the 31 March 1968 speech.

An absorbing concern remained his personal financial affairs. On retirement, Johnson became the wealthiest ex-president in American history, a multimillionaire with holdings so extensive they are hard to enumerate. By luck or skill, he was able almost to double the value of his estate during retirement, and carefully to order it and prepare his will. He and Lady Bird owned, at least in part, several Texas banks, extensive savings in tax-free municipal bonds, interest in several television stations, several small business firms in Austin, valuable subdivision lots along Lake LBJ in Austin, and land not only in several Texas counties but also in Alabama and Mexico. In 1972 he and Lady Bird sold their KTBC television station for $9 million, the largest share of which went to Lady Bird and into trust funds for the two daughters.

Johnson enjoyed all the prerogatives of great wealth. He owned a prop-jet airplane. Each February he flew with family and staff and endless supplies to Acapulco, there to luxuriate in the villa of

Miguel Alemán, the former Mexican president who was his close friend and business partner in Mexican land investments. In addition to the LBJ Ranch, the Johnsons owned a nearby ranch that had excellent accommodations for guests. In Blanco County they owned a much larger, hillier, twenty-six-hundred-acre ranch (the Scharnhorst) with a large home, good grazing, beautiful vistas, and excellent hunting. In neighboring Llano County they owned yet another ranch on the dammed-up Llano River. Here they kept a large powerboat, which Johnson drove across the lake as recklessly as he drove his Lincoln Continentals around the home ranch. These scattered ranches, plus others, made up part of a major business—the Comanche Cattle Company—owned by Johnson and A. W. Moursund and including over ten thousand acres of grazing land. Sadly, during his last year of life, he quarreled with Moursund and died unreconciled to him. Notably, in all his business activities, he still seemed to be haunted by depression memories and his years of financial stress. He never lost his lifelong desire to make more and more money. This joined with a lifelong joy in giving often lavish gifts.

Only indirectly could Johnson manage all his far-flung investments. But after retirement he directly, and in great detail, managed the home ranch, becoming emotionally involved in every detail of its operations. One can only pity his ranch manager, Dale Malechek, and the dozen or so field hands. It was as if Johnson could not give up old habits and relinquish his inclination to take charge of tasks and boss subordinates. In the small world of his ranch he still acted like a president. He had staff conferences each morning with the hands, set up daily priorities, and anxiously analyzed progress reports at the end of the day. He worried about the weather, struggled to perfect a new irrigation system, rejoiced in successful experiments or innovations, proudly showed off his prize cattle, and tried to make the ranch profitable, again as if his family depended on it. Thus, the daily egg count replaced earlier body counts. The health of his much-prized coastal Bermuda pastures replaced concern over the health of the economy. His urgent, almost frantic, efforts to procure a needed part for an irrigation pump replaced his earlier, equally frantic efforts to push an important bill through Congress.

None of these activities was enough to keep Johnson fully occupied or happy. He could be caught up in an enterprise one day, moody and depressed the next. But he largely restricted his interests to the ranch. He shunned reporters, rarely made public statements, and seldom traveled outside Texas or the South. He enjoyed University of Texas football games in Austin, attended party affairs within the state, and still held wedding anniversary parties each year in San Antonio. Of course, he had his family and friends and relished them all the more. He particularly enjoyed his grandchildren (Patrick Lyndon Nugent, born 2 June 1967, and Lucinda Desha Robb, born 24 January 1968), liked to swim in his pool, and even took up golf, characteristically bending the rules to suit his fancy. He played host to large gatherings of relatives or neighbors on holidays and, largely by letter, stayed in contact with thousands of former staff members or faithful political supporters. Among his correspondents was the former Alice Glass, who in supportive letters still addressed him as "Dearest Lyndon." His trips north were few in number and often occasioned by funerals, including those of Eisenhower and Truman. The records may be misleading, but he seems to have visited Washington only three times after retirement; President Nixon was his host on each occasion. He attended one Democratic dinner in Chicago in 1970, traveled with Lady Bird to a park dedication in California, and at Nixon's request shared the launching of the Apollo moon mission in Florida; but otherwise he traveled only within Texas or to Mexico or made private excursions to visit friends. Even this level of public involvement declined after a severe heart attack in April 1972.

If the formal correspondence is any indication, Johnson slowly warmed to President Nixon. On his part, Nixon tried to be gracious to Johnson; he or his staff sent friendly letters. Nixon came to speak at the dedication of the LBJ Library on 22 May 1971. Either he or Henry Kissinger consulted Johnson at critical junctures in the Vietnam negotiations. Kissinger twice visited at the ranch and never knew quite how to take some obvious leg-pulling by LBJ. Weekly, the Nixon administration sent by plane highly secret foreign policy briefings. All this flattered LBJ. Johnson sent special greetings to Nixon before he left for his precedent-breaking trip to Peking. Politically, Johnson deplored much of Nixon's domestic policies, hated his crew-cut staff (he let his own hair grow shoulder length and justified it as a symbolic protest), and lamented attacks on Great Society programs; but he refused to comment publicly on most policies. Generally, he supported Nixon on Vietnam and welcomed movements toward a cease-fire, but he worried that the terms would not be such as to ensure the continued independence of South Vietnam, the only goal he had ever had for fighting the war. The people of South Vietnam were now also his children. He had taken responsibility for them, and he did not want them to suffer. Because of illness in 1972, Johnson turned down repeated invitations to the White House. But he congratulated Nixon after his reelection and received a final letter from him on 4 January 1973, thanking Johnson for a Christmas print of the LBJ Ranch. In the final contact just before Johnson died, Nixon as a courtesy informed him that a cease-fire in Vietnam was imminent.

Deliberately, Johnson took no major role in Democratic party politics. He knew that his involvement would not be an asset to any candidate. As the election of 1972 approached, he kept his preferences to himself. But friends know that he favored Edmund Muskie, not primarily because of friendship but because of his belief that Muskie could beat Nixon. He despaired at the nomination of George McGovern, both because of their divergent views on Vietnam and because he believed McGovern, representing an extreme wing of the party, simply could not win. Ill health gave him an excuse for not attending the nominating convention in Miami. Actually, he was not wanted. Despite his disappointment, he supported McGovern and even entertained him at the ranch during the fall campaign.

Retirement proved dangerous to Johnson. He would probably have lived longer had he served a second term. At first, back at the ranch, he was dead tired, drained after the ordeal of the past few years. But before a year was out he was enjoying a brief interval of good health and, often, good spirits. Unfortunately, he did little to preserve his health. As in earlier periods of disengagement, he became undisciplined, indulgent. He stopped following his diet, gained weight, and in an act of insanity resumed smoking cigarettes in 1971. Periodic bouts of depression did not help his physical health. He had to enter a hospital in March 1970 because of severe chest pains. He suffered no coronary, but from this point on angina pains would haunt him almost daily. Then, in April 1972, while visiting Lynda in Charlottesville, he suffered a massive coronary and flirted with death for the second time in his life. He insisted against all medical advice on flying back to Texas for hospitalization and recuperation. Obviously, he wanted to die at home. He survived this attack, but never fully recovered. He lived thereafter with pain, always near an oxygen tank and succored by nitroglycerine tablets. He was resigned to an early death. Every trip, every obligatory social engagement, was now a heavy burden.

Even in these last months LBJ continued some activities. Walter Cronkite conducted a series of television interviews with him, the last one taking place just before Johnson's death. The programs proved revealing and moving, although Johnson was distressed at the editing of the early tapes. On 11–12 December 1972, he hosted an LBJ Library symposium on civil rights, the last major enterprise of his career. The photographs taken at the symposium show the dark lines and puffy face, suggesting Johnson was near death. No matter. He was determined to perform. With difficulty he mounted the steps to the lectern. He had to pause for a nitroglycerine tablet. But he delivered a twenty-minute speech, an eloquent one, prepared by his staff at his direction. In it, he confessed his own shifts, his own growth, in the understanding of racial issues. He referred to his Gettysburg speech of 1963, perhaps the most beloved speech of his whole career. He rejoiced in the civil rights achievements of his administration, but stressed what still had to be done, the need finally to achieve "open opportunity for all," or what amounted to the central goal of his whole political career. His ending deliberately evoked memories of his other great speech—in 1965 in support of a voting rights bill: "We have proved that great progress is possible. We know how much still remains to be done. And if our efforts continue, if our will is strong, if our hearts are right and if courage remains our constant companion, then, my fellow Americans, I am confident that *we shall overcome.*"

The crowd was enthusiastic. They sensed the cost to him of such an address. But his role was not complete. The ill-suppressed divisions among civil rights groups came into the open. Militant blacks demanded a harsh denunciation of the Nixon administration and an added agenda for the symposium. Johnson came back to the podium. Briefly the Johnson of old took over the wreck of a dying body. Once again he was the master of the divided assembly, able to find commonalities behind the sharpest discord, able to bring divided people together, to focus their concerns in such a way as to achieve goals. He told corny stories, preached tolerance, asked for reason, and urged a positive approach even to the Nixon administration. He exhausted himself and had to return to the ranch for two days of rest. It is a wonder he did not die on stage, and in a sense it is unfortunate that he did not. He would have wanted to go out with the cheers of an adoring audience. He also displayed here, for the last time, the qualities that made him seem so hard to understand. In beliefs, in values, he was not complex but so utterly simple as to be beyond most people's comprehension.

At the end of December, again against medical advice, Johnson traveled to Truman's funeral. This was his last public appearance. Not that he suffered any new attack or any clear change in his fragile health. Every day involved pain. Thus, no one sensed anything unusual on 22 January 1973. Lady Bird even went into Austin. While resting in his bed, at 3:50 P.M., Johnson suffered his final coronary. He was able to call the ranch switchboard. Secret Service guards rushed to him but failed in desperate efforts to revive him. Thus, he died alone. The body went by family plane to Brook Army Medical Center in San Antonio, where physicians certified his death. Lady Bird took the body from there to the LBJ Library, where it lay in state for a day. Then, on 24 January, the body was moved to Washington for the formalities of a state funeral. Ironically, Johnson's arrival accompanied headlines announcing the cease-fire in Vietnam and articles noting the early abolition of the Office of Economic Opportunity. In the afternoon of 24 January the casket moved from before the White House to the Capital on a horse-drawn caisson, followed by the same riderless horse that so many millions remembered from almost a decade before at Kennedy's funeral. The body lay in state for seventeen hours in the Capital rotunda; long lines of people paid their last respects, with blacks making up a reported majority of mourners. On 25 January the official funeral services took place at his old church, the National City Christian, with his former minister, George Davis, officiating. Leontyne Price sang. Former friends offered eulogies. Johnson would have appreciated the attention and the commendations, but the affair was too formal for him.

Back to the ranch! The last trip. Late on a cool, rainy Texas afternoon, relatives, friends, and neighbors gathered or else watched the motorcade as it traveled from Austin. Appropriately, his friend, the priest at nearby Stonewall, Father Wunibald Schneider, offered the eulogy. As Johnson would have wanted, both Catholics and Protestants joined in the final farewell. Billy Graham spoke at the grave site. Anita Bryant sang "The Battle Hymn of the Republic." Simple verities. So appropriate. Then burial in the family plot beside his grandparents and parents. Back in the family circle. Safe. On the banks of his beloved Pedernales.

CHRONOLOGY

27 August 1908	Born near Stonewall, Gillespie County, Texas
1912–1913	Briefly attends Junction School, near Stonewall.
September 1913	Moves with family to nearby Johnson City, Blanco County, Texas.
September 1913	Enters first grade in Johnson City Elementary School.
Spring 1920	Completes elementary school (seven grades) at Johnson City.
Summer 1920	Moves with parents back to the family farm near Stonewall.

September 1920	Begins the eighth grade at Stonewall High School.
September 1921	Begins the ninth grade at high school in Albert, Gillespie County.
Summer 1922	Course work in the Demonstration School at Southwest Texas State Teachers College, San Marcos.
Fall, 1922	Moves with family back to Johnson City home. Begins final two years of high school at Johnson City High School.
Summer 1923	Is baptized as member of the Johnson City Christian Church.
Spring 1924	Graduates from Johnson City High School.
Summer or fall 1924	Briefly attends subcollegiate classes at Southwest Texas State Teachers College.
November 1924–September 1925	Travels to California; lives with cousin Tom Martin at San Bernardino.
September 1925–February 1927	Employed in road work at or near Johnson City.
February 1927	Enrolls in six-week subcollegiate program at Southwest Texas.
March 1927	Begins college work.
September 1928	Completes first two years of college; begins nine-month teaching job at Cotulla, La Salle County, Texas.
June 1929	Resumes college work.

CHRONOLOGY

August 1930	Receives a B.S. in Education from Southwest Texas.
September 1930	Briefly teaches in public schools of Pearsall, Frio County, Texas.
October 1930	Begins teaching speech at Sam Houston High School in Houston.
November 1931	Accepts position as congressional secretary for newly elected Richard Kleberg of the Fourteenth District.
7 December 1931	Begins work and residence in Washington, D.C.
Fall 1934	Briefly attends Georgetown University Law School.
17 November 1934	Marries Claudia Alta Taylor in San Antonio.
25 July 1935	Appointed as Texas director of the National Youth Administration.
10 April 1937	Elected to the House of Representatives in special election in Tenth District.
3 May–28 June 1941	Unsuccessful campaign for the U.S. Senate, with close loss to W. Lee O'Daniel.
11 December 1941	Leave of absence from the House to assume active duty as lieutenant commander in the navy.
May–July 1942	Fact-finding mission to the South Pacific and brief military action in New Guinea.
July 1942	Goes on inactive status; returns to House.

19 March 1944	Birth of first child, Lynda Bird.
2 July 1947	Birth of second child, Luci Baines.
May–November 1948	Campaigns for U.S. Senate; wins close contested race.
January 1951	Elected Democratic whip of Senate.
1951	Acquires LBJ ranch from aunt Frank Martin.
January 1953	Elected Senate Minority Leader.
January 1955	Becomes Senate majority leader.
July 1955	Suffers severe heart attack.
14 July 1960	Selected as vice-presidential candidate by Kennedy; confirmed by Democratic convention.
22 November 1963	Assumes presidency after assassination of Kennedy.
3 November 1964	Landslide election victory over Goldwater.
July 1965	Culmination of decisions committing United States to full war in Vietnam.
31 March 1968	Announces decision not to run for president in 1968.
20 January 1969	Leaves presidency and returns to LBJ ranch.
22 January 1973	Dies at LBJ ranch.
25 January 1973	Burial in family cemetery along the Pedernales.

SOURCES

This book reflects, almost equally, the use of printed sources and of unpublished documents at the Lyndon Baines Johnson Library (LBJL). Much has already been written about Lyndon Johnson, and the books and articles continue to mount rapidly. Yet, from a biographical perspective, these published materials are still elliptical, elusive, or confusing. At almost every critical point in this biography, I had to turn to the LBJL to try to fill in missing parts of the story, to arbitrate among conflicting versions, or to verify the accuracy of received accounts. This meant that, more often than not, published materials only suggested the main story lines or raised questions that begged an answer. My work at the LBJL, on three occasions in the summers of 1984 and 1985, turned out to be very profitable, simply because I used it to search for answers to a series of reasonably clear and focused questions. Unless one so uses that library, one flounders in the sheer bulk of materials, particularly on the presidential years.

In the following brief essays I list the sources that helped me complete each chapter. I do not provide a bibliography. Because of time constraints or selective interest, I did not utilize a wide range of secondary literature that would fit any bibliography of the Johnson administration. This includes the dozens of Ph.D. dissertations so neatly filed at the LBJL. I also do not list secondary works, including a growing literature by right-wing critics and a small stack of outright apologies, that I did consult but found so clearly unreliable or simplistic as to be worthless for my purposes. In the following essays I list categories of manuscript material (collections, at times boxes) at the LBJL, not the thousands of individual documents I surveyed. Before first visiting the LBJL, I read, as I suggest anyone else read, Robert A. Divine, ed., *Exploring the Johnson Years* (Austin: University of Texas Press, 1981), an informed evaluation of the records in the LBJL and a book that remains valuable even though the library has opened several new collections since its publication.

1. PARENTAGE AND PLACE

The genealogical information comes mainly from Rebekah Baines Johnson, *A Family Album* (New York: McGraw-Hill, 1965). For anyone interested in a detailed genealogy of the Johnson or Baines families (I was not), the LBJL has almost endless sources, including several boxes of genealogical correspondence collected by Rebekah (in the Papers of Rebekah Baines Johnson), many genealogical records in the Lyndon Baines Johnson Archives (LBJA)-PA, Box 72, and family correspondence in the White House Central Files (WHC)-PP, particularly in Box 1 but scattered throughout. The fullest published background, particularly on the Bunton and Johnson families, is in Robert Caro, *The Years of Lyndon Johnson*, vol. 1 *The Path to Power* (New York: Knopf, 1982).

My description of the hill country derives largely from my own experience of both work and play on my parents-in-law's ranch in the hill country. The geographical and geological data is in William C. Poole, Emmie Craddock, and David E. Conrad, *Lyndon Baines Johnson, the Formative Years* (San Marcos: Southwest Texas State College Press, 1965). Almost everyone who has written about Johnson has given their impressions of the hill country. The quotation on page 00 is from Booth Mooney, *LBJ: An Irreverent Chronicle* (New York: Thomas Y. Crowell, 1976), p. 1.

2. LEGENDS OF YOUNG LYNDON

Piecing together Johnson's childhood turned out to be a major challenge. Legends have so camouflaged the reality as to make confident judgments very difficult. The firmest evidential base includes the surviving bits of correspondence or the mementos in the LBJL, with most of these in the Papers of Rebekah Baines Johnson. Some of this material, including early report cards, was published in Rebekah's *Family Album*. I found isolated details about young Johnson in LBJA—Family Correspondence, Boxes 1 and 2; in LBJA-PA, Boxes 72, 73, and 76; and in WHC-PP, Boxes 1, 2, 61, 68, 96 and 108. Given the paucity of papers, the early family photo albums in the LBJL photographic collection are especially valuable and allow one to infer details about young Lyndon not possible from the written records alone.

Supplementing the meager records are the quite extensive transcripts of interviews conducted by the Oral History Project at the LBJL. Most of these have to be used with great caution, for they took place from fifty to sixty years after Johnson's childhood. Very few relatives or neighbors had detailed memories, and most seemed to be guided by later legends or by information suggested by interviewers. I found the memories of Kitty Clyde Ross Leonard (interviewed by David McComb) most believable; the recollections of John F. Koeniger (by Michael Gillette) are indispensable for recovering the details of Johnson's trip to California. For specific events, or very general characterizations of young Lyndon and his family, I used transcripts of interviews with Kathryn Deadrich Loney by Douglas Cater, Louise Casparis Edwards and John B. Casparis by Michael Gillette, Emmett S. Redford by David McComb, Georgia Camach Edgworth by Michael Gillette, and Josefa Baines Saunders by Juanita Roberts. Others who tried to remember were too vague to be of much use. Merle Miller, in *Lyndon, an Oral Biography* (New York: G. P. Putnam, 1980), draws upon these transcripts and also, apparently, some interviews of his own. His use is uncritical, for any number of remembered details are proven wrong by the documentary record. Lyndon's brother, Sam Houston, regaled a ghostwriter with remembered, and often invented, details of their childhood in a completely unreliable book, *My Brother Lyndon* (New York: Cowles, 1969).

Only three biographers have tried to probe in any detail Johnson's youth. The most detailed, by far, is Robert Caro's *The Years of Lyndon Johnson*. Caro searched long and hard in order to get the chronology straight. Every future biographer will be indebted to him for many of the details he was able to discover. He based many of his judgments on interviews that he conducted personally, with the reader not having access to any transcripts. He also, at critical junctures, relied on Sam Houston Johnson and on interviews of doubtful validity recorded by Doris Kearns. He is, at best, perverse in interpreting the oral record, since he tries to force upon the child his later interpretation of a power-mad, desperately unhappy Johnson. Doris Kearns bases her account of Lyndon's youth primarily on long interviews conducted with the retired president and on his memories of his youth and even his accounts of dreams, all published in *Lyndon Johnson and the American Dream* (New York: Harper & Row, 1976). She takes quite literally the reports of a person never given to truthfulness, one who loved to tease or deceive interviewers. She also, along with Caro, makes much of small and highly suspect incidents recounted by Sam Houston Johnson, for they help her spin out a Freudian interpretation of Johnson's childhood. She does nothing to validate the psychoanalytical speculations that undergird such outdated Freudian theories. Finally, Ronnie Dugger, in *The Politician, The Life and Times of Lyndon Johnson: Drive to Power, from the Frontier to Master of the Senate* (New York: W. W. Norton, 1982), includes almost all the anecdotes available about Johnson's youth, but without any clear effort to distinguish truth from falsehood, legend from fact.

3. THE BUSINESS OF EDUCATION

Most of the sources listed for chapter 2 also encompass Johnson's college education and brief teaching career, particularly the three biographies and, in the LBJL, LBJ—Personal Correspondence and the Papers of Rebekah Baines Johnson. All earlier qualifications apply. Almost all biographers have endorsed what I believe to be a completely legendary account of Johnson's career at Southwest Texas State Teachers College. Robert Caro has, in a sense, inverted and expanded the legend, for his larger-than-life campus politician is a self-serving, cruel dictator. The records I consulted do not support this legend. The most important documents remain his registration forms, his transcript, and the student publications, the *Star* and the *Pedagogue*, all available at the LBJL in the Southwest Texas files. LBJA, Box 73, includes details about his experience in Cotulla, plus letters of recommendation from his college teachers, and WHC-PP-13-4 (Box 108) contains additional materials on

Southwest Texas. For background on the college, see Poole, Craddock, and Conrad, *Lyndon Baines Johnson, the Formative Years*.

The oral transcripts at the LBJL include interviews with most of Johnson's close associates in college, with a few former students at Cotulla and Sam Houston High, and with one of his first political supporters, Welly Hopkins (interviewed by Joe B. Frantz). Few of these are very revealing. Notably, some of the students closest to Johnson, such as Alfred T. (Boody) Johnson (interviewed by Michael Gillette) and Willard Deason (interviewed extensively by David McComb, Joe T. Frantz, Eric Goldman, and Michael Gillette) remained very vague about Johnson's publicized college achievements until pushed by leading questions from interviewers. Early faculty reports are equally restrained.

4. POLITICAL APPRENTICESHIP

Johnson's years as a congressional secretary are not well documented. Robert Caro has zealously pursued the meager evidence and has drawn the fullest inferences from it. Ronnie Dugger has a brief chapter based on the same bits of information, and a larger section on Johnson's marriage. The primary sources at the LBJL include letters in LBJ—Family Correspondence, Boxes 1 and 2; limited amounts of publicity material in LBJA, Box 73; and very revealing oral transcripts of interviews with his two assistants, Gene Latimer and Luther E. Jones, Jr. (in each case interviewed by both Michael Gillette and David McComb).

Personal data are no more extensive for Johnson's busy two years as Texas director of the National Youth Administration (NYA). But his official duties are reasonably well documented in copies of NYA files at the LBJL, Boxes 1-10. Again, the most extensive analysis of these years is in Caro. Speech material for his congressional campaign of 1937 is in LBJA, Box 1, and extensive campaign material and voting analyses in House of Representatives, 1937–1949, Box 3.

5. CONGRESSMAN JOHNSON

Beginning with his election to the House in 1937, the earlier paucity of primary sources on Johnson shifts to an economy of abundance. Instead of a few boxes of scattered materials, the LBJL has hundreds of boxes on the congressman. His public career, at least, is fully documented. Abundant, but not the most sensitive, information on his ties to Brown and Root and to George and Herman Brown, is in LBJA—Selected Names, under George Brown (Box 12) and Herman Brown (Box 13), and information on his naval career in LBJA—Subject Files, Box 73. The huge file, House of Representatives, 1937–1949, which was my main source for this chapter, includes material organized around both topics and names of correspondents. Of course, most of these files involve constituent issues. I sampled this material and surveyed boxes on topics that figured large in my chapter (Marshall Ford dam, civil rights, Johnson's voting record, the Senate campaign of 1941, the 1946 campaign against Hardy Hollers, and the Senate campaign of 1948). These topics involved selected boxes from 2 through 232. The more sensitive material on the Senate election of 1941 is in Pre-Presidential Confidential Files, Box 5, and that on the contested election of 1948 is in Boxes 6–9. LBJL also has a copy of Johnson's World War II diary, and numerous oral transcripts that at least deal in part with his congressional years. For example, the memories of Harfield Weedin (interviewed by Michael Gillette) helped me tell the early story of radio station KTBC.

Robert Caro goes overboard in tracing Johnson's congressional career from 1937 to 1941. The detours, the peripheral details, often overwhelm the central story, which is a sad story of an amoral, self-serving Johnson. Doris Kearns, in *Lyndon Johnson and the American Dream*, has a rather cursory chapter on LBJ's career in the House. Merle Miller, in *Lyndon*, has one of the fullest accounts of Johnson's wartime heroics. A more cynical account is in Dugger, *The Politician*. Dugger also has written by far the fullest story of Johnson's political career in these years, at least from a skeptical and at times vengeful Texas perspective. This includes Johnson's relationship to Brown and Root, his shifting position on national issues, and, above all, the intimate details of the contested campaign of 1948.

6. MASTER OF THE SENATE

The largest body of sources on Johnson's Senate career are in the LBJL, in U.S. Senate Files, 1948–1961. The hundreds of boxes of records are keyed to topics and to individuals. I used records related only to special topics, including communism and Senator Joseph McCarthy, civil rights, space, labor legislation, oil and natural gas regulation, and military affairs. I also sampled files on the Democratic Policy Committee, on Johnson's legislative record, and on his correspondence with selected senators. Some of the correspondence in LBJA—Selected Names overlaps his Senate years, including his later ties to the Brown brothers (Boxes 11–13); his Senate voting record is summarized in LBJA—Subject File, Box 75. Some of the oral transcripts are revealing, most of all a remarkable series of interviews with aides Harry McPherson (by T. H. Baker) and George Reedy (by Michael Gillette). Lincoln Gould (interviewed by Jerry Ness) provides the best description of Johnson's 1955 heart attack. Merle Miller, in *Lyndon*, combines interviews with narration in an extended chapter on Johnson's Senate career.

The secondary literature expanded after Johnson became a senator. Finally, he was famous. I found most useful the detailed, extended, perceptive chronicle of Johnson's Senate career in Roland Evans and Robert Novak, *Lyndon B. Johnson: The Exercise of Power* (New York: New American Library, 1966), and Doris Kearns's subtle analysis of Johnson's legislative skills in *Lyndon Johnson and the American Dream*. Kearns is much more impressive as a political scientist than as a psychoanalyst. Both McPherson, in *A Political Education* (Boston: Little, Brown, 1972), and Reedy, in *Lyndon B. Johnson: A Memoir* (New York: Andrews & McMeel, 1982), supplement their oral interpretations, although both books focus more on the presidency than on the Senate. Of the two major personal biographers (Caro and Dugger), only Dugger deals, again in a highly critical way, with Johnson as a senator.

7. IN THE SHADOW OF JFK

The best information on Johnson's vice-presidential years derives from interviews or publications largely based on them. The manuscript materials in the LBJL are extensive but not very revealing. The major file—Vice President, 1961–1963—has considerable material on the President's Committee on Economic Opportunity, and includes other material on civil rights, education, and space. The Vice President–Security File has details on all of Johnson's foreign trips. In addition, several of the oral transcripts cover these years. I particularly benefited, once again, from the insights of Harry McPherson (interviewed by F. H. Baker).

The one book on Johnson's vice presidency is Leonard Baker, *The Johnson Eclipse* (New York: Macmillan, 1966), but Evans and Novak, in *Lyndon B. Johnson: The Exercise of Power*, have almost as much detail and are more perceptive. On the controverted details of Johnson's selection as a vice-presidential candidate, I found most persuasive three somewhat divergent accounts—that by Evans and Novak, by Merle Miller in *Lyndon,* and by Arthur Schlesinger in *A Thousand Days: John F. Kennedy in the White House* (Boston: Houghton Mifflin, 1965), which is also, despite its partisan flavor, the most thorough account of the Kennedy administration.

8. PRESIDENT JOHNSON

The records of Johnson's presidency are almost overwhelming. The huge WHC Files, under dozens of headings, contain documents and correspondence on every imaginable topic, including purely personal or family matters, poll data and public relations, and millions (or so it seems) of letters to and from the president, with the most voluminous holdings under the LE (legislation) category. I did not begin even to sample all these files but used them selectively, to document specific topics. Yet, in the midst of all the information, one often looks in vain for LBJ. His letters and his speeches reflect the words of staff members. In all the WHC it is rare to discover, on the margins of letters or reports, a few words in the president's own hand. One then rejoices; he had been there. In fact, for his whole presidency the only clear, unfiltered evidence of his own thinking was in his press conferences, inept as he often was in responding to reporters' questions. Transcripts of these are available as *The Johnson Presidential Press Conferences,* 2 vols. (New York: Earl M. Coleman Enterprises, 1978). Retrospectively, Johnson's views of his presidency appear in his four television interviews with Walter Cronkite, transcripts of which are on deposit in the LBJL.

The major secondary work on Johnson's presidency is a turgid, unclearly organized, awkwardly written, but vastly informed book by Vaughn Davis Bornet, *The Presidency of Lyndon B. Johnson* (Lawrence: University of Kansas Press, 1983). I found the book reliable on details and a useful reference on bills and agencies, yet elusive in interpretation and frustrating in its lack of focus or clear transitions from one topic to another. Compared to Bornet's conscientious but pedestrian efforts, Doris Kearns's treatment of Johnson's legislative skills is superb. To previously cited memoirs (Reedy, Mooney, McPherson), I would add the judgments of two of his ablest and most trusted aides: Joseph Califano, Jr., *A Presidential Nation* (New York: Norton, 1975) and *Governing America* (New

York: Simon & Schuster, 1981), and Jack Valenti, *A Very Human President* (New York: Norton, 1975). Eric F. Goldman's, *The Tragedy of Lyndon Johnson* (New York: Alfred A. Knofpf, 1969) is a disappointing book, too tied to Goldman's beliefs and to his frustrations as an unappreciated presidential adviser and too condescending toward politicians, but an indispensable source on cultural affairs and Johnson's uneasy relationship with intellectuals. My preference, among all the firsthand reports or memoirs, is Lady Bird's delightful *A White House Diary* (New York: Holt, Rinehart & Winston, 1970), which is the major source of personal references in this chapter. She is more revealing than LBJ himself, in his *Vantage Point: Perspectives of the Presidency, 1963–1969* (New York: Holt, Rinehart & Winston, 1971).

The oral sources are rich and diverse. To earlier cited interviews, I would recommend that of John P. Roche (by Paige Mulhollan), which is full of insights into Johnson's character and intellect; of Peter Benchley (by Thomas H. Baker), which offers fascinating glimpses into the speech-writing process; of Tom Wicker (by Joe D. Frantz) and Douglas Cater (by David McComb) for analyses of Johnson's political artistry; of Larry Temple (by Joe Frantz) on LBJ's daily routine in the White House; of Peter Hurd (by Elizabeth Kaderli) for clarification of the controversy over Johnson's portrait; of George Davis (by Dorothy P. McSweeny) and Billy Graham (by Monroe Billington) on his religious beliefs and practice; and Joseph A. Pechman (by Daniel G. McComb) on economic policies. For my brief section on economic policy, I also used the official administrative history of the Council of Economic Advisers, one of many such histories housed in LBJL, and an insightful overview by Herbert Stein, *Presidential Economics, The Making of Economic Policy from Roosevelt to Reagan and Beyond* (New York: Simon & Schuster, 1984). The sharpest, most readable critique of Johnson's economic policies is in Allen J. Matusow, *The Unraveling of America: A History of Liberalism in the 1960s* (New York: Harper & Row, 1984).

9. THE GREAT SOCIETY

Strangely, despite all the literature on the Johnson presidency, I could not find a clear, straightforward description and classification of its major economic and social legislation. Evaluations of variously defined Great Societies are plentiful, but all rest on judgments about limited numbers of key bills or programs. My task was to find some patterns in the whole. This was not easy. I first worked with the *Congressional Record*. The sheer mass of legislation soon overwhelmed. In the end, I discovered that the most useful guide is in WHC-Ex and Gen LE, or the files that preface the mass of legislative documents in the LBJL. Boxes 1–10 include the White House perspective on each year's legislative agenda, with running tallies of the status of all major bills during each legislative session. This, at least, identifies the legislation taken to be crucial by the White House and reveals how much administrative effort was allocated to each bill. Beyond that, one can turn to subsequent boxes of material on each major bill or on the subject encompassed by each bill. I used this data only for the subjects and bills I treated in this chapter, and most of all for antipoverty, housing, and civil rights bills. Any one of the subjects deserves at least a book, and indeed books or dissertations have been written on each.

Of all the Johnson legislation, the Economic Opportunities Act of 1964 was the most complex and most daring; the Office of Economic Opportunity was the most controversial new agency. This antipoverty effort remains a challenge for historians. The broader perspective is clear in James T. Patterson, *America's Struggle against Poverty, 1900–1980* (Cambridge, Mass.: Harvard University Press, 1981). As yet, and by far, the most informative study of the OEO is the multivolume, reasonably critical, and historically nuanced administrative history written by OEO staffers and available in manuscript at the LBJL. It alone vindicates the decision by the Johnson administration to require such internal histories. The most effective, but ultimately unfair, criticism of OEO is in Matusow, *The Unraveling of America,* a criticism that draws from both the Right and the Left. More sympathetic is Charles R. Morris in *A Time of Passion:American 1960–1980* (New York: Harper & Row, 1984). Bornet's presidential study is often as confusing as clarifying on the administrative details of the antipoverty programs and evaluates these programs from what seems a vaguely rightist perspective. The WHC files on welfare legislation (LE-WE) is extensive. Several LBJL oral transcripts of poverty warriors flush out the story: Donald M. Baker and Bertrand Harding (by Stephen Goodell) and John A. Baker and Jack T. Conway (by Michael Gillette). Civil Rights, housing, health care, and environmental bills were often as complex, but not as innovative, as the antipoverty bills. In separate LE categories, the WHC files include abundant data on each of these subjects.

Indispensable to the Great Society legislation were the work of the various task forces. With few exceptions, the reports of these are all on deposit in the LBJL. I tried to analyze the makeup and influence of the external task forces, not the internal ones. The role of the task forces and the legislative techniques developed in the Johnson White House are clearly explored in a remarkable interview with James Gaither (by Dorothy Pierce). Next to the transcript by Harry McPherson, I found this the most valuable that I encountered at the LBJL. Gaither supplements the rich treatment of legislative strategies by Doris Kearns.

10. VIETNAM: INTO THE TRAP

The literature on the Vietnam War keeps expanding. Novelists and journalists have joined historians in trying to unlock the secrets of that agonizing war. My purpose was not a retelling of that story. It is much too complex for such a short book. My purpose had to be a limited one—to try to understand, in this chapter, why Lyndon Johnson decided by July 1965 to move into a full-scale war. My second purpose, in chapter 11, was to understand why he could not quickly win his limited goals and why in March 1968 he took the first major initiative toward peace talks and deescalation. My focus had to be on Johnson's decisions, not primarily on the war or the diplomacy that accompanied it. At present, a comprehensive treatment of the war is George C. Herring, *America's Longest War: United States and Vietnam 1950–1975* (New York: Knopf, 1979).

For my limited goals in this chapter, beyond the very general historical background, I largely used selected material from the National Security Files—Vietnam in the LBJL, supplemented by transcripts of interviews. In the last few years, perhaps thanks to the earlier published versions of the Pentagon Papers, the largest share of these 254 boxes has been opened to scholars. The detail is overwhelming, down to daily intelligence briefings. In this sense, these files simply flesh out, and extend, those already available in the Pentagon Papers. For this chapter, I focused my research on events and decisions from the Tonkin Gulf Resolution of 1964 to July 1965. The key documents on Tonkin Gulf are in Boxes 76–77. The internal memos and policy debates that led up to July 1965 are most concentrated in Boxes 13–18 and 74–75. The most detailed oral account of these decisions by a high-level participant is by William Bundy, interviewed in 1969 by Paige E. Mulhollan. Other less detailed recollections are by Maxwell Taylor (interviewed by Dorothy Pierce and Ted Gittenger) and William E. Colby (by Ted Gittenger). Johnson's retrospective vindication is in a 1969 interview by William J. Jorden. The WHC files, under the category of National Defense (ND), contain 224 boxes largely made up of letters relating to Vietnam. I only sampled a few of these boxes.

11. THE ENDLESS WAR

Most of the sources cited in chapter 10 apply here. In the NSF—Vietnam, one can trace, in great detail, the shifting course of the war. But my brief survey of the military side of Vietnam required no such heavy support, and I did not do more than look at a few of these files. I did scan Boxes 353–55 of WHC-PR16, which include all available polling data on Johnson's overall job rating and on his conduct of the war. For the critical efforts to gain negotiations, I largely relied on George C. Herring, ed., *The Secret Diplomacy of the Vietnam War: The Negotiating Volumes of the Pentagon Papers* (Austin: University of Texas Press, 1983). Just a sampling of NSF—Vietnam files reveals that, on a few of these episodes, a full record is now open to scholars at the LBJL. The most informative oral transcript is by Chester Cooper (by Paige E. Mulhollan), who was most intimately involved in the key peace effort. Supplemental to this are the memories of James C. Thompson (also by Paige Mulhollan). A counterperspective on the major peace initiatives is in William Bundy's interview (also by Mulhollan). Averell Harriman (by Mulhollan), although as intimately involved as Cooper, was much less forthcoming or else had less vivid memories of events.

The background to Johnson's 31 March speech remains a bit confused. The key decisions involved not only group discussions but personal talks between Johnson and Rusk. The perspective of participants conflict. Johnson's somewhat idiosyncratic view is in *Vantage Point*. He seems to go out of his way to dismiss the influence of Clark Clifford and of Clifford's close associates, and to make Dean Rusk the architect of all new departures. Harry McPherson (interviewed by T. H. Baker within a year of the decision) believes Clifford's reappraisal of options and his growing doubts were critical. He traces, in detail, the series of staff meetings that preceded the final speech. His view duplicates that of most other observers.

12. GENTLY INTO THE NIGHT

The LBJL, unfortunately, has not (as of 1985) screened or opened for research Johnson's postpresidential papers, except for his correspondence with Richard Nixon and with the former Alice Glass. The catalog of these papers, in itself, reveals the extent of his correspondence and documents several of his trips. The most detailed information is in Merle Miller's *Lyndon*, in Kearns's *Lyndon Johnson and the American Dream*, and in an excellent article by Leo Janos, "The Last Days of the President: LBJ in Retirement," *Atlantic* 232 (July 1973): 35–41. The details of his funeral are from newspapers and news magazines.

INDEX

314

INDEX

315

INDEX

INDEX

Texas Commission on Disciples
History, 28
Texas Gulf Sulphur Corporation, 60
Texas Railroad Commission, 70
Texas Revolution, 2
Texas, University of, 31, 71, 102, 178,
290, 293
Thailand, 167, 298
Thieu, Nguyen Van, 270
Thurman, Strom, 129
Tonkin Gulf Incident, 189, 254–56,
257, 258
Tonkin Gulf Resolution, 255–58
Trujillo, Rafael, 198
Truman, Harry F., 115, 120, 129, 130,
133, 149, 200, 213, 243, 245, 267,
268, 293, 296
truth-in-lending bills, 235
truth-in-securities bills, 235
Turkey, 168
Turner Joy, the, 255
Tydings, Millard, 131

unemployment rates, 201
United States Housing Authority, 95
Upward Bound, 222
urban legislation, 209, 213, 220, *231–
34*, 237, 241
Urban Mass Transportation Act of
1966, 231
urban riots, 217–18, 237

Valenti, Jack, 181, 183
Vance, Cyrus, 144, 284, 285
Vantage Point, The, by Lyndon B.
Johnson, 291
Veterans' Administration (VA)
housing program, 231
Vietcong (Vietnam Communist Party),
247, 248, 251, 252, 258, 259, 260,
265, 266, *272–73*, 274
Vietnam, North:
casual references, 197, 200, 293–94;
clandestine operations by, 247;
escalation of campaign in South in
1964–65, 257–62; military role in
South after 1965, 270–73; nature of
regime, 246; provocations against
before Tonkin Gulf incidents, 248–
54; response to American peace

efforts, 273–80, 283–85, 289; Tet
offensive of 1968, 281–83; Tonkin
Gulf incidents, 254–56; victory in
1975, 267–68
Vietnam, South:
casual references, 167, 168, 177,
244, 245, 293; deterioration of Diem
regime after 1960, 251–54; dire
military situation in 1965, 258–61;
efforts to create a viable
government, 270; final fate of the
country, 293–94; military role of,
271–73, 285; nature of Diem regime,
246–47, 249; problems of the Diem
regime, 248–51; relationship to
Tonkin Gulf incidents, 254–57; role
in peace negotiations, 285; Tet
offensive of 1968, 281–83; war effort
in 1967–68, 266–68
Vietnam War:
American goals in, 264–66, 268–69,
274; American military strategy in,
270–73; diplomatic initiatives by
United States, 273–80, 283–85;
financial costs of, 286; first full
involvement of American ground
troops, 261–62; incidental
references to, 184, 188, 189, 192,
194, 196, 197, 199, 201, 204, 205,
206, 217, 235, 242, 288, 296; human
suffering in, 269; Johnson's decision
to bomb the North, 258–60;
Johnson's policies before Tonkin
Gulf, 252–54; legacy of, 286;
military action after 1965, 270–73;
news coverage of, 269–70, 282;
public opinion about, 266, 267, 268,
269, 273, 280, 281, 282, 285; Tet
offensive of 1968, 281–83; Tonkin
Gulf incidents, 254–56; under John
F. Kennedy, 167, 177, 247–51;
waning congressional support for,
274–75, 280, 284, 287
Vinson, Carl, 96
Volunteers in Service to America
(VISTA), 224
voting fraud in Texas elections, 105–
106, 117–18
Voting rights. *See* Civil Rights Act of
1965

323

ABOUT THE AUTHOR

Paul K. Conkin is a Distinguished Professor of History at Vanderbilt University. A Guggenheim Fellow (1966) and a Senior Fellow of the National Endowment for the Humanities (1972–73), Professor Conkin is the author of numerous books on American intellectual history and on twentieth-century America. His published volumes include *The New Deal*; *Prophets of Prosperity: America's First Political Economists*; and *Puritans and Pragmatists: Eight Eminent American Thinkers*. Professor Conkin and his wife reside in Nashville.